THEATRE

About the Author

Arden Fingerhut served as the lighting designer for numerous plays both on and off Broadway, as well as for productions at regional theatres throughout the country. Among the many plays for which she designed the lighting are *Driving Miss Daisy* by Alfred Uhry, *Plenty* by David Hare, *Da* by Hugh Leonard, and *When She Danced* by Martin Sherman on London's West End. She worked on productions for the New York Shakespeare Festival, the Circle Repertory Company, the Manhattan Theatre Club, the Open Theatre, and the Brooklyn Academy of Music, among others. In 1982, she received an Obie Award for Sustained Excellence in Lighting Design.

Arden Fingerhut did her undergraduate work at New York University and received an M.F.A. in design from Columbia University. From 1987 until her death in 1994 she was a Professor of Theatre at Williams College and served as Chair of the Department of Theatre until 1993. Before that, she was a Master Teacher of Design at New York University, Tisch School of the Arts.

THEATRE

Choice in Action

Arden Fingerhut

Late, Williams College

HarperCollinsCollegePublishers

Acquisitions Editor: Cynthia Biron
Developmental Editor: Virginia Read
Project Editor: Rachel Youngman, Hockett Editorial Service
Art Director: Mary Archondes
Text Design: Robin Hessel Hoffmann
Cover Design: Mary Archondes
Photo Researcher: Cheryl Kucharzak
Manufacturing Manager: Willie Lane
Printer and Binder: R. R. Donnelley & Sons Company
Cover Printer: R. R. Donnelley & Sons Company
Inserts Printer: Coral Graphic Services, Inc.

THEATRE: CHOICE IN ACTION

Library of Congress Cataloging-in-Publication Data

Fingerhut, Arden.
  Theatre : choice in action / Arden Fingerhut.
    p.   cm.
  Includes bibliographical references and index.
  ISBN 0-673-46489-X
    1. Theater—Production and direction.   I. Title.
PN2053.F48   1994
792'.023—dc20   93-33846
                                                   CIP

94 95 96 97 9 8 7 6 5 4 3 2 1

Contents

PART 3
PERFORMANCE   227

Preface

This book grew out of years of teaching and professional practice in which I attempted to discover the best approach to the very complex phenomenon of theatre. Theatre, like all forms of communication (artistic or otherwise), carries meaning to its audience that is the result of careful choices. Over the years, it became clear to me that, whether a student is taking a course in theatre as a potential audience member or as a future artist, he or she must understand what the audience sees onstage and how it got there. In order to understand how those choices affect what we, the audience, ultimately see onstage during a performance, throughout this book I will examine the choices made by the many artists involved in theatrical production.

The Plays

We cannot recapture a live performance for our investigation, but we can begin where theatrical artists generally begin, with the written text. To examine the playwright's choices—about both *what* is said and *how* that theme is expressed—this text uses five plays that represent different treatments of a common subject. William Shakespeare (1564–1616) in *Macbeth,* Anton Chekhov (1860–1904) in *The Seagull,* Henrik Ibsen (1828–1906) in *Hedda Gabler,* Tennessee Williams (1911–1983) in *A Streetcar Named Desire,* and Wendy Wasserstein (b. 1949) in *The Heidi Chronicles* all wrote about people who are unable to function within the circumstances or society that surround them. Of course, those circumstances differ widely from play to play, as do the characters, the language, and what happens to those characters.

These plays were also chosen because their authors were (or *author is,* in the case of Wasserstein) major contributors to their respective periods whose plays continue to be performed today. Their use of language, dramatic situation, and theme make the plays as meaningful to contemporary audiences as they were at the time they were written. Shakespeare grapples with issues such as power, guilt, and retribution; Ibsen with creativity and frustration; Chekhov with ambition and art; Williams with the inflexibility of social beliefs; Wasserstein with equality and fulfillment; and all of them address love as it relates to those problems.

Excerpts of these plays are reprinted throughout the text, and they form the basis of our investigation. You need not have read each of the five plays in order to follow the discussion, although the choices being examined and their implications obviously will be clearer if you do so. The excerpts are meant to prompt the kinds of questions that any reader or audience member needs to ask about *any* play to understand what it means. To put the cited dialogue in context, brief summaries of each of the plays appear in an appendix. You will find it useful to read through these before beginning Chapter 1 and to refer to them as needed. Of course, the summaries are no substitute for the actual texts of the plays, and are included only to give a sense of the plots, themes, characters, and onstage events.

Production Photos

The path from individual interpretation through performance is a fascinating one. To examine how theatre artists *translate* their points of view on a particular play into a production—how they shape what we see onstage in the performance—we need to look at their work. Again, we will have to make do without the fleeting live performance. Instead, many production stills are used to illustrate theatrical choices that were made onstage in various productions. It is important to remember that these photographs, even when actually of a performance and not staged for the camera (as many production photos are), are visual records only—without sound, movement, or the living actor.

Nevertheless, although we may not be able to extrapolate the actual production interpretation from these photos—and what the audience really saw—we can use them as tools to analyze an interpretation. Again, the aim is not to re-create a past performance but to learn to examine what *we* see when we go to the theatre ourselves, and what the meaning is of the choices that are presented to us.

Interviews

One way to learn more about the genesis of an interpretation is to read what the artists say about the creation of a performance. Interviews conducted especially for this book appear throughout the text. In them, a playwright, a director, a dramaturge, an actor, a scenic designer, a lighting designer, several producers, and a stage manager discuss their work and their views of how choices are made in the theatre.

Structure

In addition to an introductory chapter devoted to how we perceive meaning, the text is divided into three parts. Part 1, called "Choice and Interpretation," is primarily concerned with the written play and with a broad view of collaboration in the theatre—thus immediately distinguishing the play as written for performance. Chapter 1, "Interpreting the Play," uses the five plays I have chosen as springboards for discussion of the traditionally defined structures of a written play and how those structures affect the interpretive process.

Part 2, "The Collaborative Artists," concerns itself with how each of the collaborators—the director, the actor, and scenic, costume, and lighting designers—make production choices understandable to an audience. Included are discussions of what each artist does, both artistically and practically, to realize these choices onstage.

Part 3, "Performance," is more directly concerned with the practicalities of production, from the desire to present a play and the producer's job, through rehearsal and the performance itself. The relationship of the audience to the performance is the subject of the final chapter, and includes discussion of kinds of performance spaces and performance styles (including musical theatre), and how the actor relates to the audience. The critic, and the critical point of view, are discussed in the conclusion.

Acknowledgments

I am indebted to the following people for their invaluable help in bringing this book to fruition: Victoria Abrash, André Bishop, Deborah Brothers, Cosmo Catalano, Pat Collins, A. Heather Doughty, Lenore Doxsee, Miata Edoga, David Eppel, John Gleason, Jane Harmon, Roy Harris, Nina Kineally, Hugh Landwehr, Wayne Lawrence, Tom Lynch, Jennifer von Mayrhauser, Dennis McHugh, Maude Mikulewicz, Allen Moyer, Al Pacino, Marshall Purdy, Ginny Read, Mary Robinson, James Scott, Tina Shepard, Paula Shoots, Wendy Wasserstein, and Robert Youdelman.

I would like to thank the following reviewers for their helpful comments on various drafts of the manuscript: Patricia Flanagan Behrend, University of Nebraska; Mary Jo Beresford, Northern Kentucky University; Georgia A. Bomar, East Texas State University; Robert Bradley, Southwest Missouri State; Richard Caram, Penn State University at Altoona; Bill G. Cook, Baylor University; David Cook, University of Tulsa; Richard Harmon, Hofstra University; Gary Heisserer, Graceland College; Marilyn J. Hoffs, Glendale Community College; Edward T. Jones, York College; Joe Karioth, Florida State University; James J. Kolb, Hofstra University; Claudia Mohler, Appalachian State University; James Norwood, University of Minnesota; Sheila Philip-Bradfield, Johnson County Community College; Ellis M. Pryce-Jones, University of Nevada; Nancy Silva, American River College; Robert Skloot, University of Wisconsin–Madison; W. Joseph Stell, University of Georgia; Douglas R. Vander Yacht, Western Washington University; and Harry C. S. Wingfield, University of Alabama.

ARDEN FINGERHUT

THEATRE

Introduction

Choice in the Theatre

Telling Stories

When an event occurs in daily life it can have a direct and enduring effect. If a flood rises or a volcano erupts, real water and real lava flow, and real people lose their homes, belongings, and possibly even their lives. The birth of a child marks the arrival of a unique person who needs to be fed and cared for. When a theatrical performance takes place, however, the members of the audience may laugh, be moved, or feel new things, but the performance presents no immediate call to action—and has no *measurable* impact on life. Theatrical performance is a kind of storytelling, and its importance lies in the unique way in which the story is presented.

A story is an image of life that provides continuity and rhythm, and that in so doing makes sense of an event or gives it meaning. A story determines which events follow which and implies that there is a reason for that sequence. It indicates what is judged important (large, loud, bright) and what is of less importance (small, quiet, dull). Unlike most events in real life, a story has a discrete conclusion. When events in life appear particularly unfathomable, we invent explanations—or stories—to give them meaning. To create a story, then, is to create meaning.

Stories work on the principle of likeness, creating parallels to life. We learn from an early age that if, for example, a bear in a bedtime story eats a child, under similar circumstances the bear will again eat the child. And because it *is* a story, we also know that "bear" connotes not only an actual bear, but any wild, powerful being, human or animal. Likewise, the child in the story is not merely a literal child, but also anyone who is innocent or powerless. The story helps us to cope with "bears" of all kinds; after hearing it, a child will think twice before antagonizing such a creature.

There aren't very many bears—talking or otherwise—in most communities, which is precisely what gives the bedtime story instructive meaning. The reader or listener is not called upon to interact with the animal, but to reflect on the meaning of the story. A story is distanced from its audience—it happens to someone else. In the *Poetics*—one of the most influential treatises ever written on theatre—Aristotle (384–322 B.C.) wrote that the invented story ("the poetic") has more force than history because it shows what *could be* rather than what is. By making those possibilities visible, a story fashions reality in such a way as to give it meaning.

From the time we are small children, stories entrance us. As we grow older, we may call them by different names—allegories, fables, metaphors, films, plays—but they are still essentially stories. In reading, listening to, or composing these stories, we prepare ourselves to face the difficulties of life head on. We give ourselves breathing space and time for reflection. We see things happening to someone else, in a time and place other than our own. Stories can be told by one person to another (as in telling a bedtime story, writing a novel, or creating a painting), by one person to many others (as in a nightclub performance or a solo concert), or by many people to many others (as in a ballet or a theatrical performance). But no matter what form they take, stories communicate qualitative judgments by offering alternative *choices* and cause-and-effect relationships. They can reinforce, clarify, and give breadth to ideas we already have, or turn our preconceived notions around completely.

All of the arts are forms of storytelling. Some use words, some pictures, some movement, some music, and some combinations of all or some of these. A painting, sculpture, or photograph may appear static and immovable when we look at it. In a sense, however, as an audience or viewer we move through it, following the choices of the artist who created it and taking meaning from those choices as we go.

Theatrical Images

Theatre is a performing art like music, dance, and film, all of which take place over time. Although we can read the written script on paper, theatre exists only in performance. There is no object that can be viewed again and again; the performance *is* the art. Theatre is a form of expression that communicates meaning from person to person by means of unique *images* that exist for only a moment, never to be repeated in exactly the same way. Theatrical images are created through the relationship of living actors to the words and actions of the play, to each other, and to theatrical space. Taken together, they establish a further relationship with the audience, a relationship that changes with each performance.

The theatre is human in scale and, by using the living actor as its central image-maker, shows the audience human choices. The actor occupies the same space, more or less, as the audience, and literally breathes the same air. This creates an immediacy unique to the theatre.

In the theatre, the audience follows the choices of the actor or characters who move through time (both real time, as we experience it in life, and the theatrical time of the performance) and space (again, both real and theatrical). Though the theatre reflects life, it is not life, and everyone—actor and audience alike—acknowledges this. The magic of theatre comes in part from the awareness that the audience could easily walk up to the stage, touch the scenery, and see that it is not real, and that the actor is not the dramatic character but an entirely different person with another life offstage. In a relatively small space, sometimes only inches from the audience, theatre is called upon to create the *illusion* of an entirely different reality. For a short period, the audience is asked to give itself over to the illusion of theatrical time and space. This process has been called the *willing suspension of disbelief.*

Making Choices in Performance

To perceive the meaning of something is to understand what choices were made to bring it into being. Listening to a musical performance in a concert hall, choices are easy to hear. The conductor (one of the *interpreters* of the music) chooses relationships of volume, tempo, phrasing, and so forth, based on choices the composer—like his or her counterpart, the playwright—made when writing the score, even before the rehearsal and performance took place. Performance allows the audience to perceive these choices in sequence, through time.

Another kind of perception occurs simultaneously. The audience hears the layers of the music—harmonies, chords, and other musical relationships—and the relationships between the instruments, or *orchestration* (this term is also used in theatre to refer to the relationship of all the individual theatrical elements to each other). Likewise, when viewing plastic art forms (such as painting or sculpture), the audience *recreates the sequence of choices* made by the artist (visually structured time).

In dance, we see the figure of the dancer move through space and time. And again, we also see the relationships between leg and arm, hand and foot, face and body. When music is added, we witness the relationship between it and the dance as a whole. When there is more than one dancer, we perceive the relationships of one individual to all the others. Together these elements add up to *choreography*—the dance analogue to orchestration.

These terms are common to all the performing arts and are used to clarify the organization of time and space. Theatre makes use of orchestrated time, choreographic time, and visually structured time. The actors move in space (through choreography, in choreographic time), create stage images (in visually structured time), and speak a text (through orchestration, in musical time). Theatre is choice in action, and performance choices are communicated to an audience through the orchestration of images in time.

Examples of Theatrical Choices, and How They Affect the Story

In theatre, as in all storytelling, we draw *general meaning* from *specific* events. In Shakespeare's *Macbeth,* the title character sees three witches who predict that he will be king. An actor playing Macbeth might choose to take their prophesy literally; his Macbeth would choose to become king because the witches told him it was fated. Another actor's Macbeth might resist the witches' prophesy or choose not to believe it; instead, he would choose to fight his destiny until it finally overtook him. In the first example, fate would actually have little to do with the outcome: Macbeth would gain the throne by murdering the reigning king. In the second case, fate is everything: Macbeth becomes king despite his efforts to avoid the crown. The two actors' choices have created significantly different meanings.

By making choices, everyone involved in a production helps to create the performance. A costume designer might dress the first Macbeth as an ambitious young gentleman, the second as a rebellious youth. The director places the characters onstage in arrangements that support or diminish the credibility of the witches in the first place. *Every choice in theatre is made to communicate specific meaning to an audience.* In life we communicate through similar choices: slamming a door to show our anger, studying for an exam to show our desire to succeed.

Imagine that a character onstage says "What's the matter with you?" to a character who is crying. The actor chooses how to say the line just as the other actor chooses how to respond to it and how to cry. How does the meaning of the line "What's the matter with you?" change if the speaker:

- Emphasizes the word *you*? The word *matter*?
- Shakes his head?
- Clicks his tongue?
- Turns his back?
- Cries?

How do these choices create meaning?

Performance Without a Written Script

If it is true that in the theatre the performance *is* the art, it is equally true that theatrical performance does not require a written play or script. Like the art of the jazz musician or the clown in the circus, theatrical performance can be *improvisational*; that is, it can be invented spontaneously, independent of the words and actions of a scripted play. Historically, one of the most popular forms of improvised theatre was a kind of clown show known as the *commedia dell'Arte,* which was already well established in Italy by 1550. Improvised around *scenarios* (outlines for performance) that included the basic plot, the location of the action, and the characters, the *commedia* was prized for its imaginative performances rather than for the novelty of its storylines. In fact, the plots of these scenarios and their *stock characters* were well known by audiences because they were used again and again. *Commedia* companies performed wherever they could gather a crowd. Today's equivalent can be found in street-corner bands, sidewalk dancers, and the occasional street-theatre performance.

Antonin Artaud—the poet, director, playwright, and theoretician—wrote *The Theater and Its Double* in 1938. In this series of essays, Artaud questioned the traditional relationship of written play to performance, asking that performance be regarded as worthy of investigation in its own right. His effect on twentieth-century theatre was profound:

> How does it happen that in the theatre . . . everything specifically theatrical, i.e., everything that cannot be expressed in speech, in words, or if you prefer, everything that is not contained in the dialogue . . . is left in the

background? . . . Dialogue—a thing written and spoken—does not belong specifically to the stage, it belongs to books. . . . In opposition to this way of looking at things . . . why not conceive of a play composed directly on the stage, realized on the stage?[1]

Jerzy Grotowski, a director whose work first became widely known during the 1960s, formed the Polish Laboratory Theater with a group of actors, designers, and writers. The company worked out treatments of written plays, changing them drastically to serve the new dramatic forms they were creating. (They also developed a method for training actors, which we will examine in Chapter 4.) Grotowski's is an extreme position, but one that cannot easily be dismissed:

Can the theater exist without costumes and sets? Yes it can. Can it exist without music to accompany the plot? Yes. Can it exist without lighting effects? Of course. And without a text? Yes; the history of the theatre confirms this. In the evolution of the theatrical art the text was one of the last elements to be added. If we place some people on a stage with a scenario they themselves have put together and let them improvise their parts as in the Commedia dell'Arte, the performance will be equally good even if the words are not articulated but simply muttered.[2]

For Grotowski, for the *commedia*, for Artaud, and for many other theatre artists throughout history, the written play was not as important as it continues to be in more traditional theatre. Today, *performance artists* combine dance, visual art, and the spoken word in a new kind of theatre that relies much less on written text or even speech itself than on the total impact of performance.

Any choice is political, social, personal, psychological, philosophical, and ethical. Choosing to follow the crowd is as clear a choice as opting to go it alone. When we make a choice in life—whether it be short term, such as what to eat for breakfast, or long term, such as what one's career will be—it can almost always be altered. Although that is also true to a degree in the theatre, a production is presented whole to the audience. It communicates by means of a series of choices that lead to a particular production. When theatre artists make choices about the interpretation of a play, these choices have an enormous impact on the audience viewing the performance. The audience can, of course, agree or disagree with the choices made—each individual brings a unique set of ideas and values to the theatre, and so interprets the choices made in performance from his or her own perspective. To decide whether or not to agree, disagree, or dismiss the choices presented on stage, each audience member must first recognize what those choices are.

In order to examine how choices are made in theatre and how they influence the meaning of a play, we will begin where most production teams begin: with the written script. One advantage of using a written text is that, since the words of a play generally remain the same from production to production, we will share a common point of reference with the theatre artists when we consider some of the choices made in actual productions. Nevertheless, it is worth restating that the written script is not the performance; every production is a translation of its own interpretation of the play—written or not—to the stage.

Part

ONE

Choice and

Interpretation

Chapter ONE

Interpreting the Play

Reading and Interpretation

What do the following words mean to you?

- night
- female
- baby

What do you visualize when you read them? Does what you "see" differ from what those around you see? How does adding these words change what you see?

- "thick night" *(Macbeth)*
- "uniquely female" *(The Heidi Chronicles)*
- "my baby sister" *(A Streetcar Named Desire)*

The written play communicates through a world confined to words. We all see the actual words on the page in a similar way, but our translation of them into a mental picture is *interpretive.* As we read, a relationship is established between the words on the page and our visual and auditory imagination, creating a perceptual context. That context, taken in relation to the words themselves, produces *meaning.* The context we create is an expression of our personal reaction to what we are reading—the words of the playwright.

The process of reading a play is primarily an *act of the imagination* through which we personalize the words on the page; the words signify something because we, as readers, *give* them that meaning. This is true whether we are reading with a view toward performance, or reading for pleasure or study.

Developing a Point of View

The text of a written play is made up of the words spoken by the characters and *stage directions,* which may provide descriptions of the characters or direct onstage actions. In the opening scene of *A Streetcar Named Desire* by Tennessee Williams, Blanche Dubois is introduced in this way in stage directions written by the playwright:

Patricia Conolly in an opening moment of the 1975 production of *A Streetcar Named Desire* at the Guthrie Theater.

Blanche comes around the corner, carrying a valise. She looks at a slip of paper, then at the building, then again at the slip and again at the building. Her expression is one of shocked disbelief. Her appearance is incongruous to this setting. She is daintily dressed in a white suit with a fluffy bodice, necklace and earrings of pearl, white gloves and hat, looking as if she were arriving at a summer tea or cocktail party in the garden district. She is about five years older than Stella. Her delicate beauty must avoid a strong light. There is something about her uncertain manner, as well as her white clothes, that suggests a moth.

Descriptions of expressions and gestures, such as "shocked disbelief" or "her uncertain manner . . . suggests a moth," when examined closely, are less specific than they might seem on first reading. Even the description of Blanche's costume, though evocative, is general. Williams's stage directions are able to provide us only with an *impression* of Blanche's character. The scene continues as follows:

EUNICE *[finally]*: What's the matter, honey? Are you lost?

BLANCHE *[with faintly hysterical humor]:* They told me to take a streetcar named Desire, and then transfer to one called Cemeteries and ride six blocks and get off at—Elysian Fields!

EUNICE: That's where you are now.

BLANCHE: At Elysian Fields?

EUNICE: This here is Elysian Fields.

BLANCHE: They mustn't have—understood—what number I wanted.

EUNICE: What number you lookin' for?

[Blanche wearily refers to the slip of paper.]

BLANCHE: Six thirty-two.

EUNICE: You don't have to look no further.

BLANCHE *[uncomprehendingly]:* I'm looking for my sister, Stella DuBois. I mean—Mrs. Stanley Kowalski.

EUNICE: That's the party.—You just did miss her, though.

BLANCHE: This—can this be—her home?

Even with the benefit of stage directions, we must carefully question this apparently simple interchange.

- Is it simply too dark for Blanche to see the address?
- Why is she confused and disconcerted by Stella's home?
- What did she expect?
- How long has she been traveling?

- Does her response mean that she thinks the place is awful? Is it, and if so, in what sense? Poor? Run-down? Squalid?
- Is her confusion a product of snobbery? exhaustion? dismay that an audience would share?

The answers to these questions form the basis for an interpretation, or *point of view.* A performance in the theatre is an interpretation *translated* to the stage. The members of the audience, in turn, "read," or view, the on-stage performance, provide a personal context, and interpret it to relate to their own lives.

In this scene, Tennessee Williams also provides important information about events that took place before the play begins, information necessary to the reader's or audience's understanding of what is to come. This material is called *exposition,* examples of which appear in boldface below in the conversation that follows after Eunice, the upstairs neighbor, lets Blanche into Stella's apartment:

EUNICE *[defensively, noticing Blanche's look]:* It's sort of messed up right now but when it's clean it's real sweet.

BLANCHE: Is it?

EUNICE: Uh, huh, I think so. So you're Stella's sister?

BLANCHE: Yes. *[Wanting to get rid of her]* Thanks for letting me in.

EUNICE: *Por nada,* as the Mexicans say, *por nada!* **Stella spoke of you.**

BLANCHE: Yes?

EUNICE: I think she said you **taught school.**

BLANCHE: Yes.

EUNICE: And you're from **Mississippi,** huh?

BLANCHE: Yes.

EUNICE: She showed me a picture of **your home-place, the plantation.**

BLANCHE: **Belle Reve?**

EUNICE: **A great big place with white columns.**

BLANCHE: Yes . . .

This important, if brief, scene raises the issues on which hinge the remainder of the play, and Blanche's future sanity. Through exposition, Tennessee Williams establishes Blanche's predicament from the moment she first appears onstage. We learn that Blanche (1) is a teacher, (2) comes from a place very unlike where she now finds herself, and (3) has been spoken about in glorified terms. Why did Blanche leave so wonderful a life to come to this particular place? The answer to that question is an interpretation.

Interpretation and the Language of the Play

Dialogue, Monologue, and Soliloquy

Tennessee Williams chose to cast these opening scenes, and most of the play, in *dialogue form.* Dramatic dialogue is a conversation or exchange of ideas between two or more characters. Dialogue embodies an underlying concept of drama: *because more than one character speaks, more than one side of an issue emerges.* Since the playwright "speaks" through more than one character via the dialogue, the playwright's own opinions or intentions are left open to broad interpretation.

In scene 4 of the same play, Blanche compares Stanley, Stella's husband, to the "brutes" who are "inheriting the earth." This speech is an example of a *monologue,* an extended speech by one character within hearing of the other characters onstage. Through this choice of dramatic device, the playwright allows Blanche to explore ideas and emotions more fully than she might in conventional dialogue:

> He acts like an animal, has an animal's habits! Eats like one, moves like one, talks like one! There's even something—sub-human—something not quite to the stage of humanity yet! Yes, something—ape-like about him. . . . Maybe we are a long way from being made in God's image, but Stella, my sister, there has been some progress made since then! Such things as art—as poetry and music—such kinds of new light have come into the world since then! In some kinds of people some tenderer feelings have had some little beginning! That we have got to make *grow!* And *cling* to, and hold as our flag! In this dark march toward whatever it is we're approaching . . . *Don't—don't hang back with the brutes!*

On the surface, this short monologue appears to support the familiar position that respects knowledge and culture over instinct, but other questions arise: Does Blanche have the right to make this speech? Is she hurting her sister? Does Stanley pose a serious threat to Stella's welfare? Will Stella be more deeply hurt if Blanche doesn't try to end her relationship with Stanley? Has Blanche gone too far in trying to protect her sister? Is Stella really listening? What is a "brute" according to Blanche? Is she right to invoke art and poetry to support her case? Is her argument a good one? What does Blanche *mean* or *intend* by this speech?

After you have given some thought to these questions, consider what you "see" when you read this scene. How does Blanche appear? How does Stella look as she listens? In what condition is the room? Does Blanche whisper for fear of being overheard? Does she speak calmly but emphatically? Loudly and hysterically? Is she forceful or tentative? Compare what you have imagined with your answers to the questions in the preceding paragraph. What does what you "see" mean? Now change, for example, the way you imagine the sound of Blanche's voice when she delivers the speech and consider how that changes her *meaning.*

The following is the prologue to act 2 of Wendy Wasserstein's *The Heidi Chronicles:*

1989. Lecture hall, Columbia University. Slides are projected during the lecture.

HEIDI: Lilla Cabot Perry, 1848 to 1933, was, along with the better known Mary Cassatt and Berthe Morisot, a major influence in American Impressionism. Her painting "Lady with a Bowl of Violets". . . *Pauses as wrong slide comes on the screen.* Lilla went through a little-known hostility period . . . Actually the painting you're looking at is "Judith Beheading Holofernes" by Artemisia Gentileschi. Please bear with me. My T.A. is taking the law boards today.

The correct slide comes on. Thank you. "Lady with a Bowl of Violets." Notice how the tones move from cool blues and violets to warmer oranges lighting up the collar of the rather flimsy negligee. Change flimsy to flouncy. But Lilla cops out when she gets to the head. Suddenly, we're back to traditional portraiture, with the lines completely delineated.

The painting I prefer is "Lady in Evening Dress," painted in 1911. Closer to her mentor Monet; Lilla here is willing to lose her edges in favor of paint and light. Go, Lilla! Now let's compare for a moment Cabot's "Lady" with Lily Martin Spencer's fading rose. There is something uniquely female about these paintings. And I'm not referring to their lovely qualities, delicate techniques, or overall charm. Oh, please! What strikes me is that both ladies seem slightly removed from the occasions at hand. They appear to watch closely and ease the way for the others to join in. I suppose it's really not unlike being an art historian. In other words, being neither the painter nor the casual observer, but a highly informed spectator.

This monologue is part of a scene in which the other characters are represented by the theatre audience. By couching the speech in what appears to be an impartial art history lecture, the playwright allows the character to comment on her role in life, something Heidi would not be likely to discuss directly in dialogue with another character.

Choosing the monologue form, the playwright raises questions of interpretation about underlying issues that, although referred to offhandedly, must weigh heavily on Heidi:

Jacqueline Kim delivering a soliloquy as the character Electra in the Guthrie Theater's 1992 production of *Agamemnon and Electra*.

- What does she feel she contributes by being neither a "casual observer" nor the painter?
- What is a "highly informed spectator"?
- Does she feel useful?
- What does her preference for the second painting show?
- Why does she apparently feel that women are "removed from the occasions at hand"?
- Why does she feel such a kinship with the women in these paintings?

What range of answers is possible for each of these questions? What other questions need to be asked?

Another dramatic form the playwright may choose to use is the *soliloquy*, an extended speech in which a character contemplates or works out what has happened and how to proceed, or how he or she feels. This device allows a more extensive investigation of emotions and ideas than does ordinary dialogue, and it relies on the audience's assumption that the character delivering the soliloquy cannot be heard by any other character onstage.

Shakespeare, and Elizabethan drama as a whole, made frequent use of the soliloquy form. Here, Lady Macbeth has just read a letter from her husband in which he describes the witches' prophesy that he will become king, and his belief that the prophecy is being fulfilled [Note that the witches had hailed Macbeth by his then-title, "Thane of Glamis"; by the title he was given shortly after meeting them, "Thane of Cawdor"; and by the words, "Macbeth, that shalt be King hereafter"]:

LADY MACBETH: Glamis thou art, and Cawdor, and shalt be
    What thou art promis'd. Yet do I fear thy nature.
    It is too full o' the milk of human kindness
    To catch the nearest way. Thou wouldst be great;
    Art not without ambition, but without
    The illness should attend it. What thou wouldst highly,
    That wouldst thou holily; wouldst not play false,
    And yet wouldst wrongly win. Thou'ldst have, great Glamis,
    That which cries, "Thus thou must do," if thou have it;
    And that which rather thou dost fear to do
    Than wishest should be undone. Hie thee hither,
    That I may pour my spirits in thine ear,
    And chastise with the valor of my tongue
    All that impedes thee from the golden round
    Which fate and metaphysical aid doth seem
    To have thee crowned withal. . .

[A messenger arrives to inform Lady Macbeth that Duncan, the king, is arriving on a visit that night.]

    Come, you spirits
    That tend on mortal thoughts, unsex me here,
    And fill me, from the crown to the toe, top-full
    Of direst cruelty! Make thick my blood;
    Stop up the access and passage to remorse,
    That no compunctious visitings of nature
    Shake my fell purpose, nor keep peace between
    The effect and it! . . . Come, thick night,
    And pall thee in the dunnest smoke of hell,
    That my keen knife see not the wound it makes,
    Nor heaven peep through the blanket of the dark,
    To cry "Hold, hold!"

Lady Macbeth fears that although her husband has been promised great success, his will is not strong enough to take power by any means necessary. When she learns that Duncan is coming to visit, she feels that the moment of opportunity has arrived and calls on the "spirits" to help in her "fell purpose" and not allow feelings of mercy or remorse to keep her from murdering the king. Just as we did with the language of *The Heidi Chronicles* and *A Streetcar Named Desire*, we can begin to think about the underlying assumptions of this passage by asking such questions as:

- Why does Lady Macbeth see the acquisition of power as the only path to glory worth pursuing? Are there others?
- Does Lady Macbeth have access to power in her world other than through her husband?
- Why does she immediately think of murder? Are there other ways to achieve power in her society?
- What view of women would prompt the writing of this speech?
- Is the drive for power natural and instinctive? Or is it learned and passed on from generation to generation?

In her extended soliloquy, Lady Macbeth explores the means to acquire the power the witches have promised—she believes that her husband does not have sufficient ambition and that she must find it within herself to drive him toward his just reward. The use of the soliloquy form itself raises some interpretive questions. How might your perception of Lady Macbeth and the issue of the acquisition of power change if the exploration had been written in dialogue form, with Lady Macbeth speaking to another character? What would need to be implied rather than stated?

Verse and Prose

Lady Macbeth's letter soliloquy, unlike the other excerpts we have examined, is written in *verse*. The verse form predominated in the Elizabethan theatre—of which *Macbeth*, written sometime around 1605, is an example. Shakespeare often combined verse and prose in one play, as in *Macbeth*, to differentiate socioeconomic status, using verse for the upper classes and prose for the lower. European drama of the seventeenth and eighteenth centuries was also usually written in verse, as were most plays prior to that time. In the latter part of the nineteenth century, when the theatre, like other art forms, became dedicated to the *representation* of life (as opposed to the more *presentational* style of earlier periods of drama and performance, which were less concerned with preserving the illusion of reality and relied on such theatrical conventions as direct address to the audience), the language of the play changed as well. Since verse is not common in everyday expression, it was not useful to a theatre that focused on recreating the surface behavior of everyday life. Therefore, the movement embracing realism in the theatre (which influenced *Hedda Gabler*, written in 1890) brought with it the use of prose.

To give an example of how the choice of dramatic language and form can influence the audience's perception of a play, imagine your response if a contemporary playwright were to write a play in verse. Would you as an audience member find it startling? What would the language signal about the world of the play? What would it mean if Stanley Kowalski delivered his lines in verse? If Blanche spoke in verse and Stanley in prose?

Interpretation and the Structure of the Play

Dramatic Conflict

Even in its everyday usage, the word *drama* indicates conflict. A situation such as a very tight deadline or a particularly difficult rescue is termed "dramatic"; we speak of a heated exchange or a child's temper tantrum as "drama." Almost by definition, drama *is* conflict. In the theatre, dramatic conflict can take place between characters, between a character and some aspect of the environment, or within a character.

In scene 4 of *A Streetcar Named Desire*, just prior to the monologue in which Blanche compares Stanley to an animal, Blanche and Stella exchange the following lines:

BLANCHE: Stella?

STELLA: Hmmh?

BLANCHE: Baby, my baby sister!

STELLA: Blanche, what is the matter with you?

BLANCHE: He's left?

STELLA: Stan? Yes.

BLANCHE: Will he be back?

STELLA: He's gone to get the car greased. Why?

BLANCHE: Why! I've been half crazy, Stella! When I found out you'd been insane enough to come back in here after what happened—I started to rush in after you!

STELLA: I'm glad you didn't.

BLANCHE: What were you thinking of? Answer me! What? What?

STELLA: Please Blanche! Sit down and stop yelling.

BLANCHE: All right, Stella. I will repeat the question quietly now. How could you come back in this place last night? Why you must have slept with him!

Even without knowing the play, or the particular incident discussed, it is clear from this dialogue that Stella and Blanche *do not agree on the meaning of events* that took place in the previous scene. They experienced the same event as did the reader (and the audience), but they "see" it very differently.

The exchange between Blanche and Stella illustrates one of the major conflicts of the play: Blanche, sensing that Stanley is dangerous, wants Stella to leave with her. Stella wants to stay with Stanley. This conflict between characters is compounded by Stella's *internal conflict:* By staying with Stanley, is she being disloyal to Blanche? By sympathizing with Blanche, is she betraying Stanley? This conflict—does she take Stanley's side or Blanche's?—remains with Stella to the very end of the play. For the reader, a deciding factor in the interpretive process might be determining whose side one is on, if anyone's, and in what measure. (In performance, the choice will be *shown* to the audience; that is, the way in which the characters are portrayed will largely illustrate the decision.)

Plot

The *plot* of a play, like that of a novel or film, is the series of actions, incidents, or situations through which the story and its implications are communicated. The scene we just looked at not only contains its own conflict, but assumes a role in the series of conflicts found in the overall plot of the play.

A plot is never the whole story—it is only those parts that the playwright has chosen in order to tell a *version* of the story to the audience. The act of plotting a play could be compared to mapping out a route by laying out key points and drawing lines that connect one point (or incident) to the next.

The plot contains the incidents that move the story forward. A plot can be *simple,* containing a single storyline with a single set of characters, or it can be *complex,* with *subplots* that run parallel to the main storyline, sometimes with entirely separate sets of characters.

The plot of the earlier scenes of *A Streetcar Named Desire* could be outlined in this way:

Scene 1: Blanche arrives unexpectedly early to visit with her sister Stella and Stella's husband, Stanley Kowalski. Blanche and Stella are reunited and Stella learns that their old home, Belle Reve, has been lost.

Scene 2: Stella and Blanche prepare to go out for the evening. Stanley questions Blanche about how she lost Belle Reve and they argue. Stella and Blanche leave as the men arrive for Stanley's poker party.

Scene 3: Stanley, Mitch, Pablo, and Steve are playing poker. Stella and Blanche arrive home from their evening out. Mitch and Blanche meet, talk, and listen to music on the radio. Stanley, drunk, rushes into the bedroom and throws the radio out the window. Stanley strikes Stella; Blanche and Stella retreat upstairs. Stanley cries for Stella, who returns to him.

Scene 4: The following morning, Blanche returns from Eunice's apartment upstairs to find Stella, and continues as we have seen in the monologue and dialogue previously cited. As Blanche becomes increasingly distressed, Stanley returns and overhears what she is saying about him.

What has Williams communicated through his plotting of this early section of the play? What has he left out? How can the movement through these incidents be interpreted? Blanche's arrival in scene 1, where she is greeted happily by Stella, ends in unhappiness and conflict. Scenes 2 and 3 begin on an upbeat note, then end in much the same way as scene 1: Scene 2 moves through discord to an uneasy peace; scene 3 progresses much more dangerously to further discord, violence, and a tortured resolution. Scene 4 contains muted discord throughout, and ends catastrophically: Blanche has insulted Stanley. How will he retaliate?

Each scene pushes Blanche further into conflict with Stanley (losing, regaining, and again losing Stella's support along the way), thus increasing the chances of being "found out"—or thrown out. Williams's careful plotting in these scenes raises many interpretive questions related to this central conflict:

- Is Blanche creating the discord? Is Stanley?
- Does Blanche need help in solving her problems?
- Is what is to be discovered about Blanche so terrible?
- Is this information best kept hidden, or would it be better for Blanche to be exposed than to continue running away?
- Is Stanley's method of investigation helpful in solving the problem?

Linear and Episodic Structure

Each scene in *A Streetcar Named Desire* is one of many relatively short scenes, covering a considerable time period (several months), that together make up the play. As such, the play's structure is called *episodic*. Like the epic poem, episodic drama tells a story through a series of scenes that show different views of the central problem of the play. The impact of this struc-

Mary Layne as Ibsen's trapped heroine, Hedda Gabler, in a 1988 production at the Hartford Stage Company. The linear structure of the play contributes to the sense of Hedda's confinement.

ture is cumulative. *Macbeth*, like all of Shakespeare's plays, employs an even more exaggerated episodic structure, with many changes in place, time, and situation. *The Heidi Chronicles* is episodic as well, covering many years, places, and situations over the course of the characters' lives.

Linear dramatic structure presents the audience with a world that possesses an internal logic, one in which each event in the play follows from the other out of what Aristotle (in describing an ideal form of tragedy, which we will explore in more detail in the next section) termed *necessity*, or cause and effect. Each part of the plot should be built logically (or necessarily) upon the last, reaching an inevitable *climax* (the point of the conflict's greatest intensity) and *resolution* (the way in which the conflict is settled). To keep this progression clear, the play usually has a limited number of settings and a brief time span. The plot revolves around a small number of characters and incidents and a single central problem.

Henrik Ibsen's *Hedda Gabler* is an example of linear dramatic structure. The plot is very tightly centered around the title character, it comprises four acts that take place within the same setting, and it covers a period of only a few days. A close cause-and-effect relationship exists in the play between Hedda's life before her marriage and her problems after it.

Ibsen uses this linear structure to support the story of Hedda's entrapment. Hedda is confined to a single place; she neither leaves nor returns during the course of the play. Whatever attempts she makes to affect her circumstances—at least until her last, desperate deed—of necessity take place away from the center of active life. All incidents in the play are connected to her specific problem and move logically from one to another. With no possible relief or alternative world shown, madness in one form or another seems inevitable.

If Ibsen had instead written *Hedda Gabler* in episodic form, how might our perception of Hedda's suicide be changed? Would her actions seem less inevitable if we had been shown her earlier life? Would we be more understanding? Less?

German dramatist and poet Bertolt Brecht (1898–1956) was one of the strongest twentieth-century proponents of episodic drama, even giving it a name: *epic theatre.* Brecht built on a playwrighting tradition predating Shakespeare, but his theories went well beyond the use of multiple scenes, place, time, and action.

Under Brecht's hand, the choice of dramatic structure took on political implications. Episodic structure, he said, should keep the audience alert to the possibility of change, in contrast to linear structure, which lulls the audience into acceptance of the cause-and-effect relationship presented in the play. By showing the audience one example or action to the exclusion of all others, Brecht felt that linear structure eliminated any basis for comparison. Epic theatre, on the other hand, makes the audience conscious participants, able to compare alternatives and make their own choices.

Brecht contrasts Aristotle's dramatic construction, a "strong centralization of plot and an organic interdependence of the separate parts," with his own epic theatre, which "could practically be cut up with a scissors into single pieces, each of which could stand alone." The audi-

ence who experiences linear theatre says: Yes, I have felt that too.—That's how I am.—That is only *natural*, while the audience experiencing epic theatre says: I wouldn't have thought that.—People shouldn't do things like that. That's extremely odd.[1]

Point of Attack

The *point of attack* is the place in the larger story at which the playwright chooses to begin the play. The earlier the point of attack, the less exposition is necessary and, generally, the more episodic the structure; the later the point of attack, the more exposition is required and the more linear the structure. The point of attack in *Macbeth* comes relatively early. The play presents all the events from a period of relative stability (winning a battle, rewarding the heroes) to restabilization (the death of Macbeth, the rise of the new king). The early point of attack and the broad scope of the play allow the audience to witness a substantial part of the Macbeths' path from glory to destruction and madness. They have many choices ahead of them at the opening of the play; the audience sees the couple make most of them.

The point of attack in *The Heidi Chronicles* is quite early as well. Heidi progresses from high school in 1965 to motherhood in 1989. The audience will witness Heidi making many of the important choices of her adult life, not just the consequences of those decisions as in *Hedda Gabler*, a play with a much later point of attack. Although its structure is episodic, *A Streetcar Named Desire* likewise has a relatively late point of attack. By the time Blanche makes her first appearance in the play, she has been through many disastrous experiences and made many unfruitful choices. Tennessee Williams opens the play with Blanche's arrival at her sister's house—in effect, the beginning of the story of her last chance—and sets Blanche closer to the consequences of her actions than, for example, Heidi or Lady Macbeth. But although we sense her peril from the opening moments of the play, the play's point of attack allows for the possibility that Blanche might save herself—unlike Hedda, who has already taken what she perceives to be her last chance.

A Streetcar Named Desire would change considerably if the point of attack were earlier and we were shown more episodes in the lives of the characters. For example, if the time frame were broadened to include Blanche's life at Belle Reve, or to show Stanley and Stella when they first met, how might your understanding of the play be affected? If the point of attack were later, for instance, when Stanley hands Blanche a bus ticket back to Laurel, how would that condensed time period and, consequently, more linear structure affect your interpretation?

Interpretation and Character

Characters speak the language of the play and, paradoxically, while embroiled in the plot they are also the forces that drive it forward. Henrik Ibsen wrote an essay entitled "The Primacy of Character" in which he describes how he writes and thinks about character: "Before I write down one word, I have to have the character in mind through and through. I must penetrate into the last wrinkle of his soul . . . But I have to have his exterior in mind also, down to the last button, how he stands and walks, how he conducts himself, what his voice sounds like. Then I do not let him go until his fate is fulfilled."[2]

Although this may be, in fact, the way Ibsen conceived of them, his characters are represented in the play through familiar means: dialogue, monologue, soliloquy, and stage directions. Characters are as much in need of interpretation as are the other elements of the play. For example, the reader might interpret Stanley Kowalski's situation in *A Streetcar Named Desire* in this way: Stanley is right to question Blanche's past and collect more information about her recent behavior. He senses that her reasons for leaving her home are ambiguous and he doubts her mental stability and her effect on his wife. He is also concerned about the welfare of his good friend Mitch and needs to protect him from Blanche's shameful past and her manipulations. Stanley's intentions are good, although the results are not necessarily in Blanche's best interests. She can no longer function on her own and needs professional guidance; until she gets outside help, she poses a threat to the happiness of their home.

Witnessing a production of *Streetcar* from this point of view, the audience gathers that Stanley's behavior, even when he strikes Stella or attacks Blanche, is somewhat justified. His actions are not typical, but a consequence of Blanche's presence. Using this interpretation, the actor performing the role of Stanley could portray him as an essentially even-tempered man who is driven to distraction trying to protect his family. He sees through Blanche's lies when his wife, blinded by her love for her sister, cannot.

Now let's turn that interpretation around. The reader might instead say that Stanley's behavior in questioning Blanche's past is reprehensible: He does it merely to build a case against her, to get her out of the house and away from Stella, and to keep her from usurping his power. He knows she is lying, and without considering why she might be doing so (out of a need for self-protection or privacy, or even out of shame), he uses those lies to destroy whatever self-esteem she has left. Stanley wishes to destroy her pretensions because Blanche has insulted him. He tries to turn his wife against her and tells Mitch about Blanche's "shameful" past solely to keep Mitch as his ally and to ruin any chance she has of making a fresh start. Stanley's intentions are strictly self-aggrandizing and serve only to maintain his tentative hold on power. His actions are brutal. The results are in Blanche's worst interests; she is already having immense difficulty functioning on her own and needs all the support she can get from her family, who are all that she has left.

This interpretation of character changes everything not only for the actors and actresses portraying the characters of Stanley, Blanche, Mitch, and

Stella, but also for the audience. The first production shows a loving couple torn apart by the intrusion of a lying, scheming, aging woman and saved at last by the sensible, if desperate, husband; the other presents a woman torn apart by a man who views power as his inviolable right.

These are but two possible interpretations of this character, of course, one of which is more plausible than the other. To conclude that Stanley is even-tempered would be very difficult for anyone reading the text carefully. Obviously, some choices are more firmly grounded in the play than others; to be taken seriously, an interpretation must be the result of careful study.

Sometimes authors leave notes about their characters to help the interpretive process along. For example, Ibsen wrote about *Hedda Gabler:*

> This married woman more and more imagines that she is an important personality, and as a consequence feels compelled to create for herself a sensational past. If an interesting female character appears in a new story or in a play, she believes that it is she who is being portrayed. . . . Hedda feels herself demoniacally attracted by the tendencies of the times. But she lacks courage. Her thoughts remain theories, ineffective dreams. The feminine imagination is not active and independently creative like the masculine. It needs a bit of reality as a help. . . ."[3]

These notes probably appear dated to most of us and not particularly pertinent to today's social problems. They might even be viewed as antifeminist, even though during his lifetime Ibsen was considered a revolutionary. But the play, produced from a contemporary perspective with a new set of notes, need not have any such problems.

Here are two contrasting interpretations of *Hedda Gabler* by two directors, Emily Mann and Maria Irene Fornes, respectively, who are also both playwrights:

> Hedda is a play I've run away from—it's terrifying. But when I finally looked at it, I saw it as a play about young people on the brink of decisions that end up being life-or-death matters. She's 29, the men are maybe 33, just establishing themselves professionally. Even Brack, who's usually played as an old man, is 45. Hedda married in a panic—she thought she had not a minute left or she would end up an old maid. I'm 35. I'm past that point, but I can so feel for her; I know what that terrible pressure is that she felt. When you make these kinds of mistakes and you've got the man's baby in your belly, then you have to have an extraordinary amount of courage to change it, walk out, or find a way to make it work. We're not talking about monsters and victims here, but about real people."[4]

> Hedda is a free agent. Something has gone askew inside. But it is not that she is restricted in this place. Ibsen presents a lovely little family in the play. The only thing wrong with them is that they're boring. But nobody said to Hedda, "Now you're ours, and you're going to sit here and be bored with us." No such thing.[5]

What are the ramifications of these differing interpretations for the other characters and issues in the play? How does each interpretation affect your understanding of Hedda's suicide? Of Brack's blackmail? Of the society as a whole? Of the role of women in that society and in ours?

Interpretation and Dramatic Genre

Categories in general provide a common vocabulary to facilitate discussion. Categories, or genres, of dramatic literature do the same. The broad categories of *tragedy, comedy,* and *tragicomedy* have been defined in different ways from period to period, even from person to person. Sometimes new categories develop when old ones are found insufficiently flexible to encompass evolving ideas. It is never wise to use categories loosely or to assume that everyone is using them the same way.

The Heidi Chronicles illustrates the difficulty of categorizing plays by genre. Although the characters deliver witty lines and snappy comebacks—the kinds of interchanges we associate with comedy—the drama also takes a serious look at the women's movement, at Heidi's feelings of betrayal, and at sexual roles in general. Still, Wasserstein's use of a comic tone causes us to listen to Heidi's speech in a different way than we did to Blanche's, and it would influence the choices made in a production of the play.

Every choice made in the course of production affects a play's meaning. A production of *Macbeth* with Elizabeth Taylor as Lady Macbeth would likely have a very different meaning than one in which Glenn Close performed the role. *A Streetcar Named Desire* set in a filthy, run-down hovel has a different meaning from one set in an old but tidy apartment. Any production of a play must consider the unique effect of the interpretation.

Conversely, the fact that a play was written in a serious or comic tone affects all production choices. It is unlikely, for example, that a production of *Macbeth* would be costumed in frothy, pastel fabrics or have flowered wallpaper on its battlements. An actress playing Lady Macbeth wouldn't breeze lightly through the performance, but that same actress playing the role of Susan in *The Heidi Chronicles* might do so, at least in the early scenes. A rainy afternoon in a production of *A Streetcar Named Desire* would differ greatly from one in *The Heidi Chronicles:* the first would probably be quiet, thick, somber; the second, crisper, simpler, lighter. Although genre does not dictate production choices—there's no such thing as "lighting for tragedy"—the tone and tempo of tragedy or comedy must be supported if the performance is to provide the audience with a unified and credible theatrical world.

Tragedy

Tragedy—the term is derived from the ancient Greek—has been the most disputed form of drama, most likely because it shows the most serious consequences of human action (although not all drama addressing serious subjects is defined as tragedy). Every period has altered its definition of tragedy, either to fit the actual practices of its playwrights or to conform to a particular social or political point of view. Those who have advocated tragedy over other dramatic genres believe it to be capable of having a considerable impact on society.

In its broadest sense, tragedy can be defined as drama that:

- Shows the consequences of inappropriate action within a particular context or set of circumstances.
- Shows the means, mechanisms, rules, or logic by which those consequences came about.
- Shows consequences that are decidedly negative or unpleasant.

With the exception of *The Heidi Chronicles,* each of the plays we are studying ends unhappily—if not violently—for at least one of it major characters. The action of each of these plays serves as the means by which this end comes about. Within a given set of circumstances, the characters make choices (shown through what they say to one another and what they do) that lead to an unhappy conclusion. Inappropriate or unacceptable behavior, toward another person or relative to some set of standards, leads these characters to that end. According to some definitions these plays would be considered tragedy, according to others simply *drama.*

The question of whether or not the actions of tragic characters must reverberate through society as a whole is a source of one of the sharpest debates over the nature of tragedy. Traditionally, tragic characters have been those whose actions could affect the entire society—in other words, important people.

ARISTOTELIAN TRAGEDY   Perhaps the single most important document dedicated to the subject of tragedy is Aristotle's *Poetics* (c. 335–323 B.C.), although only a fragment of the original survives. Many of the disputes over the definition of tragedy are based on the following passage:

> Tragedy, therefore, is an imitation of a worthy or illustrious and *perfect action,* possessing *magnitude,* in pleasing language, using separately the several species of imitation in its parts, by men *acting,* and not through narration, *through pity and fear effecting a purification from such like passions.* (emphasis added)[6]

Zöe Caldwell
as Medea and
Judith Anderson
as the Nurse in
the 1982 pro-
duction of Eu-
ripides' *Medea.*

Aristotle's concept of tragedy assumes the need for *catharsis,* or a purging of certain qualities or characteristics. What is being purged is a great error or *tragic flaw* in an illustrious or important character. *Through fear and pity, the audience members, as well, rid themselves of negative tendencies similar to those of the character in the tragedy.* The *Poetics* further states:

> It is requisite, however, in the manners as well as in the combination of the incidents, always to investigate, either the *necessary or the probable;* so that such things, *either necessarily or probably that this thing should be done after that.* It is evident, therefore, that the solutions of fables ought to happen from the fable itself, and not as in *The Medea,* from the machinery. (emphasis added)[7]

Aristotle called *The Medea,* written by Euripides (484–406/7 B.C.) in 431 B.C., a tragedy. Medea's husband, Jason, abandons her for another woman, and Medea redresses this wrong by killing her own children. Her fate—Medea is whisked away by the gods in a chariot—did not satisfy Aristotle, who thought she should be required to face the consequences of her actions. In his view, Euripides was guilty of not following the *logical outcome* of the play's actions: that which is "necessary" and "probable."

When looked at from the perspective of Aristotelian tragedy, Lady Macbeth's actions can be seen as the expression of her relentless pursuit of power, however evil the means of obtaining it. Her character fits Aristotle's profile of the illustrious figure whose flaws need to be purged for the good of society. Presumably audience members would expect to meet an equally horrible fate if they tried to change the existing power structure by the same methods. With perfect inevitability—again what Aristotle described as "the necessary and "probable"—Lady Macbeth and her husband get what they deserve.

If Aristotle had been able to examine Hedda Gabler's character, what might he have seen as her tragic flaw? Perhaps denial of her predetermined place in society? He might have considered her madness and suicide, like Lady Macbeth's, to be a just end to that denial.

TWENTIETH-CENTURY VIEWS OF TRAGEDY   Many centuries after Aristotle, John Gassner (1903–1967), an influential American critic of the drama, responded to the Aristotelian definition of tragedy in an essay that shows how deeply influenced he was by ideas from the emerging field of psychology:

> Without adhering to any specific school of psychopathology, it is safe to say that if Aristotelian catharsis is a valid definition of tragic effect (and I believe it is), it means one thing above all: In the tragic experience we temporarily expel troublesome inner complications. We expel "pity" and "fear" to use Aristotle's terms, and the terms are broad enough to cover the most pathological or near-pathological elements—namely anxieties, fears, morbid grief or self-pity, sadistic or masochistic desires, and the sense of guilt that these engender and are engendered by. In a successful tragedy we see these drives enacted on the stage directly or through their results by characters whom we can identify ourselves. They are our proxies, so to speak . . . In tragedy there is always a precipitate of final enlightenment—some inherent, cumulatively realized, understanding. . . . Enlightenment is, therefore, the third component of the process of purgation.[8]

Gassner applies Aristotle's terminology to a twentieth-century version of tragedy. Aristotle would not have recognized such terms as "near-pathological elements," "anxieties," and "sadistic or masochistic desires"—terms that are today part of our everyday vocabulary. Gassner tempers the Aristotelian purgation by specifying its effects as temporary, its results as enlightening.

The playwright Arthur Miller (b. 1915) wrote *Death of a Salesman* in 1949. The play was enormously successful in the commercial theatre and gave rise to many celebrated performances. In it Miller attempted to adapt tragedy to the changing views of the twentieth century.

Willie Loman, the main character, is an ordinary man living in an ordinary neighborhood with his ordinary, middle-class family. Willie has been a traveling salesman his entire adult life and still has nothing to show for his labors. When he was a young man, Willie believed anyone could attain success through hard work, and that with success would come love and acceptance. His circumstances worsen to the point where he can no longer believe in the American Dream, and in his despair, Willie kills himself.

Arthur Miller redefined the tragic hero for a modern industrial age:

> I believe that the common man is as apt a subject for tragedy in its highest sense as kings were . . . As a general rule, to which there may be exceptions unknown to me, I think the tragic feeling is evoked in us when we are in the presence of a character who is ready to lay down his life, if need

The original
Broadway pro-
duction of
Arthur Miller's
*Death of a
Salesman*, pro-
duced in 1949,
with Lee J. Cobb
and Mildred
Dunnock in the
leading roles.

be, to secure one thing—his sense of personal dignity. From Orestes to
Hamlet, Medea to Macbeth, the underlying struggle is that of the individual attempting to gain his "rightful" position in his society.[9]

In his book *Theatre of the Oppressed*, Augusto Boal writes a poetics for
a new theatre of political action in which he opposes, so many centuries
later, Aristotle's concept of tragedy, which he characterizes as being dedicated to inaction:

> Let there be no doubt: Aristotle formulated a very powerful purgative sys-
> tem, the objective of which is to eliminate all that is not commonly ac-
> cepted, including the revolution, before it takes place. His system appears
> in disguised form on television, in the movies, in the circus, in the
> theaters. It appears in many and varied shapes and media. But its essence
> does not change: If this is what we want, the Aristotelian system serves
> the purpose better than any other; if, on the contrary, we want to stimu-
> late the spectator to transform society, to engage in revolutionary action,
> in that case we will have to seek another poetics![10]

Boal accuses Greek tragedy of inventing the tragic flaw—that which is to be
purged—to prevent needed change in society, to purge, in fact, the impulse
for revolution.

Gassner, Miller, and Boal propose definitions of tragedy that suit the
audiences of their time. If Hedda, or Nina in *The Seagull*, are interpreted in
terms of Gassner's prescription for tragedy, they become tragic characters

because they pursue objectives impossible or at least extremely difficult for women of their time to attain. They can therefore be said to exhibit pathological, neurotic, or even masochistic characteristics.

Miller's redefinition of the tragic hero can be easily applied to the characters in *A Streetcar Named Desire*, written only a few years before *Death of a Salesman*. Blanche, Stanley, and Stella are ordinary people whose actions will not affect more than the small world around them. They each seek dignity of one sort or another, and so fit Miller's observations about the tragic character in America at midcentury.

Blanche has lost her place in society—that of a young Southern belle with money, beaus, and a big white house with columns—and has arrived unannounced, presumably with no funds, at her sister's house. She is at the mercy of the Kowalskis, and in order to preserve her sense of dignity, resorts to arrogant and vindictive behavior, which prevents her from adapting to her new situation and seeing the threat posed by Stanley. Stanley feels that Blanche is threatening his dignity, which is intimately tied to his relationship with Stella. Stella also seeks personal dignity, but is torn between two definitions of what that might be.

Augusto Boal's position is so extreme—and much more akin to Brecht's than to Aristotle's—that it is difficult to apply to the five plays being examined in this text. But if we look at the qualities Aristotle might view as being purged, we can evaluate what Boal's position might be. All of the female characters we are analyzing, and many of the male, seem to need purging of the means by which they attain their goals: power (the Macbeths); knowl-

In these two photographs, the actor Kevin Kline performs in plays of different genres. One photograph shows the actor in Shakespeare's *Tragedy of Richard III*; in the other Kline appears in a New York Shakespeare Festival Production of Shakespeare's comedy *Measure for Measure*.

edge and an equal place in society (Hedda and Heidi); love (Nina and Blanche). What might Boal have said about purging these "flaws" and their connection to revolution? Boal would probably prove his point by observing Hedda's quest for knowledge or Heidi's search for an equal place in society. If these goals are purged, then revolution cannot take place—in this case, a desirable revolution.

Using your own, more contemporary point of view, how might you rethink Aristotle's definition of tragedy in relation to Lady Macbeth's soliloquy? How might the language of the soliloquy have changed if Shakespeare had written *Macbeth* as a comedy?

For centuries, Aristotle's observations about tragedy have been fought over and redefined. It should be clear from our examples that many forms of serious drama have developed, some forming new categories, some fitting Aristotle's definition of tragedy closely, some trying unsuccessfully to fit it, some opposing it entirely and creating new forms.

MELODRAMA   One of the most abiding of these other forms of drama is the *melodrama*, a term derived from the Greek word *melos*, meaning music. Melodrama developed from a form in which music, inserted between sections of dialogue, expressed the emotional content of the scene. Melodramas lean toward an oversimplification of emotion, much the way a movie score communicates point of view in a film.

The hero or heroine in melodrama is typically entrapped by an apparently innocent, but actually villainous, character. Some characters in *Hedda Gabler* possess qualities that tie them to the melodramatic tradition. Brack certainly qualifies as the seemingly innocent friend who is revealed to be one of the play's villains. He even ties Hedda—emotionally—to the railroad tracks; unfortunately for her, the noble hero fails to arrive just in time to save her.

Today, soap operas make extensive use of music and other melodramatic conventions to underline important emotional moments. They have cliffhanging plots, although usually highly charged emotional circumstances and sexual encounters substitute for the traditional oncoming train.

Comedy

In general, theorists have had considerably less to say about comedy than about tragedy or other forms of serious drama, perhaps because comedy has historically adopted ordinary characters and everyday problems. Comedy has always been a popular form of entertainment, but because it has rarely been revered, those who write about it often do so from a defensive position, attempting to justify it as an effective alternative to tragedy for purging society of its moral illnesses.

Jean Baptiste Poquelin, known as Molière (1622–1673), wrote comedies

In productions of traditional melodramas virtually everything is enacted onstage, including spectacular scenic effects such as fires and collapsing walls. This photograph of a 1901 production of *Uncle Tom's Cabin* illustrates the scene in which Eliza crosses the frozen river. Note the use of animals onstage and the elaborate painted detail in the scenery.

A poster from a production of a turn-of-the-century melodrama entitled *Her Fatal Love*. The scene—a noble woman protecting the infant from the ill-intentioned group on the left—and the broad physical gestures are reminiscent of today's soap operas.

exclusively. Among them was *Tartuffe* (1669), which was attacked and censured when it was first performed, and was then permitted to be re-mounted. Molière had this to say about the social value of comedy in the revised preface to his play:

> . . . and we have seen that the stage possesses a great virtue as a *corrective medium.* The most beautiful passages in a serious moral are most frequently less powerful than those of a satire; and nothing admonishes the majority of people better than the portrayal of their faults. To expose vices to the ridicule of all the world is a severe blow to them. Reprehensions are easily suffered, but not so *ridicule.* People do not mind being wicked; but they object to being made ridiculous. (emphasis added)[11]

In *Tartuffe* Molière puts his theory into action. The title character, ostensibly a man of religion, has managed to install himself in the household of a Monsieur Orgon in Paris. This Orgon is very impressed with Tartuffe,

Two very different interpretations of the seduction scene in *Tartuffe*. In the photo on the *left*, Tartuffe makes rather restrained advances toward Elmire, while in the photo on the *right*, showing the same scene from a 1988 production at the Seattle Repertory Theater, his approach is far more aggressive.

who is, in fact, a fraud and a hypocrite. In one very famous scene, the pious Tartuffe is overheard trying to make love to Orgon's wife, Elmire, who, in turn, pretends to yield in order to prove Tartuffe's hypocrisy to her husband. But Orgon continues to respect Tartuffe's word, even deeding his house to the scoundrel! In the end, a message from the king is needed to resolve the situation (much like Medea's chariot) and dispatch Tartuffe to prison.

In *The Heidi Chronicles*, Wasserstein investigates the subject of hypocrisy as well. The character Scoop, a seemingly liberal son of the 1960s, treats all the women in his life, including Heidi, with something much less than the equality they demand throughout the play. Because his attitude is often presented from a comic perspective, his hypocritical behavior seems ridiculous rather than offensive or dangerous.

Like tragedy, comedy takes many forms. Two significant subcategories are the *comedy of manners* and *farce*. Comedy of manners generally takes as its subject chic, trendy, upper-class characters. The standards of behavior in these plays are highly suspect: Those who are clever win, the foolish or stupid lose. Oscar Wilde (1854–1900) was one of the great practitioners of the comedy of manners, writing such masterworks of the form as *The Importance of Being Earnest* (1894). Noël Coward (1899–1973), too, made a considerable contribution with plays such as *Hay Fever* (1925), *Private Lives* (1930), and *Blithe Spirit* (1941).

Whereas the comedy of manners makes use of witty, urbane language

A 1986 production of Noël Coward's comedy *Hay Fever*, on Broadway starring Rosemary Harris (lower right).

A production of Oscar Wilde's comedy of manners, *The Importance of Being Earnest*, with Sir John Gielgud (upper right).

and repartee, farce is comedy at its broadest, and is characterized by an emphasis on physical humor. (If *The Heidi Chronicles* were to be categorized as a comedy, it would conform more closely to the comedy of manners.) Farce often hinges on extramarital relationships; in fact, there is an entire subcategory known as *bedroom farce*. Traditional farces were written by playwrights such as Georges Feydeau (1862–1921), whose 1910 comedy, *A Flea in Her Ear*, is still frequently performed.

Tragicomedy

The centerpiece of act 1 of Chekhov's *The Seagull* is Nina's performance of a one-person play written for her by another major character, Konstantin Treplev (who, incidentally, is in love with her). The audience of the play within the play includes Konstantin's mother, Arkadina, herself an actress, who quickly becomes involved with the action onstage.

[Will o' the wisps appear on the stage.]

ARKADINA: *[softly]* This is something decadent.

KONSTANTIN: *[imploringly, and in a reproachful voice]* Please, Mother!

NINA: "I am lonely, lonely. Once in a hundred years I open my lips to speak and my voice re-echoes forlornly in this desert, and no one hears.

And you, too, pale lights, do not hear me. The stagnant marsh gives birth to you before daybreak and you wander until dawn . . . Like a prisoner cast into a deep, empty well, I know not where I am, nor what awaits me. One thing only is not hidden from me: I know that in the hard and cruel struggle with Satan, the origin of all the forces of matter, I am destined to conquer. . . Till then—horror, horror. *[Pause. Against the background of the lake two red spots appear.]* Here comes Satan, my mighty adversary. I can see his terrible blood-red eyes—"

ARKADINA: There's a smell of sulphur. Is that really necessary?. . .

In Chapter 4, we will investigate some of the interpretive issues this scene presents to the actors, but what is important here is that Chekhov has projected comic moments such as these against the background of the serious and tragic outcome of the scene—Treplev takes his mother's comments very hard and abruptly halts the performance—and the tragic outcome of the play as a whole. Because this passage is humorous to some of the characters in the scene and not to others, the reader is even more in need of interpretation. Chekhov has created the genre known as *tragicomedy.* By combining comic and tragic elements, tragicomedy reflects life, in which rarely is anything all bad or all good.

The tragicomedy has been around for a long time. Shakespeare, too, inserted comic scenes into tragedies, both to provide relief for the audience and to comment on or mirror the main plot of the play. The famous "porter scene" in *Macbeth* (act 3, scene 3) opens with a drunken porter's comically bumbling efforts to answer a knocking at the gate.

Theatre of the Absurd

The twentieth century has witnessed the emergence of forms of playwriting that do not fit neatly into any of the traditional genres. Some of these new forms use language, situation, character, and plot in new and often unconventional ways.

Theatre of the Absurd has been described as:

- Having little or no plot.
- Having often unfamiliar, sometimes almost mechanical, characters.
- Having no clear beginning, ending, or coherently resolved theme.
- Reflecting nightmares rather than everyday life.[12]

Martin Esslin began his book *The Theater of the Absurd* (1961) with a discussion of a 1957 performance of *Waiting for Godot* by Samuel Beckett (1906–1990) at San Quentin prison. (Beckett himself subtitled his play "a tragicomedy in two acts.") The production was well received by the prison inmates, perhaps because the basic theme of the play—waiting—is one with which they could easily identify.

The stage directions for act 1 of *Waiting for Godot* are: "A country road. A tree. Evening." This play could take place anywhere, in any country, on any road, under any tree, on any evening. The point of attack is almost impossible to determine; in fact, the lack of a clear beginning or end is the central subject of the play. Likewise, the structure is not easily categorized as linear *or* episodic. The characters are discovered in midaction, equally ambiguous and unexplained:

ESTRAGON: Charming spot. *(He turns, advances to front, halts, facing auditorium)* Inspiring prospects. *(He turns to Vladimir)* Let's go.

VLADIMIR: We can't.

ESTRAGON: Why not?

VLADIMIR: We're waiting for Godot.

ESTRAGON: *(despairingly)* Ah! *(Pause)* You're sure it was here?

VLADIMIR: What?

ESTRAGON: That we were to wait.

VLADIMIR: He said by the tree. *(They look at the tree)* Do you see any others?

ESTRAGON: What is it?

VLADIMIR: I don't know. A willow.

ESTRAGON: Where are the leaves?

The 1956 production of Samuel Beckett's *Waiting for Godot* with Bert Lahr (lower left).

VLADIMIR: It must be dead.

ESTRAGON: No more weeping.

VLADIMIR: Or perhaps it's not the season.

ESTRAGON: Looks to me more like a bush.

VLADIMIR: A shrub.

ESTRAGON: A bush.

VLADIMIR: A—What are you insinuating? That we've come to the wrong place?

ESTRAGON: He should be here.

VLADIMIR: He didn't say for sure he'd come.

ESTRAGON: And if he doesn't come?

VLADIMIR: We'll come back to-morrow.

ESTRAGON: And then the day after to-morrow.

VLADIMIR: Possibly.

ESTRAGON: And so on.

The original New York production in 1961 of Jean Genet's *The Blacks.*

VLADIMIR: The point is—

ESTRAGON: Until he comes.

VLADIMIR: You're merciless.

And they go on waiting for someone who never appears, in a place they sometimes recognize as the spot they were at the day before, sometimes not, waiting for "something" to happen. *Waiting for Godot* might be said to be a commentary on the human ability to survive in a godless, absurd world in which nothing happens. The plays of Edward Albee (b. 1928), Harold Pinter (b. 1930), Jean Genet (1910–1986), and Eugène Ionesco (b. 1912) are other important representatives of this form.

Every reader forms an interpretation of a play based on his or her personal reaction to it. In the next chapter we will examine how the theatre artists working together on a production extend personal interpretation into the reality of actual theatrical performance.

Suggested Readings

Aristotle, *Aristotle's Poetics,* trans. S. H. Butcher (New York: Hill and Wang), 1961.

Antonin Artaud, *The Theater and Its Double* (New York: Grove Press), 1958.

Kathleen Betsko and Rachel Koenig, *Interviews with Contemporary Women Playwrights* (New York: Beachtree Books), 1987.

Augusto Boal, *Theatre of the Oppressed* (New York: Theatre Communications Group), 1985.

Oscar G. Brockett, *History of the Theatre,* 6th ed. (Boston: Allyn and Bacon), 1991.

Barrett H. Clark, *European Theories of the Drama* (New York: Crown), 1965.

Toby Cole, ed., *Playwrights on Playwrighting* (New York: Hill and Wang), 1961.

Martin Esslin, *The Theater of the Absurd* (New York: Overlook Press), 1973.

David Savran, *In Their Own Words: Contemporary American Playwrights* (New York: Theater Communications Group), 1988.

Chapter TWO

Interpretation
and
Collaboration

*Should we respect the text? I think there is a healthy double atti-
tude, with respect on the one hand and disrespect on the other, and
the dialectic between the two is what it's all about. If you go solely
one or the other way, you lose the possibility of capturing the truth.*[1]
—Peter Brook

When a play is being read in preparation for its production on stage,
the production team needs to come to an understanding about what
eventually will be presented to the audience. This means reaching a
shared interpretation. This group of artists is responsible for whatever their production communicates to the audience. Here are a few
questions that could help to measure the impact of a particular interpretation:

• What does this interpretation imply for an audience?
• What will the audience take away from the performance? How

might the audience change the way it sees or does things, as a result of this interpretation?

- What are the ramifications of the interpretation of a single moment for the entire play?

The Production Concept

Once a shared interpretation has been roughly established, it is time to begin the process of *conceptualizing* the performance—not only what it will mean, but how that meaning will be expressed in theatrical terms. Theatrical performance, like any art form, does not articulate its meaning directly to the audience. An interpretation can be produced or expressed in many different ways. A *production concept* clarifies the specific way in which the artists working on a particular production will communicate their shared point of view to the audience. This production concept is a plan that integrates and orchestrates all the elements of the production—acting, stage space, light, costume, sound, music. The production team, equipped with its production concept, collaboratively translates ideas into theatrical images. The production concept gives everyone a common point of reference and allows each aspect of the production to be realized from a clearly stated point of view. As preparation and rehearsal move along, a production concept will undergo adjustment and become more detailed.

An Example of a Production Concept and Its Realization Onstage

Whether it is called a blueprint, a plan, or a "sense of direction"—or is not alluded to at all—the production concept is widely used in today's theatre. Elia Kazan, the director of the original Broadway production of *A Streetcar Named Desire*, developed the production concept for that play in a series of notes. In these notes Kazan expresses:

- a point of view on the whole play
- a point of view on the character of Blanche, and how that relates to the point of view on the whole
- the broad way in which that point of view was to be realized—through the production concept—in performance

First, he describes what he calls the play's theme (his point of view, or interpretation) as:

> a message from the dark interior. This little twisted, pathetic, confused bit of light and culture puts out a cry. It is snuffed out by the crude forces of violence, insensibility and vulgarity which exist in our South—and this cry is the play.[2]

That which is giving out a cry—the culture of the old South, confused as it is—is, in his point of view, violently eradicated by the new South.

Kazan goes on in his notes to describe his point of view on Blanche's character. He says she has unrealistic ideas about what a woman should be, ideas connected to the traditional Southern upbringing that is subject to this new violence. She is stuck within an ideal. Kazan believed that her self-image could not exist in the reality of the South of the play; but she tries to keep it alive in her fantasies—that is all she knows.

Finally, Kazan describes how this point of view—on the play as a whole and on the character of Blanche—might be realized on stage. At the beginning, he says, Blanche should be perceived by the audience as the "heavy." She must be seen as inconsistent: She is pushy yet unable to provide for herself; she embodies the problems of the old South. Early in the production, Blanche should be seen as a negative influence on Stella, and the audience should want Stanley to triumph in their confrontations. But then, as Stanley becomes more and more violent and strips away Blanche's defenses, the audience will begin to see how hopeless her situation truly is, how much she needs the help of those around her, and they will begin to sympathize with her. This, Kazan says, is how the audience perceives the tragedy of the death of anything—useless as it may be—especially when there is so much violence present in this play.

Here are Tennessee Williams's stage directions for scene 10 of the play:

> *It is a few hours later that night. Blanche has been drinking fairly steadily since Mitch left. She has dragged her wardrobe trunk into the center of the bedroom. It hangs open with flowery dresses thrown across it. As the drinking and packing went on, a mood of hysterical exhilaration came into her and she has decked herself out in a somewhat soiled and crumpled white satin evening gown and a pair of scuffed silver slippers with brilliants set in their heels. Now she is placing the rhinestone tiara on her head before the mirror of the dressing-table and murmuring excitedly as if to a group of spectral admirers.*

Later in this same scene, as Blanche feels Stanley threatening her, the stage directions say that she smashes a bottle on the table and faces him, "clutching the broken top." Photo 2.1, of Marlon Brando and Jessica Tandy in the original production of *A Streetcar Named Desire*, shows the con-

Photo 2.1
Marlon Brando
as Stanley
Kowalski and
Jessica Tandy as
Blanche DuBois
in scene 10 of
*A Streetcar
Named Desire.*

frontation between Blanche and Stanley alone together. How does this photograph relate to the production concept above?

In the photo, Kazan's notes about Blanche's character seem realized. She does look desperate, needy, and sincere. She seems to be pleading with Stanley. Blanche's costume is totally inappropriate for any occasion in a modern (even late 1940s) household. Its roses, lace, and satin are excessive, though the cut is refined and genteel. This is the dress of a lady of another time. It has been ironed too many times and its lace is coming off. It is not possible to equate a dress with an entire character, but we can recognize that Blanche has chosen to wear this particular dress to help her pretend she is in the past.

Stanley and Blanche each have hold of the dress—neither too strenuously, although Stanley appears less concerned than Blanche. He is dressed, not unreasonably, in an undershirt and pants.

Stanley stands over Blanche, who seems to be falling, although he is not pushing her. He looks at her as she pulls away. There is no hope for Blanche, even this early in the scene. When Stanley later tries to keep her from leaving the bedroom, he is preying upon someone already trapped. She is an ineffective, frail version of what was once a powerful feminine ideal. Blanche has taken the time to make herself look this way (her hair is neat, her tiara on straight), and this small, misplaced attempt at control over her life is set, in the photo, against Stanley's psychological and physical power.

In this production, Blanche defeats herself by her need to escape into a fantasy world, as Kazan said, of an old, outdated version of the South. Stanley need only give her a small push and she will fall over the edge. The contrast between the two costumes, the relationships established by the staging, even the height of the chair Blanche crouches on, together communicate Kazan's production concept to the audience.

Some Elements of a Production Concept

Not all theatrical performances are the result of carefully worked out production concepts. By choosing not to be limited to a single point of view at the very beginning of the rehearsal process, some productions develop through a more investigative approach. But if all the artists working on a production choose to work with a production concept, they will need to develop the shared interpretation, or a *production point of view* that can be verbally expressed. If we examine Photos 2.2 and 2.3 from two productions of *Hedda Gabler,* both show Hedda in a scene with Judge Brack. Eva le Gallienne's Hedda faces him. She is seated uncomfortably and at a lower level than he. She is backing away slightly, and is weighted with rich, elaborate

Photo 2.2
Eva le Gallienne
as Hedda
Gabler.

Photo 2.3
Claire Bloom as
Hedda Gabler.

clothing. Claire Bloom's Hedda seems almost autumnal and cool; she is detached and aloof, not responsive to an affectionate gesture. While Eva le Gallienne's Hedda seeks escape by cowering and pulling away, this Hedda looks as if all hope, even the hope of escape, has long left her.

Interpretation is communicated to the audience through *images,* the *theatrical environment,* and the *style of performance.*

IMAGE   An *image* draws a parallel between the play and the senses, translating the former from the verbal to the physical and visual. An image for a play might be an autumn day, an ice cream cake, a meat freezer, a circus tent—anything.

Appealing to the senses through images is a direct and accessible means of communicating with the audience. For example, you might say that Claire Bloom's Hedda is catlike, while Eva le Gallienne's is more like a tiny, nervous lap dog—perhaps a terrier. Bloom's Hedda is disturbing; le Gallienne's is merely an annoying distraction.

If you were to think of an image for the entire production, which of the following would be most likely to suggest the relationships reflected in the photographs?

- A steel animal trap
- A tight, boned corset

- A blue face in a dry-cleaning bag
- A balloon about to be pricked by a pin
- A helium-filled balloon floating just out of grasp

STAGE ENVIRONMENT   Establishing the environment in which the performance will take place is another major consideration in the development of a production concept. The stage world is made up of scenery, costumes, make-up, lighting, and sound. This environment will influence the way the actors move and speak onstage. What we can see of the environments or settings presented in these two photographs communicates two distinct ideas.

The environment of the le Gallienne production, although simple in overall line, is rich in detail, consisting largely of floral or plant images, and of damask, velvet, and other heavy, luxurious fabrics. The costumes are consistent with the setting.

Claire Bloom's Hedda is caught in an equally elaborate environment. While surrounded by folds of velvet, large dark furniture, and flowered damask, her clothing is simple and unaffected. This adds to her detachment (she makes *little* attempt to fit in), making her oddly less vulnerable in this production than Eva le Gallienne's Hedda is in hers.

Whether or not the production concept is written down in detail, a plan gradually develops that might do the following:

- Tell the costume designer that the color palette will be
golds and white for the le Gallienne production,
grays for Claire Bloom.
- Tell the lighting designer that the lighting will be
bright and warm for the first,
cool and rainy for the second.
- Tell the scenic designer that the setting will be
rich and grand for the first,
spare for the second.
- Tell the director that the staging will be
formal and symmetrical for the first,
with little movement for the second.
- Tell the actor that gestures and movement should be
controlled, elegant, and sophisticated for the first,
small and precise for the second.

How the artists achieve these effects and orchestrate their individual work is the subject of Part 2 of this text.

Another factor under consideration is the form of the play, its *style* or *genre*. It is important to consider how the literary form, such as tragedy, comedy, or tragicomedy, translates into theatrical performance. In both of these photographs, Ibsen's style of writing seems to be evoked. Both stages are dark, as is the overall tone of the play. Like Ibsen's dialogue, the action and the visual pictures are direct, spare, and hard. Although they differ in interpretation, each production reflects the period in which Ibsen's play was written. The style of Ibsen's world could easily inhabit either of these two productions.

Interpretation and the Rights of the Playwright

Since a play is almost always written to be performed by an infinite number of actors for an infinite number of audiences over countless years, how can there be only one interpretation? This question leads to an age-old question in the theatre: Who holds the right of interpretation? Does the writer alone decide how each moment is to be played? Is this possible if the playwright is not involved with the production? Or is it the actor who interprets and literally shows the audience a way to look at the playwright's ideas? And what about the director?

Now that the means of developing an interpretation is becoming a little clearer, what is the relationship of the playwright—or the written play that represents the playwright—to the other theatrical artists, such as the director and the actor or actress? If you as reader interact with a play from your personal point of view, can you ever *fully* understand the playwright's intention? Why is it so difficult to imagine ourselves as interpreters when we are reading plays or novels or poems? Why is finding the playwright's intention so important? Why is it so important to understand, or believe that we are trying to understand, the author's true meaning? Whatever the answers to these questions, much work in both the production process and scholarship has been devoted to understanding the playwright's intended meaning. It may simply not ever be possible either to know all the implications contained in a play or to show them all in a single production.

Henrik Ibsen described Hedda Gabler physically, as well as emotionally, in his notes:

> Hedda: Slender figure of average height. Nobly shaped, aristocratic face with fine, wax-colored skin. The eyes have a veiled expression. Hair medium brown. Not especially abundant hair. Dressed in a loose-fitting dressing gown, white with blue trimmings. Composed and relaxed in her manners. The eyes steel-gray, almost lusterless.[3]

These notes, though not as rich and exciting as the play itself, are evocative and detailed. But once carefully analyzed, they—like stage directions—yield only very broad outlines and not much specific information. Although they certainly are worth the time and effort of research, the notes require almost as much interpretation as does the play. How slender is "slender," and by whose standards? What is noble? Or aristocratic? What is a veiled expression? It is the sheer number of possibilities that makes any work exciting. Finding a meaning for today's audience, from the point of view of someone living in today's world with today's problems, keeps the work alive. A lesser play wouldn't have room for so many interpretations.

Some of our most important writers have reacted to interpretation in ways that call into question the collaborative nature of theatre. In 1985, Samuel Beckett's play *Endgame* was produced by Robert Brustein at the American Repertory Theatre. The playwright was extremely offended by the production and tried to stop its performance. Figure 2.1 shows what finally appeared in the program.

In the middle of the controversy was JoAnne Akalaitis, the director, who has observed:

> Each Beckett play is different from the others. While I think that Beckett's work is more sacred than other contemporary writers', and I pay more attention to his pauses and indications about timing than anyone else's, when I think of his work I don't necessarily think of bare spaces. For example, Beckett says *Endgame* takes place in an empty room. We set it in a subway station with a littered subway train, water, rubble. . . . You have to think what it really *means* when the writer describes the set and gives stage directions. A writer is seeing something in a physical universe that should be taken as a very useful guide.[4]

JoAnne Akalaitis's production of Beckett's *Endgame* at the American Repertory Theatre (1985) created controversy when the playwright objected to its setting: a subway station.

Figure 2.1
Statements by
Robert Brustein
of the American
Repertory
Theatre; Barney
Rossett, then
president of
Grove Press,
Samuel Beck-
ett's American
publisher; and
Samuel Beckett
himself regard-
ing the Ameri-
can Repertory
Theatre's pro-
duction of Beck-
ett's *Endgame*.

STATEMENT BY THE AMERICAN REPERTORY THEATRE

Samuel Beckett's plays are among the most powerful documents of the modern age--but except in
published form they are not etched in stone. Like
all works of theatre, productions of ENDGAME depend
upon the collective contributions of directors, actors, and designers to realize them effectively, and
normal rights of interpretation are essential in order to free the full energy and meaning of the play.
Each age, furthermore, brings fresh eyes to the
works of the past--it was Beckett's ENDGAME, ironically, that inspired Peter Brooks' radical new reading of
Shakespeare's KING LEAR. We believe that this production, despite hearsay representations to the contrary, observes the spirit and the text of Mr. Beckett's great play--far more so, in fact, than a
number of past productions, which to our knowledge
evoked no public protests from
Mr. Beckett's agents. One of these, recently performed
in Belgium in 1983, was set in a warehouse flooded
with 8,000 feet of water; another, produced in New
York in 1972, substituted American colloquialisms
for Beckett's language. Indeed, when directing his
work, Mr. Beckett makes significant revisions in his
own text and stage
directions, suggesting that even he recognizes the
need for changes with the passage of time. But even
were our own production far more revisionist or radical, it is the public that must be the final arbiter of its value. This is not the first appearance
of ENDGAME, nor is it likely to be the last. Like
all great works of theatrical art, the play is open
to many approaches, and each new production uncorks
new meanings. To threaten any deviations from a
purist rendering of this or any other play--to
insist on strict adherence to each parenthesis of
the published text--not only robs collaborating

Page One
of
ENDGAME*
as written by
SAMUEL BECKETT

Bare interior.

Grey light.

Left and right back, high up, two small windows, curtains drawn.

Front right, a door. Hanging near door, its face to wall, a picture.

Front left, touching each other, covered with an old sheet, two ashbins.

Center, in an armchair on castors, covered with an old sheet, Hamm.

Motionless by the door, his eyes fixed on Hamm, Clov. Very red face. Brief tableau.

Clov goes and stands under window left. Stiff, staggering walk. He looks up at window left. He turns and looks at window right. He goes and stands under window right. He looks up at window right. He turns and looks at window left. He goes out, comes back immediately with a small step-ladder, carries it over and sets it down under window left, gets up on it, draws back curtain. He gets down, takes six steps (for example) towards window right, goes back for ladder, carries it over and sets it down under window right, gets up on it, draws back curtain. He gets down, takes three steps towards window left, goes back for ladder, carries it over and sets it down under window left, gets up on it, looks out of window. Brief laugh. He gets down, takes one step towards window right, goes back for ladder, carries it over and sets it down under window right, gets up on it, looks out of window. Brief laugh. He gets down, goes with ladder towards ashbins, halts, turns, carries back ladder and sets it down under window right, goes to ashbins, removes sheet covering them, folds it over his arm. He raises one lid, stoops and looks into bin. Brief laugh. He closes lid. Same with other bin. He goes to Hamm, removes sheet covering him, folds it over his arm. In a dressing-gown, a stiff toque on his head, a large blood-stained handkerchief over his face, a whistle hanging from his neck, a rug over his knees, thick socks on his feet, Hamm seems to be asleep. Clov looks him over. Brief laugh. He goes to door, halts, turns towards auditorium.

CLOV *(fixed gaze, tonelessly)*:

> Finished, it's finished, nearly finished, it must be nearly finished.
> *(Pause.)*
> Grain upon grain, one by one, and one day, suddenly, there's a heap, a little heap, the impossible heap.
> *(Pause.)*
> I can't be punished any more.

*Copyright c 1958 by Grove Press, Inc.

STATEMENT BY SAMUEL BECKETT
ABOUT THIS A.R.T. PRODUCTION

"Any production of <u>Endgame</u> which ignores my stage
directions is completely unacceptable to me. My play
requires an empty room and two small windows. The
American Repertory Theatre production which dis-
misses my directions is a complete parody of the
play as conceived by me. Anybody who cares for the
work couldn't fail to be disgusted by this."

—<u>Samuel Beckett</u>

As personal friend and publisher of Samuel Beckett,
Grove Press is charged with the obligation of protecting the integrity of Samuel Beckett's work in
the United States. The audience of the American
Repertory Theatre production can judge for itself
how the stage before you differs from Beckett's directions as they are reproduced here from the
printed text. In Beckett's plays the set, the movements of the actors, the silences specified in the
text, the lighting and the costumes are as important
as the words spoken by the actors. In the author's
judgment --and ours-- this production makes a trav-
esty of his conception. A living author of Beckett's
stature should have the right to protect himself
from what he perceives to be a gross distortion of
his work. We deplore the refusal of the American
Repertory Theatre to accede to Beckett's wishes to
remove his name from this production, indicate in
some way that this staging is merely an adaption, or
stop it entirely.

-- Barney Rossett,
President, Grove Press, Inc.

Here Akalaitis investigates the relative positions of writer and director in the theatre and adds another dimension to the play. Rather than using an empty stage, as Beckett stipulates in his stage directions, she fills the space with rubble. Moving the play from an empty room to a subway station changes the audience's perceptions. Her production concept relates the play to an identifiable image of contemporary society. Does this contribute something to an audience? Does it hurt the play?

What does it mean for the theatre to have produced this play in a way different from what Beckett desired? Although this disagreement was, on the surface, about the interpretation of a stage direction, or setting, what might be the ramifications of extending it to other production elements—to how the actors act or the play is staged? What does it mean for Beckett to have reacted this way? Would you, as an audience member, want to know if a production took great liberties with—or ran counter to—a playwright's character descriptions, stage directions, or dialogue? If a playwright writes *for* the stage, isn't performance expected to be a vehicle for new and exciting interpretations? How do the other theatre artists maintain the integrity of the play and still keep it alive for a contemporary audience?

Collaboration in the Theatre

Theatre is a complicated business that requires many skills for a successful performance to be realized. Rarely, if ever, will one person possess all of these skills. The production concept, as we have seen, allows the various members of the production team to create a unified meaning or interpretation. *Collaboration* refers to the actual coordination of work by these members, and it assumes that no one person could accomplish the work as satisfactorily as all of them working together. Whether or not it is acknowledged, collaboration always exists in the theatre, most visibly between actor and audience, without which performance wouldn't exist. Sometimes the process is merely pro forma, and some types of collaborations work better for some than for others. But theatre, with its many disparate elements, needs some kind of organizing principle, and the collaborative effort serves that purpose.

In an ideal collaboration, everyone involved performs his or her job with the good of the whole process, and the ultimate success of the production, in mind. A theatrical collaboration must (1) establish and clarify the production's point of view, (2) iron out discrepancies and disagreements, and (3) come to at least a general agreement about the production concept. Using this concept as a practical blueprint, the collaborators work out the details of the actual production, determining the relationships between in-

THE OPEN THEATER

The Open Theater (1962–1973) can serve as an example of collaborative creation. On several of its projects, the company worked with playwrights such as Jean-Claude Van Itallie (b. 1936) and Megan Terry (b. l932) who, in daily consultation with the company, wrote as the actors improvised. In October 1970, the company began rehearsals for a project that was to become *The Mutation Show.* They decided to try to write the work using only the resources of the actors and directors (Joseph Chaikin and Roberta Sklar). Working without a writer called for changes in the collaborative process itself:

> One major source of material was storytelling. Company members told stories that they felt somehow related to the theme of change or that, for whatever reason, they wanted to tell the group. The ones that struck a chord were repeated and distilled. . . . They also, as before, drew on outside speakers and published writings. . . . But the core of the investigation, as always, was theatrical, an exploration through stage action. One early exercise involved showing the different facets within a single person. The company members drew up a list of the selves that they all contained: the "acceptable self," the "narcissistic self," . . . the "mask." . . . Then as Chaikin called out an item from the list, the actors tried to express that part of their personalities."[5]

Gradually, over time, an entire production developed. The actors improvised properties and scenic elements. Early in the process, the actors purchased small, inexpensive objects that meant something to them relative to the idea of "change," and used them in rehearsal. These objects either remained in the final performance or were discarded along the way and exchanged for others. Designers were brought in after the production was well under way.

dividual elements and devising complex orchestrations among them. If each artist worked alone to communicate the point of view, the individual elements, when put together, would probably not relate to one another. If, for example, in keeping with the production concept, an actress has chosen to portray a cold, calculating Hedda, the characterization might be better set off against a warm, inviting environment than a cold and forbidding one. It is the many brush strokes taken together that add up to an interpretation.

Too many changes after all the elements of a production have been brought together are time consuming and costly. For this reason, during the early stages of the collaborative process, each choice needs to be carefully weighed against all the others.

The Collaborative Process

In a typical professional working situation, the *playwright* writes a play and, with luck, becomes connected with a *producer,* who raises money and hires the *director.* The director chooses *designers*—scenic, costume, lighting, and possibly sound—and casts *actors,* and together they begin work on the production. As we will see in the chapters that follow, there are many others who must participate in the collaboration. The costume designer has collaborators: the costume shop manager, wigmaker, stitcher, draper, and cutter. Each has a hand in the process and must fully understand the designer's intention in order to contribute to the successful completion of the costume. The stage carpenter or technical director collaborates with both the scenic designer and the shop to build the scenery. Even the press agent is part of the collaborative process. Effective advertising will "sell" the important features of the production, and publicists must work with the director, designers, producers, and actors to fully understand the intention of a particular production.

Although everyone who plays even the smallest part (onstage or off) in the production is a collaborator, some are obviously more seriously involved with the ideas surrounding the production than others. Playwright, director, designers, and actors contribute most directly to the point of view and overall production concept. Much of the time they spend together is devoted to discussion and presentation of ideas. Technicians, stage managers, stage crews, painters, and costume shop personnel are more involved in executing the chosen ideas through fabric, lumber, metal, and paint, and orchestrating the presentation onstage.

Collaboration is a process that draws on individual skills, interests, and ideas. The more equal the input among individuals, the more collaborative the venture. Collaboration can be difficult and a great deal of energy is devoted to finding a balance that works for each production. The artistic teams usually vary from production to production, and therefore a new balance needs to be found for each one. To further complicate the process, many directors and designers work on more than one production at a time. They may meet about one production and then another within the space of a few hours, each time working together with a new group of collaborators.

Collaborative contributions are not always equal. Sometimes more emphasis is placed on one area than on others. Scenic elements might be more important in one show, costumes in another, and lighting in a third. Thornton Wilder's *Our Town* (1938) was written to take place on a bare stage with few properties other than some ordinary chairs that serve many purposes throughout the performance. One character, the Stage Manager, narrates the play, speaking directly to the audience. He comments on the action throughout. In such a play, more demands are placed on costumes and lighting than on scenery. Within a large, nonspecific stage environment, lighting and costume provide information about mood and atmosphere, and

The Funeral
Scene from
Thornton
Wilder's *Our
Town* (1938).

control where the audience looks—and when. A minimal setting also increases the importance of the actor's ability to establish or evoke an environment. Some productions, such as many musicals, depend on elaborate staging (where the actors are to be placed onstage and how they are to get there) and choreography, while the staging of a play like *Hedda Gabler* is more likely to result from a combination of actor's instinct and director's guidance. Staging is obviously a more complicated business, from a strictly practical point of view, when twenty people are present onstage than when there are two or three.

Let us say that a play requires that it be snowing outside. Each collaborator must help to convey this apparently simple piece of information to the audience. First, the scenic designer might put a window onstage through which the exterior can be seen, and perhaps place a fireplace onstage. The sound designer might add the sizzle of a radiator. Artificial snow might be seen falling outside the window or be projected onto a surface on the back of the window—a joint effort between the scenic and lighting designers. The lighting outside the window would be cold and wintry. An actor might look out the window early in the scene to help the audience notice the snow. Another actor might enter from outside, shivering and stamping her feet, dressed in wet winter clothes. Every member of the collaborating group is involved in what might be less than one minute of stage time.

The creation of Banquo's ghost in *Macbeth* demands a collaborative effort, even though it might at first appear to require only an actor (or puppet or dummy) looking grim and ghostlike. Some questions that must be answered about this scene include:

EDWARD GORDON CRAIG: THE DIRECTOR AND HIS ÜBER-MARIONETTES

Edward Gordon Craig (1872–1966) was an influential designer-director whose ideal of the all-powerful director was connected to a general annoyance with the human fallibility of the actor and a desire for a peculiar kind of perfection in theatrical art. Craig discredited the actor's emotionalism and felt more secure with scenic expression—something he could control. Craig, who theoretically preferred an "Über-Marionette"—a kind of human puppet—to a living actor (although he later modified that idea), expressed his opinions about theatrical collaboration in this way:

> There is nothing more outrageous than that men and women should be let loose on a platform, so that they may expose that which artists refuse to show except veiled.[6]

He questioned the actor's ability to be a true collaborator:

> But has there never been an actor . . . who has so trained his body from head to foot that it would answer to the workings of his mind without permitting the emotions even so much as to awaken?[7]

By building a case for the impossibility of true intellectual collaboration with the actor, Craig created an argument for the power of the director: "Now, then, it is impossible for a work of art ever to be produced where more than one brain is permitted to direct."[8]

Craig did, for better or for worse, have a profound influence on theatre design in the twentieth century. His belief that one vision was all that was necessary or even useful in the theatre led the way for some of today's more autonomous directors such as André Serban and Robert Wilson.

Figures 2.2 and 2.3 show Craig's sketches for act 1, scene 1 and act 2 of *Macbeth*. If you look very closely at the first sketch,

- What does the ghost look like?
- How much of the ghost does the audience see (if it sees him at all)?
- Where does the ghost stand onstage relative to the other characters and the audience?
- Is the ghost's appearance accompanied by music or other sound?

This collaboration would include the actor, scenic designer, director, lighting designer, costume designer, and composer or sound designer.

Figure 2.2
Edward Gordon Craig's sketch for act 1, scene 1 of *Macbeth.*

Figure 2.3
Edward Gordon Craig's sketch for act 2 of *Macbeth.*

it is possible to see the tiny figure of an actor at the bottom righthand corner of the tall center opening; in the second illustration, the actor is running along the righthand side. The skyscraper form of the scenery, though perhaps foreshadow-ing contemporary urban life, overwhelms the actor, rendering him nearly invisible. These sketches illustrate the implications of Craig's theories—actors could be done without altogether.

How collaboration actually works varies a great deal from production to production and from company to company. There is no guide book to follow, although perhaps there should be. The two extremes are productions in which the responsibility for decision-making is roughly equally divided among the collaborating members, and productions in which the director makes all the decisions and the rest of the company follows the plan. We will consider both of these extremes in a moment, but first let's look at a more or less typical collaborative process.

Interview

AN INTERVIEW WITH WENDY WASSERSTEIN
ABOUT HER PLAY THE HEIDI CHRONICLES

What was the genesis of the play?

I wrote it at a time when I had been away from playwrighting for awhile. I was 36 years old and had written a musical and a movie that hadn't worked out very well. I wanted to get back to playwrighting, but the play had to be about something I really cared about, like the women's movement.

I have an interest in history, I need to put events in context. I can always remember not only what is said when I talk with people, but exactly where and when. I was a history major in college; I took the first women's history course offered at Mt. Holyoke.

I actually wrote the first scene of the play while I was working on *Isn't It Romantic.* When I got back to *The Heidi Chronicles*, I at first thought it might be about the history of the women's movement; but I became interested in the characters of Peter and Scoop and saw that it could be about not just this one woman, but a whole generation.

I wrote part of the play in London where I was working on a grant. *The Heidi Chronicles* contains some overtones of that experience, like some English plays concerned with the political versus the personal. At the same time, I was angry and concerned about a woman's place onstage in the theatre.

There is a contemporary notion that a woman shouldn't be on the sidelines. She must be active, like the female killers in the movies. Why are they active? Heidi's best friend Susan changes her act every four years, but Heidi is a reflective and careful person (*and* active—she joins the women's movement, she adopts the baby).

The play also became personally important to me. Many of my closest friends are gay and I wanted to write about the affection and love possible between a gay man and a straight woman. That generation redefined a sense of family. Our friends are our families. At the end of the play, the traditional monogamous relationship is Peter and the doctor's.

Why write for the theatre? for a "collaborative" art form?

The success of a play is collaborative. If the collaboration doesn't work, it is a complete nightmare, but sitting alone in one's room is not as much fun.

    I first wrote that this play could be performed on eight folding chairs. I am terrible on sets and lights (although too detailed about costumes sometimes). When Dan Sullivan [the play's original director] asked me how I thought the scene in front of the Chicago Art Institute in the rain was to happen, I said I honestly didn't know! Tom Lynch [the original scenic designer] and Dan made a huge contribution to the play. The two made the transitions from scene to scene work and together they saved the play. In the play Heidi is always watching. Tom's set got larger and larger as the performance went along, so we could see her perspective growing. At the end of the play, Pat Collins [the original lighting designer] brought light flooding in from the left. Heidi looked as if she lived in one of the paintings she studied. Jennifer von Mayrhauser [the original costume designer] is socially very acute. She always knows, for example, exactly what form of shoe to use—the Frye boots, etc., were always just right. The audience was able to know exactly where they were.

What is your writing process?

I write alone in the house. In some ways, it's the best time, if it is going well. The hardest scene to write was the baby shower. It is sedentary, there's not much happening, and so it just demands craft. The scene in the hospital was hard because it was so emotional. The easiest to write was the speech to Miss Crain's Alumni Association (which was originally eight pages long).

How do you feel about the actor's interpretation of your work?

The character of Heidi is open to interpretation; anything is okay as long as Heidi is observing. The play was criticized by many women because Heidi seemed too passive, but there is a difference between a person who is passive and one who is an observer. Although there was discussion from each of the actresses who played the role about making Heidi more active, different actresses brought out different parts of the role:

    Joan Allen [the original Heidi at Playwrights Horizon and on Broadway] has a rich, internal life; everything registers on her.

Christine Lahti was able to connect to audiences.

Brooke Adams, who was a single mother at the time (she had adopted a baby), had a loveliness and strength about her. She also has a great sense of comedy—the funny parts played better.

Mary McDonnell brought out the Midwestern aspect of the character, someone who is happy and hearty, but got caught up in the times.

Liz Mackay, who played Heidi in the original workshop in Seattle, herself became a source for Heidi material.

When writing a play there is an original voice in my head. When you get the wrong voice it is terrible. How actors speak is very important.

How do you affect the interpretive process in production?

I don't ever talk to the actors about performances. There is a ritual, an actor's gradation of the growth of a part. I sit behind the director and can quickly do rewrites to see if something (smaller things, not major restructuring) new works. Or, I can say through the director that something doesn't work for me.

Individual Work Prior to Collaboration

Before arriving at the first meeting, individual collaborators work alone in many different ways and, again, there are no set rules. One person might read the play several times, wait to hear what the others have to say, and then clarify his or her own thoughts and images. Another might begin by making a list of the basic facts contained in the play (such as the number of windows, doors, and staircases that are mentioned; the ages of the characters; the time of day and year; the historical period; the country; and even whether or not a telephone rings). Others might develop ideas about the play's topic—or theme—bringing that point of view to the group for discussion. Some collaborators write down images that come to mind, even if they are not necessarily connected to the requirements of the play. Designers or directors might even draw a few rough sketches of what the production could look like.

Collaboration Prior to Rehearsal

An early meeting about a play might take one of several directions. Let say your theatre is producing *Hedda Gabler,* and you are attending the initial meeting. The discussion could focus on a broad but complex thematic question, such as what in Hedda's life or personality caused her to choose suicide, the kind of society the play presents, Hedda's role models, her other options, or how her decision to end her life might affect decisions in our own lives, in our society.

The discussion could also begin with such concrete questions as what Hedda or Lovborg looks like, or how they look together onstage. An early meeting might be devoted to discussing the times of day in each act and how time affects the action. It might focus on a technical problem, such as how to make it look as if the manuscript is actually burning in the stove. Usually, early meetings address both thematic and practical questions. Ideally, the result is a collaborative effort that defines the point of view of the production.

Because plays such as *Macbeth* or *The Heidi Chronicles* involve more characters and changes of scene, the initial collaborative issues they raise will differ from those of a play like *Hedda Gabler.* Some problems that arise are:

- How movement from place to place will occur
- How various places will be differentiated (through changes in scenery, costume, lighting, or all three)
- In *Macbeth,* how the various families and loyalties will be identified by the audience
- In *The Heidi Chronicles,* how changes of year will be communicated.

Even questions about how much room is available backstage and how many changes of costume there will be might come up at an early meeting.

One important issue to be determined will be the nature of the collaboration itself. Issues to be ironed out include:

- Who will make the final decisions and how
- Which areas need special attention
- The length and kind of rehearsals
- How much rewriting is anticipated if the play is new and the playwright is present
- How early—or late—costumes, scenery, and lighting will be introduced into the production.

Ideally, all elements of the production should move along at approximately the same rate. It makes no sense to decide upon a costume or setting, and have it be drawn and built, long before the actor and director decide how the character should dress or where the character should live. Still, the cost of time and materials dictates that elements such as costumes and scenery often begin to be prepared before rehearsals begin, and substantial changes are rarely possible after that point. Because of scheduling and space constraints (and consequent financial considerations), actors in this country generally do not rehearse in costume or on the actual set. This leads to two separate groups of collaborators: one composed of the director and the designers, another of the director and the actors. The director, who belongs to both groups, automatically becomes the arbiter between the two.

Later, meetings between the designers and the director center around the presentation of sketches and models; sometimes—but all too rarely—actors attend. Part of the final scene of *Hedda Gabler* can be used as a model for this stage of the collaborative process. Note the words in boldface:

TESMAN: . . . You'll have to keep Hedda company from now on, my dear Judge.

BRACK: It will give me the greatest of pleasure!

HEDDA: Thanks. But this **evening** I feel a little tired. I'll **go** and lie down on the **sofa** for a little while.

TESMAN: Yes, do that dear—eh?

> [Hedda goes into the **inner room** and **closes the portieres** after her. A short pause. Suddenly she is **heard playing a wild dance tune on the piano.**]

MRS. ELVSTED: Oh—what's that?

TESMAN: Dearest Hedda, don't play dance music tonight! Think of Aunt Rina! And of poor Eilert!

HEDDA: Aunt Juliane. And of all the rest of them—Never mind—From now on, I promise to be quiet.

TESMAN: I don't think it is a good idea for her to see us at this distressing work; I have an idea, Mrs. Elvsted. You can move over to Aunt Juliane's and then I'll come over in the evenings and we'll work there. Eh?

MRS. ELVSTED: Perhaps that would be the best thing to do.

HEDDA: **I can hear what you are saying,** Tesman. What am I to do with all those long evenings—here—by myself?

TESMAN: Oh, I am sure Judge Brack will be kind enough to drop in and see you.

BRACK: Every single evening, with the very greatest of pleasure, Mrs. Tesman! I'm sure we'll have a very jolly time together, we two.

HEDDA: Yes, that's what you hope, Judge, isn't it?—Now that you are cock of the walk—

> [**A shot is heard within.** *Tesman, Mrs. Elvsted, and Brack leap to their feet.*]

TESMAN: Now she is playing with those pistols again.

> [**He throws back the portieres** *and runs in. . . . Hedda lies stretched out on the sofa, dead. . . .*]

Shot herself! Shot herself in the temple! Think of that!

BRACK: Good God—but—people don't do such things!

The scene requires the following:

- Actors and actresses to play Hedda herself, Tesman, Brack, and Mrs. Elvsted
- Two rooms (if Hedda tried to kill herself in the same room as the others, she could be too easily stopped)
- A piano, which Hedda plays right before she commits suicide
- The sound of a piano.

The placement of the second room, the placement of the piano within that room, and the sound of the piano establish Hedda's physical relationship with the other characters. Once again, every member of the collaboration participates in the creation of the stage environment.

At this hypothetical meeting, the scenic designer will present a rough idea for the setting. Working with this design, the designers and director will come up with some possibilities for performance that will express this point of view.

The director and scenic designer might first collaborate on several central issues:

- The distance between the two rooms
- The size of the rooms relative to one another (also a function of the amount of usable stage space)
- The curtain fabric (transparent or opaque, for example)
- Whether or not Hedda closes the curtain.

These decisions will help to answer these questions: Does Hedda wish to be stopped in her suicide attempt? Will she stay close and seek help? How close? How easily can help be obtained? How attentive are the others to her distress?

Let us say, for example, that the designer has placed the piano in another room, separated by heavy drapery. In the course of the discussion, the director decides that Hedda will enter the other room, but will not close the drapery. Hedda's wild playing can therefore be easily heard by the other characters onstage, and by the audience. In this interaction with the setting, Hedda will be perceived as seeking attention—sending out a cry for help. Why wouldn't they respond to her seriously? Does this mean that they always ignore her or that her bizarre behavior is usual? Are Brack, Tesman, and Mrs. Elvsted cruel, or has Hedda been behaving like this for a long time? And if she has, why hasn't anyone paid proper attention before this?

These basic physical relationships are established through the collaboration of director, scenic designer, and sound designer. Other questions, such as what the actors and actresses wear (is this a formal or an informal evening, for example) and how dark or bright the rooms are, will also be addressed by the collaboration.

Collaboration in Rehearsal

Perhaps the most important time for collaboration comes during rehearsals. The rehearsal process is typically fairly open. Actors and director together discuss and decide upon the choices that best serve the overall concept. (Chapter 9 will explore the rehearsal process in more detail.) Let's look again at the final moments of *Hedda Gabler*, but this time with a view toward the collaborative effort in rehearsal.

Deciding on the placement of actors relative to the two rooms, to the curtains separating them, and to the sound of the piano is an important part of the collaboration. These decisions are colored by choices that have been made about the characters' response to the evening's events. For example, it is possible to arrange the main room with chairs facing away from the music room. Who turns when Hedda begins to play and who doesn't will help the audience answer questions about the characters. *How the actors use the physical environment to provide these answers is a function of rehearsals.*

Collaboration in Production

The collaborative effort continues even after the production moves into the theatre in preparation for performance. Putting all the elements together is not simply a mechanical effort. Although each enters the theatre individually and in a prescribed sequence, all the pieces need to be evaluated together once they are in place. Many details are changed at this point, but usually only the smaller and less expensive ones. All needed adjustments should be made at this time, before the production opens to the audience. For example, the color of a light might need to be changed to accommodate an unforeseen shading in a costume. (Hedda might be wearing a dress of a greener shade of blue than was originally planned, and a warm pink light might turn it gray.) The amount of light coming through the curtains when they are drawn might not be sufficient, so either the light or the curtain must be changed. The position of a chair or table might need to be adjusted to provide an actor with easier access, or to increase the appearance of communication between characters onstage. Because each element in the theatre is so dependent on every other element, collaboration should be synonymous with cooperation.

Extreme Types of Collaborations

No collaboration is typical and, as in anything else, extremes exist. Collaborative relationships differ in practical and mundane as well as in theoretical and ideological ways. They differ in how the collaborators rehearse and accomplish other tasks, in how they spend money, in how they organize their responsibilities, and even in how they schedule themselves.

At one extreme is the totally collaborative production, one that gives a nearly equal voice to every member of the company. Together, everyone is responsible for making all decisions concerning the company, its welfare, and the production itself. Obviously there are problems with this approach, such as whether or not everyone's point of view can ever—or should ever—be expressed in a single production. Usually these collaborations need lengthy rehearsal periods because everything is open for discussion. And as they need more time, generally they also require more money. During the 1950s, sixties, and seventies, many experimental theatre companies worked in this way, giving everyone in the company a voice.

Many of the members of these companies worked together for a long time, trusting each other and sharing common goals—theatrical and political. Without a long-term commitment, it is extremely difficult to establish this kind of collaboration, but it can be a very satisfying way to work. For some lucky artists, collaborations can last a lifetime. When a group of theatre artists work together over a long period, sharing in one another's lives, their work develops richness and depth. There is a common vocabulary to draw upon, and shared points of view are easier to reach.

At the other extreme is the director or producer who makes all creative decisions and arbitrates any disagreements. In this case, the actors and designers work to achieve the production goals of the director. Although this

Playwright D. L. Coburn, actor Hume Cronyn, and director Mike Nichols collaborate on a production of *The Gin Game* at the Long Wharf Theater.

sounds tyrannical, many fine productions have resulted from such "noncollaboration." Depending on the scale of the director's vision, these collaborations can sometimes translate into costly productions, but generally the potential for economy is much greater than in the totally collaborative production. Lengthy rehearsals and expensive changes can usually be eliminated because there is less discussion, less disagreement, and fewer changes. Like everything else in the theatre, most production collaborations fall somewhere between these two extremes.

As to the question of who or what really controls a production—the director, the actor's imagination, the designer's paint, the playwright's words, or all of these together—so much depends on the specific circumstances and personalities of the individual production.

The five chapters that follow in Part 2 of this text will examine the individual contributions of each of the collaborative artists—director, actor, scenic designer, costume designer, and lighting designer—and how their choices affect what we, the audience, see in performance.

Suggested Readings

Herbert Blau, *The Impossible Theater: A Manifesto* (New York: Macmillan), 1966.

Eileen Blumenthal, *Joseph Chaikin: Exploring at the Boundaries of Theater* (New York: Cambridge University Press), 1984.

Edward Gordon Craig, *On the Art of the Theater* (New York: Theater Arts Books), 1956.

Part TWO

The Collaborative

Artists

Chapter THREE

The Director

*[The] directorial problem . . . is to translate the script's words into the language of the stage where men and women of flesh and blood who move in three dimensions among real objects are to **replace description.** (emphasis added)* [1]
—Harold Clurman, *On Directing*

What the Director Does

Theatrical performance is created by the meeting of audience and actors in a mutually agreed upon space. The need for a designer or architect follows: Someone must arrange the space in which the performance takes place, choose the actor's clothing, and—if the production takes place indoors—provide illumination. Explicitly or implicitly, we take actor and designer for granted as part of the theatrical event. The role of the director is less obvious, but it seems to have existed in the theatre in one form or another for centuries, although not always as it does today.

Hamlet's advice to the players in act 3, scene 2 is often cited as an early form of stage direction:

> Speak the speech, I pray you, as I pronounced it to you, trippingly on the tongue; but if you mouth it as many of your players do, I had as lief the town-crier spoke my lines. Nor do not saw the air too much with your hand, thus, but use all gently; for in the very torrent, tempest, and, as I may say, whirlwind of your passion, you must acquire and beget a temperance that may give it smoothness.

Although Hamlet's role in this scene could be viewed as that of a critic or acting coach rather than a director, his speech does, albeit in the most general way, tell the actors *how to act the play.*

During the rehearsal process, a stage director functions as a stand-in for the audience to come, seeing and hearing what the audience will eventually see and hear during the performance. The director makes adjustments to the work of the actors and designers in order to communicate the point of view of the production as accurately and economically as possible.

What is seen onstage is never a static picture, but one that is always in motion—even if the only movement is that of the actors breathing. The art of choreographing stage movements and creating stage pictures through that movement is called *staging* or *blocking.* Life is filled with examples of staging. Most daily activities are staged without our even being aware of it. The aisles in a supermarket are carefully laid out to control the movement of shoppers and carts. Checkout counters draw us into lines for crowd control. The furniture in our living rooms is arranged to control traffic patterns in and around the areas we have chosen (consciously or not) as the focus for certain activities. The task of arranging stage pictures and stage movement in the theater has become an important part of the director's role.

The director is also an editor who looks at all the elements when they are finally put together and, along with the rest of the production team, decides which are redundant, which need clarification, which need emphasis, and which need to be played down. In so doing, the director *orchestrates* the performance. For example, in a scene involving several characters onstage at one time, the director might feel that one actor is too loud and another too soft, or that an actor playing a minor character is dressed in too brightly colored a costume and needs to be better integrated with the others onstage. The director need not necessarily know which specific color would be better, only that what appears onstage does not communicate the appropriate information to the audience.

Another of the director's tasks is to arbitrate differences of opinion, when they arise, between actor and designer. For example, an actress might feel that red, high-heeled pumps best fit her character, while the costume designer thinks that white flats would be better. It is the director's job to look at both sides and help with the decision-making process.

In preparation for these choices, the director goes through a series of steps that vary greatly from individual to individual. In general, the process looks something like this:

1. Analyze the *script* (the written play) and develop a production point of view with the other collaborators.
2. Work with the designers to develop a visual production concept.
3. Work with the actors in rehearsal.
4. *Stage* the performance.

The first two steps usually precede rehearsals, but also continue until the production is ready for an audience; the third and fourth of necessity take place in rehearsal.

Aside from this very broad outline, there is little agreement on the precise role of the theatre director. Tyrone Guthrie (1900–1971), an important midcentury British director who founded the Guthrie Theater in Minneapolis in 1963, had a strong personal vision for each production he directed, yet he played down the role of the director considerably when speaking or writing about it, as in the following passage (note that the British "producer" corresponds to the American "director"):

In 1963, Tyrone Guthrie's modern-dress production of Shakespeare's *Hamlet* opened the Guthrie Theater in Minneapolis. Here George Grizzard is shown playing Hamlet with Jessica Tandy as his mother, Gertrude, in the background.

Parallel with the creation of the actor must, I think, come the coordination of the producer. Supposing two of us are playing a scene, and one has decided that the scene must be played lightly and forcibly, and the other person takes a different view of the scene and feels that it must be managed in a very dark and very black way with long pauses. It is the business of the producer to coordinate the two without necessarily making either man [actor] feel that he has been a fool or stupid. It is a point of view which way the scene should be taken, and somebody has to be the chairman, somebody has to decide. That is really in most cases what the producer is.[2]

Guthrie saw the director as a coordinator, one who gathers together the different pieces of a production and welds them into a complete unity, working somewhat as a referee.

What the Director Looks for When Reading the Play

Analyzing the play is the process by which everyone involved with a production, including the director, finds its meaning. In Chapter 2, for example, we read about two directors' very different interpretations of *Hedda Gabler*. In each case, the director arrived at her point of view through some kind of analytical process.

Directors look for clues in the text of a play as if they were reading a mystery, trying to discover why, from their own (the directors') point of view, the characters act as they do and how their behavior results from the situations in which they find themselves in the play. Directors seek information in various categories, including:

- Character (including age and background)
- Relationships among characters
- Setting (physical, social, historical, political)
- Situation.

The product of this analysis has been called various things by various people, among them the *checklist* and *production notes*. It is important that the director gain as much information as possible while forming a point of view, so that the latter is supported by the play itself. For example, if a director cast Hedda as a 50-year-old woman or Blanche DuBois as a 23-year-old, the plays would not easily support those choices. (A 23-year-old Blanche would not, for example, be so concerned about her fading looks or so certain that coming to Stella's represented her last chance.) Let's look at some scenes from *The Seagull* and *The Heidi Chronicles* to see what is required to fulfill the needs of the play.

Fulfilling the Needs of the Play

The Seagull

The Seagull opens with the entrance of several groups of characters, Medvedenko and Masha among them, who are waiting for the performance of Treplev's play:

MEDVEDENKO: Why do you always wear black?

MASHA: Because I'm in mourning for my life. I'm unhappy.

MEDVEDENKO: Why? *[Wonderingly.]* I don't understand. . . . I mean, there's nothing wrong with your health, and though your father is not rich, he's not badly off. My life is much harder than yours. I only earn twenty-three rubles a month and my insurance is deducted from that. But I don't wear mourning.

MASHA: Money is not everything. Even a poor man can be happy. . . . The play will be starting soon.

MEDVEDENKO: Yes. Nina will be acting, and the play was written by Konstantin. They are in love. Tonight their souls will unite in an endeavor to give expression to one and the same artistic idea. But your soul and mine have no points of contact. I'm in love with you. I long for you so much that I find it impossible to stay at home. Every day I walk four miles here and four miles back, but all I get from you is indifference. . . .

MASHA: I'm touched by your love and sorry I can't return it—that's all. *[Offers her snuffbox to him.]* Help yourself. . . .

In these opening lines, we can gather general information about all of the above categories. This information is factual. *Why* these things are so is a matter for interpretation.

CHARACTER   Medvedenko is probably somewhere in his early twenties; no father is mentioned, making him the sole provider for his mother, two unmarried sisters, and a "young" brother. He counts rubles, and views himself as poor. Masha is healthy, at least according to Medvedenko; she seems to be close to his age, since he speaks as though they are equals. Her father is reasonably well off.

CHARACTER RELATIONSHIPS   Masha and Medvedenko are at odds with each other; they do not agree on what is important in life. Masha is unhappy, and expresses this unhappiness outwardly by dressing in black. Medvedenko, who does most of the talking, is caught up in trying to feed his family. He can't understand Masha's unhappiness and believes he shows a positive face to the world.

SETTING   The physical setting includes a place where a play may be presented. The location is Russia—rubles are the currency of exchange. A fact to be gathered later—that Masha's father manages Sorin's estate—indicates a time before the Russian Revolution.

SITUATION   Masha and Medvedenko meet where a play is to be performed, but they don't come together in any other way. Medvedenko tries to convince Masha of his position; she doesn't bother with much explanation. Once again, why that is so will be discovered through the production point of view.

The Heidi Chronicles

Act 1, scene 1 of Wendy Wasserstein's *The Heidi Chronicles* opens in this way:

> *1965. A high-school dance, with folding chairs, streamers, and a table with a punch bowl. Two sixteen-year-old girls enter, **Susan,** wearing a skirt and a cardigan sweater, and **Heidi** in a traditional A-line dress. The girls find a corner and look out at the dance floor as they sing and sway to the music. The "Shoop Shoop" song is playing. "Does he love me? I wanna know. How can I tell if he loves me so?"*

Susan: Is it in his eyes?

Heidi: Oh, noooooo, you'll be deceived.

Susan: Is it in his eyes?

Heidi: Oh, no, he'll make believe.

Susan: Heidi! Heidi! Look at the guy over at the radiator.

Heidi: Which one?

Susan: In the blue jeans, tweed jacket, and the Weejuns.

Heidi: They're all wearing that.

Susan: The one in the vest, blue jeans, tweed jacket, and Weejuns.

Heidi: Cute.

Susan: Looks kinda like Bobby Kennedy.

Heidi: Kinda. Yup, he's definitely cute.

Susan: Look! He can twist and smoke at the same time. I love that! *[Susan unbuttons her sweater and pulls a necklace out of her purse.]*

Heidi: Susie, what are you doing?

Susan: Heidi, men rely on first impressions. Oh, God, he's incredible! Heidi, move!

Heidi: What, Susie?

Susan: Just move! The worst thing you can do is cluster. 'Cause then it looks like you just wanna hang around with your girlfriend. But don't look desperate. Men don't dance with desperate women. Oh my God! There's one coming. Will you start moving! Trust me.

Character   Heidi and Susan seem roughly the same age. They both sing along with the music, but take substantially different points of view on how to approach "guys." Susan is the bolder of the two, but with an old-fashioned twist. Heidi is reluctant to try Susan's methods.

Character Relationships   Susan and Heidi know how to sing alternate lines of a popular song. They are, however, not familiar with each other's tactics at dances. This may be their first experience of this kind together. Heidi, as we saw, is the skeptic; Susan the activist.

SETTING   This scene takes place on one side of an evidently large space—perhaps a school gymnasium—in an era that would make easy reference to Bobby Kennedy. The characters are doing the twist.

SITUATION   This is a social gathering. Heidi and Susan are not yet at the center of it, and have different views on what that means. Nevertheless, Susan guides the conversation to the subject of boys and Heidi goes along. The single issue they agree on is what constitutes "cute."

Each of these clues needs interpretation, but no interpretation can take place without the clues. Once the director has the basic information—the product of a thorough analysis of the entire play (and not merely a few lines)—the process of interpretation begins in full.

How Directorial Choices Contribute to the Meaning of a Production

The way in which actors move through stage space and form stage pictures communicates meaning to the audience. If we examine the following production stills—with the knowledge that they are static (probably posed), and cannot capture a live performance—we can analyze the stage picture they present and what this picture communicates to the audience.

This might be a good point to mention that every element of a theatrical production is inseparable from every other and so, although our *discussion* of staging has been separated from the subject of acting, in reality the two are inseparable. In the same way, it is difficult to know where to draw the line between the director's ideas and those of the actor when examining the particular stage picture captured in a photograph. For example, if the director has an actor cross the stage for practical reasons (i.e., so the liquor bottle can be within Blanche's easy grasp), the actor must figure out a way to make the action seem in character instead of arbitrary or artificial.

In the production of *A Streetcar Named Desire* shown in Photo 3.1, Blythe Danner plays Blanche and Frank Converse is Mitch. Blanche is seated—or perched—on a stool; Mitch stands next to her, feet apart, solid and balanced. His pose is a bit too self-conscious. Being so positioned, or staged, Blanche looks up at Mitch, while he looks *out* or *down* at her. This physical relationship communicates a very specific view of male-female relationships. Blanche makes Mitch look powerful and "manly," while she appears small, dainty, and "feminine." Mitch is strong and virile, while Blanche is fragile and womanly. Blanche focuses on him; Mitch looks away, out at the world—the focus of a man's goals.

The staging in Photo 3.2 shows a heightened emphasis on the theatrical nature of the final moment of the play. The tiny room is a stage on which

Photo 3.1
Blythe Danner as Blanche and Frank Converse as Mitch in a 1988 production of *A Streetcar Named Desire* at Circle in the Square Theater in New York City. The production was directed by Nikos Psacharopoulos.

Hedda will enact her death. The picture she has created suggests her advance preparations for this moment. The other characters stand off to the sides: Tesman comforts Mrs. Elvsted; Brack stands alone on the other side. Together they complete a triangle, which has the effect of focusing attention on Hedda. Although it is possible that Hedda is not yet dead, no one rushes to her or seeks medical help.

Photo 3.2
The actress Nazimova as Hedda Gabler in a 1918 production of Ibsen's play in New York.

Photo 3.3
The 1975
production
of *A Streetcar
Named Desire*
at the Guthrie
Theater.

The stage picture in Photo 3.3 takes the form of a triangle as well, keeping the eyes of the audience moving from one character to the next, resting nowhere. Stella, almost invisible, turns from where she sits outside on the porch to overhear the scene taking place indoors. This half-inside/half-outside attitude tells us that she is not directly involved in the scene, but is anxious about its outcome. Both women are focused on Stanley: Blanche, standing, turns toward him; Stella, seated, does the same. Like Mitch in Photo 3.1, Stanley turns away from both of them.

In this staging, the women dominate in number only. Stanley holds our focus by *not* looking at either of them. Neither woman has broken her dependence on his reaction.

The Director's Work Process

Some Ways to Investigate the Play

THE SPINE   According to the director and critic Harold Clurman (1901–1980), one way to analyze a play is to look for what he calls the *spine* or main action, an expression of what the situations contained in the play mean to the director. The spine should be stated simply. Clurman stated

JoAnne Akalaitis's production of *The Balcony*, which was written by Jean Genet in 1956.

Peter Brook directed the 1966 production of Peter Weiss's *Marat/Sade*.

"What's the difference between a poor play and a good one? . . . A play in performance is a series of impressions; little dabs, one after another, fragments of information or feeling in a sequence which stirs the audience's perceptions. A good play sends many such messages, often several at a time, often crowding, jostling, overlapping one another. The intelligence, the feelings, the memory, the imagination are all stirred."

(from Peter Brook, *The Shifting Point: 1946-1987*, New York: Harper & Row, 1987.)

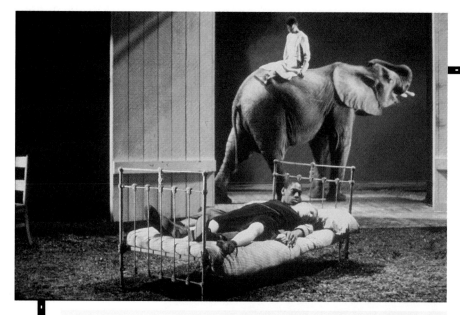

Martha Clarke directed the 1991 production of *Endangered Species* at the Brooklyn Academy of Music.

MARTHA CLARKE, whose work is a series of images combining dance and text: "I want to go to the heart of each thing and not deal with the frames on either side, as in cutting film when one wants to get directly to the action. I don't want to see anything before or after."[3]

The New York Shakespeare Festival's 1986 production of *Largo Desoloto,* directed by Richard Foreman.

RICHARD FOREMAN "There's no denying that my main interest in the theatre is compositional, that I am interested in the interplay of all the elements. I am not interested in the theatre where the audience becomes seduced by a kind of empathetic relationship to the actors."[4]

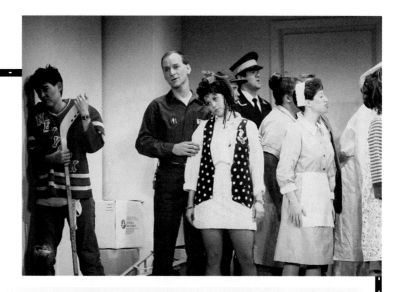

A scene from director Peter Sellars's highly innovative staging of Mozart's opera *The Marriage of Figaro.*

PETER SELLARS "While at Harvard, I founded the Explosives B, a cabaret where we did a new production every two weeks. We kept churning out the shows. I had started working on condensed Shakespeare by doing *Macbeth* with three actors. . . . Because I wanted to get another way of reading the text. You see, I've never really believed in plot that firmly because a play is about content. It's not about the story. Plot is the hook on which the playwright hangs what interests him. By entirely removing the plot I wanted to treat the play line by line, literally for 'what does this mean?' . . . In America we are totally at the mercy of the plot."[5]

Lloyd Richards directed *Ma Rainey's Black Bottom* for the 1983-1984 season at the Yale Repertory Theatre.

LLOYD RICHARDS "I accept fear as a fact. You're venturing into the unknown. You're going to try to make things happen, having no way of knowing if they can happen. But that is what makes theatre so exciting. It has a life of its own. It's going to fight back and you're going to shape that life, or those many varied lives, into your vision. That's frightening. Have you made the right choices? Are you on the right track? Have you got everything it takes to do what you want to do? Again, it's like painting. I can have a vision, but if I sit down with paint and a piece of paper, it doesn't always come out that way, and I accept that it's not going to come out that way."[6]

This production of Bertolt Brecht's *The Good Woman*, directed by Andrei Serban, uses elements from Kabuki theatre.

In 1977, Andrei Serban directed the New York Shakespeare Festival's production of Anton Chekhov's *The Cherry Orchard*, starring Irene Worth, Raul Julia, and Meryl Streep.

the spine of one play he directed as "to probe within oneself for the lost 'something.'"

After locating the spine of the play, the director looks for the spine of the individual characters. In developing or finding them, the director integrates each character into the movement of the play as a whole. The spine of each character, conceived of and stated from the *character's* point of view, can help the actor in the development of *characterization,* which Clurman defined as the inner and outer expression of character.

If we apply the spine concept to *Macbeth,* some possibilities might include:

- To seek immortality
- To ignore the cost of power
- To follow regardless of personal need.

The spine of the character of Macbeth in the first example might be "to be a man" and the spine of Lady Macbeth, "to follow her husband." In the second instance, Macbeth's spine might be to justify his kingship, and Lady Macbeth's to encourage her husband and provide support.

RESEARCH   Although Zelda Fichandler, founder of the Arena Stage in Washington, D.C., is as involved with character as was Clurman, she uses research as the springboard for her imagination.

> I always do about six months of advance research because knowledge releases my imagination. Imagination is what is there after you know everything; without knowledge, one's imagination may be too thin—lacking in strength and too fragile to build on. I need to know exactly how the characters in the play live their daily lives. It doesn't matter how abstractly, in terms of form, the information is used; I have to know what their habits of thought are, what they eat, their education, what they sit on, listen to, read, believe in. I may never use it, but it gives me a sense of reality. That's the basis of my process. . . . The words on the page are only clues to the life boiling underneath them.[7]

Just as Fichandler researches the circumstances surrounding the characters' lives, it is possible to research aspects of the playwright's life and work. A director working on a production of Chekhov's *The Seagull,* for example, could read Chekhov's other plays, letters, and short stories; a biography of both the playwright and of Konstantin Stanislavski (1863–1938), the play's original director; and Stanislavski's working scripts and notes for other productions of the play.

In some instances, a *dramaturge* may work with the director. The dramaturge provides extensive research material (on a production of *The Seagull,* for example, the dramaturge might locate and evaluate the research material suggested above), and may locate and critique different transla-

Interview

AN INTERVIEW WITH MARY ROBINSON,
ARTISTIC DIRECTOR OF THE PHILADELPHIA
DRAMA GUILD, ABOUT HER 1991
PRODUCTION OF MACBETH.

How did your personal/political views affect the way you made choices relative to the character of Lady Macbeth? Macbeth? Any of the others?

In approaching a play, I always start with what Peter Brook calls a "formless hunch," a feeling or a personal response. I try to keep it formless as long as possible; that is, I have a lot of ideas, images, and thoughts, which I jot down in a notebook as I read and re-read the play, but I try not to let anything get concrete until I've had a number of sessions with the designers, where we simply talk about what the play means to us, separately and collectively. (If I do mention specific ideas early on, they almost never end up in the final result.)

I wanted to explore the more *normal* aspects of the central relationship, to reveal that there was real love at the center rather than a manipulative bitch and a weak, hen-pecked husband. The casting of Lady Macbeth was crucial: I wanted to cast an actress who was tender and loving with Macbeth, and who pulled the audience into the conspiracy and made them real accomplices rather than judgmental observers. By casting an actor and actress who had worked together and were comfortable with each other, I hoped to get a "lived-in" sense to the relationship.

How did those choices affect the staging of scenes such as the banquet scene?

The banquet scene was one of the easiest scenes of all to stage since psychologically it is not very ambiguous. I staged it in a few hours and essentially never changed it. The aftermath of the banquet, a two-character scene, was tried in many different ways.

Staging choices evolved organically out of character work, and the two-character scenes remained fluid until late in the process, since the development of the Macbeths and their relationship was something we kept exploring even after the play had opened. The exit after "Leave all the rest to me. . ., " where she takes him by the hand and leads him off, was changed in the second week of performances to make him more of an active participant, something we'd discussed and tried many ways and perhaps never got quite right.

What kinds of images did you use in approaching the direction of the play?

Macbeth is a play that is full of images, almost all of them having to do with nature, its destruction, and rebirth. Childbirth was a central image— Macbeth's and Lady Macbeth's loving but claustrophobic relationship, their unusual childlessness and lack of connection to another generation, was one of the main aspects of the play that drew me to it as a director. This central image found its way into the design of the production as the large cradle in the witch's scene that served as the cauldron.

There are many, many references to childbirth, children, and parents. The rebirth of Scotland with the coming of Malcolm (culminating in the forest that appears on stage) was hinted at in the garden where the England scene took place. Allen Moyer, the scenic designer, was adamant about not permitting flowers to appear earlier; for instance, in the banquet scene, where we went instead for glittering, hard surfaces.

How did those images realize themselves in the design of the production?

For each project, I choose designers who I think will be right for the still vague way the production is taking shape in my mind; for instance, I sensed an eclectic approach to *Macbeth* would be the way we'd want to go, and that led to the choice of costume designer. But once the designers are chosen, the process is extremely collaborative.

The blood basins came about as a means to reveal graphically both the brutal nature of the war, and the camaraderie of the men in the aftermath as they washed together. [These basins, when emptied down drains built into the stage, were shown to be full of blood.] There are also lots of references to water and cleansing in the sleepwalking scene. There were water sounds in the sound score, usually benign and associated with Duncan. We tried to use a dripping blood sound to underscore certain scenes, but it didn't work.

tions or versions of a play, assist other collaborators with their research efforts, and attend rehearsals. The position of dramaturge is traditional in European theatre, and is often equal in stature to that of the director. A dramaturge would normally be employed by a theatre company as a regular staff member. In the United States, this is less often true, but some companies do maintain a staff position that combines the work of a *literary manager* (responsible for reading new plays and assisting in the choice of a productions for the season) with that of a dramaturge.

How the Director Chooses Actors: Auditions and Casting

The director, sometimes in conjunction with the producer and even a casting agent, is responsible for *casting,* the process that determines which actor will play which role. Auditions are difficult for the director, who may see many actors (sometimes hundreds) for a single role, as well as for the actor, who often has to face a complete stranger, receiving little feedback on the quality of the audition or the reasons for the final choice.

Many considerations go into the choice of an actor for a particular role. Sometimes actors are cast because of good work in the past or because of a recognizable name that can help sell tickets at the box office. Ideally, the choice is based on:

- The actor's suitability to the kind or style of play being presented
- The actor's skills and training
- The actor's ability to work with other actors
- The actor's appropriateness to the role.

Appropriate casting is very important to the realization of the point of view of a production. For example, a director who sees Hedda as cold, unsympathetic, and spoiled might cast the role in a number of ways:

- Casting an actress who easily projects those qualities
- Casting "against type," and using an actress who projects warmth and sympathy to throw the coldness of the character into relief
- Casting an actress who works well with the other actors cast, who has particular flexibility of skills, who is physically right for the production (for instance, in terms of height), or who simply works well with the director.

With regard to other issues, however, there are fewer alternatives. For example, if the point of view demands that Hedda be old enough to feel that she must take her last chance at marriage (as in Emily Mann's interpretation), casting a very young actress would be inappropriate.

Another major consideration in casting is the relationship of individual characters to one another. If Hedda is to be perceived by the audience as cold, then what might be the requirements for the actor playing Tesman or Brack? If Blanche is, in her view, old enough to need to hide her age, how old should Stanley and Mitch be? All characteristics, physical and otherwise, need to be evaluated in this way.

How the Director Works with Actors

A large part of the director's job is to let the actor know what is being communicated from the audience's point of view, how close the actor's work is to the intention of the overall production, and how the actor can make choices or adjustments to clarify the intention or point of view of the production. Some directors allow the actor as much creative freedom as possible in this process, and respond to actors' contributions rather than dictating limits at the outset. Other directors ask actors for specific results within tight limitations. The results in production can be quite different.

Konstantin Stanislavski, the Russian actor and director, had an enormous effect on virtually every aspect of twentieth-century theatre, especially the way in which the director works with actors. His most important contributions were to the training and rehearsal of the actor (Chapter 4 will examine this in more detail).

Stanislavski saw the emergence of two kinds of directors: *directors of the result* and *directors of the root.* As his work progressed, he shifted his focus from the external to what he called the *inner meaning* of the play. Stanislavski looked for what was authentic (the root)—what might actually be credible in reality, not just onstage. His meticulous creation of physical and psychological realism became the cornerstone of his school of directing, and remains as important today as it was in his own time.

Figure 3.1 on pages 92–95 shows sample pages from Stanislavski's prompt script for *The Seagull,* the first of Chekhov's plays to be directed by Stanislavski and the beginning of one of the most famous of theatrical collaborations. The prompt script was prepared before rehearsals began. Stanislavski's notes contain more than simple instructions about where actors should be onstage. In addition to indicating exactly when Nina opens the door, when the sound of wind is heard, when there are pauses, and so forth, Stanislavski explains the emotional life of the characters, with statements such as: "This is where he *really* dies"; and "Nina freezes in one pose. She does not seem to be addressing anybody in particular, but seems to be *speaking to herself,* her gaze fixed on one point"; "Talks in a dead voice, *without life, without hope."* (emphasis added)[8] Stanislavski later grew more concerned with the actor's development of the role in rehearsal, although still under the director's guidance.

Harold Clurman also believed in the preparation of a working script, which he considered his "score." He was meticulous in the way in which he laid out the script, arranging the actor's actions in three columns:

Interview

SOME NOTES BY DRAMATURGE VICTORIA ABRASH ON THE PHILADELPHIA DRAMA GUILD PRODUCTION OF MACBETH

A dramaturge approaching a play like *Macbeth* must begin by asking questions. For starters, why are we doing this play? And what does this play mean—to me, to the director, the theatre, the audience, the community—at this moment in time? Shakespeare's plays are so enduring precisely because they are wide open to interpretation, which is a challenge not to take anything about the plays for granted.

So, in approaching *Macbeth*, I began by reading and re-reading the play, and thinking about my own responses—what interested me, what seemed problematic, what questions the text raised. Then, since it is the dramaturge's job to support and enrich the director's vision, I talked to the director about why she had chosen this play and what her responses were. If we differed in our reactions, we talked through the differences. As dramaturge, I know that the ultimate decision is always the director's, but it is incumbent on me to make my thoughts clear; perhaps I have information or a perspective that the director hasn't thought of.

We arrived quite quickly at a fundamental "take" on *Macbeth*—what the play was about to us—for this production, as well as a number of questions that needed to be addressed, including, but by no means limited to: What is a witch? What do we do about Birnham Wood? How do we deal with all the bloodshed?

As we formulated our thoughts, we researched the play. A production history told us what other stagings had made of Shakespeare's text. The late seventeenth century produced a version featuring new songs and dances for the witches. Other productions have emphasized the spectacle, the supernatural, the psychology, the violence, the Scottish setting. We watched film adaptations from Orson Welles's to Akira Kurosawa's to *Men of Respect*, which placed the story in a contemporary Mafia setting. We read a lot of criticism and scholarly thought on the play. But as we got deeper and deeper into *Macbeth*, we found that we were increasingly drawn to the criticism that reinforced our own thoughts, dismissing the rest as interesting but irrelevant.

Our reading of *Macbeth*, in a nutshell, was that it is a play about generations. There is endless talk of children, of heirs, of family and lineage. Macbeth and Lady Macbeth talk of having children. Macbeth steps up his butchery because, even though he has no children, he can't bear to think of Banquo's heirs—not his—inheriting the throne. The violence progresses in its horror from the wrongful murder of old King Duncan to the failed attempt to kill the youthful Fleance to the appalling murder of Macduff's young son. Even the play's conclusion centers around the circumstances of Macduff's birth. And, in reading through the play from this perspective, one finds countless other examples of this preoccupation with children and the generational cycle of birth and death.

We also saw this focus on generation played out in *Macbeth*'s imagery. Most of the play, which is full of barrenness and the slaughter of innocents, is unnaturally dark. But the scene in England, in which Malcolm, Duncan's heir, plans his return, is green. We had no idea what to do about Birnham Wood and the green boughs called for at the end of the play until we realized the significance of greenery, life, and regeneration after the darkness and murder Macbeth has unleashed.

Our reading of the play led to a number of specific production decisions. Macbeth and Lady Macbeth could not be as old as they are often cast if they truly hope to have a child. Macbeth needs to be believable as a great soldier, which suggests youth, and Lady Macbeth has to be in her child-bearing years. We even considered having Lady Macbeth be pregnant at the start, and miscarry at the time of Duncan's murder, but decided it was too self-conscious a choice. At the same time, we felt that the hope for a child was a clue that this was not the story of a diabolically evil couple, but of a very loving marriage that becomes twisted into evil actions.

Some of the questions about the witches were answered by our reading of the play, but many weren't. We have associations with the word *witch* today that are at odds with those of Shakespeare's day, in which witchcraft was a capital offense. I did a lot of research into witchcraft through the ages, and the director, designers, and I had endless discussions about what the witches were. We decided they had to be real people—not spectacular effects, supernatural visions, or hags in pointy hats. And we decided that they should be played by three generations of women—a child, a middle-aged woman, and an older woman. We toyed with having them all be children, but abandoned that idea for both practical and thematic reasons. I don't think we ever cracked the witches completely, and those sections remained problematic in our production. We were hoping to discover more in rehearsal than we were able to. Some ideas we employed, such as replacing the rather clichéd cauldron with a cradle, were exciting, but the witches never took on the cohesive identity they needed in our production.

Overall, my job as dramaturge on *Macbeth* was to work with the director to realize her vision of the play. That included research, textual work (for instance, we cut Hecate's scenes since they are widely seen as interpolations and were not relevant to our interpretation; for a production stressing the role of the witches, I might have *added* material for Hecate from other sources), and a lot of discussion with the director and designers about the play. During rehearsals I was available as a sounding board for the director, as an "outside eye" responding to what I saw as the show came together, and as a resource for the actors and director as questions arose. During previews, I continued to give feedback about what was working and what wasn't and what might be done to strengthen the production.

Column one described *what* is to be done. Clurman stated this in terms of active verbs in order to avoid generalizations such as "getting angry," "being modest," "feeling hurt," which he found unproductive for the actor. If a character is feeling hurt, the director must help the actor to find a positive action with which to make that clear—such as "holding back tears."

Column two described the *manner* in which the action is to be carried out. For example, an actor can hold back tears defiantly, forlornly, fearfully, etc.

Column three described the *physical means* by which what is to be done is done. An actor might hold back tears by contorting his face, turning his head, pressing his eyes, etc. He can strike out angrily, hitting another character, or turn his back and walk offstage.

The third column was always quite sparse because Clurman left much of the actual staging to be developed with the actors in rehearsal. In other words, he did not know in advance what the performance would look like onstage. He joined Stanislavski in his willingness to include the actor in decisions about the look of the final production.

German director Max Reinhardt (1873–1943), a contemporary of Stanislavski, planned the physicalization of each moment precisely. His plans were carefully noted in his prompt scripts, known as *Regiebuches*.

Everything has been taken into consideration, from the most important feature to the least: the atmosphere of every scene, of every conversation in that scene, of every sentence in that conversation. Expression, intonation, every position of the actor, every emotion, the indication of every interval, the effect on the other actors—all these details are mapped out in clear, concise words. At the beginning of each scene, there is a minute description of all the decorations, generally accompanied by drawings, together with a sketch of the stage with full explanations; there is an accurate description of the costume for every new actor, all the crossings within a scene are not only mentioned, but also sketched; the lighting and all the changes in the illumination are described; there are notes on the significance, expression, length, and volume of the music; notes on the different noises; and notes on the way in which the change of scenes is to proceed. The book of stage directions, the playbook, which contains all these elements, reminds me of a closely woven rug; in its explanations, it is a complete work without any gaps.[9]

George II, Duke of Saxe-Meiningen (1826–1914), is usually considered the first modern stage director. His directorial work began when he formed a private theatrical company adjoining his court in Germany. On May 1, 1874, the Meiningen Company performed in Berlin and the age of the director was born.

The company's goals were rooted in a revolution against the popular "declamatory" style from the time in which the actor performed without paying particular attention to the other actors onstage or to the scenic environment. There was no *ensemble*, an expression that refers to the integration of actors and environment, in the service of the play as a whole. To create such an ensemble, the Duke found the position of director a necessity; this position had not been required earlier when every play was staged in roughly the same manner.

As a director with substantial knowledge of the theatre, Saxe-Meiningen had very specific ideas about what should happen onstage to achieve unity. Central to this unity is the human figure of the actor in motion, performing not in front of a painted backdrop, but within a three-dimensional space. To make both actor and space seem natural, Saxe-Meiningen proposed:

- The use of asymmetrical stage groupings (which appear to be less consciously formed and more lifelike)

- The use of movement as an integral part of the process of telling a story

- The integration of actor and stage setting.

Onstage crowds, previously characterized as screaming mobs or "revolutionaries," became a collection of individual characters, each of whom was an important part of the scene.[10]

Figure 3.1
Pages from
Stanislavski's
prompt script
for *The Seagull.*

NINA *(bewildered)*: Why does he talk like this? Why does he talk like this?

KONSTANTIN: [119] I am alone in the world, Nina. I have no one whose affection might warm me. I'm cold, cold, as though I lived in some underground dungeon, and everything I write is dry, harsh, gloomy. Please, stay Nina, I implore you! Or let me go away with you!

NINA quickly puts on her hat and cloak. [120]

KONSTANTIN: Nina, why? For God's sake—*(Looks at her as she puts her things on; a pause.)* [121]

NINA: My cab is waiting for me at the gate . . . Don't see me out, please. I'll find my way alone . . . *(Bursts into tears.)* [122] Could you give me some water, please? [123]

KONSTANTIN *(gives NINA a glass of water)*: Where are you going now?

NINA: To the town. *(Pause.)* [124] Is your mother here? [125]

KONSTANTIN: Yes, she's here . . . [126] Uncle was taken ill on Thursday, so we wired her to come. [127]

NINA: Why did you say that you kissed the ground on which I'd walked? I deserve to be killed. *(Bends over the table.)* On, I'm so tired! I want to rest—rest! *(Rasies her head.)* [128] I'm a seagull. No, that's not it. I'm an actress. Yes!* *(Hearing MISS ARKADINA and TRIGORIN laughing, she listens for a minute, then runs to the door on left and looks through the keyhole.)*

* The words "I'm a seagull. No, that's not it. I'm an actress. Yes." are crossed out by Stanislavsky. (S.B.)

119. (Konstantín seizes her hand ecstatically and covers it with kisses. Nina tries to free her hand and turns away so that he should not see her face. Konstantín is drawn to her more and more.)*

120. Nina runs across the whole length of the stage to the french window and puts on her hat and cloak there. Konstantín follows her.

121. No pause here under any circumstances.

122. She opens french window to go out (noise of the wind rushing into the room). Then she stops—leans against the jamb of the door and bursts into sobs. Konstantín, who is leaning against the lamp-post, stands motionless, gazing at Nina. Whistling of wind from the open door. "Could you give me some water, please?" is spoken between her sobs.

123. Konstantín walks off slowly (the jug of water is near the mirror in the front of the stage), pours some water into a glass (sound of glass knocking against jug), and gives it to her. A pause. Nina drinks. (Conversation in the dining-room.)

124. Nina wipes her tears with a handkerchief and smothers her sobs. Konstantín stands motionless, glass in hand, leaning against the lamp-post, staring lifelessly at one point. This is where he really dies.

125. Nina speaks restraining her sobs.

126. A pause. (Conversation in the dining-room.)

127. A pause.

128. A pause. Nina leans her head weakly against the door. Both stand as though rooted to the ground for about ten seconds. Trigórin's voice is heard clearly. Nina, stung to the quick, straightens herself. She listens, then takes a few steps toward the dining-room.

*Stanislavsky's note has been crossed out with a black pencil, evidently by Nemirovich-Danchenko. (S.B.)

So he's here too . . . *(Returning to* KONSTANTIN.*)* Oh, well—it doesn't matter. **129** No, he didn't believe in the theatre. He was always laughing at my dreams, and little by little I stopped believing in them and lost heart . . . Besides, I had the worries of love to cope with, jealousy, constant anxiety for my little one . . . I grew trivial, cheap. And I acted badly . . . Didn't know what to do with my hands, how to stand on the stage, how to control my voice. Oh, you've no idea what it feels like to know that you're acting abominably! **130** I'm a seagull—no, that's not it. Remember you shot a seagull? A man came along, saw it, and—just for the fun of it—destroyed it . . . An idea for a short story . . . No, I don't mean that . . . *(Rubs her forehead.)* **131** What was I saying? I was talking about the stage. Well, I'm different now . . . I'm a real actress now. I enjoy my acting. I revel in it. The stage intoxicates me. I feel that I am—peerless. But now, while I've been here, I've been walking about a lot and thinking—thinking— and feeling that the powers of my mind and soul are growing stronger every day . . . Now I know, now I understand, my dear, that in our calling, whether we act on the stage or write, what matters is not fame, nor glory, nor the things I used to dream of. No. What matters is knowing how to endure. Know how to bear your cross and have faith. I have faith, and it no longer hurts so much. And when I think of my calling, I'm no longer afraid of life.

KONSTANTIN *(sadly)*: **132** You have found your path in life. You know which way you are going. But I am still whirled about in a maze of dreams and images, without knowing what it is all about or who wants it. I have no faith, and I do not know what my calling is. **133**

NINA *(listening)*: Sh-sh—I'm going. Good-bye. When I'm a famous actress, come and see me in a play. Promise? And now . . . — *(Presses his hand.)* It's late. I can hardly stand on my feet—I'm worn out—famished . . .

KONSTANTIN: **134** Won't you stay and have some supper? Please, do . . .

129. Nina sinks into a chair (by the card table, where Shamráyev sat). Konstantín is still standing motionless with the glass in his hand. Nina freezes in one pose. She does not seem to be addressing anybody in particular, but seems to be speaking to herself, her gaze fixed on one point.

130. Propping up her elbow on the table, she puts her weary head on her hand. She is exhausted.

131. Sits up.

132. Without altering his pose. Talks in a dead voice, without life, without hope.

133. A pause of ten seconds. (A sudden noise in the dining-room: two or three chairs being pushed back. Nina jumps to her feet and runs to the door.)

134. His last hope.

Creating the Stage Picture

The stage picture is affected by all the elements of production, including the physical relationships among the actors, as we have seen. Photo 3.4 shows the final moment of the original 1947 Broadway production of *A Streetcar Named Desire*. The eye of the audience is guided by:

- The staging (both the physical placement of actors on the set and the actors' gestures within that placement)
- The setting in which the the actors are arranged
- The lighting
- The value and color of costumes (*value* is the relative brightness of an object, established by the addition or subtraction of black or white along a gray scale).

An analysis of each element's contribution to the stage picture is helpful to further understand not only the director's staging choices, but how the other contributing artists, whose work we will presently study in more detail, support those choices.

THE STAGING   Onstage are three groups of actors who are separated from each other. Any hope of reconciliation seems remote.

Group 1, the poker group, downstage left (see Figure 3.2), although set up for a card party, is not playing cards. Mitch's face is buried in his arms, presumably because he cannot look at what he has allowed to happen to Blanche. The other card players look away from Blanche as well—perhaps they cannot bear to see Mitch's grief.

Group 2, the stage-right group, includes Eunice, Stella, and Stanley. Within this cluster are two subgroups: Eunice stands apart and Stanley holds Stella, who buries her face in his chest. Eunice looks in Blanche's direction as Blanche disappears, and Stella and Stanley look away—Stanley at Stella, Stella into her tears.

Group 3, comprising Blanche, the Doctor, and the Nurse, who follows upstage left, function as a moving unit. Blanche, ironically, is "protected" by the Doctor.

How would the audience's perception of the characters' fate change if the director had chosen to place Stanley, Stella, and Eunice near or at the poker table? How would the perception of guilt change if Stella looked at Blanche as she walked away? If Blanche turned back?

THE SET AND THE STAGING   The set is composed of two principal spaces, the interior and exterior of the apartment. The set also contains two levels, upstairs and down. (A third level, the step on which Stanley embraces and comforts Stella, literally places Stella on a pedestal, free from her sister's

Photo 3.4
The final moment from the original 1947 Broadway production of *A Streetcar Named Desire,* directed by Elia Kazan.

fate.) Mitch and the other poker players are inside the house; everyone else is outside. Eunice, Stella, and Stanley, probably in that order, have followed Blanche out of the apartment. By splitting the stage unequally right and left, the designer has allowed a broad view of the space; therefore, at this moment Stella, Stanley, and Eunice are easily visible to the audience, while still separated from the poker players and Blanche. (This same device allows the audience to see both Stanley and Blanche, and Stella listening to them in scene 2.) The designer has also permitted Blanche to be seen at this critical moment by making the walls of material that can be made to seem transparent (known as *scrim*). The audience knows that, even though Blanche is visible, she is not actually in the same room as the poker players, but can be seen relative to them. This heightens the audience's awareness of the potential relationship between Mitch and Blanche at the time of the first poker game, and what has become of it now.

How would this moment and what it means differ if the designer (and director) had chosen to make the walls of the house opaque, not reminding the audience about those relationships as Blanche is taken away? How would they differ if there was no exterior-interior relationship, if only the inside of the apartment could be seen?

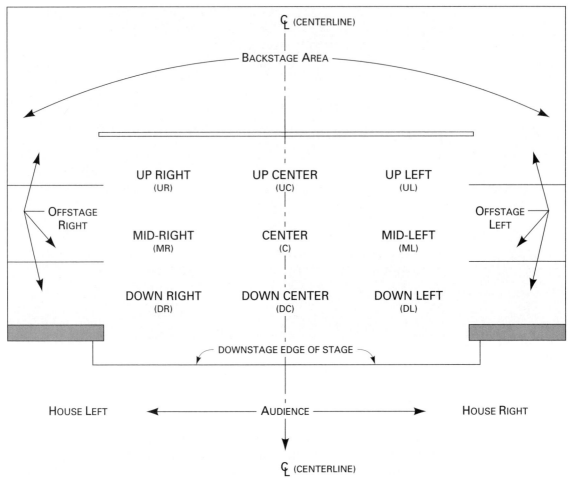

Figure 3.2
Stage directions. Before staging can begin, everyone must have a common vocabulary. A director telling an actor where to move on stage uses language not used anywhere else in the world. Stage directions always refer to the actor's onstage orientation, facing the audience. Thus, *stage right* and *stage left* are opposite to the audience's right and left (which are called *house right* and *house left* and used more often by designers, ushers, and so on). *Downstage* and *upstage* are terms that originated at a time when the stage floor tilted down toward the audience. *Downstage* means "toward the audience," *upstage* "away from the audience." *Offstage* indicates any space not visible to the audience.

LIGHTING AND STAGING Each of the three groups is sharply delineated against a fairly dark background, reinforcing the relationship between the three groups. Exterior light comes from the direction in which Blanche is moving, etching her out of the background and giving her an almost celestial glow as she walks into the light. Eunice is illuminated by the same light—they balance the stage, like bookends. The house itself is relatively dark; only its important features are outlined. Stella and Stanley, and the poker players, are duller and less distinct than Eunice and Blanche. They are seen as groups rather than individuals.

How would the meaning of the staging change if the most sharply delineated characters were Blanche and Mitch rather than Blanche and Eunice? What if the lighting isolated these groups even more, rather than blending them into a unified stage painting?

COSTUME AND STAGING   The three elements of the stage picture are grouped by costume color and value as well. Stella, Blanche, and Mitch, in the lightest values, establish the three primary points of focus and guide the audience's eyes from one group to the next and back again.

How would the staging be affected if the costumes of the minor characters were of lighter values as well? What if the value of Mitch's costume were more consistent with those of the other poker players than with Stella's and Blanche's? How would this change the meaning of the staging?

As we study each of the other areas of production (acting and set, costume, and lighting design), we will examine in more specific detail *how* these effects are accomplished.

Creating Stage Business

In addition to setting the staging, or blocking, the director works with the actor to fill out the world of the characters onstage with lesser activity called *stage business*. In the opening scene of *Hedda Gabler* Miss Tesman and Berte, the maid, speak about Hedda and Tesman. What else are they doing? Does Berte immediately take the flowers Miss Tesman has bought? Does she place them in a vase already onstage or must she go into another room—offstage—to get one? How is this "business" used to convey the meaning or intention of the scene?

In the opening scene of *The Heidi Chronicles*, what might Heidi and Susan be doing aside from what is specified in the dialogue? Are they sipping cups of punch? Eating pretzels or potato chips? Do they fuss with their clothes? When Heidi gives her art history lecture, does she point to the slides she refers to? When the lecture is over, does she pick up papers or a handbag and walk off? Does she put on a coat? How much stage business is required, and does the amount vary depending on whether Heidi is alone onstage or with another character?

Stage business tends toward more detail in plays like *Hedda Gabler, A Streetcar Named Desire,* and *The Seagull,* than in *Macbeth,* or, to a lesser degree, *The Heidi Chronicles.* Prose drama composed within a linear structure demands a more convincing reality onstage, and detailed stage business helps to support that illusion.

Imagine the difference in stage business between the scene in which Lady Macbeth reads Macbeth's letter aloud and then comments on it, and the scene in *The Seagull* in which, while packing to leave, Trigorin asks Arkadina to let him go. Lady Macbeth is given such rich and detailed language that additional activities (what else could she be doing?) would be unnecessary and distracting. In *The Seagull*, trunks move in and out, bonnets are pinned on, food is packed and consumed, and books are lost and found, all of which is important to the creation of illusion and meaning. The poignancy and pain Arkadina feels is cleverly set against the pressing but everyday tasks of packing and departing.

The Importance of the Director in Today's Theatre

Before the turn of the century, the central figure controlling the production also served as actor (known as the *actor/manager*), producer, playwright, designer, or some combination thereof. Directors like Max Reinhardt had an almost mystical power over their companies and ruled their productions with an iron hand. Many directors today follow that pattern, others temper it with charm, compassion, or both, and still others are true collaborators. In the theatre, any discussion about the power of the director is carried on with great passion, but without any definite conclusion ever being reached.

The ascent of the director to the point of controlling every aspect of the production nearly coincides with the ascent of the motion picture. In film, theatrical practice is paired with the camera, making a director a virtual necessity: Only one person can look through the lens of the camera at a time. Following in the footsteps of the film industry, live theatre became more and more involved in new technical effects, and the director became more and more important. Someone had to oversee the stage, if only to keep the actors from being run over by the scenery or blown up by an explosion!

But theatre, unlike film, does not have an infinite capacity for technical effects; its real strength lies in the immediacy of the living actor. So the theatre director's function has become largely one of developing an interpretation, guiding the actors through rehearsals, and making certain that the production's point of view is conveyed to the audience through the actors' performances and the designers' images. We cannot know whether or not actors today are as central to the experience and creation of theatre as they were before the introduction of the director, or whether the great nineteenth-century actors, working without directors, presented a hodgepodge of styles and ideas or brilliant interpretations. Nor can we know how audiences perceived those performances.

Today, the primary position of the theatre director is not only assumed, but has become a virtual necessity as economics increasingly dictate that every production be the most efficient possible.

Suggested Readings

Arthur Bartow, *The Director's Voice* (New York: Theater Communications Group), 1988.

Edward Braun, *The Director and the Stage: From Naturalism to Grotowski* (New York: Methuen), 1982.

Peter Brook, *The Shifting Point: Forty Years of Theatrical Exploration 1946–1987* (New York: Harper & Row), 1987.

Harold Clurman, *On Directing* (New York: Macmillan), 1972.

Toby Cole and Helen Krich Chinoy, eds., *Directors on Directing* (New York: Bobbs Merrill), 1963.

Tyrone Guthrie, *A Life in the Theater* (London: McGraw-Hill), 1959.

James Roose-Evans, *Experimental Theater: From Stanislavski to Peter Brook* (New York: Universe Books), 1984.

Oliver Sayler, ed., *Max Reinhardt and His Theater* (New York: Benjamin Blom), 1968.

Konstantin Stanislavski, *My Life in Art,* trans. J.J. Robbins (Boston: Meridian Books), 1956.

Chapter

FOUR

The Actor

Imitation has nothing to do with creativity.[1]
—Konstantin Stanislavski

It is the act of laying oneself bare, of tearing off the mask
of daily life, of exteriorizing oneself. . . . It is a serious
and solemn act of revelation.[2]
—Jerzy Grotowski

I have a notion that what attracts people to the theater is a kind of
discomfort with the limitations of life as it is lived. . . . We present
what we think is possible in society according to what is possible in
the imagination. When the theater is limited to the socially possible,
it is confined by the same forces which limit society.[3]
—Joseph Chaikin, *The Presence of the Actor*

What the Actor Does

Acting in the theatre is a process that makes choices of interpretation visible to an audience through the use of the human body, voice, and emotions. Acting is a carefully rehearsed artistic endeavor, separate and distinct from an actor's real life. Max Reinhardt, known primarily for his directorial extravagances, also had some interesting things to say about acting. Life and our upbringing, he says, teach us to hide what goes on within us. We are not to let it be seen that we are suffering or happy, hungry, or thirsty. Manners and the social code have "crippled the actor, whose business it is to body forth feeling." Reinhardt also points out that although we have many technical devices with which to communicate (like telephones and television sets), ". . . the way to the human being next to us is still as far as to the stars."[4] Although many things have changed since Reinhardt wrote these words in 1929, the job of the actor remains to bridge that gap.

In order to perform at all, an actor must first be cast in a production. There are two basic kinds of auditions: *open calls,* which anyone may attend, and scheduled auditions for actors whose agents have submitted them for the role. Auditioning is often considered an art in itself. In an audition, an actor or actress usually performs before a completely unfamiliar set of people, including the director and occasionally stage managers, producers, the playwright, composers, and designers—anyone who has an interest in who will be cast. Audition times vary, but are usually scheduled at fifteen-minute intervals—not much time in which to demonstrate what one might do with the role.

The actor or actress will probably first "read" for a role with someone who is not an actor (usually the stage manager), compounding the difficulty of sparking the director's interest. If the play is new, an actor or actress may have to give a "cold" reading, meaning that the actor or actress reads aloud from a scene that he or she has never before seen or heard.

The second stage of auditions is referred to as *callbacks.* If the initial reading has impressed the director and producer, the actor or actress may be called back to audition again, this time perhaps reading with candidates for the other roles. The actor or actress might also be asked to prepare a specific scene for this second audition.

Once cast, an actor begins the process of rehearsing, a subject that will be considered more carefully in Chapter 9. Rehearsals usually extend over a period of many weeks, during which time the actor is responsible for learning lines and blocking, and researching the play and the play's characters. Many changes are made during the course of this period, each to be learned anew. If the playwright is present and rewriting problem areas during rehearsals, the actor may have to learn new lines and investigate new scenes, sometimes every day.

After weeks of auditions and rehearsals, an actor may spend countless additional hours in the theatre before each performance, applying make-up, putting on costumes, and warming up the voice and body. The performance itself demands tremendous energy and commitment from the actor. A professional actor often performs the same role for months, even years, and must keep each performance fresh and alive for the audience. What may look like play to the audience is the actor's business.

Actors, like directors and designers, have only the dialogue on the page and the occasional stage direction with which to prepare the performance. An actor interprets the words of the playwright by creating the underlying life of the character and then behaving (walking, talking, listening) onstage in ways—sometimes prosaic, sometimes fantastic—that are appropriate to the character. Often an actor must create this magic eight times a week. What is it exactly that actors do, and how do they do it?

What the Actor Looks for When Reading the Play

A director looks at character and character relationships through a lens that takes in all aspects of the play. Designers, as we will see in the following chapters, look for clues specific to the play's physical environment. An actor looks in close detail at what the play has to say about a particular character. To take a simple example, if a scene takes place outdoors in summer, the director might think about the overall picture (Is it a lawn party? A picnic? Are different groups involved in various activities such as baseball or barbecues?), and the designer might think about how hot it is and whether there is any shade. The actor might think about whether or not the character likes hot weather and how the heat will affect his or her behavior during the scene.

Returning to the play within the play in act 1 of *The Seagull,* we can see how complicated a process this really is. Just some of the questions that arise for the actress playing Arkadina might be:

- In saying that her son's production is "something decadent" is she merely being funny? At whose expense?
- Is this a nasty comment meant to establish her superiority, as Treplev assumes, or is she simply teasing him, trying to make contact?
- Is her reference to the smell of sulfur intended to draw attention to herself or to point out that the smell is really obnoxious?
- Is she commenting on contemporary production techniques?

- Do her continual interruptions mean that she has to be the center of attention? That the play is boring? Or is she protecting her son by providing entertainment?

After Treplev brings down the curtain, is Arkadina's response naive? Does she understand that she has hurt his feelings? And if so, why does she cover it up? Does she really believe that she was serving Treplev's best interests by treating the play as a joke? Did she understand the play at all? Is she threatened by its novelty?

An actor or actress investigating these questions is searching for the subtext, an interpretation based not on what is written or spoken, but on what motivates the spoken words. By answering, or at least posing these questions, the actor or actress playing the role begins to shape his or her own point of view on the character: in this case, the degree of Arkadina's selfishness, childishness, maternal feelings, attitude toward aging, and so on. The answers to these questions will also affect every other production choice.

Fulfilling the Needs of the Play

Like the director in Chapter 3, the actress playing Heidi in scene 1 of *The Heidi Chronicles* might look for information under the categories of *character, character relationship, setting,* and *situation.* For the actor or actress, like all the other artists, these categories are not exclusive—a question related to one will inevitably lead to another.

- Does Heidi often go to dances? Is she afraid to be there? Why?
- Why did Heidi come to a dance with Susan, who seems to have very different ideas about this sort of event? Was she Heidi's only choice? Does she believe she will learn something from Susan? Does she think Susan can learn from her?
- How did they get to the dance? Did they arrive together or did they meet at the dance? Would Heidi have come on her own?
- What kind of room is this? How warm or cool is it? How does temperature affect Heidi's discomfort? Is the room crowded? Has the dance just begun?
- How has Heidi dressed for the occasion? How is Susan dressed? Did they confer ahead of time about what to wear?
- Is Heidi pleased when Peter comes up to her? Is she interested in him? Is she merely relieved not to be left alone with her book?

How would the interpretation of this scene, and perhaps the play as a whole, be affected by a positive response to the last question?

How Acting Choices Contribute to the Meaning of a Production

Looking at production photographs is not the ideal way to examine an actor's performance. The beauty and magic of acting lies precisely in its inability to be caught in time. But pictures are all that remain of a performance, and through them we can try to understand something about acting choices—even if not precisely those of the actual production shown.

Photos 4.1, 4.2, and 4.3 show three actresses—Jessica Tandy, Judith Evelyn, and Patricia Conolly—as Blanche DuBois at the moment before Stanley returns from the hospital where Stella is giving birth.

We know instinctively just from glancing at the photographs that these actresses have adopted different points of view on this scene, and on what immediately preceded it (which the audience has not seen). Through her performance, each actress communicates the character's mental state based upon what has just taken place. To provide a framework for this process, we can look at the question of whether or not these three Blanches believe in her fantasy.

Jessica Tandy's Blanche gestures in a small, tight, and restrained way. Her arms are close to her body. Her hair and dress are neatly arranged. She has probably looked at herself in the mirror. She raises her head, looking

for—or at—something in the distance. As she raises her glass in a toast, her expression is wistful. What we understand from this movement is that this woman is straining to reach her past. It is hard to believe that she trusts in the story she is about to tell Stanley: that she has had a call from an old beau, Shep Huntleigh, and that he will take her away from all of this.

Judith Evelyn's Blanche gestures on a grander scale. She, too, raises her glass, but she does so joyously. She looks boldly ahead, not up and away. She appears happy and buoyant though her situation at this moment is certainly not hopeful: Mitch has left after insulting her and Stanley has given her a bus ticket back to Laurel, Mississippi, where she is less than welcome. Given those circumstances, her happiness must come from something internal. Her celebratory mood might spring from the belief that she actually has received a phone call that will save her. She has withdrawn into the past.

Patricia Conolly's Blanche is sly and sexy, alert to all possibilities that might fulfill her fantasy. She is, in a way, the most desperate of the three, the most dependent on past behavior, the most coy (wrapped in her curtain), while wildly searching for Shep Huntleigh. Her strain to believe in her fantasy—shown most keenly in her tight smile—is even greater than that of Ms. Tandy. The past is only present in this photograph in her exaggerated, even absurd, mannerisms.

Photo 4.1, left, opposite
Jessica Tandy as Blanche DuBois in the original production of *A Streetcar Named Desire.*

Photo 4.2, right, opposite
Judith Evelyn as Blanche.

Photo 4.3, left
Patricia Conolly as Blanche.

Photo 4.4
The Barry Jackson production of *Macbeth,* staged in London in 1928.

Photo 4.5
Maurice Evans and Judith Anderson in a 1941 production of *Macbeth.*

Photos 4.4 and 4.5 show two interpretations of the relationship between Macbeth and Lady Macbeth. The first, from the 1928 Barry Jackson production in London, appears to show the moment immediately after the murder of Duncan. The second, from the 1941 production featuring Maurice Evans and Judith Anderson, probably captures a moment in the play before the murder.

Because each photograph is a complete stage picture, the relationship is revealed in many ways. Costumes are a major factor, illustrating both different periods and different conceptions of the characters. Settings are also very different—the first seems to be set at the time of the production, in 1928, while the other is closer to the time the play was written. Let us look at the question of how each of these Lady Macbeths has chosen to help her husband achieve the crown, and how these photographs communicate that information.

In the first photograph, Lady Macbeth, although concerned, seems somewhat detached from her husband's despair. She stands back from him, perhaps afraid to bloody her clothing. She touches him gingerly on the shoulder, but maintains a considerable distance between them. She seems to be waiting for him to respond in some way, to show a sign of life before she proceeds. This Lady Macbeth has probably followed her husband's lead all along. Her look is fierce, but she has a cautious touch.

The couple in Photo 4.5 is encumbered by their heavy costumes; their royalty literally loads them down. This Lady Macbeth physically enfolds her husband, protecting and mothering him. Her relationship to Macbeth must be very different from that of the Lady Macbeth in the other photo. She projects strength, warmth, and fortitude. Hers is a nurturing presence—she would only do what is best for Macbeth and he seems to accept her protection readily. She also appears to await her husband's action, but we suspect that she has already given him whatever encouragement he needs to proceed. When the deed is done, we expect this Lady Macbeth to remain in control; her careening fall into madness will therefore be all the more surprising.

The Actor's Work Process

Robert Lewis (b. 1909), an important teacher of acting, defines what an actor should be able to do. An actor's job consists of "transmitting to an audience what you are experiencing when you are acting: your feelings, your thinking, your sensitivity, your humor, etc."[5] Looking at an actor's performance, an audience gathers clues about the meaning of the play. Revealing these clues to the audience is not something that comes naturally or automatically to an actor, although obviously it is easier for some people than others. For actors to be able to act, they must have a way of working.

Ways to Investigate a Character: The Major Dispute About Acting

Historically, actors trained by working with and watching older, more experienced actors. For obvious reasons—desire for success being one of them—young actors needed to know not only what an actor did onstage, but how he did it. A major dispute developed over how "good" (presumably meaning believable and moving) acting was achieved. In this dispute, an actor was said to either (1) use and display real passion onstage or (2) be an empty vessel through which the character emerged. In the first instance the actor was "hot" and "impassioned," in the second, "cool" and "analytical." The passionate actor worked from (inner) feelings to the creation of the liv-

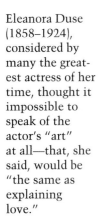

Eleanora Duse (1858–1924), considered by many the greatest actress of her time, thought it impossible to speak of the actor's "art" at all—that, she said, would be "the same as explaining love."

ing (outer) character onstage. The cool actor worked from (outer) observation to the character's (inner) feelings.

As this dispute continued into the twentieth century, new issues were incorporated. Stanislavski focused on the internal, but not necessarily passionate, process of acting. Michael Chekhov (1891–1955), another influential acting theorist, was one of many who focused on working from the outside in.

Other questions arising from this disagreement are:

- In performance, how aware is the actor of being an actor?

- How much of the actor's own passion or emotion is actually used in performance?

- Does an actor create the emotions of the imaginary character from his or her own feelings or by observing and imitating others (for example, their voice, walk, and gestures)? How much does an actor rely on each of these and is there really a difference?

- How personally committed must an actor be to the central idea or politics of the play?

Working from the Inside

Like Stanislavski, Lee Strasberg (1901–1982), a founding member of the Actor's Studio from which many important mid-twentieth-century actors emerged, emphasized the inner life of the actor. Because actors working in this way contributed so much from their own personal investigations of the character, they became, in a sense, co-authors. The actor working from the inner character to the outer uses the playwright's work as a jumping-off point, spending considerable time in his or her imagination, away from the play itself, and then returning to it much later.

INTENTIONS AND OBJECTIVES: THE ACTOR'S CHOICES   One of Stanislavski's major contributions was to define acting as a conscious process, emphasizing the need to bring logic and truthfulness to the character being portrayed. Physical actions and emotions would eventually be produced by coherent internal ideas. According to Stanislavski, feelings can't be performed—an actor cannot enact "fear" in a general way; it must be connected to specific circumstances (fear of a dog, Arkadina's fear of being eclipsed by a younger actress, Blanche's fear of her past surfacing).

In order to understand the progress of a character through a play, the actor finds the *core* of the play—what Clurman termed the "spine" and Stanislavski the "super-objective." To be manageable, the core must be broken down into small *units.* The actress playing Blanche isn't faced with the final outcome of the play from the moment she comes onstage, but builds toward that end moment by moment, or unit by unit. The objective of the first unit might be as simple as finding Stella's street. Later, after Eunice lets Blanche into the house, Blanche's objective might be "to get Eunice out of the house so she can have a drink" or "to calm down."

Stanley's super-objective might be "to get Blanche out of the house" or "to hold on to Stella"; Heidi's super-objective might be to "carve out her own way in the world." Hedda's objective in the last scene of that play might be "to escape Brack" or "to escape public humiliation."

To truthfully present a character on stage, each line or action must be done *for a purpose.* The actor or actress must know why he or she is doing or saying whatever is being said or done, and he or she must be able to justify it. An objective must be specific to the character and truthful to the play, and most important, it must be *active.* It should be expressed in the form of a verb. An objective should not be to produce an effect on the audience members, for example, to please them or make them laugh.

CREATING PARALLELS TO LIFE EXPERIENCES   Tomaso Salvini (1829–1915) was an actor known for the violence of his attack in the murder scene of Shakespeare's *Othello.* Salvini believed that *actors themselves actually experience the character's emotions.*

Stanislavski didn't believe there was any such thing as actual passion on the stage; if there were, the results could be very dangerous. (How far would Salvini actually go?) Stanislavski argued that actors make use of emotions or passions that parallel the emotions of the character. He referred to this process as *sense memory.* Drawing parallels allows the actor to re-experience these feelings each time the role is played.

Interview

TINA SHEPARD ON ACTING AND
HER WORK WITH JOSEPH CHAIKIN
AND THE OPEN THEATER

Shepard played the role of Nina in Chaikin's 1974 production of The
Seagull.

I knew I wanted to be an actor from the eighth grade on. I was in a play. I
had been in other plays before but this one was different. We were studying
Greek, Elizabethan, and modern theatre. I had a great teacher who directed
these plays as we studied them. She divided the class into three groups:
one to work on a Greek play, one on Shakespeare, one on the modern play.
I was in the group that did *Antigone*. We had been studying about the chorus, and she had us each write down what role we wanted to perform. I
wrote down that I wanted to be in the chorus. But my teacher asked me to
play Antigone. And so I found myself on the stage knowing everyone's
lines, and knowing exactly what I was doing. I was at home for the first
time in my life. I had found my focus.

I was in a lot of plays. Then I went to Sarah Lawrence College. Even
though I hadn't imagined myself there, I did like it. There were good teachers and the theatre department was great. We were a handful of students
and we had to do everything on the productions. We learned how to do
everything: directing, designing, acting.

Then I had to graduate and decide what to do. I decided to become a
lighting designer. Being an actor was too much: Where would I study?
Where could I go? The summer after graduation I was in New York running and designing lights for a theatre on St. Mark's Place [off-off Broad-
way]. Two performers—mimes—came to perform at the theatre. I got to
know them because I did their lights. They told me they were going to
start a school and wanted me to come and study. I said I had no money and
they asked me to be their scholarship student. I figured that was okay, because I could focus on the movement part of acting, not the talking part. I
didn't have to tackle *all* of acting. It was wonderful training in clarity.

Moni Yakim, the head of the school, said, "You can only do one thing
at a time. You can't have two choices going at the same time." And this is
true. There may be many things going on but you can only *activate* one of
them at a time. All the choices you didn't make are reverberating around
you.

There is a wonderful exercise of Brecht's. You go through a scene moment by moment and say of your character, "She says not this, this, this, *but* she says," and then you give the character's line. You determine everything that could have been written but wasn't. The audience becomes aware of all the other possibilities that are in the air because the actor has thought of them.

I trained as a mime for three years. Finally, we put together a company from the school and developed some pieces. This was the fall of 1966. Just as we were about to set out on tour, the San Francisco Mime Troupe came to New York. They were doing very political work, and we were doing all this stuff about boys and girls, and handkerchiefs. I began to think that I should be doing something else.

When we returned to New York. I went to sit in on, and then participated in, a training workshop in Open Theater exercises, which was being taught by one of the actors in the company. Joe [Chaikin] came to watch the workshop one day and afterwords invited me to join the work that he had started several weeks earlier with the Open Theater. He wanted to develop a piece about the life of Christ: what was going on in the missing years. We started in Genesis—and never got out. The piece became *The Serpent.*

Actress Tina Shepard in two very different performances. Both, however, show her background in mime and her extraordinary physical training, which she uses as a powerful emotional force on stage.

I entered this very chaotic exploration. Joe was saying we could only work for three or four hours a day or we wouldn't have any life from which to bring material to the work. This was a great release for me after my work with the mime company; it was another notion of discipline in the theatre.

I was completely in awe of what was going on, but every now and then I would get up and try something. We were working in a loft space over a movie theater on Bleecker Street. I remember that the floor was painted black and that the paint came up all over us. We scrubbed the floor for three days because Grotowski was coming to do a workshop with us. I was stumbling along, but Joe was somehow seeing in me a person who was doing something that intrigued him.

As I went on working with him, he would say try this, and I would try it, but I still had no notion of the legitimacy of my work. That didn't come for a couple more years. The other actors seemed to have so much to draw on, and I thought I didn't have anything. My denial about my own life experiences was unprecedented. Even though I was totally unaware of what I was doing, it was apparently coming out in my work.

We started working on *Terminal,* then touring and performing it. When we came back, Joe cut the company down to a small group. . . . We started work on *Mutations Show.* We were a small, concentrated group of actors. We were receiving funding (we were actually on salary!) and had a loft on Thirty-Sixth Street. This was an extraordinary time. We worked four days a week: from 10:30 to 12:00 training sessions, dance classes, etc.; in the afternoons we worked on developing material. Joe wrote a lot and we brought in our own material as well. We were wrestling with this material, trying to determine what it was. Every now and then Joe would sit us down and talk to us, reading from notes he had made during work sessions. They were ideas and suggestions about acting and theatre, not necessarily about the piece itself. He would say actors shouldn't do this—they should do that. I would think, how does he know that? Then I realized that he knew because he was watching me and the other actors do it. There was this trade back and forth. In addition to being a director, Joe functioned as the eyes I couldn't have. It was a really close collaboration, an extraordinary collaboration that always led me on to discover what I knew—and didn't know. For me, Joe was the person who could put into words thoughts that I couldn't quite think yet. He would allow me to jump in time.

During the last year of the Open Theater [the company disbanded in the winter of 1973], sessions were held to work on scenes from legitimate plays; *The Seagull* was one of them. . . . When Joe decided do the production [of *The Seagull* in 1974], the whole thing became an enormous struggle for me. I was feeling like a cardboard cutout again (which I still do every time I start on a piece, but I know now that is okay, that it is part of

Raul Julia played Macbeth in the 1989 production by the New York Shakespeare Festival. At left, Lady Macbeth (Melinda Mullins) tells her husband of her plan. Below, Macbeth consults with the three witches.

Two scenes from the 1992
production of *Hedda
Gabler* at the Seattle
Repertory Theatre, di-
rected by Douglas Hughes.
At right, Hedda talks with
Lovborg and Thea Elvsted,
while Judge Brack and her
husband can be seen shar-
ing a drink upstage. Below,
Hedda speaks with her
husband's Aunt Julia.

Hedda gives Lovborg one of her father's pistols in
this scene from the American Repertory Theatre's
production of *Hedda Gabler*, directed by Adrian Hall.

Two scenes from the Intiman Theatre's 1991 production of *A Streetcar Named Desire,* directed by Elizabeth Huddle. At left, Blanche (Julia Fletcher) entreats her sister, Stella (Suzanne Bouchard), to leave, unaware that Stanley (Scott Macdonald) is listening. Below, Stanley and Blanche alone.

Two scenes from the American Repertory Theatre's production of *The Seagull*, directed by Ron Daniels. Above, Madame Arkadina (Christine Estabrook) and Sorin (Jeremy Geidt). Below, Nina (Stephanie Roth) performs Treplev's play.

the job to go from this two-dimensional thing gradually into the performance). For several years I had been doing this work with which I was at home and here I was working with the same director, and I was cheating again. I knew it was Chekhov, and Stanislavski, and I wasn't doing it right!

I made a list of the struggles I had with that role:

- For the first time in years I was working with actors with whom I had never worked before. I was speechless and sweaty.

- For the first time, I was in a play in which you had to wait backstage, then come on in the middle. Then you went away again. Most actors think that is how actors work, but I was appalled. I didn't know what the event was for the audience. Working with the Open Theater we were always all present onstage all the time. We were in the same room and the same moment with the audience. Backstage there was a completely different life going on.

- Gwen Fabricant, the costume designer, designed a velvet gown for me after I had been rehearsing in a bohemian costume I had done myself. I didn't understand this new costume, so I thought I had to behave in some other way.

- I was performing a character written on a page for the first time in a long time. In all Open Theater projects we didn't work with character but with essence, or the emblematic expression of human possibility in a moment. Sometimes there were characters connected to that but what we were after was the essential hunger of that moment or that person. The focus was the hunger, not the continuity of the person. So we were working out of time. When you take that and put it in time it becomes character, but we were not threading circumstances together. It wasn't a story of if, if, if—and then.

There were two moments in *The Seagull* when I felt okay. The first was when Nina is alone onstage during the second act. I thought, a woman doesn't talk like this to herself, she must be talking to the audience, and it all fell into place. The second was when Arkadina says she is leaving. We all talked at once in a sudden explosion onstage.

The play within the play always worked in rehearsal because Joe would stand there and giggle at what I was doing. The audience wouldn't giggle and I didn't know what to do. Whenever I came into the theatre happy I could do the end of the play. Whenever I came into the theatre unhappy I could do the beginning. I don't know if I ever got it all right.

In order to work on *The Seagull* I had to struggle to make a bridge between the work I had done and this work. I didn't know that all of that previous work made it possible for me to do classical theatre. I thought they were entirely different. I believe my teaching is about that—getting in touch with raw impulses and seeing how that feeds classical texts.

An actress of the appropriate age playing Heidi in 1968 might draw on emotions aroused by similar circumstances in her past. An actor playing Arkadina might be able to convey her fear of losing her lover by finding parallel losses in her own life—the loss of a friend, a lover, a precious memento. Stanislavski suggested that another way was to ask, what if one were actually in the position of the character in the play? What if I were in Lady Macbeth's situation? What would I think? How would I move? What would I wear? The use of this "magic if" can spark the actor's imagination to create an onstage performance that has the depth of real life.

FINDING THE GIVEN CIRCUMSTANCES   Establishing the facts of a play is also important to the actor working from the inside out, because those facts keep the actor within the specific situation of the play, and therefore believable.

Stanislavski calls these facts the *given circumstances* and defines them as the story of the play, its *conditions* (period, time, place, etc.) and *interpretations* (the director's, actor's, and playwright's choices), and the *stage setting* and *production elements* (costumes, properties, lighting, and sound). Those circumstances that are external to the actor are referred to as the *external circumstances* (setting, period, weather, etc.); those that are related to feelings (the actor's and director's interpretations and the resulting emotions) are the *internal circumstances.*

In the opening scene of *A Streetcar Named Desire,* Blanche sees Stella's apartment for the first time. The size, condition, and decor of the apartment combine to create a set of external circumstances for the scene. Blanche's response to the apartment is based upon these external circumstances. The apartment might be cramped, dirty, neglected, and unattractive. Blanche's internal circumstances—such as her need to be saved at any cost—might give her the strength to endure anything. Relating these internal circumstances to the external circumstances of the apartment creates a living scene on the stage.

To summarize the inside-out approach, we can say that behavior, or physical action, is the result of developing the inner life of the character relative to the outer circumstances of the play and production.

Working from the Outside

Two important twentieth-century English actors, John Gielgud (b. 1904) and Laurence Olivier (1907–1989), have spoken of working from the outside in. Gielgud notes the importance of his appearance, costume, and make-up and their effect on his characterization. Olivier wrote:

> Theater deals primarily in practicability; there is no room for genius. If
> you as a performer have a sudden flash of genius, when do you express it?
> Do you keep the members of the audience waiting patiently till Act IV,

Scene V of *King Lear* and then hit them with one flash of genius and say, "That's all I can do today"? I don't think so. . . . On the other hand, if you're practiced, rehearsed, and thoroughly versed, you have something to offer. You know what the lines are about but you haven't waited for the final, ultimate way of saying them or handling a single moment. . . . You must produce something; that's the job. You must present a mirror or an echo; otherwise the audience will run screaming for their money back or shower the stage with tomatoes. You take care of the play and let the genius take care of itself. . . .

If I'm directing someone and I see he is in difficulties, I can suggest a technique that will help him. Sometimes it's almost ludicrously simple. . . . So often you can get the most fantastic results by saying, "Darling, try twice the pace," and reality falls upon the actor like a cloak. Well, that's a trick that you learn with experience.[6]

Denis Diderot (1713–1784), an eighteenth-century playwright and scholar, said an actor should be emptied of his own emotion in order to be able to "take on" the emotions of the character he is portraying. The actor should be unmoved and disinterested, and equally able to play any character. (According to this approach, any actor should be able to play Macbeth, Stanley, or Scoop by determining their characteristics and assuming them.)

In Diderot's view, an actor was responsible for "mastering nature," and the only way to do that was through *observation* and *imitation.* An actress playing Heidi in the first scene of the play might observe teenage girls at a

Sir Laurence Olivier as Macbeth, with Judith Anderson as Lady Macbeth, 1937.

dance. An actress playing Arkadina might observe another actress approaching middle age, perhaps performing with a younger woman. The actresses would imitate those characteristics and translate them to the stage.

Both Sides Together

Harold Clurman, though a follower of Stanislavski's method, felt that the different approaches to portraying a character were not mutually exclusive; every actor uses some of each. The true actor, he says, works from the inside and the outside at the same time. Good acting is a balance between the two approaches.

Sarah Siddons (1755–1831) played Lady Macbeth in 1812. Writing about the role, she explained how external characteristics brought her to an understanding of the character and the play. Here she describes how *external behavior* (in boldface) and *internal states* (in italics) act together to tell the story of a woman covering up for her husband's bizarre behavior:

> *Dying with fear*, yet assuming the utmost **composure**, she returns to her stately canopy; and, with *trembling nerves*, having **tottered up the steps** to her throne . . . she **entertains** her wondering guests with **frightful smiles**, with **overacted attention**, and with **fitful graciousness**; *painfully, yet incessantly, laboring to divert their attention from her husband.*[7]

Ellen McLaughlin, who played Hedda at the Berkeley Repertory Theater in 1986, also speaks about how outside factors help to create the inside of the character:

> With Hedda, for example, the costume helped enormously—the corset, the dress that was like a sheath, the high boots that grabbed your feet, all tight, confining, inescapable. . . . She's pregnant and not letting her corset out a notch. She has no means of release.[8]

The costume strangles her, the shoes hold her feet down—both presumably symbolic of the society that confines her. The outside helps create the inside, the inside helps create the outside.

Portraying a Character

Whether passion guides performance from the inside, observation creates character from the outside, or some combination of both, "traditional" actors view their responsibility as the portrayal of a character other than themselves. How an actor persuades or convinces the audience of the reality of that character is the chief concern and focus of training and rehearsal. An actor portraying a character must create the "illusion of the first time," that is, he must make the situations in the play appear as if they were happening at that moment for the first time.

Act 5.   MACBETH.   Line 33.

J.Rhamberg del.   *Delattre sc.*

Mrs SIDDONS in LADY MACBETH.
"Yet here's a Spot"

Printed for John Bell British Library London Aug.t 26 1784

Sarah Siddons as
Lady Macbeth.

In order to create this illusion, the actor acts in the present, making decisions based upon the events of each moment rather than the play as a
whole. (For example, the actress playing Hedda Gabler making peace with
her husband focuses on that situation and does not anticipate what is to
come.) In order to do that, the actor maintains a nonjudgmental attitude toward the character and the play.

Confronting the Character: Brecht, Chaikin, and Grotowski

Bertolt Brecht wanted actors to work not only from the point of view of the
individual character, but with reference to the whole play—showing character and story together to the audience. The actor played a central part in
Brecht's conception of a new kind of theatre.

   One of the goals of Brecht's theatre was to change human beings by allowing the audience to see and judge what is done by society. This meant
that actors, who traditionally portrayed characters as unchanging and unchangeable, had to arrive at a new attitude toward their work, and that attitude had to encompass the ability of people to change. To Brecht, an actor
"acting" represented the essential change he wanted to take place in society. Actors who work in a Brechtian manner can be said to *confront* their
characters rather than *portray* them.

Ellen McLauglin as Hedda in the 1986 production of *Hedda Gabler* at the Berkeley Repertory Theatre. Her uncomfortable posture shows how confined she is by her tight corset and the weight and fit of her costume.

To act in a theatre that requires confrontation, actors must change their goals and methods. Brecht developed a method of cutting through illusion that he called the *alienation effect.* To create this effect, the actor faces and speaks directly to the audience, behaving much like a witness who reports to the crowd how the victim of an accident behaved in the past—not in the present. Brecht's actor quotes the character rather than portraying him. There is no transformation: The actor is the actor, the character is the character. The actor or actress doesn't identify him- or herself with the character, and doesn't look for parallels in his or her own life to bring the character into existence. When an actor confronts a character, according to Brecht nothing about that character is "given" or to be expected. Everything about the character could be some other way.

An actor confronting a role from a Brechtian point of view might comment on the character by means of a physical movement, such as a particular walk. A Brechtian Heidi's walk might be a slow shuffle, Arkadina's a series of tiny steps going round in a circle, Blanche's a swagger. These movements have little to do with how the characters would walk in reality.

Joseph Chaikin (b. 1935), director and founder of the Open Theater, wished to change the static relationship of audience to actor. Chaikin looks for what people have in common rather than what sets them apart. Like Brecht, he wants to remove disguises, but he also wants to allow the actor to move into deeper "zones" and reveal something more elemental to the audience than everyday behavior. Under Chaikin's guidance, an actress performing the role of Blanche might show her rage at being confined to a feminine role, Heidi might race on a treadmill, Nina might mourn the loss of her talent.

Olympia Dukakis performs the leading role in Brecht's play *Mother Courage* in a Williamstown Theatre production. In this play, Mother Courage and her family confront the realities of war by providing the armies of the Thirty Years' War with their daily needs. As the play progresses, however, it becomes clear that war is living off Mother Courage as well—she loses all her children. In this photograph we see her drawing her wagon alone.

When an actor confronts, rather than portrays, a character, the story of the play itself is called into question. The actor judges both the story and the character, creating *social and political commentary.* To act in this manner is not lifelike in the traditional sense. Instead, the actor puts on a show for the audience, and is always conscious of being a part of that show. The actor does not create the illusion of the first time.

Stanislavski's method focuses primarily on the individual character's intentions, preventing the actor from judging the character. Brecht and Chaikin ask actors to use their judgment and not simply allow themselves to be empty vessels.

Like Chaikin, Grotowski was "interested in the actor because he is a human being." The actor's job is to dissect him- or herself as a human being, for other human beings:

> It is not a question of portraying himself under certain given circumstances, or of "living" a part. . . . The important thing is to use the role as a trampoline, an instrument with which to study what is hidden behind our everyday mask—the innermost core of our personality.[9]

How is the actor to accomplish this apparently impossible task? Besides intensive and extremely complex training, one of Grotowski's methods is

Actor Ray Barry in Joseph Chaikin's production *Mutation Show.*

A workshop performed by members of the Open Theater in preparation for *The Serpent.*

the use of what he terms an *organic mask.* The actor or actress, by means of highly trained facial muscles, creates a mask for the character that he or she wears throughout the performance. "While the entire body moves in accordance with the circumstances, the mask remains set in an expression of despair, suffering, and indifference."[10] The desired result is a depersonalization of the characters. Strongly influenced by Asian theatre, Grotowski makes detailed characterization virtually nonexistent, and presents a broader view of the human characteristics we share.

Training

Lee Strasberg describes the two basic types of actors in this way:

1. The actor of experience, trained in the "inner technique"
2. The actor of skill, very good at external work.

As we have seen, debate over the importance of one aspect over the other is part of virtually every theory of acting. It is generally agreed, however, that in order to accomplish anything onstage—whether imitation or revelation of the character's inner life—the actor must have resources both physical *and* emotional.

NON-WESTERN APPROACHES TO ACTING

Traditional theatre in India, China, and Japan is based upon recognition by the audience of very precise symbols that have developed over many centuries. The Noh drama began in Japan in the late-fourteenth century. *Noh* means talent or the display of talent before an audience. The talent displayed is that of the actor. In the Noh, most actors are masked. When the actor or actress puts on a mask, he or she believes there is a god within it and it is this god who guides the performance.

The mask helps the actor with the portrayal of characters, which is traditional and has remained the same for centuries. If a character is performed without a mask, it is done without changing the expression of the face. (This is one source of Grotowski's face mask.)

The art of acting, according to the Noh tradition, exists in the mind of the actor and can only be realized after years of study and endless repetition of the same exercises. Young Noh actors use older, more experienced actors as their text-

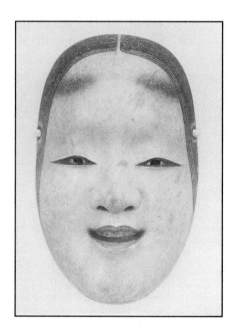

A Noh mask used for the character of a "young woman." Since each mask was uniquely crafted, each had its variations, but a mask like this one would be instantly recognizable as representative of its type.

A ritual scene from a Noh production at the Kanze School.

books. The heart of their training is observation: The Noh actor repeats exactly what every other actor that came before has done. This process works from the outside to the inside and is based upon the concept of *suggestion* rather than *representation*. Gestures developed over centuries delineate an emotional state.

Here is a description of the gesture for "noticing something":

> The actor brings together his opened fan from his right hand to his left hand; slowly lifts fan diagonally upwards, lowers his left hand diagonally to the left as his gaze falls on the object.[11]

This gesture is recognized immediately by the audience; it *always* means "noticing something."

Tadashi Suzuki, one of the foremost contemporary Japanese theatre directors, is especially well known for his training methods, which are a hybrid of modern psychology and ancient Japanese acting traditions. The basis of his theatre is the Noh, but the result is completely different and completely modern. His best-known work as director and writer are adaptations of Western classics, such as Greek tragedy, Shakespeare's *King Lear*, and Chekhov's *The Cherry Orchard*. In his productions, the basic plot of these plays remains intact—although drastically cut and rearranged, much like Grotowski's work—but the performances bear no resemblance to Western productions.

Suzuki focuses his work on the actor's body. The actor directly faces the audi-

A Noh actor performs a gesture that signifies grief.

The actress Shiraishi in Tadashi Suzuki's production of *The Bacchae*.

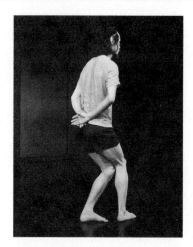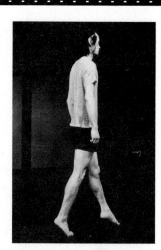

Three examples of the "walks" used by Suzuki's actor's in their training. They are executed quickly and rigorously across a wide expanse of floor. Each walk symbolizes a time of life.

ence (in the Japanese tradition of facing the gods at all times to show respect) and creates physical movements that are directly connected to the words of the play. These movements have been codified by Suzuki and reduced to a number of recognizable gestures that symbolize human responses rather than represent them.

Stanislavski felt that in order to properly and precisely express the inner life of the character to the audience, the actor needs to have an "unusually responsive, excellently prepared vocal and physical apparatus." At the other extreme, Grotowski founded his laboratory to remove resistance to psychic, or internal, impulses from the actor's body. Thus, the audience sees a series of impulses, with no everyday behavior getting in the way. Training to clear this channel is not a matter of "collecting skills" but of ridding oneself of blocks.

Different goals produce different methods of training, but whatever the goal and whatever the method, an actor must have certain skills that are different from those of other artists.

Training the Voice

An actor needs to be heard, and this is not simply a matter of volume. An actor must have a trained voice—one that can be heard over a great distance, for long periods of time, without the aid of microphones, and without strain. Every school of acting understands the importance of a trained

Actor Al Pacino as King Herod in Oscar Wilde's *Salome* and as a modern down-and-out character in the play *Chinese Coffee.* These works were performed in repertory, usually alternating daily.

I think one develops one's own style and method of approaching a part over the years, but I suppose I've been most influenced by the "method" approach which means, I guess, understanding the play, researching it, and trying to interpret what you think the author was getting at—and take it from there. . . . But, my approach has definitely changed and evolved over time . . . I would say I was influenced by various teachers throughout my life, some who were actual acting teachers, some directors and writers; but influenced in the sense that I responded to their ruminations. Lee Strasberg is an example. He could speak for hours at a time on the subject of music and that would somehow affect one's performance . . . I don't start work on a play with a point of view that I'm looking to express. My point of view comes from reading through the play. I have many different points of view and different plays connect to different views.   —Al Pacino on his approach to acting

voice. Even the Actor's Studio, which devotes most of its training to work on the actor's inner life, takes for granted the need for vocal training.

As far back as the sixteenth century, actors were concerned with proper training of the voice and with proper diction, which is as important as projection. Leone di Somi (1527–1592), actor-manager, director, and general man of the theatre in sixteenth-century Mantua, Italy, wrote a series of "Dialogues on Stage Affairs" in which he addressed diction. He wrote that an actor must speak slowly, pronounce words deliberately, and take care not to let his voice drop at the end of syllables. The last is important because "through this fault the spectators often lose the ends of sentences." This is as true today as it was then, and is one of a multitude of matters involved in vocal training for the actor.

Training the Body

In addition to a trained voice, an actor must have a trained body. The actor's body, too, must project itself to the last row of the audience. An actor onstage invests even routine movements such as sitting and standing with an extra energy. In order to sustain a performance of two and a half hours or more, an actor must have a strong, flexible body.

Grotowski's method for training actors is the most physical—and rigorous—of all the ones we have mentioned; in fact, it is so physical that it can be dangerous if not properly supervised. His goal is to decrease the distance from inner impulse to outward expression, and to do that the actor's body must be capable of expressing anything. Some Grotowski exercises are:

- Running on tiptoe
- Walking with knees bent
- Relaxation exercises such as "the cat," in which the student mimics the waking, stretching, and arching motions of a cat
- Upside-down exercises based on Yoga positions
- Leaps and somersaults
- Foot exercises such as walking pigeon-toed and walking on the edges of one's feet
- The study of mime
- Plastic exercises, such as this one described by Grotowski: "Give yourself a concrete task such as opposing one side of the body to the other. The right side is graceful, deft, beautiful, with movements that are attractive and harmonious. The left side jealously watches the right side, expressing in its movements its feelings of resentment and hate."[12]

The body of a well-trained Grotowski actor can create a drama within itself. Grotowski also developed many exercises to train the voice, to develop breathing, and to help with the creation of his *organic* facial mask.

An actor must be receptive to everything taking place onstage. To do this he or she must learn *relaxation.* John Gielgud even went so far as to claim that relaxation is the secret to all good acting. Stanislavski also considered relaxation very important in an actor's training and, in *An Actor*

Prepares, describes an exercise in which the actors take a variety of poses, noting which muscles are tensed in each. Only those muscles needed to hold each pose were allowed to remain contracted, and only as much as necessary.

Robert Lewis uses a similar exercise that begins by completely relaxing the body and then isolating and tightening a single muscle. These and other *isolation exercises* are an invaluable way to identify unnecessary tension and to gain control over each separate part of the body. To tense the entire body needlessly (in anger, for example) is to give up a large part of the actor's choice-making mechanism.

Ways to Develop the Inner Life

Actors need exercises that develop their minds and emotions as well as their voices and bodies. We have already seen how an actor begins to build units and objectives, creating a throughline, or consistent innerlife, for a character. To accomplish this, an actor must be able to concentrate. There are many exercises that can help an actor work on concentration.

Stanislavski said it is necessary for an actor to maintain a state of "solitude in public." If the actor's object is to create the illusion that the stage action is "real" and happening at that moment for the first time, the actor's attention must remain focused within the world of the play. Stanislavski developed an exercise in which the actor draws circles that contain the subjects of concentration. Circles of attention can be of any size. An actress working on the role of Hedda might begin with a small circle of attention such as Miss Tesman, gradually widening the circle to include George, the flowers, the hat, and the sunlight.

Concentration can be directed in or out. Outward concentration is the ability to look at something onstage and really see it. Onstage listening also requires superb concentration. Here is one of Robert Lewis's concentration exercises:

> Let's divide the class into two groups. Group A, on a signal from me, is going to count, to themselves, in their heads, upwards by eights (8, 16, 24, etc.). Group B is going to try to distract them by calling out numbers at random (preferably not divisible by eight). You may get up and go over to them, but don't touch them. Just try to break their concentration vocally.[13]

This exercise shows how difficult concentration is for an actor. Onstage with other actors, the set, and the audience, the actor must work very hard to focus as well on inner circumstances. The ability to concentrate helps control the audience's focus—what they see, hear, and understand as significant.

Whatever the theory and whatever the social, political, or psychological goals on which it is based, there are certain basic requirements of the art of acting. The actor needs to be a keen observer of human life. Actors must *communicate* the *meaning* that they have chosen *to the audience* and to do this, they must be clearly seen and heard. Although Stanislavski, Brecht, Grotowski, Strasberg, and Chaikin brought very different ideas on acting to the field, they are in agreement on the fundamental importance of training the actor's body, voice, and internal resources so that they are able to present whatever is required by the character and the play to the audience.

Suggested Readings

Robert Benedetti, *The Actor at Work* (Englewood Cliffs, N.J.: Prentice-Hall), 1986.

Bertolt Brecht, *Brecht on Theater*, trans. John Willett (New York: Hill and Wang), 1964.

Joseph Chaikin, *The Presence of the Actor* (New York: Atheneum), 1972.

Toby Cole and Helen Krich Chinoy, eds., *Actors on Acting* (New York: Crown), 1970.

John Geilgud, *Early Stages* (San Francisco: Mercury House), 1989 (rev. ed).

Jerzy Grotowski, *Towards a Poor Theater* (New York: Simon & Schuster), 1970.

Foster Hirsh, *A Method to Their Madness* (New York: Da Capo) 1984.

Donald Keene, *Nō: The Classic Theater of Japan* (New York: Kodansha International Ltd.), 1970.

Robert Lewis, *Advice to the Players* (New York: Theater Communications Group), 1980.

Laurence Olivier, *On Acting* (New York: Simon and Schuster), 1986.

Konstantín Stanislavski, *An Actor Prepares* (New York: Theater Arts Books), 1948.

Tadashi Suzuki, *The Way of Acting* (New York: TCG Publications), 1986.

Chapter FIVE

The Scenic Designer

*A chair is a chair. It is in the arrangement
of the chairs that the magic lies.*
—Robert Edmond Jones
The Dramatic Imagination[1]

What Scenery Does

Scenery, like playwrighting, directing, and acting, has many roots in everyday life. How we determine the structure of houses, why we choose to live in one house and not another, how neighborhoods are laid out, how we arrange furniture, how we arrange objects on and around that furniture are all, in their way, scenic choices that express our traditions, family backgrounds, likes and dislikes, even our hopes, fears, and ambitions. A heavily draped window communicates something about the person who chose it; an undraped window indicates something else. A small room filled with plants communicates something very different than a large space with a single, dramatically placed piece of sculpture.

For example, a person going for a job interview is influenced first by where the office is located, even by what floor it is on. Once inside the office, the interviewee notes the arrangement of the furniture. If the interviewer sits behind a huge desk with three constantly ringing telephones, the interviewee is being told that a particular hierarchy exists in this place. A sofa and chair with a coffee table express another relationship, or that the interviewer is attempting to create a casual impression for a more relaxed interview. Contemporary Italian leather furniture and chrome-trimmed desks communicate one set of values and expectations, while heavy, polished wooden boardroom tables communicate another. Color will influence the atmosphere of the interview as well. An office decorated in shades of pastels with large, gauze-covered windows expresses one mood, while a room with dark greens and browns and heavy velvet draperies projects another.

In real-life situations we process this kind of information very quickly. We pick up on what kind of place we are in, whose place it is, what the owner wishes to communicate (or what he or she doesn't want communicated), and many more detailed pieces of information. In the theatre, as in life, scenic choices provide crucial points of reference for making judgments about a situation.

What Stage Scenery Does

The total theatrical environment can:

- Inform the audience about the reality in which the play takes place
- Communicate information, such as time, country, and season
- Provide information about the characters inhabiting the set
- Project a mood or atmosphere.

Information Provided by Scenery

When the lights come up on a performance, what the audience sees is real and concrete; the audience knows the set can be touched and weighed, its contents analyzed—just like the theatre seat they occupy. They put trust in the literalness of the materials that make up the setting. Whether the scenery represents a kitchen, the Garden of Eden, or a dream, it answers the question, "What kind of place is this?"

Scenery for *A Streetcar Named Desire* communicates information about the city in which it takes place. Building styles in New Orleans differed greatly from those in Minnesota or Argentina during the same period in history. The hot, muggy weather dictates such architectural features as shuttered windows that can provide both shade and air circulation. The setting also communicates information about the specific neighborhood within New Orleans. None of this need be realistically detailed—as it would be in life—but must be credible to the audience as a world in which this play *could* take place.

Scenery can help to tell the audience when the play takes place, which is very important to understanding the ideas and problems that concern it. Any production of *Hedda Gabler,* for example, must be specific about its choice of period. If the production were set in 1972, instead of 1890 when the play was written, what would you conclude about Hedda's problems and her position in her household?

A Streetcar Named Desire takes place in the late 1940s in New Orleans, but the house itself is probably much older. Architectural detail, such as elaborate wrought-iron work, helps to indicate the age of a building. Similarly, the architecture of Tesman's house will communicate the general *period*, but furnishings and decor communicate it more specifically. Sometimes directors and designers change the period of the play to draw parallels to other periods, or for other conceptual reasons.

George Tsypin's set for a La Jolla Playhouse production of Moliere's *The Misanthrope,* directed by Robert Falls. Although the play was written in 1668, Tsypin's design places the characters in the setting of a contemporary apartment.

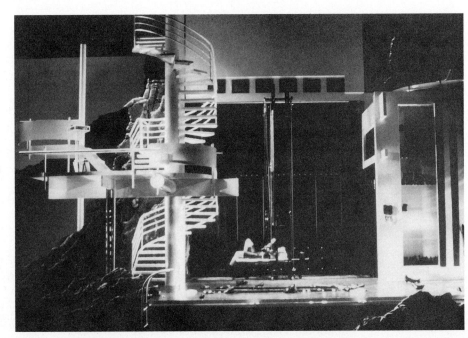

Scenery also communicates information about the *conditions* under which people live. Are they poor? Wealthy? Have they lived a long or a short time in this place? Are they vagabonds? Landowners? Is it very cold, very hot? How effectively are the characters able to control these conditions?

Scenery for *A Streetcar Named Desire* tells the audience not only how old but also how well maintained the house is, and even how long it might remain standing. It can indicate when Stanley and Stella's apartment was last redecorated, how long they have had their refrigerator, how often the apartment is cleaned and how well, and how the two rooms were used in the original building.

The setting for *Hedda Gabler* communicates conditions of life in a period that differs even more significantly from our own than does that of *A Streetcar Named Desire*. During the course of the play, the issue of whether or not the Tesmans can afford their house is raised. Since they have not occupied the house for very long, the truth of their financial or economic situation will be communicated through architecture, furniture, and various other objects onstage. Careful design will help the audience to understand the conditions of the Tesman's life and assess their anxieties. How might you construct a visual relationship that would establish the Tesman's precarious financial state? How might you indicate financial security?

Information About Character

A critical question to ask about any play is "Who made the choices that together create the environment?" Places are affected and changed by choices made by the characters who live in or occupy them.

The architecture and decor of the dining room in act 3 of *The Seagull* (taken together with the characters' response to it), helps in answering some questions about the characters. If, for example, the dining room contains objects that are clean but worn and aged, the audience will know that

- The servants work hard to make Arkadina happy
- Arkadina either does not have enough money to help her brother and son buy new things or she does not see the need for new things.

Act 4 of *The Seagull* takes place in the study of a troubled writer who in the end commits suicide. The room provides a framework for his state of mind. If he is in a state of mental chaos, the study might be neat as a pin except for his disorderly papers and desk. If his mind and habits have become rigid and inflexible, neatly stacked papers and pencils laid precisely side by side could communicate that fact. The study that reflects this compulsive orderliness could be a family room that has seen many happy times.

Macbeth and Lady Macbeth live at the upper echelons of society. Again, the scenery chosen will communicate something about the characters to the audience. Where and how they choose to live will relate to their ambitiousness. Is their dwelling a modest house or a grandiose castle? Do they belong to the medieval equivalent of the middle class? The upper class? Are they seeking power, money, and prestige?

Obviously, communicating information of this kind within the context of a period setting demands that the designer not only tell the audience when the play is taking place, but also how a setting that is unfamiliar to most members of the audience is located economically and socially within that period.

In *A Streetcar Named Desire*, Stella and Stanley have presumably chosen to live in their apartment. What does this choice tell us about them? If the apartment is simply old-fashioned, their choice may indicate an attachment to the charms of another era. But if the building is old and dilapidated, the audience can assume that they chose it because of limited funds. If the interior is messy, we can assume that housekeeping is not a priority. If it is dirty as well as messy, we can assume that they simply don't care about cleanliness. Then we would ask: What *do* they care about? Has Stella given up the values of her childhood in the Old South? Why?

Information About Mood or Atmosphere

Besides giving an audience information about time, place, and character, scenery has a story or life of its own that contributes to the mood and atmosphere of the production. The great twentieth-century designer Robert Edmond Jones called this an "expectancy . . . like a mixture of chemical elements held in solution. The actor adds the one element that releases the hidden energy of the whole." Jones, best known for his designs for the plays of Eugene O'Neill (1888–1953), says that no matter how "real" or credible the scenery is, it still remains the "magical element which can be seen," and so reminds us that the event we are witnessing is theatre. "A setting is not just a beautiful thing, a collection of beautiful things. It is a presence, a mood, a warm wind fanning the drama to flame. . . . It is an expectancy, a foreboding, a tension."[2]

Photo 5.1 of a production of another of Chekhov's plays, *The Cherry Orchard* (1904), shows a relatively simple setting, made up of walls and furniture, but one that creates an almost tangible atmosphere. With great delicacy the designer has worked the mood of the production into every element, down to the wallpaper. The subject of the play is the fate of a family. Will their land be sold to raise the money they need to survive, necessitating the destruction of their cherry orchard, or will the orchard remain, plunging them into poverty? The height of the walls, combined with the tree-patterned wallpaper, evokes the central problem of the play and lends a dreamlike mood to the production.

Photo 5.1
The original 1904 Moscow Art Theater production of Chekhov's *The Cherry Orchard.*

What the Scenic Designer Does

The total production, which includes actor, play, and theatrical environment, communicates meaning to the audience through the production concept. A theatrical environment is never neutral, but is the physical and visual balance to the words of the play and the actor's performance. The scenic designer is first and foremost responsible for working with the director and the other designers to create an environment that will communicate the meaning of a specific production and in which living actors can perform the play. Scenery, lighting, and costumes cannot "tell" the meaning of the play without the presence of the actor; conversely, the actor cannot "tell" the meaning of the play without a place in which to tell it.

There is a long road from the initial vision of the production to its realization onstage. The theatrical environment is created in very concrete ways: walls are built, backdrops painted, furniture arranged, trees and fountains grouped to suggest a park—even moons, stars, and planets are fashioned out of wood, Styrofoam, steel, or papier-mâché—all to suit the needs of the actors and the play. Each fabric, detail, and color is carefully chosen to communicate the nature of the environment to the audience.

The scenic designer is responsible not only for creating stage pictures, but also for communicating the necessary information to the people who actually build and paint the scenery. The scenic designer begins with rough drawings and sketches, then creates the scaled drawings from which the scenery is eventually constructed. These drawings communicate the specifics of the scenery—the actual dimensions of each piece. Later in this chapter we will see how these drawings are used by the carpenter building the scenery.

Scenery is built in a scene shop. Sometimes this is a space built specifically for that purpose, sometimes it is makeshift. Shops can be large or small, well equipped or not. Often the designer works closely with the shop during the construction and painting of the set. The designer is also responsible for designing most of the properties onstage. A *property* (or "prop") is any object that can be picked up by an actor, or any piece of furniture. (A prop belonging to a costume—eyeglasses, a cane, an umbrella, etc.—is the responsibility of the costume designer and is called a *costume prop*.) The scenic designer may help in acquiring props or may provide drawings for their construction.

Scenery and properties cost money. Like all the designers on a production, the scenic designer is responsible for staying within a set budget. This budget may be $500,000, $500, $50, or, occasionally, nothing at all. A designer's future work may well depend on whether or not the budget was adhered to.

What the Scenic Designer Looks for When Reading the Play

A designer will typically read the play many times from different points of view before the designs are completed. Reading as a designer is a special skill, and the different designers read with an eye toward different problems and requirements.

A scenic designer reads a play looking for some very practical information, including:

- Number of locations (and possibly settings)
- Kinds of settings
- Kinds of materials.

Macbeth and *The Heidi Chronicles* have many locations, *The Seagull* has four, *Hedda Gabler* and *A Streetcar Named Desire* have one. The setting for *Macbeth* could be a single, broadly defined performance space or many smaller ones; *Hedda Gabler* requires one setting that is specific in period and architectural requirements; *A Streetcar Named Desire* requires a street in New Orleans and a house in which both the downstairs and upstairs can be used by the actors. Scenery can be primarily painted on flat cloth or have constructed detail like doors, windows, cornices, and foliage—or any combination of these.

Designers, like directors and actors, also read a play for less practical information, such as tone, mood, and overall atmosphere or spirit. They convey these imaginative elements to the audience by the way they choose to design the more specific material requirements of the play.

Fulfilling the Needs of the Play

Aside from the imaginative aspects of scenic design that incorporate personal conceptual choices, the scenic designer is responsible, first, for fulfilling basic requirements of the play. After reading the play to become familiar with the plot, it is necessary for the scenic designer to make a checklist, what designer John Gleason calls a *shopping list,* consisting of all of the *physical requirements* of the play. To create this list, the designer reads the stage directions and dialogue with special care, noting every reference to physical objects.

A Streetcar Named Desire   Here is an example of such a checklist from the stage directions and dialogue of the first scene of *A Streetcar Named Desire.* The stage directions have been broken down into smaller units, but note that nearly all the information contained in these stage directions is also present in the dialogue.

1. *The exterior of a two-story corner building on a street in New Orleans . . .*

2. *. . . and runs between the L & N tracks and the river*

3. *The houses are mostly white frame, weathered grey, with . . . outside stairs and galleries . . . ornamented gables.*

4. *This building contains two flats, upstairs and down.*

5. *. . . stairs ascend to the entrances of both*

6. *Two rooms can be seen. . . . The one first entered is primarily a kitchen but contains a folding bed to be used by Blanche. The room beyond this is a bedroom. Off this room is a narrow door to a bathroom.*

7. STELLA: Don't holler at me like that. [Wherever Stella is inside, it is either relatively easy to hear what goes on outside, or Stanley is very loud.]

8. STANLEY: Catch! Meat. [Either the two of them are enough of a distance apart to warrant Stanley's throwing the package or he throws things because of the kind of fellow he is.]

9. STELLA: Stanley! Where are you going?

   STANLEY: Bowling! [Where is there to go? How do they enter and leave, and how does that relate to the house? Is the bowling alley visible?]

10. BLANCHE: This—can this be—her home? [In Chapter 3 we saw what broader issues arise from this sequence of lines. Blanche's question implies that there is something peculiar about Stella's house. Is there?]

    EUNICE: She's got the downstairs here and I got the up. [Eunice confirms for the audience who lives where, and that there are two floors.]

11. EUNICE: We own this place so I can let you in. [Is there a key? Is the door locked? If not, what kind of door is it and where is it located? Is there a door at all?]

12. EUNICE. It's sort of messed up right now but when it's clean it's real sweet. [Is Eunice simply responding to Blanche's reaction or is the place a mess? If it is a mess, how bad is it? Is it cluttered or is it squalid?]

This list provides information about the concrete requirements of the play and provides a springboard for establishing a conceptual relationship to it.

As an example of the conceptual relationship to which the scenic designer makes a major contribution, we can examine the last item in the checklist, which raises the question of whether or not Stanley's and Stella's apartment is a mess. The nature of this mess, if there is one, can be determined by analyzing what Eunice and Blanche say or do in response to it. Blanche says nothing initially; Eunice responds only to something that Williams refers to in the stage direction as "Blanche's look." After Eunice's line, Blanche responds: "Is it?," implying that at the moment, in her eyes, the apartment is not at all "sweet." To learn the nature and scale of the mess, it is necessary to understand Blanche's expectations (just how clean does a place need to be?) and the degree of Eunice's self-consciousness, if any. The mess itself, therefore, is dependent upon our understanding of the two characters.

- Is Eunice unable to see (or is she not bothered by) piles of trash?
- Is Blanche so refined that the presence of beer bottles, even if neatly aligned, would upset her?

Imagine some component of this mess and try to determine its impact on an audience's understanding of these characters and what they say.

Each physical object referred to in the play must be analyzed in this way. A shopping list for *Macbeth* would obviously look quite different from the one for *Streetcar.*

The Heidi Chronicles   Act 2, scene 5 of the play opens in the following way (emphasis added):

HEIDI: Excuse me. Can you help me? I just have **one more box**.

RAY: What?

HEIDI: I just have one . . .

RAY: I'm sorry, the **children's ward** is closed to visitors after nine o'clock. Can you come back tomorrow?

HEIDI: Actually, no, I can't. Well, I want to make a donation. So I'd like to, uh, drop this off tonight. Maybe if you could tell Dr. Patrone.

RAY: I'm sorry, he's on the **phone**.

PETER: Heidi!

HEIDI: Peter.

This dialogue, while providing us with some information, leaves much to interpretation. Questions arising from just these few lines might be:

- Where has Heidi come from? How many boxes does she have, what do they contain, and how did she get them here? Is there an elevator? What floor is she on?
- Is there a door into this room?
- What kind of room is it? Is it a waiting room or the ward itself? Where is the children's ward if this room isn't it?
- What is Ray doing in the room? Where is Peter? Can Ray see him or does he know by some other means that Peter is on the phone? Can his conversation be heard from this room?
- Can Heidi see Peter on the phone? If she sees Peter, why doesn't she go to him immediately, moving around Ray? Is she afraid she won't be well received?
- Does Peter see Heidi before he enters? If so, does he quickly come to her aid? What does that say about their relationship?

One of the basic questions regarding the beginning of this scene is why Heidi has dragged these boxes herself, after midnight, to the children's ward of the hospital at which Peter works. Why didn't she let him know she was coming? She says later in the scene that she tried to reach him, but did she? How does the way these two rooms are arranged relative to one another help to answer this question?

How Scenic Choices Contribute to the Meaning of the Play

Photos 5.2 through 5.6 are production stills of *The Seagull* taken, respectively, from designs by V. A. Simov for the original Moscow Art Theater production in 1898; Robert Edmond Jones for the 1938 Broadway production featuring the prominent American actors Alfred Lunt and Lynn Fontanne; Josef Svoboda for a March 1960 production in Prague, Czechoslovakia; George Tsypin for director Peter Sellars's adaptation of the play (renamed *A Seagull*) in 1985; and John Arnone for the La Jolla Playhouse's production, also in 1985, directed by Garland Wright. These five designs communicate five different points of view about the play.

We know from the script that the opening scene of *The Seagull* takes place in a clearing of some sort, near a lake, during the summer. Whether or not there are actual trees or an actual lake onstage, the scenery, at the very least, must help to communicate that the characters are outside (and not inside) and that they are near a lake. The set must do this so that when a line of dialogue refers to the physical environment, the character delivering it does not appear delusional to the audience; the stage world in this particular case should be believable.

Simov's design for the original production is painted on mostly flat cutout pieces, but even so manages to communicate the atmosphere of a dark and forbidding forest. The many tall trees, the tops of which are out of

Photo 5.2
The original 1898 Moscow Art Theater production of *The Seagull.*

sight range, imply that the characters are surrounded by an ancient wood. The trees are untrimmed, left to grow wild. The whole look is primitive; even the benches are rough-hewn. During the play within the play, there is reference to the effect of the "red eyes" of the devil. Even without sophisticated lighting, this place is frightening enough to render such an effect almost believable.

This is where Treplev has boldly placed his stage. The light color of the billowing curtain stands out crisply from the surrounding trees, causing the forest to appear even darker. The curtain is as primitive as the forest surrounding it, but easily holds the focus of the scene. The designer has placed the benches so that the backs of the stage audience face the real audience, reinforcing the focus on Treplev's play.

This setting communicates something of Treplev's battle to free art from artificiality, and from its effort to control nature. In Simov's design, the forest and Treplev's makeshift settings seem untamed.

Robert Edmond Jones's design is significantly lighter than that of the original production. The spot opens onto a lake and a luminous backdrop. Less obviously menacing, it also establishes a strong relationship between light and dark. The trees, though clearly theatrical, are old and tall, hanging darkly, almost lyrically overhead. The benches are casually arranged and look as if they belong in a rather elegant park, so we know this place is used for events other than theatrical performances. The setting evokes innocent, almost childlike pastimes. Treplev's performance will probably be received in that spirit as well.

Photo 5.3
Robert Edmond Jones's design for the 1938 Broadway production of *The Seagull.*

Photo 5.4
Josef Svoboda's
design for a
1960 production
of *The Seagull*
in Prague.

Josef Svoboda's design is more filled with foreboding than either of the previous two. He surrounds the setting in all four acts with deep black velour, and branches appear from the shadows. There is no clear delineation of interior and exterior, as Jones and Simov provide. This is a fluid world with no boundaries. It is shadowed, soft, ambiguous, and inescapable. The woods, penetrating every room in Svoboda's design, are transformed and theatricalized into a deep, black void.

Like Svoboda, George Tsypin creates a stage world with no defined boundaries. Are the characters inside, outside, or both? The designer even makes an ironic comment through a tear in a painted drop of the sky, which underscores that it, too, like everything else onstage, is artificial. Although this setting might appear at first to be a vast, light space, it is dark at floor level and lighter above, making the actors look as if they are at the bottom of a dark well. The elements, though simple, overwhelm the characters. The setting exudes a deep sense of pessimism.

John Arnone has created a setting that is not primarily interior or exterior, or even specific to any place at all. Like Svoboda and Tsypin, he combines architectural and natural elements, which reflect one another. This is a limitless world, one in which all boundaries are unclear. Arnone's set partially accomplishes this by establishing a strong relationship between light background and dark foreground, as do the designs by Robert Edmond Jones

Photo 5.5
George Tsypin's
design for Peter
Sellars's adapta-
tion of *The
Seagull* in 1985.

Photo 5.6
John Arnone's
design for Gar-
land Wright's
production of
The Seagull at
the La Jolla
Playhouse in
1985.

and George Tsypin. This setting, too, creates a sense of mystery and apprehension. In contrast to the extraordinary brightness of the sky, the dark is gloomy and deep. The characters, like shadows moving under water, seemalmost anonymous.

Although each of these settings is, to some extent, dark and forbidding, there are subtle differences in mood.

> V. A. Simov sets a rough stage in the middle of a primitive forest, expressing naivete; the pessimism of the environment becomes clear only at the end of the play. What are the ramifications of this setting for the rest of the play?

> Robert Edmond Jones creates a delightfully simple and lyrical picture of the Russian countryside. Gradually it becomes apparent that a perhaps insurmountable darkness looms overhead. What lies beyond this little park? Is it safe to go there?

> Svoboda's darkness is large, deep, and dense. To step out of his setting is to fall off the edge of the world into a bottomless pit; life within this darkness is stilted and cramped.

> George Tsypin's world is a bare, pristine, and boundless stage. It is a pit with light above that can be seen but probably never reached. As the tiny figures of the actors move, we question their (and our) sanity. In this setting, what is real? How far does one have to dig to find out?

> Arnone's setting is like a formal garden whose view is blocked. The light is far away upstage, accessible only through a maze. If they would only try hard enough, the characters might be able to escape the trance of this world. What, then, holds them there?

The questions raised by these settings must be answered in performance.

The Scenic Designer's Work Process

The Elements of Scenic Design

Like other visual artists, the scenic designer uses composition, color, value, shape, line, texture, and space to express meaning.

Robert Edmond Jones, whose design for *The Seagull* we have just examined, also designed many productions of Shakespeare's plays, including director/producer Arthur Hopkins's 1921 production of *Macbeth* starring Lionel Barrymore. Later, Jones sketched additional ideas for several scenes. Figure 5.1 shows the working model for Lady Macbeth's sleepwalking scene (act 5, scene 1) for the 1921 production. Figure 5.2 shows another design for

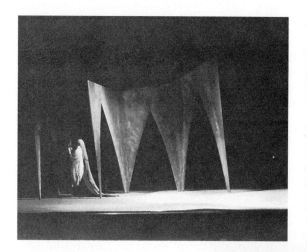

Figure 5.1, above
Robert Edmond Jones's model
for the sleepwalking scene in
the 1921 Arthur Hopkins production of *Macbeth*.

Figure 5.2, right
Robert Edmond Jones's sketch
for the sleepwalking scene,
date unknown.

Figure 5.3, above right
Robert Edmond Jones's design
for the same scene from a 1946
production.

the same scene in an undated project, and Figure 5.3 a design for an unpro-
duced project in 1946. We can use these designs to examine the different
choices Jones made and how he sought to establish meaning for the audience.

Jones uses unadorned elements and simple *compositional relationships*
in all three settings. The figure of Lady Macbeth is at the center in all three,
but in 5.1 and 5.3 the scenic pieces are asymmetrically arranged; in 5.2 they
are symmetrical. In the asymmetrical arrangements, Lady Macbeth is surrounded by a disturbing place; in the symmetrical composition, her personal confusion is set off against the balanced effect of the setting.

There is no question but that it is night in all three of these settings. A
strong, dark background sets off lighter *values* illuminated by candlelight.
Figure 5.2 places Lady Macbeth, a light value, in and against other, equally
light values. She is lost in her surroundings. In Figures 5.1 and 5.3 she is set

apart: Jones isolates her against the darkest value in the background, distinguishing her from her observers in an almost clinical arrangement.

Texture plays an important part in Figures 5.2 and 5.3. Mirrors, in the former, multiply Lady Macbeth's image, creating confusion for her but not for those observing her. In Figure 5.3, cold, hard stone separates Lady Macbeth in another way from her surroundings, by its contrast with warm human flesh.

Jones's use of *shape* and *line* in these designs was influenced by a movement in the visual arts known as *Expressionism*, which sought to express the artist's internal, emotional experience. In all three designs, distorted, expressionistic versions of an arch are used.

Each of these designs influences the audience's point of view on the character of Lady Macbeth. In all of them, Lady Macbeth is surrounded by menacing shapes, but only in Figure 5.3 does reality really seem menacing. The other two allow for escape, if only she could see what lies around her; what she does see are only reflections of her own disordered mind. In Figure 5.1 she is perhaps least sympathetic. Shape and scale show her fear to be a symptom of her mental state. In this setting, someone who was not already afraid would be frightened only by the dark surrounding night. Figure 5.2 presents a somewhat more sympathetic picture: a mirrored space, reflecting one's own shape over and over, would create confusion for anyone. But this setting is not terribly dark, and the placement of the other figures is somewhat reassuring.

Figure 5.3 shows a setting so sinister that the figure of Lady Macbeth becomes sympathetic. The reversal of value relationships, a sharply enclosed space, cold stone, and an apparently endless repetition of archways make the situation look inescapable. Within this framework, Lady Macbeth seems a victim.

Stages of the Scenic Designer's Work Process

A scenic designer progresses through some or all of the following stages in the process of designing: *research, drawing, rendering, model building,* and *drafting.* Each has its own place in the production process.

A scenic designer working on the first scene of *A Streetcar Named Desire* would probably begin by doing research on the New Orleans of 1947 in order to learn what kind of building and in what neighborhood people of Stanley's and Stella's economic means might have lived. The designer would look at the age of the building, what it would have been like when it was first built, and what it might have become over time. Research would also need to include specific elements of the setting such as railroad tracks, bowling alleys, other stores and shops, the proximity of other buildings, signs, street lights, sidewalk construction, wallpaper, floor coverings, furniture, refrigerators, water faucets, sinks, bathtubs, and so on.

Most designers also use research as a creative tool. (See Figure 5.4.) Sources of research can be paintings, photographs, nature itself—almost

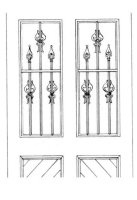

Figure 5.4
Photos and a sketch of the architecture of New Orleans. A designer might consult similar sketches and photographs while conducting research for a production of *A Streetcar Named Desire.*

anything that helps the designer to create an image for the overall production, the first step toward the design. What might be useful as research for a production of *Macbeth?* What kinds of photographs? Architecture?

As design work progresses, ideas gradually become more specific. Many designers use drawing, sketching, and painting to work out the problems of the scenery. Designer Adrianne Lobel notes, "I'll just sketch and sketch and sketch, and hope that something interesting will eventually show up. . . . It's really like thinking with a pencil."[3]

The sketch and *rendering* (a painted, two-dimensional representation of a setting or costume, or of the lighting design) not only make the design concrete for the designer, but also serve as communication tools for the director and other designers. An even more specific means is the *model*, a scaled representation (usually one-half inch on the model to one foot onstage) of the actual scenery. This model, either in color or black-and-white, placed within a model of the theatre in which it will be presented, shows the director, actor, and other designers how the scenery will look in three-dimensional space. Changes that need to be made can be accomplished much more easily and economically at the model stage than when full-scale scenery is already in the theatre. Some designers work almost exclu-

Alan Moyer's model for Mary Robinson's 1990 production of *Macbeth* at the Philadelphia Drama Guild.

sively with models, believing that sketches alone cannot accurately represent space, and that they can even be deceptive.

To provide for the actual construction of the scenery, the designer drafts the scenery to scale. These drawings are called *true views*, meaning that they show things in their true measurements, not as they would appear in a perspective drawing. They are carefully dimensioned because stage carpenters will use these drawings to build the scenery. Accurately rendering every line is critical. Scenery, made of real materials, must fit into a theatre made of solid walls, and the two must mesh perfectly.

Once the drawings are complete and the costs have been worked out, the scenic designer oversees actual construction in the shop. At a college theatre or off-off Broadway, the designer and stage carpenter may be the same person; on Broadway, the designer is literally not allowed to touch the scenery—a member of the stagehands' union must do so, under the designer's guidance.

Likewise, the designer will sometimes paint the scenery, but in other cases a *scenic artist* will do so. If the scenery is to be painted by someone else, the designer must provide a set of *paint elevations*, which are scaled drawings painted exactly as the scenery will appear.

Finally, once the scenery and props have been built, painted, and taken from the shop, they are brought to the theatre. The designer is responsible for being present at the time of the *load-in*, or installation of the scenery in the theatre. The designer is often aided here by a design assistant. During technical and dress rehearsals (which will be discussed in more detail in

Chapter 9), the scenic designer notes problems and alterations, supervises set changes, and is generally available to the costume and lighting designers for ongoing consultation.

Creating Movement Through the Setting

A *ground plan* is a map of the elements of a setting as viewed from above. It shows whatever the actor encounters: walls, doors, chairs, tables, plants, windows, etc. Department stores often have ground plans that make it difficult to find the exit or relative placement of departments within the store. Obviously, it is good business to keep the customer in the store for as long as possible! The placement of objects onstage likewise influences where and how the actors move around the set and establishes physical relationships that affect the meaning of the play.

Imagine a scene in which a young man and woman have returned to the woman's home, where she lives with her parents, and are seated on the sofa. The young woman's parents are due to arrive home at any moment. If, in the ground plan, the sofa faces a front window and the street, the problem of seeing the parents arrive becomes relatively inconsequential. But, if the ground plan has the back of the sofa facing the window, the dramatic—and comic—possibilities are substantially increased. Actors playing the

The final scene of *The Heidi Chronicles* as realized onstage.

Heidi Chronicles   Apartment

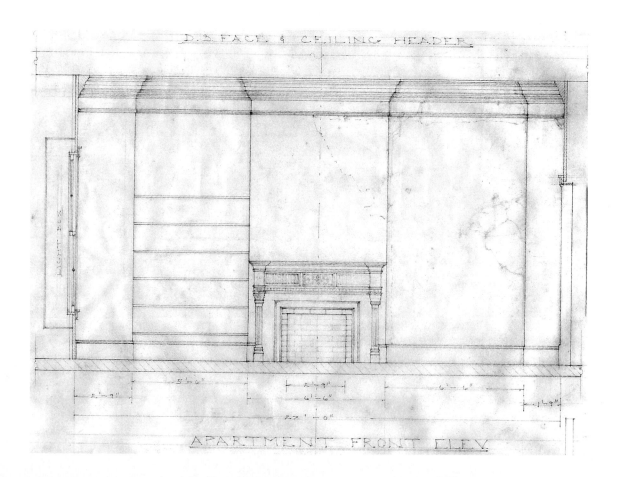

D.S. FACE & CEILING HEADER

APARTMENT FRONT ELEV.

young man and woman will be forced to turn around constantly to look out the window, interrupting their principal focus.

The cowboy in a Western movie shootout is similarly affected by ground plan. How does he stay hidden and shoot at the same time? Get closer to his target? Cross all that open space?

In Chapter 3, we saw how Jo Mielziner's setting for the original production of *A Streetcar Named Desire* helped create a strong visual ending for the production. The ground plan established by this set shows the actual relationship, *in scale,* of the floors and platforms, walls, stairs, and furniture that together created that picture. Imagine looking at the production photograph of the final moment of *Streetcar* from above—a view similar to a ground plan. Imagine how Blanche would move from the bedroom, through the kitchen, out the front door, and around the back of the house. Then imagine how the others would follow her. How does the ground plan affect their movement? What options are available other than the one we see in the picture? How flexible is the ground plan?

Scenery and Style

The stage environment has an important effect on the way in which the audience receives information about how reality has been transformed to provide the world in which the play will take place. The settings in the following illustrations show five different styles of scenery. Without attempting to name them, it is nevertheless possible to note their use of realistic detail and how close or far each is from our idea of everyday life. It should be noted that the plays for which the scenery was designed were written in different styles, which, in turn, called for different *styles of production.*

Charles McClennahan's design for Stage West's production of August Wilson's play *Fences* is made up of very realistic details. In fact, without the heads of the audience at the bottom, this might seem to be a photograph of an actual street. The next illustration, of Adrianne Lobel's design for Harry Kondoleon's *Anteroom,* looks at first glance as realistically representational in its stylistic conception as does the first. But there is something disconcerting about it. After looking at the setting for a few minutes, we see some other-than-realistic elements emerging. The cupboards, for ex-

Figure 5.5, opposite
Sketch and *elevation* for *The Heidi Chronicles.* A sketch is a perspective view of the scenery, drawn by the designer and used to communicate the look of the setting to the director, actors, other designers, and the producer. An elevation is a "true" front view of one unit or piece of scenery at a time, used for construction purposes. Courtesy of Tom Lynch.

Right: Charles McClennahan's design for a production of August Wilson's *Fences.* The production was directed by Clinton Turner Davis at StageWest in Springfield, Massachusetts.

Below, left: Adrienne Lobel's setting for Harry Kondoleon's play *Anteroom.*

Below, right: Hugh Landwehr's design for a production of Chekhov's *Uncle Vanya,* directed by Jack O'Brien for the Old Globe Theater.

ample, are considerably taller than they would be in an average kitchen. Who could reach them? They could be real—or not. The design is also extraordinarily symmetrical. Is any real space composed in such a way—with pairs of refrigerators? Clearly, the room was composed, even if from elements that seem realistic.

Hugh Landwehr's design for another of Chekhov's plays, *Uncle Vanya* (1897), shows a setting that would, in reality, have walls, but—for reasons to be revealed in the course of the performance—walls are not present. What we see is an overall structure reminiscent of a room, but not itself a room. The settings required by the play move from exterior to three different interiors and could, with minor changes, be accommodated in this open setting. As with Mielziner's setting for *A Streetcar Named Desire,* the audience fills in the missing walls for themselves.

The next two illustrations (Norman Bel Geddes's design for Shakespeare's *King Lear* and Michael Yeargan's design for *A Midsummer Night's*

Above, left: Micheal Yeargan's design for Shakespeare's *A Midsummer Night's Dream* at the Hartford Stage Company.

Above, right: Norman Bel Geddes's design for Shakespeare's *King Lear.*

Dream) depart dramatically in style from the first two illustrations, and somewhat from the third. It is not surprising that these settings are so free of representational detail. Even after all these centuries, much is left in the production of Shakespeare's plays to the descriptive skill of the actor and the text, and to the imagination of the audience.

Bel Geddes's set is remarkable for its single, strong sculptural element. The place it describes is wholly imaginary. The setting is presentational and looks as if a religious ceremony could take place in it. Yeargan's setting, created for a different kind of play, is more playfully mysterious. *A Midsummer Night's Dream* concerns itself with the relationship between love in the real world and love in the fairy world. Yeargan's setting is, of the five, the least realistic, and aided by the lighting, takes on an almost underwater atmosphere.

Painted Scenery

Styles of scenery can be categorized in many ways, but how scenery is constructed, profoundly affects our perception of it. If it is possible to build piece of scenery so that it looks almost as it would in reality, why use painted scenery? The simple answer is that flat, painted scenery can (thanks to various methods to be discussed in Chapter 9,) be quickly gotten out of the way and replaced by another set. It is also less expensive than scenery with dimensional detail.

Above: An example of the highly realistic detail that can be achieved by today's scenic artist. This kind of traditional painting is referred to as *trompe l'oeil,* or "fooling the eye."

Left: A scenic artist at the Paris Opera follows the scenic designer's paint elevation to create a backdrop.

In earlier periods, most scenery was painted. Highly skilled scene painters used techniques that made painted scenery look almost three-dimensional. Today's *scenic artists* practice many of the same techniques as their predecessors, on both flat and dimensionally built scenery. Today, a setting composed totally of painted scenery is usually found only in productions of musicals, if at all.

Using painted scenery alone, it is possible to achieve a total stage environment. To do so, however, requires the use of several carefully placed pieces. At the back of the stage is a *backdrop*—a painted or unpainted sheetlike affair that covers the upstage wall of the theater from one side to the other. (A *drop* is the same thing, but can be placed anywhere, not just on the upstage wall.) A painted *wing* is a vertical piece of scenery that meets a drop and masks actors entering and exiting the backstage area. Above, the wing or drop meets a *border* that, in turn, masks everything overhead. When put together, the resulting setting is called *wing and border,* and it has had a long and illustrious history in the theatre. As a simple method for masking the stage, a wing-and-border arrangement can be used effectively where a quick setup is needed, for example, in touring situations in which very little time is allowed for setting up and taking down the production.

Some painted scenery is meant to look painted and not like a three-di-

A *cyclorama*, or unpainted "sky" drop, appears brightly lit behind the actor. Black velour wings (also called *legs*) and borders complete the general stage picture.

Figure 5.6
Leon Bakst's 1910 setting for *Scheherazade*, Ballets Russes, Paris.

Figure 5.7
Serlio's tragic scene.

Figure 5.8
Serlio's comic scene.

Sebastian Serlio (1475–1554), an Italian painter, architect, and stage designer, produced a group of painted settings based on a treatise, *De Architectura*, written by the Roman Vitruvius (70–15 B.C.).

Figure 5.9
Serlio's pastoral scene.

Serlio's settings (Figures 5.7, 5.8, 5.9) were designed to be used generically for tragedy, comedy, and pastoral drama (a poetic dramatic form that made use of rustic subjects). In them Serlio employs the Renaissance method of conceiving a picture from the point of view of a single observer. Set up in halls of state or in palaces, scenery painted in single-point perspective like Serlio's was arranged so that the one correct view was from the seat of the person in power.

Stages were built to reinforce this perspective. The downstage area was used by the actors and was level. The upstage section was primarily for the scenery and was raked upward. This plan kept the actors away from the painting, which, as it moved upstage, became smaller and smaller and thus out of scale; it also rein-

Figure 5.10   *Figure 5.11*

Two settings by Inigo Jones for *The Masque of Oberon,* presented January 1, 1611.

forced the illusion created by the per-spective drawing.

The use of painted scenery continued into the seventeenth and eighteenth centuries, with designers like the Bibiena family in Italy and artists like Inigo Jones (1573–1652) in England.

Jones's designs shown above for a court masque—a kind of performance that celebrated English royalty in dance, poetry, and music—makes use of painted backdrops and shutters (moveable wings) that opened to reveal a new painted setting behind them. The setting by Bibiena,

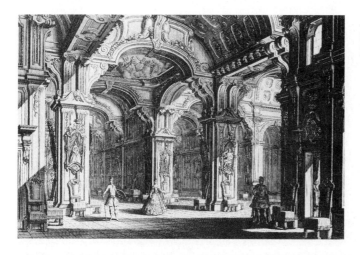

Figure 5.12
Setting by Guiseppe Galli
Bibiena, 1719.

A setting for Shakespeare's *Othello* at the Comédie Française in 1899.

over one hundred years later, illustrates the use of multiple vanishing points.

The setting shown above for Shakespeare's *Othello*, produced at the Comédie Française in 1899, provides a fascinating comparison with what the play might have looked like in Shakespeare's Globe Theater. The proscenium stage, combined with a mania dating back to the Renaissance for creating the illusion of three-dimensional space on a two-dimensional surface, brings Shakespeare's play a long way from the essentially bare stage for which it was written.

Theatre today also uses painted wing-and-border settings. Tony Straiges's settings for *Sunday in the Park with George* makes use of a series of *portals* (joined wings and borders) to achieve a look similar to the wing-and-border settings used by Serlio, Bibiena, and Inigo Jones.

Sunday in the Park with George. The painter Georges Seurat (played by Mandy Patinkin) creates his painting on stage with the support of scenery made up of a series of wings and borders.

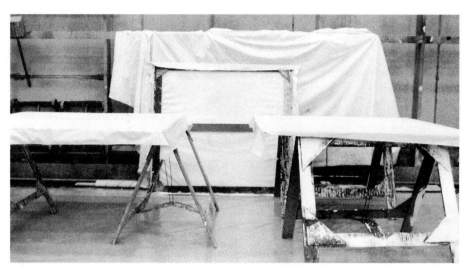

Figure 5.13
A flat and its construction. A *flat* is a scenic module, several of which, placed next to one another and joined together, might make up a section of wall onstage. A flat consists of a frame and a *covering*—the side that faces the audience. The covering can be soft (like muslin or canvas) or hard (like plywood) and covered with muslin or canvas.

mensional environment at all. The setting by the famous designer Leon Bakst in Figure 5.6 is like a painting. There is no attempt to make it look like a real place; rather it is a painting of a place in the imagination.

Dimensional Scenery

If a setting can be painted to look like the real thing, why not do that? After all, dimensional scenery doesn't have the practical advantages of painted scenery: it is difficult to move and store offstage, and generally is more expensive than painted scenery. When dimensional scenery is used, it means that a way of relating the actor to three-dimensional space is needed. Today, most scenery not intended to resemble a painting is built with dimension. Although once it was common to see a wall with pots and pans painted on it, today the pots will most likely be real.

Figure 5.14
A basic platform. Like the flat, a platform used in the theatre is often modular and therefore easy to move about. A platform consists of a frame, which gives it stability, and a strong surface that can hold actors and other scenery. One standard platform size is 4 feet by 8 feet—the size of a standard sheet of plywood.

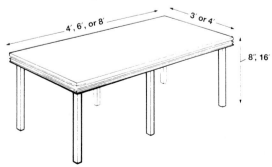

Interview

AN INTERVIEW WITH TOM LYNCH, SCENIC
DESIGNER FOR THE ORIGINAL PRODUCTION
OF THE HEIDI CHRONICLES AT PLAYWRIGHTS
HORIZONS, ON BROADWAY, AND ON TOUR.

I remember first reading *The Heidi Chronicles.* It was very, very touching to me, emotionally touching more than anything else, partly because it felt like a piece of writing right in line with my own experience. I felt, "This is my class, my generation." It rang true. Part of that comes from an assumed political stance, a shared kind of liberalism. Wendy and I are very close to the same age, and both went to college in the late sixtiess, early seventies. We shared an assumed political sympathy.

The intriguing thing about this play for me as a designer was to find how to organize a series of emotional pictures that are being stated in an almost satirical way. I needed to be able to highlight, in a way, the serious-ness and the legitimacy of the play. It was like figuring out a puzzle, trying to put a structure on very nonstructured things. The more specifically po-litical side of the play began to feel more like a payoff only when audiences started to listen to it. All my energy went toward trying to find the visual and emotional organization.

The writing is so likable. Wendy is so good at the sound of dialogue and she writes great jokes. The audiences were truly touched by the play: older audiences recognized their children, younger audiences recognized themselves. You are surprised by the play; it makes you listen.

[Working on] *The Heidi Chronicles* is a good example of the design process. In the play there is a very varied set of emotional points or states that the audience goes through. The designer's job is to make a physical context in which that can happen easily. The designer must identify what that context is—which is tricky—and find the requirements of how to tell the story. I don't know exactly what the link is between pinning down a feeling about a scene, and then organizing it relative to the other scenes. Right there, in pinning things down, is where the designer's work happens.

Dan Sullivan [the director] and I talked about the play in only one or two meetings. Then Dan went away. He came back to see what I had come up with, made a few suggestions, and that was it. We decided that the early part of the play was like a memory and we might use less space and less physical detail; the latter part of the play would have the true depth of reality, while the earlier scenes would be shallow. The last scene used the full depth of the stage and felt the most real in terms of detail. This was the most conscious design strategy we used.

The collaborative process is so important to me. My work is only going to be as valuable or as good as the director's work. I never think of my design work being able to stand alone. It is not very interesting by itself, but rather depends on what the director does with it. In the case of *The Heidi Chronicles*, Dan could use what I supplied as sort of chips that he was putting down to tell a story. He made it seem inevitable, in a way invisible, which it should be.

Starting at Playwrights Horizons, we had to do the play with a minimum of design elements. When it was decided to move the production to Broadway, there was something in the small space that we wanted to preserve. At Playwrights we had created a geometric solution to the emotional puzzle of the play. Expanding that in scale meant completely changing physical strategies, yet maintaining the same ideas. For example, if it takes five seconds to move a piece of furniture nine feet at Playwrights, it would take much longer to move it twenty-eight feet at the Plymouth Theater [on Broadway]. We still wanted to maintain a sense of a snapshot. Having decided on an emotional solution, it became a mechanical puzzle as to how to achieve it. The solution was a fairly elaborate mechanical setting, more like that used in a small musical than a straight play.

We used two adjacent *slip stages* downstage, which together were fifty-five feet wide. The trick was to get the next set of furniture to center stage (none of the scene changes took more than six seconds). The slip stages moved very fast, and the actors were changing clothes at the same time. Walls and rear projection screens were flying in and out (at the rate of eight feet per second). What was amazing was that there were no accidents, thanks to smart, attentive actors and stage management. We did crush some chairs during technical rehearsals; in fact, we went through several sets of them. They had to be in exactly the right place.

The audience did not see how the scene changes happened. Some took place in front of slides, some were in complete view but just slid away with someone standing in front of it. The feeling was like TV editing. The mechanics, which were very complicated and expensive, made the piece seem clever and unpretentious, just as it was at Playwrights Horizons. At Playwrights the scenery was moved by hand, by overhead tracking, and the actors sometimes moved some of the furniture. On Broadway, the actors had to get out of the way of moving furniture instead. It was like having an emergency at every scene change.

Pat Collins [the lighting designer] created the look and solved the puzzle of how to make these scenes vivid so as to give each a real identity. It was a big technical problem because the stage was so crowded and tight.

The process of designing is making an emotional progression through technical solutions. In the case of *The Heidi Chronicles*, that kind of solution could only happen with certain financial resources. Finally, it takes pretty sophisticated equipment and technicians who can consistently make that happen, without accidents, for a year-and-one-half run.

Jim Walsh, the producer of *The Heidi Chronicles* on Broadway, respected the fact that I was thinking about the problem, and I really respected him for not trying to dismantle the production, but to keep it intact. The process was very clear. We were all doing the same thing and attention was not diverted toward money problems. Together we were just making it as good as we could.

Dimensional scenery is not constructed like a house—it is not built to last (Figures 5.13 and 5.14). Even if it stays put from opening to closing night, scenery must still be carted into the theatre, set up in a relatively short amount of time, and taken apart quickly for disposal. Scenery cannot

The setting for the play *Victoria Regina* by Laurence Housman, produced in New York in 1935, illustrates what can be done with a box set. Wallpaper, windows, drapes, pictures, picture frames, and appropriate furniture together come close to creating the illusion of an actual room. Note that the side walls do not meet the back wall at a 90-degree angle, but are angled or raked to allow the audience a view of the entire room.

The box set for the Broadway production of Marsha Norman's *'Night Mother*, designed by Heide Landesman, illustrates the definitive use of built, realistic detail. The kitchen—only half of the total setting (the rest is not visible in this photograph)—surrounds the actors just like an average suburban kitchen. There is very little painted detail on this setting; every detail is constructed from the actual materials that would be used to build a real kitchen.

Constructed almost entirely of Styrofoam, Ming Cho Lee's setting for the play *K-2* looks as close to a real mountain as one could imagine, with the help of some wonderful lighting. Although the surface is treated and painted, the emphasis is on extraordinarily realistic construction.

require a year or even a month's installation time, and ideally it doesn't cost as much as a house (though often it does, and more).

Although dimensional scenery is in its golden age today, it is not an exclusively twentieth-century idea. In the Middle Ages, performance spaces known as *mansion stages* housed dimensional scenery that incorporated fantastic effects and devices, such as the "hell mouth." Sometimes built in the shape of a monster's head, the hell mouth appeared to swallow the characters who came near it, accompanied by fire, smoke, noise, and other sound effects.

After the Middle Ages, truly dimensional scenery was not in regular use in Europe until the late nineteenth century, when the *box set* became a regular feature. This interior setting surrounds the actor with walls on three sides, creating a box. The introduction of the box set allowed the use of real windows and doors, pictures in real picture frames, and real pots hanging on the "walls."

Single Settings, Multiple Settings, and Unit Settings

Scenery, whether painted or dimensionally built, fulfills the requirements of place in many productions. If a production requires only one location, a *single setting* will fulfill that need. If more than one location is required, the designer can create *multiple settings,* which provide a different setting for each location, or a *unit setting,* which is an overall structure into which and from which smaller pieces of scenery and props are moved, creating easily identifiable transitions for the audience. An extreme example was the Elizabethan theatre, where the stage itself formed a "unit"—a setting that evidently remained essentially the same for every production.

Unit settings (like those represented in Figure 5.15) also include those settings that show more than one location at a time, for example, more than one room within a single building. This is also referred to as a *split stage.*

Figure 5.15
Shakespeare's *Measure for Measure,* designed by Hugh Landwehr and directed by Douglas Hughes for the Seattle Repertory Theater, 1989. The "unit" consisted of a single space shared by actors and audience in seating risers. Fourteen marble columns topped by bronze statues of angels, a marble floor, and a roughly white-washed wall scored with black horizontal lines filled the space. When scenes changed, stagehands repositioned the basic furniture, moved a metal gate across the space, and lowered lightbulbs. The "unit" was also changed by recomposing groups of actors.

Here David Belasco, an important early twentieth-century American director and producer, "splits" the stage with what in reality would have been a wall. Viewed at its edge, the wall is used to divide the action, allowing the audience to see simultaneously both a stage in a theatre and an offstage dressing room. Although the two sides are next to each other, the audience accepts that what occurs on one side cannot be seen or heard by the characters on the other. The production is *Zaza* (1900).

As we saw earlier, Jo Mielziner's design for Williams's *A Streetcar Named Desire* presented exterior and interior at once—a unit setting with a split stage. At the opening, Blanche enters carrying her suitcase and speaks with Eunice. As she tries to find her sister's house, she "looks" at the exterior, which isn't there. The audience accepts that Blanche cannot see into the house even if they can. When she enters the house, Blanche can see only the kitchen, although the audience can see the bedroom as well. Throughout the play, Williams pays careful attention to what the characters can and cannot overhear and can and cannot see, depending on the dramatic needs of the scene. The audience, however, can always see and hear everything.

The Stage as Scenery

As we saw in the Broadway production of *Our Town* discussed in Chapter 2, sometimes the theatre structure itself is used as the basis or unit of the setting. The large, quiet, rather romantic emptiness of the backstage supports the mood of that particular play.

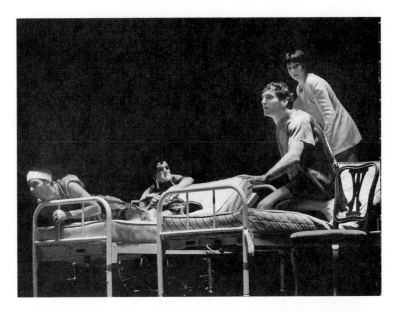

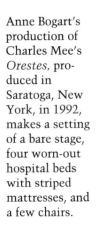

Anne Bogart's production of Charles Mee's *Orestes*, produced in Saratoga, New York, in 1992, makes a setting of a bare stage, four worn-out hospital beds with striped mattresses, and a few chairs.

Whether for reasons of economy, ease of transportation, aesthetics, or a combination of all three, many experimental theatre companies of the past several decades have chosen to use just a few properties, making no attempt to represent an environment other than that of the theatre itself. For example, the Open Theater's production of *Nightwalk* (last performed in 1973) used rolling carts to create a fluid, ever-changing environment.

Scenery, and the scenic designer, have an enormous impact on what the audience sees onstage. Not only does the scenic designer create a visual picture to support the work of the other collaborators, he or she also determines how the actors move through the space.

In a production of a play such as *Hedda Gabler* or *A Streetcar Named Desire*, in which one setting remains throughout, the scenic designer contributes most to the overall look of the room and to the ground plan. In a production of a play such as *The Seagull*, the designer must develop an overall design scheme that provides movement from one act (or setting) to the next, and does so convincingly: each must somehow differ from the other. Plays like *Macbeth* and *The Heidi Chronicles* demand from their scenic designers an even more elaborate design scheme, one that fulfills not only the audience's need for information, but the production concept as well. In the interview with Wendy Wasserstein in Chapter 2, the playwright says that Tom Lynch's setting became larger as the performance went along, allowing the audience to observe the growth in Heidi's perspective. The designer had to convey this idea, while at the same time allowing each individual setting to assert its own identity.

Suggested Readings

Adolphe Appia, *The Work of Living Art: A Theory of the Theatre and Man Is the Measure of All Things* (Miama: University of Miami Press), 1969.

Arnold Aronson, *American Stage Design* (New York: TCG Publications), 1985.

Denis Bablet, *Edward Gordon Craig* (Paris: Editions du Centre National de la Recherche Scientique), 1984.

Howard Bay, *Stage Design* (New York: Drama Book Specialist), 1974.

Jarka Burian, *The Scenography of Josef Svoboda* (Middletown, Conn.: Wesleyan University Press), 1971.

Harold Burris-Meyer and Edward C. Cole, *Scenery for the Theatre: The Organization, Processes, Materials, and Techniques Used to Set the Stage*, rev. ed. (Boston: Little, Brown), 1971.

Edward Gordon Craig, *On the Art of Theater* (New York: Theatre Arts Books), 1956.

Walter R. Fuerst and Samuel J. Hume, *Twentieth Century Stage Decoration*, two vols. (London: Dover), 1967.

Robert Edmond Jones, *The Dramatic Imagination* (New York: Theater Arts Books), 1941.

Mordecai Gorelik, *New Theaters for Old* (New York: S. French), 1940.

Kenneth Macgowan and Robert E. Jones, *Continental Stagecraft* (New York: Harcourt Brace), 1922.

D. M. Oenslager, *Stage Design: Four Centuries of Scenic Invention* (New Haven, Conn.: Yale University Press), 1964.

Richard Schechner, *Environmental Theater* (New York: Hawthorn Books), 1973.

Ronn Smith, *American Set Design 2* (New York: TCG Publications), 1991.

Chapter SIX

The Costume Designer

We all have considerable experience with costumes in our lives. Every day we are faced with the choice of what to wear, every day we look at what others have chosen. Clothing affects our relationship with the environment (when it is cold, hot, raining, etc.) and with society. We choose to dress a certain way because of many complex factors, not the least of which is the perennial desire to be fashionable and successful, to be accepted by a particular group.

What do we think we know when we look at how a person is dressed? If we return to the job interview scenario from Chapter 5, we can imagine our response to how the interviewer is dressed. Photo.s 6.1, 6.2, and 6.3 show three relatively credible sets of apparel for a person conducting a job interview in a large corporation. You, the interviewee, have ridden an elevator to the twentieth floor of a modern skyscraper and are waiting patiently, under the watchful eye of the receptionist. A door opens and one of the three people illustrated welcomes you to your interview.

The interviewer in Photo 6.1 is clearly self-assured, carefree, and reasonably affluent. Fashionable and classic at once, her clothing

Photo 6.1, left
This woman's choice of clothing might lead you to expect an unconventional job interview.

Photo 6.2, below left
You would expect an interviewer dressed in a suit like this one to be casual yet sophisticated.

Photo 6.3, below right
An interviewer dressed in a conservative suit like this one worn by Richard Nixon probably would conduct an interview very differently from someone wearing clothes like those pictured elsewhere on this page.

has been carefully chosen. It would probably make you concerned about your own. This interviewer most likely doesn't always follow the pack, and you might expect your interview to be somewhat out of the ordinary.

Photo 6.2 shows a fashionably dressed interviewer, younger in spirit (if not in actual age) than the one in Photo 6.3 and deliberately more relaxed. His suit, shirt, and tie are expensive but, unlike those in Photo 6.3 are designed to be casual in a very sophisticated way. The suit in Photo 6.3 is very traditional and might or might not be terribly expensive. Most men wear suits like this, some costly and of expensive material, some not.

What about each of these three "costumes" might change your expectations for the interview? Which interview is likely to *seem* casual? Which, if any, will actually *be* casual? Which will demand more input from you? Which of the three will make you most comfortable? Least comfortable?

What Stage Costumes Tell Us

Our understanding of character is made up of many assembled details. Costumes, like scenery, provide specific information for the audience. *Place, character, character relationships,* and *socioeconomic level* are some categories of information provided by costumes. If scenery answers the question "What kind of place is this?," costumes help answer that question while also asking another: "What kind of people are these?"

Place

Before we can understand who the characters are, we must provide a context for them; where and when they live affect how they dress, and it is within that context that we must be able to distinguish one character from another. Scenery, costumes, and lighting together help establish where the characters are. Costume choices indicate where the play takes place—in what *historical period*, in what *climate*, and sometimes even the *occasion* or *time of day*. Costumes for *Macbeth*, for example, must tell the audience where the play takes place, in what period, whether the climate is warm or cold, whether the characters are indoors or out, and how those characters present themselves to others.

Later in this chapter we will explore *how* the costume designer communicates this and other information.

Character

Once we, as the audience, are clear about the context of the play, we must be able to clearly distinguish one character from another within that context. If we know, for example, that *A Streetcar Named Desire* takes place in New Orleans, in spring, in the late 1940s, we can make some determinations about the characters who live in this setting. When Mitch, for example, in a climate that is extremely hot and humid, dresses in a winter-weight suit, we know that for him personal comfort is not a priority.

When we gain information about a character through a costume, we are really gaining an understanding of the character's self-image and how he or she chooses to be seen, in addition to specific physical information such as age, sex, and body type. In many cases, this choice is largely determined by social and economic circumstances. A homeless person has very little choice in what to wear, whereas Lady Macbeth would have a substantial range of choices, although still limited by the fashions and customs of her time. The Scarlett O'Hara in Photo 6.4 chooses to be perceived as girlish and attractive, privileged, flirtatious, and light-hearted. Her dress is low cut, bright, and difficult to move in; her face is charmingly framed by her hat. She is bearing up very well under the hot weather. Elizabeth Taylor's Martha (Photo 6.5), in Edward Albee's *Who's Afraid of Virginia Woolf?*, chooses to be seen as more voluptuous, younger, and wealthier than she is. George (Richard Burton) doesn't seem impressed with any of these quali-

Photo 6.4
Vivian Leigh as Scarlett O'Hara in the movie *Gone With the Wind.* The costumes provide information about these categories:
- *location:* the American South
- *time:* nineteenth century
- *weather:* a hot day (Scarlett's large hat protects her from the sun)
- *setting:* some kind of festive event or party.

Photo 6.5
Elizabeth Taylor and Richard Burton in the movie version of Edward Albee's play
Who's Afraid of Virginia Woolf? (1966). Their clothing tells us that the two characters probably live in a northern climate (the man is wearing a sweater indoors), are
in the middle class, and do not agree on the nature of the occasion (she is dressed
for a party; his outfit is more appropriate for a quiet evening at home).

ties, but would like to be seen as professorial, poor, and unappreciated.
Their clothing communicates this information to the audience before the
characters speak their first lines.

Character Relationships

The nature of Scarlett O'Hara's costume suggests her relationship with the
men in the picture, a relationship that would be fairly typical of that period.
George and Martha, with their different ways of presenting themselves at
whatever occasion is taking place at the time of the picture, probably disagree often.

Hedda and Mrs. Elvsted live in a society that specifically defines
women's roles for them. In Chapter 2 we read two points of view on Hedda
for two productions of the play, one directed by Emily Mann, the other by
Maria Irene Fornes. Ms. Mann's Hedda is a 29-year-old who married in a
panic and is trapped by society's expectations. Ms. Fornes's Hedda is a free
agent, not trapped at all, but somehow unable to move.

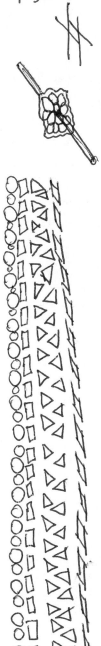

In Ms. Mann's production, Mrs. Elvsted might be close to Hedda's age, but less panicked, more comfortable with her role in society, and supportive of the men in her life. Although this relationship becomes clear to the audience through the performances, costume plays a role as well. Perhaps Hedda, out of habit, dresses more coyly and sweetly than Mrs. Elvsted. Or she might dress more elegantly than the occasion warrants, while Mrs. Elvsted shows less concern for occasion.

Ms. Fornes's production point of view creates some interesting problems for the costume designer. Hedda, though not actually trapped by society, perceives herself to be so. Mrs. Elvsted, in contrast, might see herself as trapped, but she tries to gain the most freedom possible within the system. How would their costumes differ?

Nazimova's costume for Hedda (see Photo 3.2) seems appropriate for Fornes's point of view, although perhaps somewhat extreme. Casting herself in the role of a trapped victim, Hedda would dress to emphasize the hopelessness of her situation. Mrs. Elvsted, in contrast, might choose a less constraining, more practical garment, one better suited to the context that the men create. Perhaps her costume would be the late-nineteenth-century equivalent of a contemporary woman's business suit.

Economic and Social Status

From our knowledge of society in general, we know the difference between the "look of success" and the "look of failure." Look at the society pages of any newspaper and study the outfits of wealthy and successful people. Are the fabrics expensive? The cut of the garments good? Do the shoes appear to be handsewn and of fine, polished leather? Does the jewelry look valuable? What about hairstyles?

We use our ability to assess social and economic status in theatrical costumes as well. We know, although they belong to two entirely different periods, that Scarlett is well to do and Martha is not. Of the two Heddas discussed, which would be more apparently wealthy or successful? How might a woman's costume of that period communicate this information? It is the costume designer's responsibility to answer these subtle questions.

What the Costume Designer Does

The costume designer is responsible for clothing each actor in a manner appropriate to character and production. As straightforward as this sounds, the job is often profoundly complex. The costume designer must possess not only design skills, but interpersonal skills as well. Actors often, and rightly, have strong feelings about the characters they are playing, but because they are a part of it, they cannot see the whole stage picture. The costume designer, along with the director, must be able to negotiate choices to everyone's satisfaction.

The costume designer works with the director to find ways of expressing the production's point of view through clothing. Along with the other designers, the costume designer makes choices about the shape, color, line, texture, value, and detail of all the costumes as they will appear onstage under lights and against the set. A costume also affects how the actor wearing it will move. A corseted character in *Hedda Gabler* will walk, sit, and even talk differently than a loosely draped character in *Macbeth* or Heidi in the 1980s.

A costume designer need not be an expert at sewing. In fact, many professional costume designers are not "stitchers" at all. But they must know how a costume is put together. That information is vital to the final appearance of the garment. Costumes are generally constructed in a costume shop, and the designer is responsible for providing the shop with the necessary information—usually through costume sketches or renderings.

Costume shops, like scene shops, are either built specifically for a particular university or regional theatre, or they are independent operations that construct costumes for many theatres and productions simultane-

Figure 6.1

Sketch of a costume for the character of Arkadina from *The Seagull*. On this sketch the costume designer has provided the costume shop with information that might not be immediately evident from the sketch alone. The notes regarding the kinds of fabrics the designer desires, such as the references to brocade of different scales; detail and decoration, such as the use of lace and fabric flowers; and supplemental garments, such as the capelet, all provide the person constructing the costume with a more detailed sense of what the final garment should look like. Courtesy of Deborah Brothers.

ously. After providing detailed sketches and fabrics to the shop, the costume designer must be available for consultations with the *costumer,* who oversees the actual process of putting the garments together. Often changes take place during rehearsal that need to be communicated immediately to the costume shop, before too many dollars are spent. Keeping a close watch on the process in the shop also allows the designer to fine-tune the design as the garment is being cut and sewn.

Like the other designers, the costume designer is responsible for the budget for his or her area of responsibility. The budget can range from many thousands of dollars to nothing at all. In case of the latter, the actors may bring their own clothes, from which the designer picks something appropriate. Or the designer may choose from the theatre's stock of costumes or borrow clothing from some other source.

There are many details involved in what an actor wears onstage, and the costume designer is responsible for the choice of every button, shoe, and snap. The garment itself may involve undergarments, such as petticoats, hoops, bustles, and corsets. In addition, the total effect of a costume may require wigs, facial hair such as beards and mustaches, particular haircuts and styles, make-up, and personal costume props such as canes, eyeglasses, wallets, pill boxes, and handkerchiefs. In a production such as the musical *Cats,* a make-up designer might be hired to work with the costume designer. Wig designers are also common on high-budget productions.

What the Costume Designer Looks for When Reading the Play

Like the director, actors, and other designers, the costume designer reads the play for plot, action, and point of view (Figure 6.1). However, as in all the other design areas, the final decisions are strongly affected by the practical considerations of scope and budget.

Scope of the Production

HOW MANY COSTUMES?   The costume designer is first of all concerned with the number of costumes needed. The designer looks at how many characters are in the play (*A Streetcar Named Desire* has 12 characters, *Macbeth* at least 28, *The Seagull* at least 13). This determines the minimum number of costumes to be designed or secured.

HOW MANY COSTUME CHANGES?   A costume designer must know when and how often a character changes clothing. This information will depend on changes in place, time (one day to another), event (for example, a party), season, etc. This number is not necessarily written in stone, and can vary from production to production. In general, however, a designer would not keep a character in the same costume for several scenes in which major time shifts occur unless it were justified by the text of the play.

Heidi appears in every one of the 13 scenes of *The Heidi Chronicles*. It is unlikely that she would wear the same clothing at each of the two art history lectures given in the two prologues, and it might confuse the audience if she did. The other scenes take place in the following circumstances:

Act One
Scene One: Chicago, 1965, the high school dance
Scene Two: Manchester, New Hampshire, 1968: dance for Eugene McCarthy, the New Hampshire primary
Scene Three: Ann Arbor, Michigan, 1970: a church basement, it is snowing outside
Scene Four: Chicago, 1974: outside the Chicago Art Institute in the rain
Scene Five: New York, 1977: anteroom to Pierre Hotel ballroom—a wedding reception.

Act Two
Scene One: An apartment, 1980: Scoop and Lisa's apartment, the baby shower
Scene Two: a TV studio, 1982
Scene Three: A trendy New York restaurant, 1984.
Scene Four: The Plaza Hotel, 1986: Heidi is presenting a speech to her old school's alumnae association
Scene Five: A pediatrics ward, 1987: Christmas, after midnight
Scene Six: An apartment, 1989

Here, situation, time, and weather change from scene to scene. The costume designer must find a way to make these differences clear to the audience.

A Streetcar Named Desire takes place in 11 scenes over several months' time. Given the economic status of the characters, it may not be necessary to have different clothing for each scene, but a character probably wouldn't repeat a costume from one scene to the next except in those cases when the scenes take place in the same day (e.g., Blanche and Stella go out before the poker party begins, then return in the next scene which takes place later the same evening). Blanche, who previously had a more lucrative job than the others and seems to be much more concerned with physical appearance, might have more costumes than the other characters.

The Seagull has four acts, two outside in summer, one indoors in summer, and one indoors in the fall. Textual references to clothing suggest that most of the characters, with the exception of the servants, change clothing regularly even within a single day.

WHEN DO COSTUME CHANGES OCCUR?   Timing is a concern because it affects how the costumes will be constructed. If a costume change must happen quickly, the garment must be made so that it can easily be put on and taken off, and wardrobe people may be needed backstage to help.

PERIOD   The period in history in which the play takes place influences the costume design just as it does the scenic design. Clothing not only looks different from one period to another (clothing in medieval Scotland looked nothing like American clothing in New Orleans in 1947), but is constructed differently as well.

Budget

The budget will affect all of the preceding considerations. A costume for Macbeth, designed perhaps in the Elizabethan period (in which the play was written) or even in the Middle Ages, will be more expensive than Stanley Kowalski's work pants. Costumes for Arkadina—a professional actress who has to buy her own costumes—will be more costly than those for Medvedenko, who is a schoolmaster. Heidi's clothing is probably more consistently inexpensive than Susan's or Scoop's—two characters making their way up the economic ladder.

The cost of costumes is affected by the cost of materials and labor. Blanche's clothing, dating from a time in her life when she had more money, will probably be made of materials like satin and silk crepe, and will be more expensive than the cotton housedresses Eunice probably wears. A costume that can be purchased new is usually less expensive than one constructed in a costume shop (an exception being high-fashion clothing for a contemporary play). A costume will also be more expensive if its construction is particularly difficult and time-consuming. Eunice's housedress will be less costly, in terms of labor, than Lady Macbeth's Elizabethan or medieval dress for the banquet scene.

Fulfilling the Needs of the Play

The costume designer reads the play for clues about each character's age, physical characteristics, speech, personality, and self-image. This information, taken from the play's text, helps the designer to balance the needs of the play, including its mood or tone, with the interpretation. The choice of costumes is based on these considerations taken together.

In the first scene of *A Streetcar Named Desire,* Stella returns from the bowling alley to find Blanche sitting alone in the kitchen.

BLANCHE: *[faintly to herse f]* I've got to keep hold of myself.
STELLA: *[calling out joyfu y]* Blanche!
BLANCHE: Stella, oh, Stella, Stella! Stella for Star!

[She begins to speak with feverish vivacity as if she feared for either of them to stop and think. They catch each other in a spasmodic embrace.]

> Now, then, **let me look at you. But don't you look at me** Stella, no, no, no, not till later, **not till I've bathed and rested!** And turn that over-light off! Turn that off! **I won't be looked at** in this merciless glare! *[Stella laughs and complies]*

The issue of Blanche's physical condition, introduced here, recurs in this scene and throughout the play.

BLANCHE: No coke, honey, **not with my nerves** tonight! Where—where—where is—?
STELLA: Stanley? Bowling! He loves it. They're having a—found some soda!—tournament. . . .
BLANCHE: Just water, baby, to chase it! Now don't get worried, your sister **hasn't turned into a drunkard,** she's just **all shaken up and hot and tired and dirty!** You sit down, now, and explain this place to me! What are you doing in a place like this?

What is Blanche's mental state in this scene? Is she nervous, unbalanced, deranged? How does the way Blanche looks affect the audience's perception of that condition? Is she merely hot and tired? Or does the audience see more than that? Should Blanche really be concerned about the glare of the overhead light? How will the way she looks now affect the audience's perception of her in the scene in which Mitch shines the bulb in her face? How will her present condition affect the audience's perception of her in the last scene, when she is taken away by the doctor?

Does Blanche's costume reflect her condition and is it consistent with her looks? Is she wearing a lovely dress, one that is in good condition but disheveled from her trip? Or is it an old dress or one that was a mess before she left?

How do these choices affect the meaning of the scene? How does Stella look? What is she wearing? The choice of Stella's costumes will affect Blanche's perception of her. A little later on in the scene, the following interchange takes place:

BLANCHE: You haven't said a word about my **appearance.**

STELLA: **You look just fine.**

BLANCHE: God love you for a liar! **Daylight never exposed so total a ruin! But you—you've put on some weight, yes, you're just as plump as a little partridge! And it's so becoming to you!**

STELLA: Now, Blanche—

BLANCHE: **Yes, it is, it is or I wouldn't say it! You just have to watch around the hips a little.** Stand up.

The costume designer, along with the director, is responsible for conveying the meaning of this scene, which to some extent depends on whether or not Stella is, in fact, plump around the hips. If she is, then Blanche is either teasing her, complimenting her, or insulting her. If she is not plump, or is only barely so, then Blanche is either trying to put her sister in her place or else she is overly, even obsessively, concerned with the issue of weight, fig-

This suit makes a fashion statement. If Blanche were dressed in this suit, she would be aiming to impress her sister and Stanley by obviously false means.

The suit on the right, while still fashionable, is less obviously so. It is neater and more appropriate for the occasion—travel. The dress on the left falls somewhere in between.

ure, age, and attractiveness. What kinds of clothing choices would communicate these different meanings to an audience today?

Information communicated to the audience must come from the specific context of the scene. The costume designer for this scene must communicate whatever meaning has been chosen (for example, that Blanche is disheveled but not over the edge, that Stella is plump and her sister is teasing her) along with other critical information. Season, weather, time of day, historical period, are all important to this scene as well. How would they affect the choice of Blanche's costume? How hot is it? Is her costume appropriate to the weather and if not, does that add to her disheveled look? How long has she been traveling? How late is it? Which of the following examples of traveling suits dating from the period of *Streetcar* would you choose to support your interpretation of this scene?

Which of the following would you choose for Stella?

Photo 6.6 shows Rosemary Harris as Blanche in the opening scene of the 1973 production of the play at the Vivian Beaumont Theater in New York. How has Blanche chosen to present herself to her sister and to Stanley, whom she has not previously met? How disheveled is she? How long has she been traveling? What else do you know about Blanche from this costume? What expectations do you have about her?

In act 3 of *The Seagull,* Arkadina and her aging brother Sorin exchange the following lines about her son Treplev, the young playwright who has recently attempted suicide:

Photo 6.6
Rosemary Harris
as Blanche in
the 1973 pro-
duction of *A
Streetcar
Named Desire.*

ARKADINA: Oh, what a trial that boy is to me! I wish he'd get himself a job. In the Civil Service or something.

SORIN: I think it wouldn't be a bad idea if you—er—if you let him have a little money. You see, he really should—I mean, **he really does want some decent clothes,** and so on. **He's been wearing the same old coat for the last three years. Walks about without an overcoat.** And it wouldn't be a bad thing for the young man to . . . go abroad for a while. It wouldn't cost a lot, would it?

ARKADINA: Well, I don't know. **I suppose I might manage a new suit,** but as for going abroad—no, that's out of the question. **I don't think I can even afford a suit just now. I haven't any money! I've no money!**

SORIN: I see. I'm sorry, my dear. Don't be angry with me. I—I believe you. **You're such a warmhearted generous woman.**

ARKADINA: **I have no money!**

SORIN: Of course, if I had any money, I'd give him some myself, but **I haven't anything—not a penny! My agent grabs all my pension and spends it on the estate.** He rears cattle, keeps bees, and all my money just goes down the drain. The damned bees die, the damned cows die, and when I ask for a carriage, the horses are wanted for something else.

ARKADINA: Of course, **I have some money, but you must realize that I'm an actress. My dresses alone are enough to ruin me.**

Even if, as she suggests, Arkadina must buy her own costumes (as an actress of that period might be required to do), do you believe that neither she nor Sorin can afford to buy clothing for her son? Or that the solutions Sorin proposes will solve Treplev's real problem? Is Treplev really dressed so wretchedly? If Arkadina had sufficient means to help him but did not do so out of selfishness, how might she herself be dressed? What if she had some money but feared poverty? How might that change the costume choice? And what about Sorin? Does he have money? Is he a miser? Is he merely trying to goad his sister or is he sincerely interested in the young man's welfare? How would different interpretations of Sorin's character affect what he might wear?

How Costumes Contribute to the Meaning of the Play

Photos 6.7 through 6.12 show the actresses from six productions of *Hedda Gabler* between 1903 and 1988. The costumes reveal different points of view on the character of Hedda as well as different points of view on the

Photo 6.7
Mrs. Fiske as
Hedda Gabler.

period in which the play takes place. Generally, as we move toward the second half of the twentieth century, Hedda becomes more and more tightly wrapped and confined in her costume, surely a statement about the confines of the time in which she lived—relative to our own.

Photo 6.7 shows Mrs. Fiske, an important American actress at the turn of the century. Her costume, though revealing, is subdued. The lines are simple and soft; the dress seems quite proper, as does her pose. The rich fabric with its woven detail tells the audience that this is a woman who dresses splendidly. The costume as a whole suggests that she has, at least partially, accepted her social role.

Photo 6.8 shows Emily Stevens as Hedda in a 1926 production at the Comedy Theater in New York. Clothed in a loose-fitting morning gown, this Hedda seems trapped in its folds. Although the costume suggests, once again, a partial acceptance of her role, its weight presents a depressing picture. The costume is light in value, but heavy in texture, and looks as if it would trail behind or trip her up if she tried to move quickly in it. This costume is not far removed from Mrs. Fiske's "doll" costume, but its weight requires the wearer to take on the role of lady of the house, regardless of her desire.

Photo 6.9 is a striking picture of the actress Nazimova in a 1936 production. This Hedda is wrapped so tightly in her austere dress that she

Photo 6.8
Emily Stevens (on the left) as Hedda Gabler.

Photo 6.9
The actress Nazimova as Hedda Gabler, 1936.

seems to be strangling. The way she holds her head suggests someone searching for light at the end of a tunnel. The dress is so lacking in detail that it suggests neither the period nor Hedda's circumstances. This costume suggests that Hedda has not accepted her role in society. She is straining at its confines, but without success. The costume is like a straitjacket.

Photo 6.10 shows the great American actress Eva Le Gallienne in the Civic Repertory Theater production. The dress she wears is made of an elegant, light-colored brocade, enhancing the languid pose she takes at the window. Like the others, this costume is heavy; moving in it would present some difficulties. This is also an expensive dress, implying that either they are better off than Tesman implies or the finances of their household are strained by the purchase of this particular ensemble. This costume shows us a more sophisticated doll than the other Heddas, but one who still accepts her role, albeit with slight adjustments. The dress is also a reflection of the period in which it was produced (the 1930s).

Photo 6.11 shows Claire Bloom in the 1971 production of *Hedda Gabler.* Simple and almost childlike in its artlessness, her costume presents a very different view of Hedda, and one that gives the audience a new

Interview

AN INTERVIEW WITH JENNIFER VON
MAYRHAUSER ABOUT HER COSTUMES FOR
THE PLAYWRIGHTS HORIZONS AND BROADWAY
PRODUCTIONS OF THE HEIDI CHRONICLES.

The timing of what the character Heidi went through was exactly parallel to my own experience. I graduated from high school in 1965—the same year the dance in scene one takes place. Each of the scenes of the play follows a chronicle that, although not specifically my own, shows the high points of a shared history.

So, there were a lot of personal things that affected my designing of this play, and on many levels. Having lived through the sixties and that whole political experience, it was interesting to go back and design the clothes. I would have to say that perhaps all the clothes were the fantasy of my own memory. Even the black velvet jumper and the cream silk blouse in the first few scenes are bound up in my own fantasy. The clothes wound up being what I liked and responded to in my own life, even to the Laura Ashley dresses for the pregnant women in the 1980s scenes.

When I first designed the show, the 1970s were kind of recent and everyone hated them (now there is a seventies revival so the feeling is different). The wedding scene at the Hotel Pierre was one of the only places where Heidi is not part of a puzzle of quick scenes. While looking at research, I tried to find a way to allow the audience to relate to Heidi without having a horrible reaction [to the styles of the seventies]. I designed a dress from my memory of the most beautiful dress of the seventies, one that was still beautiful to me. The dress had to represent the seventies of my imagination, not what they actually were.

I was always aware of this about the seventies dress for the wedding—that it was pretty much tied up with my own life. (The first shows I did with Wendy were *Uncommon Women* in the mid-seventies and then *Isn't It Romantic,* so I had traveled that route with her through those plays, through the seventies.) The encounter group came more from my memory of other people, but actually, now that I think about it, there were parts that were very personal. Heidi wore a long scarf that my own mother actually crocheted for me. I did use some of my own clothes in the production at Playwrights Horizons (there was very little money). The original velvet jumper and cream blouse came from my mother's attic. The character of Heidi had taken a different route in life than I had, but in the visual world we were similar. I felt something in common with her. This is what you hope to accomplish in doing research: involving yourself as deeply as I was able to do with *Heidi;* but it was easy to do it there, and it is not always so.

Normally I work in different ways depending on circumstance, but I always tie up my designs with the play, the character, and the actor who is playing the part. The last has an enormous effect on the design. When I talk to an actor, I assume a kind of partnership: it is Jennifer designing for that person. Of course, there are exceptions, and those are very painful. The other day a producer asked me if a certain actor was "very opinionated." We all are opinionated! That is part of the partnership. In my designs there is no way to determine who did what—what I did versus what the actor did.

Since the production of *Heidi,* I have been designing for film, where there is much less time and less of a tendency to engage in that kind of partnership, but I do still find that it is the way to go. Working on a film called *Captain Ron,* Kurt Russell and I together evolved a wonderful faded, off-center costume. The studio freaked out. They wanted him to look like their image of Kurt Russell. We fought the battle and we won because we had developed the costume together. The strength of that partnership and work paid off.

I am currently designing the television series *Law and Order.* The series is a lot about character but, because of the television schedule, there is not enough time for in-depth character work with the actors. As a designer, I have to say, "Well, this is your character," but since I am most involved with "character" and am good at it, I can work in such a concentrated way. It is like a bouillon cube: there is no extra stuff. This process fine-tunes my instincts.

Photo 6.10
Eva Le Gallienne as Hedda Gabler.

Photo 6.11
Claire Bloom as Hedda Gabler, 1971.

look at how Hedda might view herself. This time the tight collar is decorated with a bow, and the high neck is made of a delicate embroidered eyelet. The shape of the jacket is conventional, and the softly rolled velvet collar unassertive. This Hedda has chosen to look her role of a conventional matron, either because she has given up entirely or because she is craftily hiding her true intentions.

Photo 6.12 shows Mary Layne in a 1988 production directed by Mark Lamos at the Hartford Stage Company. This is the airiest of the costumes and the most childlike. It would be possible to put such a dress on Nina in the second act of *The Seagull*. It is the dress of a young woman. Everything about it is light and cheery, and so makes Hedda's journey through the play the more heartbreaking. The costume suggests that she tries to hide her problems, perhaps even from herself. This Hedda's despair and failure would be very painful to watch.

Costumes (like scenery, lighting, or staging) can never convey the meaning of a production without the final ingredient of the actor's perfor-

Photo 6.12
Mary Layne as
Hedda Gabler in
the 1988 pro-
duction at the
Hartford Stage
Company.

mance. But even within the limitations of a still photograph, certain judgments can be made about those performances based on what we can sur-
mise of the intended meaning of the costumes.

The Costume Designer's Work Process

Elements of Costume Design

A costume design emerges from the organization and composition of silhouette, color, value, texture, fabric, detail and ornamentation, the shape of
the actor's body and face, and the fit and drape of the costume. The choice
of these elements depends on understanding the historical period, which is
then interpreted or changed to express the meaning of the production.

We examined the costume of Nazimova's Hedda and how it expressed
something of Hedda's inability to accept her role. Because this costume is
so spectacular, it is a good example of how the designer uses all the design
elements to create the desired effect.

The costume's *silhouette* is extreme. It is tight fitting; even the sleeves
typical of the period have been considerably narrowed. The actress's sleek
head and hair are part of the overall tubelike shape. Standing, the actress

would look thin, even gaunt. The dress is so long that no suggestion of a foot is visible. Movement in this dress would be very difficult.

Nazimova's costume is of a dark *value,* and because it is unrelieved by any detail or ornamentation, the dress has a brooding quality. The *color* is probably black or a dark shade that would produce the effect of black. There is virtually no surface *texture* to the fabric, further enhancing the funereal aspect of the dress. When compared with the rich brocade of Eva Le Gallienne's dress or the prissy eyelet of Claire Bloom's, this costume seems to hold back nothing; there is no question of presenting an artificial front to the world.

The *fabric* appears stiff, as it would need to be to hold the shape of the sleeves. Although it is difficult to analyze the fabric content from a photograph, it seems gauzy, perhaps organza, giving those areas that stand away from the body a transparent, ghostlike quality. The fabric itself has no pattern or print to speak of, reinforcing the starkness of the silhouette.

Ornamentation is minimal in this costume. Again, compared with the series of laces down the back of Eva Le Gallienne's costume, or even the bowed, embroidered, and belted look of Claire Bloom's dress, this garment is austere. The only bit of ornamentation is a necklace, whose very prominence strikes an ominous note. No button or zipper is in evidence, no stockings or shoes, none of the expected, everyday details. This contributes to the otherworldliness of the costume, its lack of connection with daily life.

The costume focuses on the length and slenderness of the actress's slim *body and face.* Nazimova's own neck must be very long to give the impression it does, but the dress certainly contributes to the effect: it makes her look taller and thinner, the height of the collar forces her to raise her chin, the close-cropped hair gives her face an emaciated look.

The *fit* of this costume supports all of the other elements. A loosely fitted garment, like that of Emily Stevens or even Mrs. Fiske, would not create the frozen, bound effect of this one. Although the skirt does seem to have a bit of fullness to it, the bodice, the lower part of the sleeves, and the neck are closely fitted to Hedda's body, reinforcing the image of a trap.

Research

Hedda Gabler was written by Ibsen in 1890 and takes place in the same period. Any costume designer working on a production of the play would need to have knowledge of the fashion of that time, if only to purposefully deviate from it. Figure 6.3 shows dresses from a fashion plate published in 1890. Although not from Norway and meant for a very different occasion, these styles suggest the dress Nazimova is wearing.

A high collar is featured in all four of the dresses shown in Figures 6.2 through 6.5, but none is so extremely high as that in the production photo-

Figure 6.4
J. Beraud's *Place de la Concorde*, c. 1895.

Figure 6.3
Fashion plate published in 1890.

Figure 6.2
John Singer Sargent's *Mme Edouard Pailleron*, 1879.

graph. The dress in Figure 6.2 (taken from a painting by John Singer Sargent), with its tight skirt, absence of bustle or hoop, and high (although white) neck, comes closest to evoking the overall mood of Nazimova's dress. Note that the painting was completed in 1879, more than ten years earlier than the play.

Figure 6.3 shows some puff to the sleeves, but they are not nearly as exaggerated as those in the photo. The sleeves in Figure 6.4 produce a similarly unnatural effect but are more balloonlike in form.

The designer of Nazimova's costume has borrowed from many periods while creating an impression of the late nineteenth century. In fact, the dress shares more qualities with dresses of the period in which the play was produced—the 1930s—than with those of the 1890s. The sleek silhouette is more reminiscent of Hollywood movie stars than late-nineteenth-century matrons. Combining elements of two periods alters the meaning of the costume and of the character. A nineteenth-century matron evoking the qualities of a thirties star is surely and very sadly trapped. (See Figure 6.5.)

Figure 6.5
A 1930s evening dress. The high dramatic collar and long, slim silhouette suggests a mood similar to that of Nazimova's dark, sleek costume.

Stages of the Design Process

Costume designers communicate with directors, the other designers, the actors, and the costume shop. They express their ideas using sketches, finished renderings (also called costume plates), fabric swatches, and costume plots.

A costume designer *sketches* in much the same way as a scenic designer, finding through the drawing process ways to add to the design. Rough sketches can also serve as an excellent communication tool, and one that can be easily changed. A costume designer often shows both front and back views. Smaller elements, like shoes, can be sketched in slightly larger scale so that details are clearer. Most costume sketches also contain written notes to clarify what can only be seen in the full-scale costume itself.

Finished renderings, or *costume plates,* also serve an important function. The costume shop will construct the costumes from these renderings, with only minimal additional input from the designer. Therefore, in addition to being beautiful to look at and informative for the director and actors, the renderings must be accurate and detailed enough to communicate specific information to the costume maker.

The costume designer chooses fabrics for each of the costumes. This choice is critical. None of the costumes we have analyzed could look the way they do if the fabrics were different. (Imagine Claire Bloom's costume in burlap or Nazimova's in cotton!) After shopping for fabrics, the costume designer provides the shop with *swatches* of the base fabrics and any decoration, such as lace, buttons, belts of a different fabric, even shoe coverings.

While all of this activity is taking place, the costume designer assembles the *costume plot.* This lays out costumes by character and by scene, in an orderly manner, so that anyone can see which character is in which scenes and when each character changes costumes. This helps everyone on the production to keep track of what has been done, what still remains to be done, and what the problems might be in running the show backstage.

Costumes are not always constructed anew for each production of a play. Costume rental houses have many thousands of costumes available for much less than what it would cost to build the design from scratch. If a production is to be "rented," it is the responsibility of the costume designer to contact rental houses and to choose costumes from those available. A designer must balance the needs of the particular production point of view with the available budget. Many productions, as a result, are a combination of rented and constructed costumes.

If the designer is responsible for running a costume shop as well as designing (as is the case at some universities), he or she must know more about draping, pattern drafting, and cutting than does a designer who basi-

In a typical costume rental shop, the aisle of costumes on the left and the shoes or accessories in the boxes on the right would be only part of a vast collection. The costumes are usually organized by period.

Photo 6.13
A draper carefully fits a costume to a dummy that matches the size of the actress who will wear the costume on stage.

cally works with a shop. *Draping* is the process of shaping fabric to a three-dimensional dressmaking dummy that is the size of the actor who will be wearing the costume (Photo 6.13). Figure 6.6 shows the drafted pattern for a coat that might appear in a production of *Hedda Gabler. Pattern drafting* is the process that flattens the costume into two-dimensional pieces that are then laid out and cut from fabric, like home dressmaking patterns.

Once the costumes have been built (whether by a stitcher in a costume shop or by the designer), the costume designer oversees all of the finishing. Any added details such as embroidery, beading, buttons, or fastenings must be carefully chosen. The costume designer must also see to items such as shoes, socks, underwear, wigs, hairpieces, facial hair, and personal props. At fittings, the costume is tailored to the actor who is to wear it. Nazimova's costume, which is so form-fitting, would need to be altered several times as the production approaches so that no unsightly wrinkling or buckling could be seen.

Like the other designers, the costume designer attends rehearsals, makes changes, attends dress rehearsals, and consults with the director. Changes are made right up to the last minute. The costume designer must be present to oversee these changes and to give the actors confidence, and sometimes instruction in how to wear their costumes. The costumes for *Hedda Gabler* that we have seen bear no resemblance to what a contemporary actress would wear offstage. The actresses must practice moving in long dresses with corsets, bustles, and hoops underneath so that they look as if they have worn them every day of their lives.

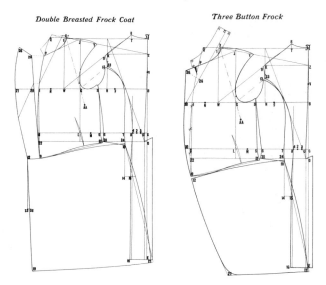

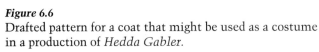

Figure 6.6
Drafted pattern for a coat that might be used as a costume in a production of *Hedda Gabler*.

Like the scenic designer, the costume designer contributes to the overall look of the production, but more than that, he or she directly affects the way in which an actor performs a role. Working closely with the cast, the costume designer provides the audience with information not only about time, weather, situation, and period, but also about how the characters choose to be seen. The costume designer must be able to look inside the characters with the production's point of view in mind, and communicate these choices quickly and with an economy of means. The orchestration of all the costumes in any given production involves a complex interweaving of social, cultural, historical, and psychological considerations.

Suggested Readings

Françoise Boucher, *20,000 Years of Fashion: The History of Costume and Personal Adornment*, exp. ed. (New York: Abrams), 1987.

Richard Corson, *Stage Makeup*, 8th ed. (Englewood Cliffs, N.J.: Prentice-Hall), 1975.

Rosemary Ingham and Liz Covey, *The Costume Designer's Handbook* (Englewood Cliffs, N.J.: Prentice-Hall), 1983.

Motley, *Designing and Making Stage Costumes* (London: Studio Vista), 1964.

Chapter
SEVEN

The Lighting Designer

What Light Does

Light assures us of the rhythms of life. One of the few certainties in today's fast-paced world is that the sun rises and sets—and that it does so in a completely predictable way, season after season, day after day. When natural light from the sun is present, we can see the world around us with clarity. Before the advent of electric light, the bulk of our work was therefore performed during daylight hours.

Natural light also provides us with information about the seasons. Even if we lived our lives totally indoors and at a constant temperature (and many people who work in offices virtually do live this way), we could differentiate the seasons merely by the quality of light through a window. Days are of different lengths at different times of the year. In the northern hemisphere, the light is cooler and crisper in autumn and winter, clearer and thinner in spring, and denser in summer. Light changes when a sunny day turns cloudy and rain begins to fall. Looking out a window, we can tell a great deal about the season and weather from the quality of the light alone.

We can also tell the time by looking at light. We know where the sun rises and where it sets and the range in between. We can see differences in the color and quality of light between dawn and dusk even though the sun's position is relatively the same at the horizon. Light provides other rhythms to the day as well. Changes in light—and temperature—in the course of a day tell us when to speed up, when to rest, and when to stop. Crisp morning light prepares us for activity; in some countries, strong, hot light directly overhead at midday demands a siesta. Afternoon light begins to fade as the working day ends. To escape from this natural cycle, we use electric light to extend our waking hours into nighttime and to bring an artificial daylight inside.

Artificial light also communicates information. Candlelight, gaslight, kerosene lanterns, and firelight hearken back to other, earlier times. A campfire evokes our ancestral bond to nature. We are drawn to the warmth and safety of a fire in a hearth. Gaslight evokes the nineteenth century— perhaps music halls or the world of Sherlock Holmes.

Incandescent light, invented by Thomas Edison, illuminates most of our homes and is the standard source of light in the theatre, as well. A crystal chandelier fills a room with glittering light. A bare bulb hanging from the ceiling of a seedy hotel room (like the bedroom in *A Streetcar Named Desire* after Mitch has torn off the paper shade) suggests desolation. Soft lamplight creates pools and pockets of light reminiscent of fire in a grate. Light at a desk focuses attention on a task, leaving the rest of the room in darkness. We have adapted Edison's lightbulb in hundreds of ways to create the quality of light we want.

Fluorescent light, which floods offices, factories, and other work spaces with an even blanket of light, communicates an entirely different message. The source of fluorescent light is broader, more powerful, and more even than that of incandescent light. There is no direction to fluorescent light, and it wipes out the sense of composition we expect of natural light. It is colder than incandescent light as well. No wonder it is associated with modern times.

When we walk into a new friend's apartment, or an office or even a supermarket, light offers a clue as to what kind of place we have entered. How objects and spaces are illuminated—how they are seen—is a potent and visceral source of information. Our associations with particular kinds of light contribute to this synthesis of information. We take much of this data for granted, processing it rapidly and without much thought.

What Stage Lighting Does

Information from Stage Lighting

Like the other design areas, the design of stage light provides the audience with information. The categories of this information are:

- What is important onstage, and what is not
- Time of day and year
- Location
- Atmosphere and mood.

As in life, light in the theatre allows the audience to see. Light and objects are interdependent: light can't be discerned without a surface to reflect it, and a surface can't be seen without light. Illuminating the stage so that the audience can see is the lighting designer's most important job.

Illumination has many distinctions in the theatre as in everyday life. Some days are brighter, others duller; some rooms are brighter, some darker. Scene 9 of *A Streetcar Named Desire* requires three degrees of illumination: a darkened room, light shaded by the paper lantern, and the glare of a bare bulb. The lighting designer must determine these *levels of illumination* relative to one another.

- How dark is the room before the light is turned on? Even though it is described as very dark, the actors must still be visible to the audience.
- How much illumination does the bulb with the paper lantern provide?
- How much light does the bare bulb contribute?

Regardless of the point of view, the actors must be clearly visible to the audience even after the light has been turned off, when the room is relatively darker (a dark hallway appears darker to an eye accustomed to a brightly lit room than to one accustomed to a dimly lit room).

If a play requires specific information about *time of day* and *season*, the lighting designer must provide the audience with some of it. In *Macbeth* and *The Heidi Chronicles* this information is probably less important than it is in *Hedda Gabler*, *A Streetcar Named Desire*, and *The Seagull*. Time of day is critical in *Streetcar*. Does Blanche really only go out at night? How bright is it when Mitch picks her up for their date?

As we saw earlier, season is important in *The Seagull*. Summer is a time of relaxation for Arkadina, when she returns to the countryside to get away from her hectic life. Bringing Trigorin with her, she seeks rest but finds disaster instead. In the light of summer, Nina falls in love with Trigorin. When they return in the fall, everything has changed. Chekhov uses this change of season to paint a picture of their loss. How bad is the storm from which Nina emerges?

To some extent, light can help to reinforce the location of a setting. Color, direction, intensity—the whole quality of light differs from place to place. Light in Norway is not the same as light in Scotland; light in New York City is not like light in New Orleans. Even without having visited these places, we can get a sense of where these plays are meant to take place.

A sunset in Norway is cool, clean, and crisp.

Sunset or late day in New Orleans accents high heat and sharp shadows.

Sunset at the tip of Manhattan. The quality of light indicates an industrial, smog-laden atmosphere.

Perhaps the information most difficult to pin down is *mood* or *atmo-sphere*. In an attempt to specify the overall quality of light, we tend to use words such as "romantic," "stuffy," "crisp," and "soft," although the atmosphere each of these words suggests is hard to define.

Light can provide a familiar framework for the audience, within which the emotional states of the characters can be highlighted. In fact, the mood of the lighting need not reflect the mood of the scene, and might serve even better as a foil to it. The atmosphere of Blanche's birthday party could be hot, humid, and stifling, making all her attempts to lighten the mood doubly difficult. An airy cheeriness in act 2 of *The Seagull* would make the serious disruption of the relationship that is about to occur more shocking.

Adolphe Appia (1862–1928) had perhaps the greatest influence on the creation of mood in modern stage lighting. Appia believed that lighting could be the device that unified an entire production: actor, movement, music, scenery. He introduced the still very popular idea that lighting is as sensitive in creating mood as music, and that it is capable of paralleling the subtlest of emotional and psychological states (Figures 7.1 and 7.2).

Lighting shows the audience the very air the characters are breathing, and along with the actors, can help create the sense that the performance is taking place now, in the present moment. Because theatrical light can mimic the movement of natural light, it sets up the rhythms of life onstage. The audience believes in the passage of time because the light is actually moving, sometimes as imperceptibly as natural light. Light can also change in quality as it moves, conveying additional information.

Figures 7.1 and 7.2
These two examples of Adolphe Appia's designs show his interest in the rhythmic relationships of light and dark, and how those relationships in turn expose and articulate a physical landscape.

What the Lighting Designer Does

When Hedda says that the light through the French doors is too bright and asks to have the drapes closed, when Blanche tells Mitch to turn off that unforgiving overhead lightbulb, or when Masha feels the heaviness in the air, it is the lighting designer's job to create an environment that helps the audience to interpret these statements. As in the other design areas, a character's reference to specific physical conditions—in this case ones connected to lighting—is measured by the audience against the conditions suggested on the stage. The lighting designer must decide:

- How bright and harsh is the light through Hedda's window?
- How glaring is the bulb shined on Blanche's face and how old does it make her look?
- How damp is that Russian country evening?

To create such precise lighting requires careful planning and extended rehearsal time. Today, stage lighting can be controlled in sophisticated and complex ways. Light can move as quickly as the eye can perceive it, and technology provides lighting designers, more than any other theatrical designers, with the ability to create an almost infinite variety of moods or environments, and to change from one to another in less than a second. In this, theatrical lighting is most closely allied to film. Unlike film, however,

stage lighting cannot change the picture frame itself, which is created by the theatre architecture and scenery. For example, theatrical lighting cannot actually bring the actor closer to the audience, the way the camera can in a close-up. These limitations make the challenges to the lighting designer different from the challenges of film.

The lighting designer works with the director and the other designers to establish the point of view of the production and to work out how the lighting will function to convey it. Lighting alone does not have meaning; it does so only in relation to the actors, the play, and the other design elements.

The lighting designer most often communicates verbally with his or her collaborators. Some designers work from sketches that are then transformed into scaled drawings and charts (to be discussed later in the chapter). These provide the production electrician and lighting rental shop with sufficient information to put the lights together in the theatre.

Lighting equipment is essentially the same regardless of the production; it is what is *done* to the light—its color and brightness and where it is aimed, for example—that makes it specific. The lighting designer's responsibility in the shop is therefore a less complex matter than it is for the scenic or costume designer. Sometimes a shop rents equipment to productions, and sometimes a theatre owns its own equipment. Careful maintenance is a large part of the job of shop personnel.

Lighting budgets vary greatly depending on the circumstances of the production. When lighting equipment is rented from a shop for a single production (as is common in Broadway and off-Broadway productions and road tours), budgets can be quite high. When equipment is owned by the theatre and is used again and again, the budget for an individual production can be kept low (Figure 7.3).

Theatrical lighting takes as many forms as theatre itself. A Broadway musical is usually full of color and rapid and exciting changes of mood and locale. It often uses *special effects* such as neon, lasers, chase lights, projections of snow and rain—anything one can imagine. Used to create instantaneous reactions in the audience, lighting for musicals generally is not concerned with sustaining an emotion. Like the music and moods it reinforces, lighting for musicals is vibrant, energetic, and rarely understated (see the color insert following page 210).

At the other end of the spectrum is lighting for experimental theatre, which, like the musical, is also often removed from everyday experience but has a very different set of intentions. Harder, cooler, and more sharply focused, this kind of lighting complements an often ambiguous environment to create an abstract visual world. Similar to the lighting used in modern dance (and often designed by the same artists), this kind of lighting is meant to establish an emotional or intellectual, rather than a realistic, environment.

Between these extremes lies lighting which, although different for each production, provides a framework for the action of the nontraditional play.

LN#	QUANT	PRODUCT CODE	PRODUCT DESCRIPTION
(99)	2	580-020	20' ZETEX BORDER
(100)	10	515-105 750 W	6" FRESNEL
(101)	4	515-110 1000 W QUARTZ	8" FRESNEL
(102)	6	520-100 1000 W WFL	PAR 64 CAN
(103)	4	535-100 750 W	MINI-LITE 10
(104)	10	545-110	6" 4 WAY BARN DOOR
(105)	10	545-115	8" 4 WAY BARN DOOR
(106)	90	545-135	6" TOP HAT
(107)	20	545-142	6" TOP HAT-HALF ROUND BARREL
(108)	6	255-300 EYC 75W FLOOD	6' - 0" MR16 3 CIR STRIP LIGHT

Figure 7.3
A sample equipment list for a recent off-Broadway production. The rental costs for this list would be approximately $12,600.00 for the first three weeks; $1,800.00 per week thereafter. The current list value for this equipment is $230,000.00. (Courtesy Production Arts Lighting)

A Sample Lighting Budget for a Mainstage Show

Item	Amount
Color (15 Sheets @ 4.95)	$74.25
Equipment Rental (12 PAR 64, MFL for 3 wks)	$200.00
Templates (12 @ 11.50)	$138.00
	$412.25

Estimated Maintenance expenditures, Electric, Adams Memorial Theater, Williams College '92/'93

Item	Amount
Lamps	$1,301.00
Repair (in house)	
Labor (100hrs)	$500.00
Parts	$318.00
Repair (out of house, parts & labor)	$510.00
Contract Maint. (control system & dimmers)	$710.00
	$3,339.00

Figure 7.3, continued
Sample lighting budget and maintenance costs for a university production.

This photo of the actor Jack Lemmon in Eugene O'Neill's *Long Day's Journey into Night* (in a production on Broadway in 1986) illustrates a fairly traditional use of stage lighting. The source of light is clearly coming from his right and most probably relates to a window or other natural source.

The lighting of this Hartford Stage Company production of *Hamlet* helps to create a frightening emotional environment, not a literal one.

What the Lighting Designer Looks for When Reading the Play

Many of the lighting designer's concerns are similar to those of the scenic designer and involve the size and scope of the production.

Locations and Settings

In today's theatre, a scenic designer might provide a single setting for a play such as *Macbeth*. It then becomes the job of the lighting designer to establish different places, or movement from place to place, within that setting. On the other hand, a production of *The Seagull* will probably have four distinct, identifiable settings to represent the four locations in the play. In that case, it is the lighting designer's responsibility to create a lighting environment that is consistent with the scenery.

Interview

JOHN GLEASON ON HIS LIGHTING FOR THE 1973 VIVIAN BEAUMONT PRODUCTION OF A STREETCAR NAMED DESIRE

I designed another production of *A Streetcar Named Desire* just before this one. It was done in a rather traditional way—the lighting was very soft, etc.—because I had always been told about the "poor put-upon little southern lady" forced to live in a dreadful situation created by an unkind world. I didn't agree with that interpretation because the language of the play can't support it. So when the Beaumont production came along [directed by Ellis Raab, with Rosemary Harris and James Farentino], I really sat down and looked at the script more closely. I began to feel that this woman [Blanche] was a manipulator; as if Don't believe what I do, believe what I say—the adage about understanding characters turned around.

She contradicts herself. Blanche DuBois is a liar, in what she does as well as what she says. She must always be in control, so she supports her intended persona by saying that she likes artists that paint in bold colors, she doesn't like wishy-washy people, etc. She takes events and makes them what she wants them to be rather than what they are. *She disguises herself and the environment in which she exists.* Blanche manipulates the environment—puts lanterns on lightbulbs, doesn't go out until after dark, lights candles when she and Mitch come back from their date. Williams describes her as a moth. My visual image is a moth in the guise of a butterfly—an image that is a lie—and light destroys a moth.

In the opening scene of the play, Blanche arrives, searches around, finds liquor, has a drink, washes out the glass, and then hides the liquor. When Stella comes in and turns on the overhead light, Blanche—and this is the beginning of understanding who this lady is—immediately turns it off because, she says, her life at Belle Reve has made her into this "wreck." This scene defines her for the rest of the play.

Before she enters the house she already has a plan; the lie has been developed in her own head. [In the Beaumont production] the area around the house was overcast, showing beams of light where magnificent moonlight broke through. Blanche enters down a long ramp with backlight behind her. She does her opening speech in a single shaft of moonlight. She is already performing for these people on the apartment stoop. The place is not what she expected it to be: magic surrounds the apartment but inside it is cold (illuminated in blue-gray, as opposed to the magical colors of New Orleans). When Stella comes in and turns on the light, it glares. As the rest of the scene progresses, Blanche starts to control the situation and the light takes on a more textured, colored look. She manipulates the environment; her plans are working for her. Throughout the production, whenever Blanche is seemingly in control, the world around her is textured and colored. When she is not in control, we have raw, white light.

The most crucial example of this is the morning after the poker party, the only bright daylight scene in the production. Blanche is completely out of control at that moment and Stella controls the scene. Blanche can't understand why Stella takes Stanley back. The lighting was a totally white-light version of daylight. Another example is when Mitch pulls the lamp shade off the lightbulb, exposing Blanche's real image. The bulb itself was at a high level of intensity. The textured poetry of that previously darkened room disappeared and stayed that way, even after the bulb was turned off. The poetry was gone; gray darkness remained.

When Stanley returns from the hospital, he goes around the apartment turning on all the lights. Blanche's act didn't work. In the last scene, [while the others are] waiting for the doctor and nurse to arrive, Blanche has to get through the kitchen to escape. But the kitchen is lit with hard, white daylight coming through the window, while the bedroom light is soft and warm. When Eunice goes to meet the doctor and nurse at the front door, the light coming into the kitchen becomes harder yet.

Although I used heavy color, it did not make the lighting abstract. It always stayed within the "shopping list" of the play: the time of day, year, etc. Color was used as accent around the playing area.

If I were to redesign a production of *Streetcar* today, I wouldn't do it much differently. My feelings on this point of view are even stronger. But technically the design might change, because I have changed as a designer. I would allow more shadows, be more extreme.

Seasons and Times of Day

Within each location, the lighting designer must also create different times of day and weather conditions if the play and the production require it. In *The Seagull*, there are three times of day (two evenings, afternoon, noon) and two seasons (summer, autumn). As we discussed in the previous chapter, all seasons and almost all weather conditions are present in *The Heidi Chronicles*, along with every conceivable time of day—from midnight to late afternoon, both inside and out.

These requirements give the designer a feeling for the number of lights that will be needed, as well as how sophisticated the control of those lights needs to be. Generally speaking, the more complex the requirements, the greater the number of lights, the higher the budget, and the more time the designer must spend in the theatre.

Fulfilling the Needs of the Play

Although lighting can be fantastic, like scenery and costumes it must take into consideration the requirements of the play. In the previous chapter, we looked at the reunion of Stella and Blanche in scene 1 of *A Streetcar Named Desire*, concentrating on the ramifications of textual references for the costume designer. Let's look at these same lines from the lighting designer's point of view, again noting the dialogue set here in bold type.

A Streetcar Named Desire

BLANCHE: *[faintly to herself]* I've got to keep hold of myself!

STELLA: *[calling out joyfully]* Blanche!

BLANCHE: Stella, oh, Stella, Stella! Stella for Star! Now, then, **let me look at you. But don't you look at me,** Stella, no, no, no, not till later, not till I've bathed and rested! And **turn that over-light off! Turn that off! I won't be looked at in this merciless glare!** Come back here now! Oh, my baby! Stella, Stella for Star! I thought you would never come back to this **horrible place!**

Just as the costumer is required to design clothing and make-up for Blanche that will communicate the production's interpretation of her character, so must the lighting designer answer the following questions prompted by these few lines.

- How dark is the room when Stella comes in? If it is actually quite dark, then Stella is right to turn the light on to see her sister. If it is barely dark, why does she turn it on?

- How bright is the overhead light? And how glaring is it? Is it really "merciless" or is Blanche simply too sensitive about her age? (This question was asked relative to choice of costume as well, and the answers in production must support each other. The costume designer creates the costume and make-up, the lighting designer the actual "merciless" or not-so-merciless light.)

- Is the place really "horrible" in the light? Is it the darkness that makes the place horrible to Blanche? Is the light itself horrible? How horrible?

How do the various choices in answer to these questions change the meaning of the scene and the audience's understanding of the characters? Let's look at similar issues in another scene we have referred to several times, again paying special attention to the dialogue set in boldface.

MITCH: **It's dark in here.**

BLANCHE: **I like it dark. The dark is comforting to me.**

MITCH: I don't think I've ever seen you **in the light.** That's a fact!

BLANCHE: Is it?

MITCH: I've never seen you in the **afternoon.**

BLANCHE: Whose fault is that?

MITCH: You never want to go out in the **afternoon.**

BLANCHE: Why, Mitch, you're at the plant in the **afternoon.**

MITCH: Not Sunday **afternoon.** . . . You never want to go out till after six and then it's always **some place that's not lighted much.**

BLANCHE: There is some obscure meaning in this but I fail to catch it.

MITCH: What it means is **I've never had a real good look at you,** Blanche. **Let's turn the light on here.**

BLANCHE: **Light? Which light?** What for?

MITCH: **This one with the paper thing on it.**

   [He tears the paper lantern off the lightbulb. She utters a frightened gasp.]

BLANCHE: What did you do that for?

MITCH: So I can **take a look at you good and plain!**

BLANCHE: Of course you don't really mean to be insulting!

MITCH: No, just realistic.

BLANCHE: I don't want realism. I want magic! Yes, yes, magic! I try to give that to people, I misrepresent things to them. I don't tell truth, I tell what ought to be truth. And if that is sinful, then let me be damned for it! **Don't turn the light on!**

In this scene, light is used as a tool by one character to wrench the truth out of another. Williams uses light as a means by which the production can comment on the characters. The requirements for the lighting are therefore fairly precise. First, both Blanche and Mitch acknowledge that it is dark in the room, although Blanche fiercely defends her desire to keep it that way. Mitch begins to build his case for turning on the light; almost every line that follows contains a reference to light (the word "afternoon" alone is repeated four times in quick succession). Finally, after the tension has built to the breaking point, Mitch suggests turning on the light. By asking which one, Blanche is either stalling for time, or indicating that there is at least one light in the room other than the one with the "paper thing on it" (a reference back to scene 3, in which Mitch helps Blanche put the paper lantern on the lightbulb when they first meet—a scene with a very different mood), or both. After Mitch rips off the shade, he switches the light on and then off again. Mitch defines Blanche's entire being as what he has seen by the light of a single bulb.

The lighting requirements for this scene are:

- A dark room at two in the morning (Are there streetlights, neon signs, moonlight through windows, lights from another room?)
- A lightbulb with a paper lantern over it (Of what color and texture? How attractive is the light with the shade on it? How much glare comes from the bulb? How does this affect Blanche's reaction to the bulb in scene 1?)
- A light switch (Where is it? How far is Mitch from Blanche when he sees her in the "light of day"?).

If Mitch's cruelty is meant to be impressed upon the audience, the room should not be excessively dark, and might even seem romantic. The fixture when turned on should be quite bright. The paper lantern should be charming; it should seem perfectly reasonable that Blanche would try to mask the ugliness of a bare bulb. The light switch could be far from where Blanche is standing.

THE SEAGULL   By making design choices about the precise nature of light, many questions about characters and their behavior can be addressed. In *The Seagull,* Chekhov creates a cycle that encompasses two hot mornings (acts 2 and 3) and two nights (acts 1 and 4). The nights stand in contrast to one another as well, much as Williams contrasts the romance of the paper lantern with its destruction. Night in act 1 is an early evening in summer; night in act 4 is autumnal, rainy, windy, and dark. Though other characters are involved, each act hinges on the meeting and relationship of Nina and Treplev. The two night settings frame the two very different meetings.

Chekhov also uses time and weather early in act 1, this time to contrast three relationships (the first of which we examined in the chapter on directing):

- Masha and Medvedenko
- Nina and Treplev
- Paulina and Dorn

In the scene between Masha and Medvendeko, Masha refers to the weather: "It's awfully **close. I expect there'll be a thunderstorm."** A little while later, when Nina and Treplev are alone together, Nina asks, **"Why is it so dark?"** and Treplev explains, **"Well, it's evening. Everything's getting dark.** Don't rush away after the play, please don't." Darkness worries him because Nina must then leave for home. A few lines later on, Treplev asks Yakov, one of his stagehands, **"Is the moon rising?"** to which Yakov replies, **"Yes** sir." Nina and Treplev go off to prepare for the play, while Paulina and Dorn arrive. Paulina says, **"It's getting damp.** Do go back and put on your galoshes." Dorn replies, **"I'm hot."**

Although none of these statements about the weather (and about the light, which communicates the weather to the audience) is actually contradictory, each is different and makes a different comment about the various relationships. The characters use the weather and the light to communicate their concerns to one another. For example, if it is truly damp, the audience will draw these conclusions:

- Masha feels trapped by the dampness and sees her problems as external.
- Treplev doesn't feel the damp; he is worried about time passing too quickly for romance and about the success of his play (also connected to his love for Nina).
- Paulina wants to protect Dorn and he fights her, even at the risk of his health.

These references provide excellent material for the lighting designer, but once again, all choices must meet the requirements of the scene: a moonlit summer night near a lake.

How would our understanding of the relationships between these characters change if the lighting showed a clear, starry night?

MACBETH   Not surprisingly, Shakespeare's own lighting requirements are generally minimal, since the Elizabethan theatres for which he wrote had open roofs and plays were performed in daylight. The actor in the Elizabethan theatre was responsible for *evoking* the setting almost exclusively through words and action, and the performance space changed very little for each production. The following dialogue is taken from what is known as the "sleepwalking scene" (act 5, scene 1) of *Macbeth*:

DOCTOR: I have **two nights watched** with you, but can perceive no truth in your report. When was it she last walked?

GENTLEWOMAN: Since his Majesty went into the field, I have **seen her** rise from her bed, throw her nightgown upon her, unlock her closet, take forth paper, fold it, write upon't, read it, afterwards seal it, and again return to bed; yet all this while in a most fast sleep.

DOCTOR: A great perturbation in nature, **to receive at once the benefit of sleep and do the effects of watching!** In this slumb'ry agitation, besides her walking and other actual performances, what, at any time, have you heard her say?

Finally, Lady Macbeth herself enters, carrying a taper (candle):

GENTLEWOMAN: Lo you, **here she comes!** This is her very quest, and upon my life, **fast asleep! Observe her;** stand close.

DOCTOR: How came she by that **light**?

GENTLEWOMAN: Why **it stood by her. She has light by her continually. 'Tis her command.**

The Doctor and Gentlewoman stand in the dark, but can see. Lady Macbeth holds a candle but, asleep, sees only what lies in her imagination. Shakespeare uses the relationship of light and dark as a fulcrum for the scene. Lady Macbeth has a candle by her at all times, presumably to ward off the spirit of the dead. The simple requirements of the scene for the lighting designer—night darkness and a candle—are expanded into an important image. It is the job of the designer to create lighting that will throw into focus the choices of a given production relative to these conditions. Some of the questions that need to be explored include:

- How well can the Doctor and Gentlewoman see? By what light?
- If the light is supplied by Lady Macbeth's candle alone, can they see well enough by it to justify the conclusions they draw?
- If they have a torch or candle, how will that affect our perception of Lady Macbeth's sleep (for example, the brighter the torch, the deeper her slumber)?
- If they have no light with them, will the audience perceive them as stealing upon Lady Macbeth? As being less than detached observers?
- Which choices are likely to make us sympathize more with Lady Macbeth? Which would lead us to sympathize with her less?

In this scene, the dialogue by itself quickly and economically establishes the time of day (night), Lady Macbeth's actions while sleepwalking, and the mood of the scene. Elizabethan playwrights and actors relied heavily upon the imagination of the audience, and in doing so were free to move from one location to another without giving any indication of setting or lighting other than that provided by the actors.[1] But lighting Shakespeare's plays today requires a different approach—both our theatre buildings and our expectations have changed.

```
MS. JORDAN BAKER

Chemise: PDG

Petticoat: PDG

Robe and sash: PDG

shoes: PDG

Ivory piano shawl: JMS

Taupe skirt: PDG

Taupe bodice with white mink trim: PDG

White silk blouse: PDG

Nightgown: PDG

Gloves: JMS

Plain pearl necklace: PDG

Pearl earrings: PDG

Fancy pearl necklace: Phila. Opera

Rhinestone necklace (attached to
above): JMS

Rhinestone Earrings: Phila. Opera

Wedding ring: JMS
```

A page from a costume plot (left) and sketches by James Scott (below and following page) for the Philadelphia Drama Guild's 1990 production of *Macbeth*. There are many ways to organize a costume plot. This plot costumes by actor, listing each item of clothing to be worn by the character portrayed, along with the wardrobe source.

Additional costume sketches by James Scott for the Philadelphia Drama Guild's production of *Macbeth*.

a.

b.

The same fabric as photographed under white (a), blue (b), green (c), and red (d) light. Notice how the appearance changes under each different color.

c.

d.

Left, Jo Mielziner's lighting sketch for the porch scene in *Look Homeward, Angel* shows a cool background behind a warmly lit figure.

In contrast, Mielziner's sketch of a side street off Broadway for the musical *Guys and Dolls* shows a warmly lit background and a cool foreground.

Sketch of lighting design by Linda Essig for *The Hairy Ape*, produced at the University of Wisconsin-Madison, and directed by Barbara Clayton. Set design by Andrei Both. (Courtesy of Linda Essig)

Lighting sketch by Lenore Doxsee for Giuseppe Verdi's opera *La Traviata*. (Courtesy of Lenore Doxsee).

How Lighting Choices Contribute to the Meaning of the Play

To analyze a lighting design for the choices it reveals, it is necessary to ask:

- What kind of place is represented?
- How does the lighting help to create that place?
- How do the play and characters relate to that place and the quality of its light?

Photo 7.1 shows Hedda burning Lovborg's manuscript at the end of act 3 of *Hedda Gabler*. The most important light shines directly on Hedda's face and is coming from within the stove itself. It is harsh and very tightly focused so that her maniacal expression is clearly visible. Everything else falls off into a grayish haze. Only two surfaces other than her face seem to reflect any ambient light: the stove and a painting, probably the looming portrait of General Gabler, her father. The room is dark and heavy. Its boundaries are in shadow, but not invisible. This is a dark, dreary place.

This photograph shows clearly how the lighting—so tight and clear on Hedda's face, so diffuse and dim in the rest of the room—contributes to the

Photo 7.1
In this 1929 production of *Hedda Gabler* by Le Petit Theatre du Vieux Carre, lighting is used effectively to focus the audience's attention on the moment when Hedda burns Lovborg's manuscript.

sense of place. Through the lighting, the audience knows that either the time is late at night or the room is naturally very dark. (Other sources of information, such as words spoken in the play itself, will clarify this information and make it specific.)

Further, the lighting communicates the emotional reality of the moment, which is closely tied to the activity of burning the manuscript: Hedda's intense focus is echoed by the intensity of the fire in the stove that consumes the manuscript. The comparatively dull surroundings mean nothing to her at this moment, or to the audience. The lighting helps to shut out everything but the moment at hand.

If we look again at Eva Le Gallienne as Hedda (Photo 6.11), we find fairly high-contrast lighting. Reflected by the white, shiny fabric of the costume, the light slices across Hedda's face and body. Light is brighter and dark darker than in Photo 7.1. The room is gloomy and heavy; only the surface of the piano behind her, of a deep, highly polished wood, is picked up by the light. The light itself seems cold and harsh. Within this context, Hedda's choices seem limited to a cold, dark interior or a harsh exterior.

In Photo 6.12, light enters from the side as in the previous examples, but is filtered and softened by a gauze curtain at the window (If this were the curtain that Hedda asks to be drawn, its delicacy and translucence would suggest something quite different about her character than the opaque curtain in Photo 6.11 on page 186, which would completely block the light if drawn). Here, too, there is a slant of sunlight on Ms. Bloom's face, but its edge is harder to pinpoint. The light is composed of shades of gray, giving this place a softer quality, more hidden from the outside. This is a carefully controlled environment in which nothing jars or unsettles, including the light. Claire Bloom's Hedda has been placed in a nest that wraps around and protects her. The light filtered through the curtain, and the soft reflected light in the room itself, contribute to this atmosphere.

The Lighting Designer's Work Process

Elements of Lighting Design

The lighting designer creates a picture by careful manipulation of:

- Color
- Composition, angle, and direction
- Intensity
- Texture.

Returning to the photograph of Claire Bloom's Hedda looking out the window, we can analyze the light in terms of the creative tools used by the lighting designer (with the exception of color). Light composes the picture by illuminating different surfaces in different ways. Ms. Bloom's face is unevenly illuminated: the left (stage right) side of her face is in relative shadow. The light is perceived as coming from the window. This particular balance of light, its *composition, direction,* and *angle* (i.e., a low angle of light is produced at sunrise or sunset; a high angle at noon; one angle when the sun is coming from behind, over an actor's shoulder, etc.), communicates something of the meaning of the entire scene. Imagine how differently we would understand the scene's meaning if the light were equally balanced right and left, or if all the light came from the front or the back.

The *intensity* of neither the light nor the shadow is particularly great in this photograph. An already dim room is further darkened by curtains shutting out some of the light. Imagine if this room were very bright, or if, as in the photograph of Eva Le Gallienne, one side were very bright and the other very dark. How would that change the meaning of the stage picture?

Texture in light is something we can see but whose feel we can only imagine. In *The Seagull,* the dampness is texture. Fog, humidity, even the smell of spring flowers contribute to the texture of light. In the photograph of Ms. Bloom, the texture might be characterized as soft. The lack of contrast between the right and left sides of her face contributes to this feeling, as does the fairly strong light filtered by the curtain. The light is also slightly thick or dense.

Research aids for a production of *Hedda Gabler* would certainly include photographs of Norway in different light at different seasons. While we may think that light has remained the same since the universe began, factors such as industrialization and air pollution have wrought great changes in its general quality. There is a significant difference between the quality of air and light in the city and in the country. And, as we saw earlier, light also differs from place to place. A sunset in New Mexico differs from a sunset in New York or Moscow, and noon in India differs greatly from noon in New Orleans or Paris. Likewise, the morning after the poker party in *A Streetcar Named Desire* is a different morning from Hedda's, if only because of its geographical location.

Designers from all three design areas share research materials. Sometimes a particular painting or painter is the source of a visual point of view for the production. Paintings are useful in that they contain all the elements used in stage design, but in two dimensions rather than three. Color, shape, line, composition, and light are elements of all paintings, both realistic and abstract. The musical *Sunday in the Park with George* took a painting by Georges Seurat (1859–91) as the starting point for the entire production, including the book and score. The painting was virtually reproduced onstage and brought to life.

Light in paintings and photographs can also be helpful to lighting designers. Painters work from a light, blank surface and lighting designers from a dark one, but painters, too, carve shapes out of the canvas by means of light and shadow, color, and shape, just as lighting designers do out of the space of a darkened theatre.

The most practical and important sources of ideas for the lighting designer, however, are observation and imagination. Every day, right outside our windows, light changes and moves.

Lighting Technology

Scenic and costume design generally rely on the same creative tools as they did centuries ago. Although the mechanics and construction of scenery have changed and improved (computerized mechanisms move scenery; metals, foams, and plastics often replace wood), paint remains paint and fabric is fabric. A costume from Shakespeare's time, minus a zipper or a snap, is much like a costume today.

Lighting design, however, is vastly different from what it was in the past. Lighting design technology derives from two basic factors. One is the way in which the light source itself (be it candle, oil lamp, or lightbulb) "burns" or creates light. The second is the way in which that source is controlled. Lighting before the invention of the electric lightbulb obviously differed tremendously from lighting today. The greatest advances in stage lighting have occurred as a result of the use of electricity, which also made control much more sophisticated.

Until the sixteenth century, most theatrical performances were held outdoors. Daylight was the standard and simplest means of lighting the stage. Playwrights handled the problem of times of day in various ways. In the sleepwalking scene of *Macbeth*, for example, Shakespeare indicates that it is night through the dialogue and through the presence of candles or torches onstage.

Today, stage lighting is created by means of specialized theatrical lighting equipment, which controls the relationship of light to the actor onstage.

LIGHTING EQUIPMENT   Lighting equipment is designed and built expressly for the purposes of the stage and performs two basic functions: *light output* and *light control. Lighting instruments* (for light output) are based on a lightbulb, or *lamp,* enclosed in a shield (the source of light), and sometimes include devices to control the shape, quality, and color of light. Lighting instruments are of two basic types: *floodlight* and *spotlight.*

Floodlighting, produced by instruments comprising nothing but a shield and a reflector, produces a general wash of light. This kind of lighting is used for illuminating backdrops and broad areas of the stage. Floodlighting allows little control over the stage picture.

Spotlighting is produced by instruments that have a lens system (somewhat like that of a projector or camera, but not as complex or refined) to control and shape the light. This kind of instrument allows the lighting designer to have more control over discrete areas of the stage. With spotlighting equipment, a designer for *Macbeth*, for example, can isolate an actor from the rest of the stage for a soliloquy. Spotlights are usually rigged permanently in position for each production, each light illuminating the same area of the stage throughout.

Followspots are a type of spotlight that can move with the actor around the stage. In most cases, followspots require an operator (unless they are computer controlled, which is not only very costly but allows the actor no freedom of movement whatsoever).

Pictured at left and below right are examples of two varieties of floodlight: a 2000-watt SoftLite (left) and an ellipsoidal reflector floodlight with a wattage of 300 to 500. Both produce a soft, blendable light.

An ellipsoidal reflector spotlight, such as that pictured below left, can produce a sharp, unblendable edge, useful for maintaining sharp focus onstage.

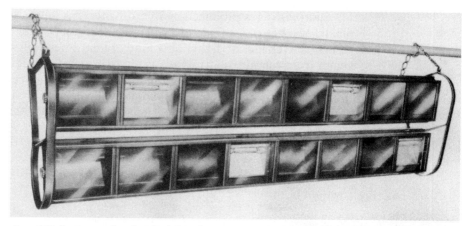

A striplight is another kind of floodlight and comes in many sizes. Each lamp can range from 75 to 1000 watts. Striplights are usually laid out end on end to cover a large space such as the backdrop. They are generally wired to allow every third or fourth light to come on as a unit, providing interesting color control.

Lighting control systems are made up of a series of *dimmers*, each of which controls the amount of electricity flowing to a given lighting instrument. Each instrument is connected to a dimmer by means of electrical wire or cable. When the dimmer (or control) is turned on, electricity flows to the light in varying amounts, and the filament glows proportionately; the more electricity flows, the brighter the light.

LIGHT AND THE ACTOR   The most important function of stage lighting is to provide illumination by which the audience can see the actor within the stage environment. There are many technical terms ("lumen output," "footcandles," etc.), which describe the potential brightness or intensity of different lighting instruments, but precise measurement is not really necessary in the theatre. Unlike cinematic photography, in which the film itself receives light and then transmits it to the eye of the viewer, live theatre transmits light to the audience directly. How well or poorly the audience can see is determined by how well the designer can see.

Many elements besides brightness, such as color and composition, influence vision as well. Onstage *focus* is the place to which the eye is drawn, and the more carefully focused the stage picture, the easier it is for the audience to see. The lighting designer usually achieves focus by increasing the light in the places on stage where the actors are playing a scene and decreasing the light in other areas. (The most extreme example of focus is the use of a followspot or a single light on an actor or singer, leaving the rest of the stage in darkness.)

Focus can also be achieved through color. A cool background behind a warmly lit figure will make the figure more visible than if the relationship were reversed. Scenic and costume designers also contribute to focus were reversed. Scenic and costume designers also contribute to focus through their use of value, color, and texture—as does the director through the staging.

The way in which light hits the actors contributes to how they are seen as well. These directions of light also have their own vocabulary. Light coming from the general direction of the audience is called *frontlight,* from behind the actor *backlight,* from the sides *sidelight,* and from above *downlight.* Photos 7.2 through 7.6 show how these directions of light affect the way in which we see the actor onstage. In most cases, several directions of light are combined to create the overall stage picture.

Photo 7.2, above left
Light from the front (and slightly to the side) reveals more of the basic form of this setting for the opera *Faust* than if it were lit from the back or the side only.

Photo 7.3, left
The director Joseph Chaikin speaks with an actress. Backlight—here in a natural setting—highlights the outline or silhouette of the "characters."

Photo 7.4, above right
The actress Mary Layne, portraying Hedda Gabler, is shown here in *silhouette,* a lighting condition that provides light on the backdrop alone, with none on the major figure. With an accent light on the portrait of General Gabler, the designer has chosen to highlight certain theatrical relationships.

Photo 7.5
In this production of *Camille,* sidelight etches the surrounding figures from the background, which, in this case, remains dark. The major figure is accented by light from above.

Photo 7.6
Downlight produces an eerie and harsh effect on the performers in this 1992 production of *Iphigeneia at Aulis* by the Guthrie Theater. What appear to be masks are highlighted and made more frightening by the virtual obliteration of eyes and other facial features.

Creating the Design on Paper

Although the lighting designer can sketch and paint his or her ideas just as scenic and costume designers do, it presents some unusual difficulties. Since light is not tangible without surfaces to reflect off of, the lighting designer must sketch or paint the surfaces that are illuminated in order to render light. This places special demands on the graphic skills of the lighting designer, but is sometimes worth the time and effort.

Once the design has been sketched in some manner (Figures 7.4 and 7.5), the lighting designer draws schematics of the design, sometimes called *magic sheets.* These drawings break down the sketches into their component points of view:

- From above, the *plan view*
- From the side, the *section view*
- From the front, the *elevation view.*

Figure 7.4
Lighting sketch by Jo Mielziner for a 1945 production of *The Glass Menagerie.*

Figure 7.5
Lighting sketch by Jo Mielziner for the original 1947 production of *A Streetcar Named Desire.*

These schematics help the designer to determine compositional relationships in three dimensions. Color is usually indicated on rough magic sheets as well. The finished magic sheet is used for easy reference when lighting the production (Figure 7.6).

Many colleges have a lighting lab in which to work out lighting problems before the production is put together in the theatre. The lab provides space for experimentation. For the beginner, visualizing light in three dimensions is difficult enough; visualizing color in light is nearly impossible.

Interview

AN INTERVIEW WITH PAT COLLINS ABOUT HER LIGHTING FOR THE HEIDI CHRONICLES

How did your personal/political views affect the way in which you made design choices?

That is a very difficult question. I have no agenda—it is subconscious if I do have one. I feel very strongly that work that is not informed by your subconscious is propaganda, a forebrain idea that makes you a pamphleteer. I loathe ideology. I try not to put forward frankly political work because it gets very flat and uninformed. Anything that involves taking sides is more interesting if a dialogue is maintained. I work for a more poetic approach. I have political and social opinions; I will argue them at the dinner table anytime, but in my work I don't even try. Those ideas dive under to a more subconscious level.

It is possible to work in an ideologically driven theatre, one that drums an idea at the audience, but that is not what *all* theatre is about. If I am designing a scene such as the one on the steps of the museum in the rain, in that specific place I am aware that hugely diverse things can occur: a person can be taking a child to an exhibit or meeting a friend, or a murder can take place, etc. In that same locale, the specific life of the world of the play works itself out. I feel it would be inappropriate for me to add another agenda. All we can do at our best is to prompt people to ask their own questions of the playwright's work.

Playwrights seem to write out of an attempt to discover something within themselves. In the best of their plays, they come at subject matter in a very ambivalent way, because they both enjoy the mystery and fear the pursuit of self-discovery. Wendy [Wasserstein]'s work sneaks up on you. It makes people see things they don't want to look at. She seems to believe that life is far too complex to be described by political or ideological issues alone. There are many ways to approach the complex problems of a life. We can't just throw in the towel, insisting that in some politicl or ideological way we can make things right. Ultimately, we have to look at life with a compassionate eye as Wendy does. For example, in the family relationships she creates, there are often tiny explosions that can totally smash these relationships, without [those involved] ever knowing they are gone. She can crystallize ordinary moments and break your heart. And she is generous with her characters, not didactic.

Wendy set the characters of *Heidi* in particular locales for her particular reasons and I, as a designer, respond to that. She set them there in order for them to come together in a certain spirit. Those locales are emotional spaces. Wendy chooses places in which people work their way out of certain purgatories they have made for themselves. She does not give a huge amount of detail about place. All the spaces are like time capsules for people. Tom Lynch [the scenic designer] was brilliant in the distillation of these multiple spaces out of that repository of images.

My work on *The Heidi Chronicles* was not political in intent. The lighting for the final scene was everything I love about a West Side New York apartment, as it exists in the minds of many other people as well. It was a place in which one could express the possibility of comfort, in which contemplative people could find themselves comfortable. When Wendy says "a West Side apartment," a certain amount of living brings me to a certain understanding of what that is.

Tom captured that apartment brilliantly. He put a window close to the fireplace, and after that the lighting kind of designed itself. All I did was to come at a kind of visual truth about light in certain New York apartments—because Tom set it in a particular way. Heidi probably couldn't afford the front apartment, so it seemed to be in the back; but it could still provide a kind of elegance, an empty place, with no choices made yet. It represented a brand new look at life, a place of possibility.

In designing a production I am looking for a series of truthful, resonating spaces, for recognizability. I am looking for a visual image about which the audience can say, "Oh yes, I think I remember what it is like to be *there.*"

For a designer, images leap out of the accumulation of perceptions about the world that surrounds one every day. One has to draw from one's interpretations of life, to try to touch those things that will resonate for other people in a certain way as well. If a designer does not tap that, the audience won't believe the emotional and physical context of the actors.

Did seeing what the actors were creating affect what you were doing?

Not exactly. My job is to help set the characters in terms of my perceptions of their physical world. For example, there is a scene in *Heidi* set in the children's ward of a Harlem hospital, where every effort has been made to increase the quality of life for the children. It is 3 A.M. in this place. What does that mean to me as a designer? Is the hallway bright? Yes, probably, because that is where the majority of activity takes place at that hour. The young doctor is half asleep in the light of a TV set. He has been on duty too long. The characters play out their lives in this place. This scene has no objective reality, only a subjective one that comes out of a life of observation by the designer. It comes out of the designer's life experience.

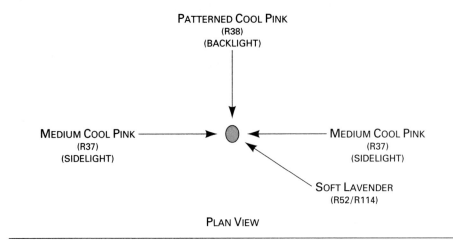

PATTERNED COOL PINK
(R38)
(BACKLIGHT)

MEDIUM COOL PINK
(R37)
(SIDELIGHT)

MEDIUM COOL PINK
(R37)
(SIDELIGHT)

SOFT LAVENDER
(R52/R114)

PLAN VIEW

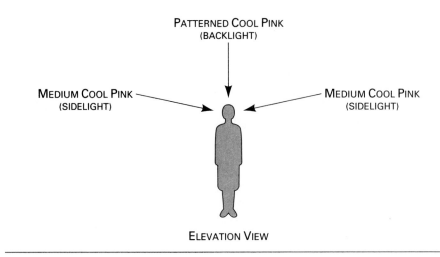

PATTERNED COOL PINK
(BACKLIGHT)

MEDIUM COOL PINK
(SIDELIGHT)

MEDIUM COOL PINK
(SIDELIGHT)

ELEVATION VIEW

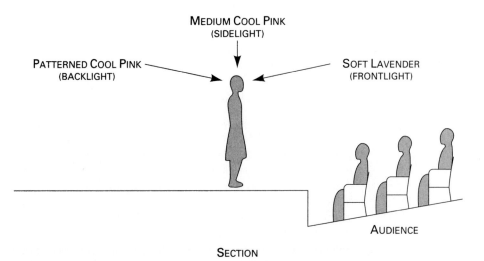

MEDIUM COOL PINK
(SIDELIGHT)

PATTERNED COOL PINK
(BACKLIGHT)

SOFT LAVENDER
(FRONTLIGHT)

AUDIENCE

SECTION

Figure 7.6
A magic sheet
from *Driving
Miss Daisy* by
Alfred Uhry,
1987.

Color in light does not work the way it does in paint. In the lab, a color medium is placed in front of a light source, allowing only a particular color to pass through (red if the medium is red; green if it is green, etc.). By using the actual light and color, the designer can determine in advance what the color will look like onstage next to other colors.

Sketches, schematics, and light labs are important in the development of a design. Through them the designer works out the color, intensity, and angle of light, all of which together create the lighting picture. They are useful for developing the design in a general way, and can also be used to communicate with the director and the other designers (suggesting, for example, that a color be tested on fabric or on sample set pieces).

To realize the design in the theatre, however, drawings and charts of a more specific nature are required. The lighting designer drafts a *light plot* (and sometimes a *lighting section*) and creates a *channel hookup* or *dimmer hookup*. A document known as an *instrument schedule*, which organizes the lights by their position in the theatre, is sometimes also used.

THE LIGHT PLOT   This is a scaled drawing (usually one-half inch to the foot) that tells the electrician or technical director (in most cases one or both of these people are responsible for actually hanging the lights onstage,

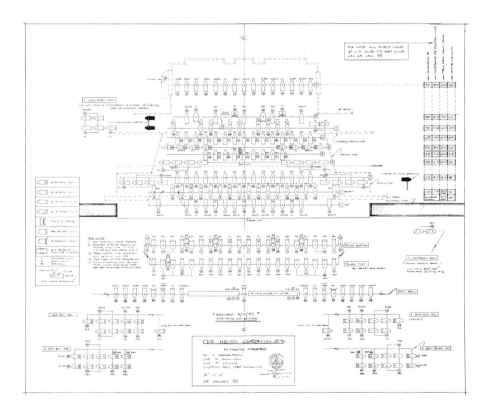

Figure 7.7
Light plot for the production of *The Heidi Chronicles* on Broadway, 1989. (Courtesy of Pat Collins)

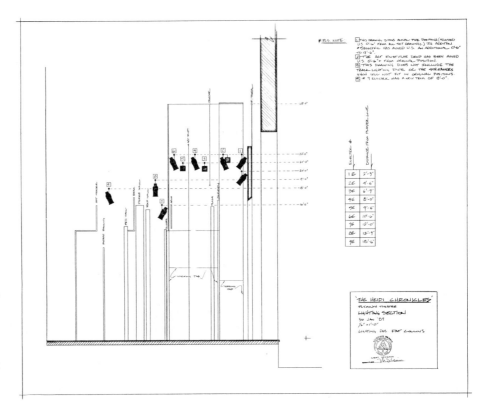

Figure 7.8
Lighting section
from the Broad-
way production
of *The Heidi
Chronicles*.
(Courtesy of Pat
Collins)

although sometimes the lighting designer does so) exactly where lights are to be put and in what configuration. The light plot must be carefully laid out so that the electrician and crew can hang the lights even in the absence of the designer (Figure 7.7).

The light plot is dimensioned and shows the relationship of the lights and lighting positions to the scenery, allowing any problems to be worked out before moving into the theatre. A drafted *lighting section* illustrates the height of lighting positions relative to scenery, actors, and audience (Figure 7.8).

THE DIMMER HOOKUP   This is a chart that tells the electrician three other vital pieces of information not found on the light plot:

- How each light is to be connected and controlled
- Where onstage the light is to be focused
- The color of each light.

As you can see in Figure 7.9, the hookup is numbered by dimmer, showing which lights are grouped together. Referring to both the dimmer hookup and the light plot, the electrician has all the information needed to put the lights into the theatre.

CH.	CIR.	LOCATION	TYPE	FOCUS	COLOR
		HOOKUP			PAGE 1
	03-10-1989		THE HEIDI CHRONICLES		Pat Collins
1	53	Truss Bot-1	6x16 Axial 1K	Area 1	R60
	53	Truss Bot-10	6x16 Axial 1K	Area 1	R60
2	48	Truss Bot-4	6x16 Axial 1K	Area 2	R60
	48	Truss Bot-13	6x16 Axial 1K	Area 2	R60
3	49	Truss Bot-6	6x16 Axial 1K	Area 3	R60
	49	Truss Bot-15	6x16 Axial 1K	Area 3	R60
4	51	Truss Bot-8	6x16 Axial 1K	Area 4	R60
	51	Truss Bot-17	6x16 Axial 1K	Area 4	R60
5	54	Truss Bot-11	6x16 Axial 1K	Area 5	R60
	54	Truss Bot-20	6x16 Axial 1K	Area 5	R60
6	33	Truss Top-1	6x16 Axial 1K	Area 6	R60
	33	Truss Top-10	6x16 Axial 1K	Area 6	R60
7	37	Truss Top-4	6x16 Axial 1K	Area 7	R60
	37	Truss Top-13	6x16 Axial 1K	Area 7	R60
8	38	Truss Top-6	6x16 Axial 1K	Area 8	R60
	38	Truss Top-15	6x16 Axial 1K	Area 8	R60
9	40	Truss Top-8	6x16 Axial 1K	Area 9	R60
	40	Truss Top-17	6x16 Axial 1K	Area 9	R60
10	42	Truss Top-11	6x16 Axial 1K	Area 10	R60
	42	Truss Top-20	6x16 Axial 1K	Area 10	R60
11	67	1 E Bot-1	6x12 Axial 1K	Area 11	R60
	67	1 E Bot-7	6x12 Axial 1K	Area 11	R60
12	69	1 E Bot-3	6x12 Axial 1K	Area 12	R60
	69	1 E Bot-10	6x12 Axial 1K	Area 12	R60
Plymouth Theatre				M.E. - Donny Beck	
				A.L.D. - Mimi Sherin	

Figure 7.9 Channel hook-ups for light plot shown in Figure 7.8. *(Courtesy of Pat Collins)*

The lighting designer, like all the other collaborative artists, uses the production concept to make choices about interpretation and then uses the tools of lighting design to make those choices visible to an audience. Decisions about how a dimmer hookup is organized and which lights are placed where are based upon those interpretive choices. If the school gymnasium in act 1, scene 1 of *The Heidi Chronicles* is illuminated in bright, flashing colors, Heidi's and Susan's quest for "cute" boys will be understood in terms of their ability to see the boys at all. If Blanche can't easily make out the numbers on Stella's door when looking for her sister's apartment, our perception of her attitude will change. It is the art and craft of the lighting designer that communicates these choices to the audience.

Suggested Readings

Adolphe Appia, *Music and the Art of the Theater*, translated by Robert W. Corrigan and Mary D. Dirks (Miami: University of Miami Press), 1963

Jo Mielziner, *Designing for the Theater* (New York: Clarkson N. Potter), 1965.

Richard Pilbrow, *Stage Lighting* (New York: Drama Book Specialists), 1979.

Jean Rosenthal and Lael Wertenbaker, *The Magic of Light* (Boston: Little, Brown),1972.

William Warfel, *Handbook of Stage Lighting Graphics* (New York: Drama Book Specialists), 1974.

Part

THREE

Performance

Chapter
EIGHT

The Producer

Throughout the history of theatre there has always been some separation of responsibilities in production. One part of any theatrical organization is devoted to *creating the work* and another part to *attracting an audience* and *raising the money* to make the work possible in the first place. Although the line separating these functions is not always clear—actors have been producers, directors have been actors, designers have raised money for productions, and so forth—most theatrical organizations today do separate the two because of the degree of skill required in each. Those who create the work are the *artists*—the playwright, director, designers, and actors—and the *production staff*—the carpenters, shop managers, electricians, costume fitters, stage managers, etc. Those who raise and manage the money and develop the audience are the *producers.* Just as the writer is the initiator of the play, the producer is the initiator of the production.

What the Producer Does

Initiating the Production

A play will not be produced unless someone has an interest in presenting it. There is no way to calculate what makes a producer choose to produce a play, but two obvious reasons are a commitment to the merits of a particular work and a desire to make money (whether on behalf of a theatre or for personal gain). One of the fascinations of producing is that it almost always combines aspects of both. Some producers are dedicated to a particular social agenda, others to developing the work of new playwrights or to presenting the ongoing efforts of more established ones.

There are many ways in which plays are produced today. A producer can choose to present a single play in either an open-ended or a limited run. In an *open-ended run*, the production must generate enough income at the box office to meet its expenses and make a profit. In a *limited run*, a production is scheduled for a predetermined number of weeks or months, depending on certain conditions such as the availability of a particular actor or theatre. Productions imported from other countries are often presented under limited-run agreements.

All producers are responsible for bringing together the production's collaborators and, in this way, have considerable artistic input. The producer may exercise control over the choice of play or plays, the choice of director, the choice of venue, and sometimes the choice of designers and actors. Once they have made these important decisions, however, producers generally leave most of the remaining artistic choices to others.

What the Producer Looks for When Reading the Play

Since the producer is responsible for funding the production, the choice of play is always contingent on cost. Whether in the commercial or nonprofit theatre, a producer must know how much money can realistically be expected to be raised for any given production, and he or she must balance that amount against the scale of production necessary for a given play. Producing a play with four characters and one setting is obviously more economical than producing a musical that needs a full orchestra and a cast of thirty.

We have seen how directors, actors, and designers read the script to determine what is required to fulfill the needs of the play. The producer's checklist represents the sum total of all the artists' lists put together. The cost of any production is determined by the following general considerations:

- Payment to the playwright (or the playwright's estate) for the right to produce the play
- Size of the cast
- Number and variety of personnel
- Rehearsal time and space
- Amount and kind of scenery
- Number and kind of costumes
- Size of the theatre
- Cost of advertising.

The size of the cast is obviously of tremendous concern to the commercial and nonprofit producer alike. Hiring twenty-five actors is more costly than hiring five, but sheer numbers are not the sole factor when determining costs. A well-known actor, or "star," in a small production can far outweigh the cost of a larger cast with less highly paid actors. Likewise, some directors and designers are paid more than others.

A musical presents special challenges for the producer, as the talents of a vast array of artists and craftspeople may be involved. In addition to the director, the producer must hire a choreographer, a musical director (and possibly an orchestrator), and musicians. Musicals also tend to have more elaborate sets, costumes, and special effects than straight dramas.

The kinds of scenery and costumes needed and their numbers have an effect on personnel as well. As we will see in the next chapter, when quick costume changes are necessary, a *wardrobe crew* must be hired. When scenery has to be changed, a *stage crew* is required.

The size of the production can also determine the theatre chosen, and vice versa. If a theatre is being rented for a commercial production, the larger it is, the more it will generally cost. Some productions simply will not fit into some theatres, because the offstage space is too small to accommodate the sets.

Advertising is another major concern for any production. The city where a production is being shown, the major outlets available for advertising (newspapers, radio, television, mailings, posters), and the accessibility of the audience all affect the advertising budget.

The producer's greatest dilemma is reconciling the desire to produce a particular play with the costs involved. Figure 8.1 shows the first page of each of the plays we have been analyzing. From the producer's point of view, each of these would, to varying degrees, present some economic difficulties for production today.

Macbeth, with its large number of characters, will be costly in terms of actors, costumes, and possibly scenery. A backstage wardrobe crew might be required, and possibly a crew to move the scenery. Lighting or scenery, or both, will be expensive—one of these will have to communicate changes of place to the audience. A small theatre might have difficulty accommo-

Dramatis Personae.

Duncan, King of Scotland.
Malcolm,
Donalbain, his son.
Macbeth,
Banquo, Generals of the Scottish Army.
Macduff,
Lennox,
Ross,
Menteith,
Angus,
Caithness, Noblemen of Scotland.
Fleance, son to Banquo.
Siward, Earl of Northumberland, General of
    the English forces.
Young Siward, his son.
Seyton, an Officer attending on Macbeth.
Boy, son to *Macduff*.
A Captain.
An English Doctor.

A Scottish Doctor.
A Porter.
An Old Man.
Lady Macbeth.
Lady Macduff.
A Gentlewoman, attending on *Lady Mac-
    beth.*

Hecate.
Three Witches.
The Ghost of *Banquo*.

Apparitions.
Lords, Gentlemen, Officers, Soldiers, Mur-
    derers, Messengers, Attendants.

Scene: *Scotland and England.*

Figure 8.1
Opening pages
of the published
editions of
(clockwise from
above) *Macbeth,
The Heidi
Chronicles,
Hedda Gabler,
A Streetcar
Named Desire,
and The Seagull.*

CHARACTERS

Irina Nikolaevna Arkadina, *married name Treplyov,
    an actress*
Konstantin Gavrilovich Treplyov, *her son, a young
    man*
Peter (Pyotr) Nikolaevich Sorin, *her brother*
Nina Mikhailovna Zarechnaya, *a young girl, daughter
    of a rich landowner*
Ilya Afanasyevich Shamrayev, *a retired army
    lieutenant, Sorin's estate agent*
Pauline (Polina) Andreyevna, *his wife*
Masha, *his daughter*
Boris Alexandrovich Trigorin, *a novelist*
Eugene (Yevgeny) Sergeyevich Dorn, *a doctor*
Simon (Semyon Semyonovich) Medvedenko, *a school-
    master*
Yakov, *a workman*
A Cook
A Maid

*The action takes place on Sorin's country estate. Be-
tween Acts Three and Four there is an interval of two
years.*

CHARACTERS

In order of appearance:
HEIDI HOLLAND
SUSAN JOHNSTON
CHRIS BOXER
PETER PATRONE
SCOOP ROSENBAUM
JILL
FRAN
BECKY GROVES
DEBBIE
CLARA
MARK
MOLLY MC BRIDE
LISA FRIEDLANDER
DENISE
BETSY
TV ATTENDANT
APRIL LAMBERT
WAITER
SANDRA ZUCKER-HALL
RAY

ACT ONE

Prologue: A lecture hall, New York, 1989
Scene 1: Chicago, 1965
Scene 2: Manchester, New Hampshire, 1968
Scene 3: Ann Arbor, Michigan, 1970
Scene 4: Chicago, 1974
Scene 5: New York, 1977

ACT TWO

All scenes take place in New York.
Prologue: A lecture hall, 1989
Scene 1: An apartment, 1980
Scene 2: A TV studio, 1982
Scene 3: A restaurant, 1984
Scene 4: The Plaza Hotel, 1986
Scene 5: A pediatrics ward, 1987
Scene 6: An apartment, 1989

THE CHARACTERS

BLANCHE
STELLA
STANLEY
MITCH
EUNICE
STEVE
PABLO
A NEGRO WOMAN
A DOCTOR
A NURSE
A YOUNG COLLECTOR
A MEXICAN WOMAN

CHARACTERS

JÖRGEN TESMAN,* *holder of a scholarship for research in the History of Civilization*

MRS. HEDDA GABLER TESMAN, *his wife*

MISS JULIANE TESMAN, *his aunt*

MRS. THEA RYSING ELVSTED

JUDGE BRACK

EJLERT LOVBORG

BERTE, *maid at the Tesmans'*

The action takes place in Tesman's villa on the west side of the city (Oslo).

*In performance, the form GEORGE is always used.

dating this many actors and generating enough box office income to cover production costs. "Selling" Shakespeare may not be as easy as selling a simpler work, but the play is well known.

The number of characters in *The Seagull* is not unreasonable, but the play does require four distinct settings and turn-of-the-century Russian costumes, together representing a fairly costly production. In both areas, stage crews will be necessary. The play is not necessarily well known—Shakespeare is more recognizable than Chekhov—and, unless a known actor stars, will need substantial advertising to bring in an audience.

Hedda Gabler takes place in one interior period setting and has a limited number of characters, but costumes could represent some additional, though not astronomical, costs. *A Streetcar Named Desire*, with a larger cast, requires less expensive costumes. Its single setting requires an interior, exterior, and access to an upstairs level. Depending on the design, this setting could be quite expensive. Tennessee Williams has long been a celebrated American writer and revivals of this play have proven popular with audiences. *The Heidi Chronicles* is economical in its use of one actor to play several roles (called *doubling*) and may or may not be costly from a scenic point of view. Because of the play's recent commercial and critical success—it won the Pulitzer Prize for Drama in 1989—it should not be difficult to sell to an audience.

The producer weighs all these considerations against the potential box-office revenue or available funding for the production. Making the decision to go ahead with a production means that, on balance, the project is not only important, but economically feasible.

The Producer's Work Process

The Nonprofit Producer

For a producer who has chosen to work in the nonprofit theatre, making money is not the main goal; rather, the object is presumably to produce works of artistic or social merit. It is very difficult, if not impossible, to make a profit at the box office with productions of plays that will not attract a large audience.

The nonprofit producer normally produces a season of plays, each of which runs for a limited period of time (Figure 8.2). A full season of productions can provide an audience with variety and the assurance that theatre of a certain quality will consistently be available. Over the course of several years, a theatre will be even better able to meet the needs of its particular audience, offering seasons of breadth and depth. An audience for a nonprofit theatre could conceivably see *Macbeth*, *A Streetcar Named De-*

Figure 8.2
The 1993–94 season of plays at the Arena Stage in Washington, D.C.

"*Washington theater-lovers are fortunate in having a world-class director like Doug Wager in this city. There is really no one quite like him.*"
Lloyd Rose,
The Washington Post

THE 1993-94 SEASON
TWELFTH NIGHT
By William Shakespeare

DANCING AT LUGHNASA by Brian Friel

A COMMUNITY CAROL
Adapted from
A Christmas Carol
by Alison Carey, Edward P. Jones, Laurence Maslon, and Bill Rauch

LONG DAY'S JOURNEY INTO NIGHT
by Eugene O'Neill

THE REVENGERS' COMEDIES Parts I & II
by Alan Ayckbourn

A SMALL WORLD
by Mustapha Matura

HEDDA GABLER
by Henrik Ibsen

Dear Friends,

Never underestimate the power of theater to refresh, rejuvenate and restore your spirit.

At Arena Stage all of the elements to make great theater come together at each and every performance—an internationally recognized acting company, an expansive spectrum of classic and new dramatic literature, award-winning scenery, lighting and costumes to enhance the world of the play, and most importantly you, our audience.

Join Arena's audience community. Give yourself a gift that keeps on giving all year long . . . a subscription to Arena Stage.

The 1993-94 Season is springing to life, and I am eager to share with you our plans for an exciting and entertaining cavalcade of plays that will shake the rafters with laughter, raise the roof with song, and stir your soul with an artful abundance of penetrating drama.

As always, we will endeavor to produce a high quality, dynamic and enthralling 8-play series of storytelling events that you won't want to miss. Now, more than ever, we need your support and your advocacy.

Please take the time now and be a part of our imaginative enterprise. It's more than just a subscription; it's a creative way of life, for us here at Arena, and, most importantly, for you.

Plan ahead and to do yourself some good; after all, we think you deserve it.

SINCERELY,

DOUGLAS C. WAGER
ARTISTIC DIRECTOR

sire, *The Seagull, Hedda Gabler,* and *The Heidi Chronicles* in a single season. The theatre publicizes the upcoming season well enough in advance that the audience can plan its theatre going up to a year ahead.

Many regional nonprofit theatres in the United States are members of the League of Resident Theaters (LORT). The league's collective bargaining agreement with Actors' Equity (see the discussion of unions on p. 243) assigns ratings based on a theatre's adjusted potential box office averaged over a three-year period. In other words, theatres are categorized by the amount of income their ticket sales can generate. These ratings (LORT A, B, C, etc., with A being the highest box-office potential) affect contracts for all the artists who work in the theatres. For example, the Guthrie Theater in Minneapolis and the Arena Stage in Washington, D.C., are LORT A houses; the Philadelphia Drama Guild is a LORT B; the Portland Stage Company in Maine a LORT D.

Although the vast majority of LORT houses are in cities of medium size where one theatre may serve a substantial constituency, in major cities such as New York City, Chicago, and Los Angeles, several theatres of this type may coexist, providing great variety for their patrons.

While some not-for-profit theatres engage a *producing director* who is responsible for both artistic and financial matters, responsibilities are more often divided between an *artistic director* and a *managing director* (sometimes known as an *executive director*). Responsibilities of each are relatively consistent from theatre to theatre.

THE ARTISTIC DIRECTOR   Although choices are made by each of the various artists involved in a project, the artistic director is ultimately responsible for the finished production. The artistic director in the nonprofit theatre chooses the season of plays, and usually directs several of them. To find original works to produce, the artistic director, sometimes with the aid of a *literary manager*, may read plays submitted to the theatre by playwrights and their agents, and "scout" new works at readings and workshops. Some nonprofit theatres commission new plays; others, like Actors Theatre of Louisville, sponsor play festivals. Playwrights are invited to submit their work; if chosen, the play is produced at the theatre, usually with the playwright in attendance during rehearsals.

In a theatre such as the New York Shakespeare Festival in New York City, all the productions in a given season might be new plays (Figure 8.3). Another theatre might offer a mix of new plays and revivals, such as the Guthrie's 1991–92 season, which presented seven plays, including Arthur Miller's *Death of a Salesman,* Shakespeare's *The Tempest,* and a stage adaptation of Charles Dickens's *A Christmas Carol.* Some theatres produce additional plays less elaborately in smaller spaces. The Arena Stage puts on as many as nine productions on three stages in a single season and, in addition, has "outreach" productions that tour local schools and community centers.

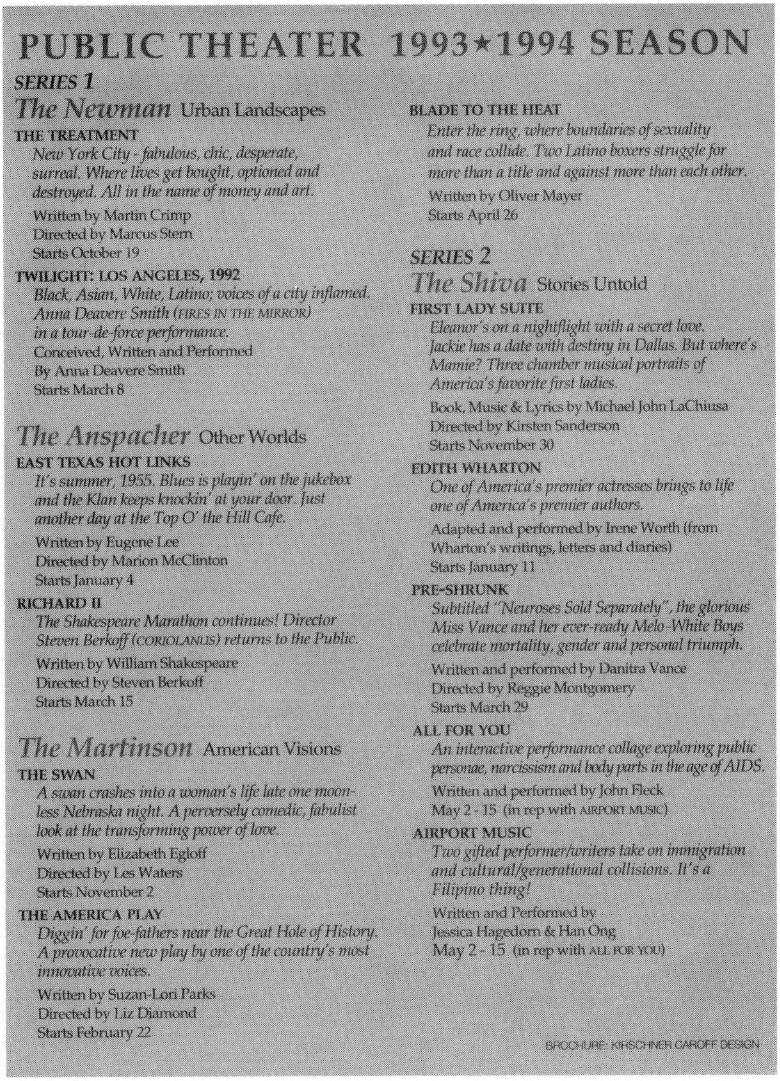

Figure 8.3
The 1993–94 season of plays at the New York Shakespeare Festival.

PUBLIC THEATER 1993★1994 SEASON

SERIES 1

The Newman Urban Landscapes

THE TREATMENT

New York City - fabulous, chic, desperate, surreal. Where lives get bought, optioned and destroyed. All in the name of money and art.

Written by Martin Crimp
Directed by Marcus Stern
Starts October 19

TWILIGHT: LOS ANGELES, 1992

Black, Asian, White, Latino; voices of a city inflamed. Anna Deavere Smith (FIRES IN THE MIRROR) in a tour-de-force performance.

Conceived, Written and Performed
By Anna Deavere Smith
Starts March 8

The Anspacher Other Worlds

EAST TEXAS HOT LINKS

It's summer, 1955. Blues is playin' on the jukebox and the Klan keeps knockin' at your door. Just another day at the Top O' the Hill Cafe.

Written by Eugene Lee
Directed by Marion McClinton
Starts January 4

RICHARD II

The Shakespeare Marathon continues! Director Steven Berkoff (CORIOLANUS) returns to the Public.

Written by William Shakespeare
Directed by Steven Berkoff
Starts March 15

The Martinson American Visions

THE SWAN

A swan crashes into a woman's life late one moonless Nebraska night. A perversely comedic, fabulist look at the transforming power of love.

Written by Elizabeth Egloff
Directed by Les Waters
Starts November 2

THE AMERICA PLAY

Diggin' for foe-fathers near the Great Hole of History. A provocative new play by one of the country's most innovative voices.

Written by Suzan-Lori Parks
Directed by Liz Diamond
Starts February 22

BLADE TO THE HEAT

Enter the ring, where boundaries of sexuality and race collide. Two Latino boxers struggle for more than a title and against more than each other.

Written by Oliver Mayer
Starts April 26

SERIES 2

The Shiva Stories Untold

FIRST LADY SUITE

Eleanor's on a nightflight with a secret love. Jackie has a date with destiny in Dallas. But where's Mamie? Three chamber musical portraits of America's favorite first ladies.

Book, Music & Lyrics by Michael John LaChiusa
Directed by Kirsten Sanderson
Starts November 30

EDITH WHARTON

One of America's premier actresses brings to life one of America's premier authors.

Adapted and performed by Irene Worth (from Wharton's writings, letters and diaries)
Starts January 11

PRE-SHRUNK

Subtitled "Neuroses Sold Separately", the glorious Miss Vance and her ever-ready Melo-White Boys celebrate mortality, gender and personal triumph.

Written and performed by Danitra Vance
Directed by Reggie Montgomery
Starts March 29

ALL FOR YOU

An interactive performance collage exploring public personae, narcissism and body parts in the age of AIDS.

Written and performed by John Fleck
May 2 - 15 (in rep with AIRPORT MUSIC)

AIRPORT MUSIC

Two gifted performer/writers take on immigration and cultural/generational collisions. It's a Filipino thing!

Written and Performed by
Jessica Hagedorn & Han Ong
May 2 - 15 (in rep with ALL FOR YOU)

BROCHURE: KIRSCHNER CAROFF DESIGN

Once a season's plays have been chosen, the artistic director chooses the artists who will be involved in each production. Usually the director is chosen first. Then, in consultation with the director, the artistic director chooses the designers. Not all designers' styles are equally appropriate for all plays, and some directors always work with the same group of designers, making the selection process much simpler.

Casting is a much more complex process, and is undertaken by artistic director and director together. Some regional theatres have *resident companies*, a group of actors hired to appear in many plays each season. An actor in a resident company may play a major role in one production and a

Interview

AN INTERVIEW WITH ANDRÉ BISHOP,
ARTISTIC DIRECTOR OF THE LINCOLN CENTER
THEATER IN NEW YORK CITY, FORMERLY
ARTISTIC DIRECTOR OF PLAYWRIGHTS HORIZONS

What personal or political points of view guide your choice of productions?

I think the way I choose plays to produce is largely by instinct. Like some actors who are superstitious about discussing technique, afraid they might lose it by talking about it, I try to avoid analyzing why I make the choices I do. Any producer responds to a play or a writer as we do to anything in life. (Someone once told me that I picked plays that had versions of me in the lead!)

What do I respond to in a play? What do I look for? I love plays in which the personal and social are allied. I have always valued idiosyncratic voices in the theatre. I love playwrights whose world view and subject matter come out in a very distinctive style. I love plays with bravura roles for actors, perhaps because I was an actor myself and my training was as an actor. Above all other considerations, I read and choose plays that are performable.

I love comedy. I tend to look at the world through humorous eyes. Comedy is hard to produce and write and act, but can be easily dismissed. Americans think that what is serious is sad; that if something is funny, it is not lofty. *The Heidi Chronicles* is a perfect example of this—a play that is funny, but whose content cannot be easily dismissed.

My work at Playwrights Horizons was about the freedom to produce whatever seemed important. The commercial success of many of the projects gave me confidence. If I had a success, I can take a chance and have a failure. But you never really know what will be a success, because by simply reading the play you can't know what the production will be, and the production creates the success.

The responsibility of doing a new play for the first time is very great. If a production is a failure, the critics often take it out on the play. In only two instances was I sure of the future success of the play. One was *Driving Miss Daisy* and the other was *The Heidi Chronicles.* I always knew it would do well. I knew it was a good play, both funny and serious. Here clearly was an author stretching herself. I had worked with Wendy for many years and watched that progress take place.

Writers put their lives in the hands of a production team. A producer can sense what a good director will do, but this sense is not always consistent. We can plan very carefully, and it doesn't work, and the opposite. We can work very hard and still be a failure. The production is very important. When you think of *A Streetcar Named Desire,* you think of the original and most famous production, of Kazan, and of Brando. The productions become as famous as the play.

What do you feel is your responsibility to your audience?

Working in the not-for-profit sector at Playwrights Horizons, I could act on my own taste and hope that others would follow. I didn't have to worry about whether something would be a big success. At Lincoln Center [also a nonprofit theatre], I have to remember what theatre we are performing in. If it is a big space like the Vivian Beaumont, that will inform my choice of director even more than the choice of writer.

I feel responsible for producing something that will do something for everyone. There are lots of well-to-do people, and lots of not so well-to-do. I think the ticket price should be kept low. I want them to love everything. I don't want them to walk out in a huff—but that is not to say that audiences cannot be unbelievably dumb! But in general, they are unbelievably smart and if something is good, they will recognize it.

When I began, commercial theatre and nonprofit theatre were very distinct entities. Playwrights' original charter even stated that its goal was "to support the work of playwrights *away from the pressure of the commercial theatre.*" Now Broadway has completely failed for the production of new work. The lines are blurred and the nonprofit theatre has become mainstream. Broadway is the fringe, in terms of creating new work. No one made much of a living in commercial theatre when it was at its peak. The bulk of American theatre was in the middle—productions that did not have to make huge amounts of money. Right now, it is still possible to have the middle in the nonprofit theatre, but not in the commercial theatre. Nonprofit theatre picked up regular theatregoers mostly for reasons of cost, and because it provides a wider range of productions.

What makes a good producer?

Everyone has a different opinion about producing. Producing is "the intelligent exertion of one's own taste." I am not a director, so I have been able to be the third pair of eyes. I don't know how others direct and produce at the same time. Although I know a lot about writing, I work more closely with directors, with whom I have good relations because I am not perceived as a threat. My version of the play is their version of the play. I see it through their eyes and help make it better.

I was very lucky. My generation (I am 44 years old) coincided with the growing up of the nonprofit theatre. I got in more or less at the beginning and I grew as Playwrights Horizons grew, as the movement across the country grew. There were no seminars then and no one wrote books about people like me. Just as Broadway wound down as cities grew, the nonprofit system cannot be taken for granted either. I hope my generation will be role models for the younger generation, but they need to keep reinventing the wheel.

While at Playwrights Horizons, André Bishop was responsible for developing the work of such playwrights as Wendy Wasserstein, Alfred Uhry, Peter Parnell, William Finn, Christopher Durang, and Jon Robin Baitz.

minor one in the next. When no resident company exists, each role in every play must be cast by audition or by invitation to an actor whose work is already well known. Some artistic directors like to work with favorite actors again and again.

THE MANAGING DIRECTOR   In the not-for-profit theatre, the managing director is responsible for all financial matters. A general formula is that the artistic director chooses what is to be produced and the managing director finds a way to pay for those choices. In the best of situations, artistic director and managing director agree on budgeting priorities.

Undertaking a complete season in a not-for-profit setting is an enormous task. Budgets can range upwards of ten million dollars. The managing director's staff is responsible for securing funds and for balancing remaining costs against projected earnings at the box office. The managing director is also responsible to the *board of trustees* for the long-term financial well-being of the institution. The board, in turn, advises the theatre on financial matters and helps raise money.

Funding for a nonprofit theatre comes from many sources: grants from federal, state, and local government; grants from private corporations; individual donations; and box-office income (Figure 8.4).

Once funding for the season is in place, the managing director, with advice from the artistic director, hires the artists for each production and negotiates their contracts. The managing director is also responsible for maintaining a full-time, year-round staff to carry out this work. As with casting, the choice of staff will depend on the managing director's personal views and preferences and on how he or she wants the work done. The overall harmony of the theatre, as well as its success, is vitally dependent on these decisions.

The not-for-profit theatre makes a long-term commitment to a community. Ideally, theatre and community define each other. The center of theatre in the United States as late as the 1960s (and before a construction boom resulted in major theatres being built in every large city in the country) was New York City. For those who could not get to "the great white way" of Broadway, there were touring companies that made their way around the country by train or bus. Such companies still exist, but thanks to nonprofit resident companies, theatre has become more accessible and more a part of the fabric of individual communities.

OMB No. 3135-0102 Expires 7/31/95 33

Theater

Fiscal Year 1994

Project Grant Application Form NEA-3 (Rev.)

Applications must be submitted in triplicate and mailed together with other required materials to: Information Management Division/TH, 8th floor, National Endowment for the Arts, Nancy Hanks Center, 1100 Pennsylvania Avenue, N.W., Washington, DC 20506-0001 (overnight mail zip code: 20004).

I. Applicant name (legal/IRS), address, zip:

Phone: ( )

II. Category under which support is requested:

☐ Professional Theater Companies
☐ Professional Theater Training
☐ Services to the Field

III. Period of support requested:

Starting ____ **month day year**

Ending ____ **month day year**

IV. Employer I.D. number:

V. Summary of project activity (Complete in space provided. DO NOT reduce copy or continue on additional pages.):

VI. Estimated number of persons expected to benefit from this activity:

VII. Summary of estimated costs detailed in Section X:

	Total costs of activity (Rounded to the nearest $100)
A. Direct costs	
1. Salaries and wages	$
Fringe benefits	$
2. Supplies and materials	$
3. Travel	$
4. Permanent equipment	$
5. Fees and other	$
Total direct costs	$
B. Indirect costs	$
Total project costs	$

VIII. Total amount requested from the National Endowment for the Arts .... $

NOTE: Amount requested from Arts Endowment (VIII.): $

PLUS Total contributions, grants, and revenues (XI., page 3): +

MUST EQUAL Total project costs (VII. above): =

How much of this amount could you absorb in Treasury Funds (see page 28)? $

IX. Organization total operating fiscal activity:	Actual FY92 (92-93)	FY93 (93-94)
A. Operating expenses	$	$
B. Operating contributions, grants, and revenues	$	$

(Continued on reverse)

X. Budget breakdown of summary of estimated costs: **2**

A. Direct costs.

1. Salaries and wages (INCLUDE ARTISTS' COMPENSATION IF PAID ON A SALARY BASIS):

Title and/or type of personnel	# of personnel	Annual or average salary range exclusive of incidentals	% of time devoted to this project	Amount
				$

Total salaries and wages $
Add fringe benefits $
Total salaries and wages including fringe benefits $

2. Supplies and materials (list each major type separately):

	Amount
	$

Total supplies and materials $

3. Travel:

Transportation of personnel

# of travelers	from	to	Amount
			$

Total transportation of personnel $

Subsistence

# of travelers	# of days	Daily rate	
			$

Total subsistence $
Total travel $

(Continued on next page)
34

Figure 8.4
Part of an application for a grant from the National Endowment for the Arts.

The Commercial Producer

Unlike the artistic and managing directors in the nonprofit theatre, the commercial producer usually works on a project-by-project basis. One producer might work simultaneously on several plays at various stages of production, and any given production will generally have several producers.

Most commercial producers are responsible for raising money and showing a profit at the box office. Depending on personality, one will be more involved with artistic decisions, one with advertising, one with tour arrangements, and so on.

At least one of the producers on a commercial show maintains a full-time staff and an office. Major producers such as Emanuel Azenberg (who has produced many of Neil Simon's plays) have complex organizational and financial responsibilities for all of their productions; many of these can be "running" at once, some in New York, others around the country, others around the world.

A producer's first responsibility is to find a play to produce. Again, playwrights and playwrights' agents send plays to established producers. Producers also look for new plays by attending workshops or readings or other productions. If the producer is interested in producing a play, the next step is to *option* it. An option is a contract with the playwright, stipulating that for a specified period of time, only that producer has the right to present the play.

The process of raising funds for a commercial production differs from that for not-for-profit theatre chiefly in that the commercial producer raises money from individuals or corporations and is legally responsible to the investor (known as the *backer* or *angel*) for that money. The producer must show that the production is making a profit at the box office and that the investor can be paid back (ideally with a profit), or that the show is losing money and cannot be repaid. The government, under the auspices of the Securities and Exchange Commission and the state's attorney general's office, carefully monitors all the financial dealings of commercial productions.

University Theatre and Community Theatre

The organization of university and community theatres resembles that of the not-for-profit theatre. The university theatre, although part of a not-for-profit institution, sometimes depends on box-office revenue for its continued existence. Community theatre is almost always dependent on box-office success; in fact, proceeds from one production generally fund the next. Overall, as nonprofessional companies, university and community theatres have less formal organization than commercial or other nonprofit organizations, because their finances are not as carefully monitored by the government. Making a profit is not the primary issue. The goal of community

DESIGNING *THE HEIDI CHRONICLES*

```
JOAN ALLEN--HEIDI
I-5
rose silk dress
white floral chiffon shawl
beige pumps

PETER FRIEDMAN--SCOOP
I-5
white formal shirt
grey morning coat
   "     "    pants
   "     "    vest
striped cravat
black shoes
wedding band, studs, cuff-
   links
suspenders
```

Jennifer von Mayrhauser's costume plots and photos as they appeared onstage in the Broadway production of *The Heidi Chronicles.*

```
JOAN ALLEN--HEIDI
II-5
overcoat w/ scarf
grey  shoulder bag
breakaway skirt

BOYD GAINES - Peter
2-5
purple plaid shirt
knit tie
light brown corduroy trousers
Doctor's coat
I.D.tag
socks loafers w/tassles
black belt
```

Set designer Tom Lynch's sketch of the baby shower scene (Act 2, scene 1) and the scene as it appeared onstage in the Playwrights Horizons production of *The Heidi Chronicles* (sketch courtesy of Tom Lynch).

The rally at the Chicago Art Institute (Act 1, Scene 4), as sketched by Tom Lynch and as seen onstage in performance (sketch courtesy of Tom Lynch).

Peter, Heidi, and Scoop being interviewed together on a television talk show in Act 2, scene 2 of *The Heidi Chronicles* in the Playwrights Horizons production.

The intriguing thing about this play for me as a designer was to find how to organize a series of emotional pictures that are being stated in an almost satirical way. I needed to be able to highlight, in a way, the seriousness and the legitimacy of the play. It was like figuring out a puzzle, trying to put a structure on very nonstructured things. The more specifically political side of the play began to feel more like a payoff only when audiences started to listen to it. All my energy went toward trying to find the visual and emotional organization.

Tom Lynch, set designer

A paint draw-down from *The Heidi Chronicles*.

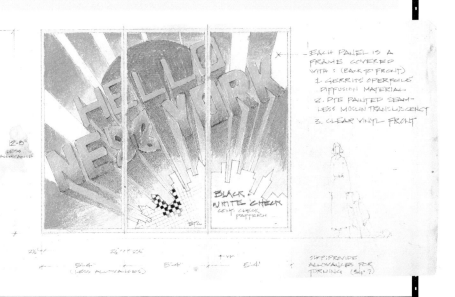

Joan Allen as Heidi in the final scene of the play in the Broadway production of *The Heidi Chronicles.*

The lighting for the final scene was everything I love about a West Side New York apartment, as it exists in the minds of many other people as well. It was a place in which one could express the possibility of comfort, in which contemplative people would find themselves comfortable. When Wendy says "a West Side apartment," a certain amount of living brings me to a certain understanding of what that is.

Tom captured that apartment brilliantly. He put a window close to the fireplace, and after that the lighting kind of design itself. All I did was to come at a kind of visual truth about (light in) certain New York apartments—and because Tom set it in a particular way. Heidi probably couldn't afford the front apartment, so it seemed to be in the back; but it could still provide a kind of elegance, an empty place, with no choices made yet. It represented a brand new look at life, a place of possibility.

Pat Collins, lighting designer

theatre is usually the enjoyment of the work; university theatre focuses on educational value.

The goals of these theatres also affect how decisions are made. In university theatre, faculty and staff choose the season, cast the plays, and make design considerations based on the ongoing learning process and each student's educational needs over four years' time. Students in many universities also run their own theatres, where they have more say in choosing and producing the plays. In community theatre, decisions are based on many of the same factors that apply in professional theatre, but with the welfare of its members being a primary consideration.

Hiring and Firing

Producers are responsible for *contracting* all members of a production company; that is, creating an agreement that stipulates the responsibilities of both parties relative to the production. A contract in the theatre is as binding as any other contract and covers certain basic areas of concern to the producer and the employee.

First, the contract states how much and when the employee will be paid by the producer. Actors, stagehands, musicians, press representatives—all those working on the production on a continuing basis—are paid by the week. Directors, choreographers, and designers are generally paid a one-time fee for their work and, in addition, are sometimes paid a weekly *royalty*, or percentage of box-office receipts, for the run of the production.

All contracts in the theatre have an *out clause* that indicates how much notice an employee must give before leaving the production. This allows the producer time to replace that person without harming the production. A contract will also provide each party with other protections, such as the designer's right to reproduce a design, the choreographer's ownership of a dance sequence, or the producer's right to maintain an acceptable budget. Contracts also cover issues that range from dressing rooms (their location, appointments, etc.) to billing to assistants.

The producer, as employer, also has control over firing. As in any other business, if an employee does not carry out the responsibilities stipulated in the contract, he or she can be dismissed.

Theatrical Unions

The professional theatre has unions that were organized to protect its workers and to ensure their expertise (members must demonstrate a certain level of competence before being admitted). These unions draw up contracts that stipulate minimum allowable wages, health or pension ben-

Interview

PRODUCERS JANE HARMON AND
NINA KENEALLY ON CHOICE

As producers, we look for unique or new voices in the theatre. The material has to intrigue and involve us and to speak honestly about the human condition. Our reactions are initially visceral. Since we deal primarily with American writers and new material (nonrevivals), we have an affinity for socially relevant issues, dilemmas, and situations.

To successfully exploit a play's potential we adhere to the highest standards of production, so the choice of artistic and technical personnel (that is, designers) is crucial to us. Equally as important as putting together the appropriate artistic and creative company are the choices involved in assembling another group of people not normally perceived as part of the creative team: press agents, the advertising agency, general management, and stage management. We feel, however, that their contributions are equally creative in their own specialties.

We also take into consideration:

- What is the most appropriate venue for the play?
- What is the best route for the play at this particular stage of development and is it ready to withstand critical exposure?
- Production costs.

efits, and the conditions under which a member employed on a production can be dismissed. The major theatrical unions have contracts that cover Broadway, off-Broadway, and resident theatres, and have special agreements for use in unusual circumstances. Each contract differs according to the needs and problems of those venues, and is negotiated with a different group of producers. There are seven major unions for theatrical employees.

Actors' Equity Association

This union protects actors and stage managers in all professional theatre situations. Its contracts cover such issues as hours, working conditions, and even how changes can be made in rehearsal schedules (Figure 8.5). Rules governing actors' contracts are contained in the Equity Rulebook, a copy of

Periodically, we will develop a play in conjunction with a not-for-profit theatre (for example, *Driving Miss Daisy* and *The Substance of Fire*). Even if a play has been successfully produced at a not-for-profit, there are many factors that contribute to the decision as to whether a commercial move is indeed the best next step or whether a play is better served staying in not-for-profit venues.

Our exercise of choice is part of our day-to-day dealings with all these additional elements: how to advertise—the logo, copy, scheduling print, TV, and cable; and where to market—placement of paid advertising, the target audience, group sales; and how to keep cast and crew happy night after night in "sitdown" companies or on tour through our company and stage management.

All these personnel choices are important to us because they inform and prepare the audience for the experience that we and the creative team have realized onstage.

Most recently, Jane Harmon and Nina Keneally were responsible for pro-ducing the Pulitzer Prize–winning play Driving Miss Daisy *by Alfred Uhry (which ran successfully in New York (and abroad) for several years, had many road companies, and was made into an Academy Award–win-ning movie) and* The Substance of Fire *by Jon Robin Baitz (initially pro-duced in collaboration with Playwrights Horizons, subsequently pro-duced by Lincoln Center at the Mitzi Newhouse Theater).*

which is always at hand on the stage manager's desk. The cast of each Equity production elects an "equity deputy" as its representative to see that the rules are properly adhered to and to arbitrate changes.

The Dramatists Guild

This guild (it is not technically a union) was organized for the protection of playwrights. Like the theatrical unions, it stipulates how and when a member's work can be used, the minimum amount a playwright can be paid for use of his or her play in different venues, and how, when, and under what conditions the production can be remounted or licensed. The Dramatists Guild has no contract with LORT; it can only make recommendations. Individual theatres, however, have their own contracts with playwrights.

Society of Stage Directors and Choreographers

This union (the SSD&C) represents directors and choreographers and has contracts with all the major producing units (LORT and the League of American Theatres and Producers in New York, which covers Broadway houses). It is a considerably smaller union than Actors' Equity, and therefore has considerably less power in negotiations. It also stipulates minimum fees that can be paid for work in different venues.

United Scenic Artists of the Brotherhood of Painters and Allied Trades

This union represents scenic, lighting, and costume designers and their assistants, and scenic artists (who paint the scenery in unionized paint shops). Unlike its counterparts in acting, directing, and playwrighting, this union also represents production designers, art directors, costume designers, and scenic artists working in the film and television industries.

The International Alliance of Theatrical Stage Employees

This union (IATSE) negotiates contracts for all stagehands (who handle all kinds of scenery, including flying scenery and properties) and electricians in union theatres, which are generally large theatres (like Broadway houses) in major cities and touring theatres in such cities as Chicago, Boston, Philadelphia, and Los Angeles. Several of the larger nonprofit resident theatres also employ unionized stagehands.

American Federation of Musicians

This union represents professional musicians, including those who work in the theatre. Like the other theatrical unions, the musicians' union protects its members from excessive hours, low pay, and substandard working conditions. Contracts with producers also stipulate the minimum number of musicians that can be used in musical productions, and how taped music is to be used (in the Broadway theatre, only a limited number of minutes of taped music are allowed before the musicians must be paid).

Association of Theatrical Press Agents and Managers

This union protects those who work as theatrical press agents, general managers, house managers, and company managers (who will be discussed in the next section).

There are also other theatrical unions, such as the usher's union (Legitimate Theater Employees Union), the wardrobe union (Theatrical Wardrobe Attendants Union), and the union for box-office personnel (Treasurers and Ticket Sellers Union), that serve a more limited constituency, like those who work in Broadway theatres.

Money Management

Financial management is an important part of the producer's job. Once the money for a production has been raised, it must be delivered to various departments and its use regularly supervised. There are several categories of money manager in the theatre.

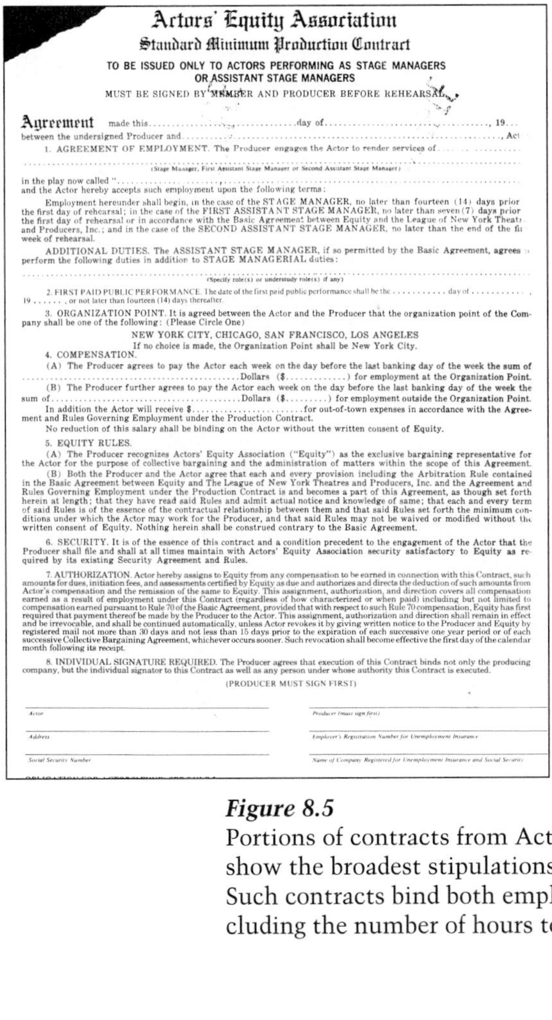

Actors' Equity Association

Standard Minimum Production Contract

TO BE ISSUED ONLY TO ACTORS PERFORMING AS STAGE MANAGERS OR ASSISTANT STAGE MANAGERS

MUST BE SIGNED BY MEMBER AND PRODUCER BEFORE REHEARSAL

Agreement made this .... day of .... , 19...
between the undersigned Producer and .... , Act

1. AGREEMENT OF EMPLOYMENT. The Producer engages the Actor to render services of ....
(Stage Manager, First Assistant Stage Manager or Second Assistant Stage Manager)

in the play now called "....................
and the Actor hereby accepts such employment upon the following terms:

Employment hereunder shall begin, in the case of the STAGE MANAGER, no later than fourteen (14) days prior the first day of rehearsal; in the case of the FIRST ASSISTANT STAGE MANAGER, no later than seven (7) days prior the first day of rehearsal or in accordance with the Basic Agreement between Equity and the League of New York Theat and Producers, Inc.; and in the case of the SECOND ASSISTANT STAGE MANAGER, no later than the end of the fi week of rehearsal.

ADDITIONAL DUTIES. The ASSISTANT STAGE MANAGER, if so permitted by the Basic Agreement, agrees perform the following duties in addition to STAGE MANAGERIAL duties:

....
(Specify role(s) or understudy role(s) if any)

2. FIRST PAID PUBLIC PERFORMANCE. The date of the first paid public performance shall be the .... day of .... , 19 ...... , or not later than fourteen (14) days thereafter.

3. ORGANIZATION POINT. It is agreed between the Actor and the Producer that the organization point of the Company shall be one of the following: (Please Circle One)

NEW YORK CITY, CHICAGO, SAN FRANCISCO, LOS ANGELES
If no choice is made, the Organization Point shall be New York City.

4. COMPENSATION.

(A) The Producer agrees to pay the Actor each week on the day before the last banking day of the week the sum of .... Dollars ($..........) for employment at the Organization Point.

(B) The Producer further agrees to pay the Actor each week on the day before the last banking day of the week the sum of .... Dollars ($.........) for employment outside the Organization Point.

In addition the Actor will receive $.................... for out-of-town expenses in accordance with the Agreement and Rules Governing Employment under the Production Contract.

No reduction of this salary shall be binding on the Actor without the written consent of Equity.

5. EQUITY RULES.

(A) The Producer recognizes Actors' Equity Association ("Equity") as the exclusive bargaining representative for the Actor for the purpose of collective bargaining and the administration of matters within the scope of this Agreement.

(B) Both the Producer and the Actor agree that each and every provision including the Arbitration Rule contained in the Basic Agreement between Equity and The League of New York Theatres and Producers, Inc. and the Agreement and Rules Governing Employment under the Production Contract is and becomes a part of this Agreement, as though set forth herein at length; that they have read said Rules and admit actual notice and knowledge of same; that each and every term of said Rules is of the essence of the contractual relationship between them and that said Rules set forth the minimum conditions under which the Actor may work for the Producer, and that said Rules may not be waived or modified without the written consent of Equity. Nothing herein shall be construed contrary to the Basic Agreement.

6. SECURITY. It is of the essence of this contract and a condition precedent to the engagement of the Actor that the Producer shall file and shall at all times maintain with Actors' Equity Association security satisfactory to Equity as required by its existing Security Agreement and Rules.

7. AUTHORIZATION. Actor hereby assigns to Equity from any compensation to be earned in connection with this Contract, such amounts for dues, initiation fees, and assessments certified by Equity as due and authorizes and directs the deduction of such amounts from Actor's compensation and the remission of the same to Equity. This assignment, authorization, and direction covers all compensation earned as a result of employment under this Contract (regardless of how characterized or when paid) including but not limited to compensation earned pursuant to Rule 70 of the Basic Agreement, provided that with respect to such Rule 70 compensation, Equity has first required that payment thereof be made by the Producer to the Actor. This assignment, authorization and direction shall remain in effect and be irrevocable, and shall be continued automatically, unless Actor revokes it by giving written notice to the Producer and Equity by registered mail not more than 30 days and not less than 15 days prior to the expiration of each successive one year period or of each successive Collective Bargaining Agreement, whichever occurs sooner. Such revocation shall become effective the first day of the calendar month following its receipt.

8. INDIVIDUAL SIGNATURE REQUIRED. The Producer agrees that execution of this Contract binds not only the producing company, but the individual signator to this Contract as well as any person under whose authority this Contract is executed.

(PRODUCER MUST SIGN FIRST)

Actor — Producer (must sign first)
Address — Employer's Registration Number for Unemployment Insurance
Social Security Number — Name of Company Registered for Unemployment Insurance and Social Security

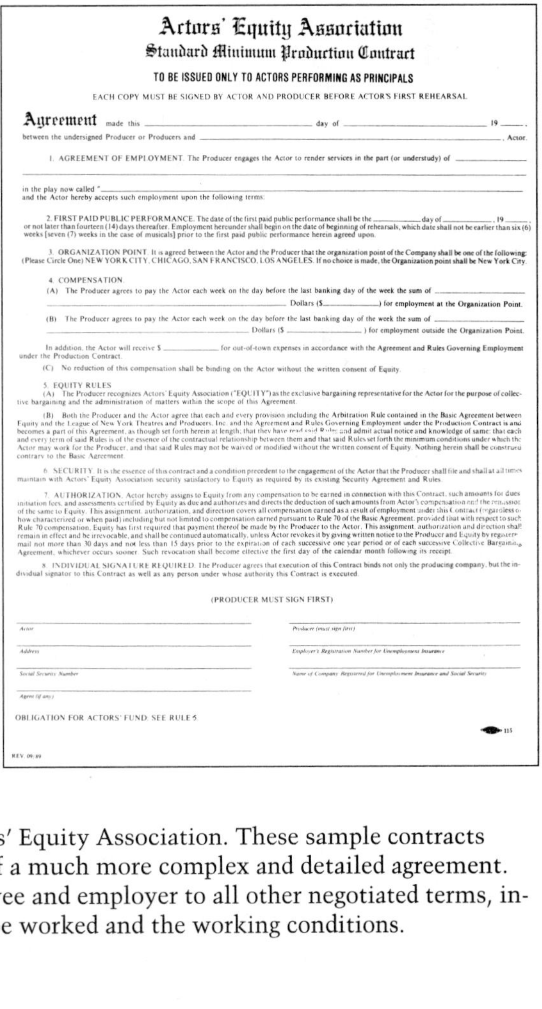

Actors' Equity Association

Standard Minimum Production Contract

TO BE ISSUED ONLY TO ACTORS PERFORMING AS PRINCIPALS

EACH COPY MUST BE SIGNED BY ACTOR AND PRODUCER BEFORE ACTOR'S FIRST REHEARSAL

Agreement made this ________ day of ________ 19 ____,
between the undersigned Producer or Producers and ________, Actor.

1. AGREEMENT OF EMPLOYMENT. The Producer engages the Actor to render services in the part (or understudy) of ________

in the play now called "________
and the Actor hereby accepts such employment upon the following terms:

2. FIRST PAID PUBLIC PERFORMANCE. The date of the first paid public performance shall be the ________ day of ________, 19 ____, or not later than fourteen (14) days thereafter. Employment hereunder shall begin on the date of beginning of rehearsals, which date shall not be earlier than six (6) weeks [seven (7) weeks in the case of musicals] prior to the first paid public performance herein agreed upon.

3. ORGANIZATION POINT. It is agreed between the Actor and the Producer that the organization point of the Company shall be one of the following: (Please Circle One) NEW YORK CITY, CHICAGO, SAN FRANCISCO, LOS ANGELES. If no choice is made, the Organization point shall be New York City.

4. COMPENSATION.

(A) The Producer agrees to pay the Actor each week on the day before the last banking day of the week the sum of ________ Dollars ($________) for employment at the Organization Point.

(B) The Producer agrees to pay the Actor each week on the day before the last banking day of the week the sum of ________ Dollars ($ ________) for employment outside the Organization Point.

In addition, the Actor will receive $ ________ for out-of-town expenses in accordance with the Agreement and Rules Governing Employment under the Production Contract.

(C) No reduction of this compensation shall be binding on the Actor without the written consent of Equity.

5. EQUITY RULES

(A) The Producer recognizes Actors' Equity Association ("EQUITY") as the exclusive bargaining representative for the Actor for the purpose of collective bargaining and the administration of matters within the scope of this Agreement.

(B) Both the Producer and the Actor agree that each and every provision including the Arbitration Rule contained in the Basic Agreement between Equity and the League of New York Theatres and Producers, Inc. and the Agreement and Rules Governing Employment under the Production Contract is and becomes a part of this Agreement, as though set forth herein at length; that they have read said Rules and admit actual notice and knowledge of same; that each and every term of said Rules is of the essence of the contractual relationship between them and that said Rules set forth the minimum conditions under which the Actor may work for the Producer, and that said Rules may not be waived or modified without the written consent of Equity. Nothing herein shall be construed contrary to the Basic Agreement.

6. SECURITY. It is the essence of this contract and a condition precedent to the engagement of the Actor that the Producer shall file and shall at all times maintain with Actors' Equity Association security satisfactory to Equity as required by its existing Security Agreement and Rules.

7. AUTHORIZATION. Actor hereby assigns to Equity from any compensation to be earned in connection with this Contract, such amounts for dues initiation fees, and assessments certified by Equity as due and authorizes and directs the deduction of such amounts from Actor's compensation and the remission of the same to Equity. This assignment, authorization, and direction covers all compensation earned as a result of employment under this Contract (regardless of how characterized or when paid) including but not limited to compensation earned pursuant to Rule 70 of the Basic Agreement, provided that with respect to such Rule 70 compensation, Equity has first required that payment thereof be made by the Producer to the Actor. This assignment, authorization and direction shall remain in effect and be irrevocable, and shall be continued automatically, unless Actor revokes it by giving written notice to the Producer and Equity by registered mail not more than 30 days and not less than 15 days prior to the expiration of each successive one year period or of each successive Collective Bargaining Agreement, whichever occurs sooner. Such revocation shall become effective the first day of the calendar month following its receipt.

8. INDIVIDUAL SIGNATURE REQUIRED. The Producer agrees that execution of this Contract binds not only the producing company, but the individual signator to this Contract as well as any person under whose authority this Contract is executed.

(PRODUCER MUST SIGN FIRST)

Actor — Producer (must sign first)
Address — Employer's Registration Number for Unemployment Insurance
Social Security Number — Name of Company Registered for Unemployment Insurance and Social Security
Agent (if any)

OBLIGATION FOR ACTORS' FUND: SEE RULE 5

115

REV. 09/89

Figure 8.5
Portions of contracts from Actors' Equity Association. These sample contracts show the broadest stipulations of a much more complex and detailed agreement. Such contracts bind both employee and employer to all other negotiated terms, including the number of hours to be worked and the working conditions.

General managers are hired by the commercial producer to oversee the entire budget and the production process. They are responsible for setting the budget and monitoring all expenditures, and for overseeing the funds spent on advertising and audience development.

Company managers work under the general manager and are employees of the production company. These managers oversee the weekly payroll and tend to the ongoing needs of the performers, stage managers, and everyone else connected with the actual run of the production.

Figure 8.6

Covers of the playbills for the Playwrights Horizons and Broadway productions of *The Heidi Chronicles*. The original production of *The Heidi Chronicles* was produced under the auspices of a not-for-profit theatre, Playwrights Horizons. The cover of its program emphasizes the play's content. For the Plymouth Theatre production on Broadway, however, the program cover emphasizes the "star" quality of the leading performer, Joan Allen. A different audience is clearly being targeted.

Box-office managers are responsible for ticket sales and are accountable for revenue taken in at the box office. They keep daily statements so that the producers can closely monitor the amount of money earned—or lost—on a production.

Business managers, who are generally found in the nonprofit theatre, are responsible for the actual money flow. Either they keep the accounts themselves or they supervise bookkeepers, depending on the size of the organization.

Production managers, also found in the nonprofit theatre, are responsible for scheduling and funds connected to the production itself—for rehearsals, scenery, costumes, lighting, technical rehearsals—excluding advertising and audience development.

Audience Development

As we saw earlier in this chapter, a producer is responsible for finding an audience, a task that is becoming more and more difficult. Ticket prices have skyrocketed and people have gotten out of the habit of going to the theatre. If it is to draw an audience at all, a theatre needs to spend a great deal of money simply to entice people away from their homes and video recorders. As the need to draw an audience increases, the organization of theatres is weighted more and more heavily toward management, development, and marketing, sometimes at the expense of artistic concerns (Figure 8.6).

Often a large proportion of the production budget goes to advertising. The commercial production hires a *press agent,* on a show-by-show basis, who is responsible for publicizing the production. The press agent consults with the artistic team as well as with the producer to better promote the production.

Most not-for-profit theatres go beyond the traditional advertising relied upon by commercial theatrical enterprises in an attempt to build an audience for individual productions and entire seasons. "Talk backs" are scheduled after performances to involve the audience in the process of theatre; volunteer organizations help sell subscriptions and build audience support; creative marketing efforts like discounted tickets and special guest speakers are employed to attract those who have never attended a production at a particular theatre. The theatre goes to the audience as well, touring schools, hospitals, and community centers.

House managers are present in every theatre in the country, even if only informally, and are responsible for the well-being of the audience in the theatre. They welcome the audience, supervise ushers, and maintain a clean, safe, and pleasant atmosphere; this is important not only for a particular performance, but for future attendance as well. House managers also note the general physical condition of the theatre and cope with ticket discrepancies and emergencies during performance.

From the time of the ancient Greeks, producers have funded the production of plays. Historically, they have been important and wealthy members of the community, and they have had a tremendous impact on what was produced and what was not, what was popular, and what has remained with us as valuable dramatic literature. (What would have happened to Shakespeare's work if it had never been produced?) The range of producers in this country has grown. We now have commercial producers working alongside not-for-profit artistic and managing directors, developing productions in resident theatres that travel to Broadway. The late Joseph Papp, founder of the New York Shakespeare Festival, became a producer hybrid by developing productions such as *A Chorus Line* in his off-Broadway, not-for-profit theatre and then remounting them on Broadway, where they helped support the work of many playwrights back at the Festival.

Suggested Readings

Stephen Langley, *Theatre Management and Production in America: Producing for the Commercial, Stock, Resident, College and Community Theatre* (New York: Drama Book Specialists), 1980.

—*Producers on Producing* (New York: Drama Book Specialists), 1976.

Todd London, *The Artistic Home: Discussions with Artistic Directors of America's Institutional Theaters* (New York: Theater Communications Group), 1988.

Chapter NINE

Rehearsing the Production

Rehearsals are the period in which the point of view and production concept are transformed from idea into reality through the work of actors, director, and designers. This transformation gradually takes shape as choice after choice is made and discarded, until the production coheres. Rehearsals are of several types:

- Acting rehearsals
- Technical rehearsals
- Dress rehearsals
- Preview performances.

Once the producer has found and optioned the play, located a theatre to put it in, and hired the director, designers, actors, stage managers, and some of the technical staff, the rehearsal period can begin. The length of this period depends upon the economic circumstances of the production, among other factors.

An average rehearsal period in the professional theatre in the United States is from three to four weeks. A work week in the professional theatre is six days long; work days are usually eight hours long. Many theatre artists find this insufficient. Legend has it that Bertolt Brecht once rehearsed a play for nearly a year and then decided to start over again because everything was wrong! In today's economic climate, that kind of luxury is normally out of the question. Occasionally, grants will allow a theatre company to develop a work over a long period of time, but productions are generally forced to keep to a basic four-week schedule. Most commercial and some nonprofit productions add preview performances to provide some extra rehearsal time before opening the production to the critics.

Each type of rehearsal serves a part of the transformation process. Acting rehearsals allow actors and directors to establish the intentions of the play relative to the production point of view, and then to stage it for that purpose. Technical rehearsals facilitate the creation of the onstage visual world of the production by scenic and lighting designers, stage managers, and technicians. Dress rehearsals do the same for the costume designer. Preview performances allow everyone involved with the production, including the producer, to look at everything in concert and make adjustments accordingly. Previews also offer the invaluable input of audience reaction.

Pre-Production

Pre-production refers to the period of work on a production, apart from rehearsals, before it enters the actual theatre. Many activities take place during this time that affect the final production. In addition to the designer's pre-production work examined in Chapters 5 through 7, stage managers, scene shops, costume shops, and lighting shops are very busy as well.

Some of the people responsible for the following pre-production tasks were introduced in earlier chapters, and some were not.

- Scenery and properties are built in the scene shop by the head carpenter or technical director and prop master, or under their supervision. Scenery is painted by either the designer or a scenic artist (see Chapter 5).
- Additional properties are purchased or rented under the supervision of the prop master.
- Costumes are constructed by costume shop personnel or rented by the designer from a costume rental house (see Chapter 6). Costume fittings are supervised by the costume designer and the head of the costume shop.
- Wigs are constructed by a wigmaster or are purchased.

- Lights are prepared in the shop by the head or master electrician.
- Theatres are evaluated in terms of such considerations as dressing rooms, access to the stage, power supply for lighting and sound, backstage space, distance between audience and stage, and lobby and lobby displays.

All of these, as well as the design and distribution of publicity and the sale of tickets, are overseen by the production managers, general managers, and producers.

Some theatrical unions have contracts with scenic and lighting shops. Contracting with a union shop for a production can greatly increase costs. Hourly wages are considerably higher for union shop personnel, and in union shops, designers are not allowed to execute any of the work themselves. A producer usually contracts with a union shop when there is no other workable choice. For example, in certain areas such as Broadway, union shops have sole jurisdiction; in other locations, unions have agreements—some of very long standing—with the resident theatres. The majority of theatres in this country, however, work with nonunion shops. Usually, the staff members who oversee work in the shops are also responsible for it inside the theatre.

Rehearsal Halls and Spaces

In many countries, rehearsals take place in the theatre, with the actual set and lighting. To accommodate this, scenery is constructed and lighting set up prior to the beginning of rehearsals. Sometimes costumes are used as well. In the United States, it is much too costly to rent a theatre for such an extended period of time (before ticket sale revenue has been received), so a rehearsal hall is necessary.

There are many kinds of rehearsal halls, some of the drafty and romantic sort still in existence in New York, some very elaborate, with every modern convenience including microwave ovens. Rehearsal halls for dancers must be large, and they must come equipped with mirrors and a piano. Many not-for-profit theatre complexes have several of their own rehearsal halls; most commercial productions rent rehearsal spaces by the week.

In the rehearsal hall, the ground plan of the set is indicated by tape marks on the floor. Rehearsal furniture of roughly the size and shape of what will be used in performance is placed on this ground plan. If period dresses are to be used in performance, rehearsal skirts are provided, sometimes with corsets or shoes that might pose a particular difficulty for the actor or actress. Small properties are also present in one form or another, but usually not the actual ones that will be used in performance.

Actors rehearsing in a rehearsal hall. Note that one actor wears a hat and scarf, which are part of the actual costume. Because these costume elements might get in the way of certain actions, the actor needs to rehearse wearing them. On the floor the ground plan of the setting is indicated with tape.

Choreographer Bob Fosse rehearses a dancer, who works in rehearsal clothes. Once again, one costume element—the hat—is utilized in rehearsal. It appears to be an important aspect of the choreography.

The Stage Manager

The stage manager is responsible for the overall organization of everything that pertains to rehearsal and performance, including making sure that everything needed for the performance is where it should be at all times. Most professional productions have more than one stage manager. A Broadway production can have a production stage manager (who is responsible for the overall show) and several assistant stage managers. One assistant will be responsible for "calling" the show—telling actors, stagehands, dressers, etc. exactly what is to happen and when—and another will supervise property and/or scene changes backstage. Stage managers in not-for-profit, university, and community theatre function in the same way; the requirements for making a show run are essentially the same everywhere. The differences lie in the nature of the specific responsibilities delegated to each stage manager and the number of stage managers working on the production.

One or all of the stage managers are present at all the rehearsals in the rehearsal hall, at all the technical and dress rehearsals, and, like the actors, at all the performances. Stage managers "run" performances as well as rehearsals, but in the rehearsal hall the stage manager is guided by the desires of the director.

Once the production has been cast, the stage manager's first task is to set rehearsal and production schedules. Rehearsal schedules are set with the director, but the stage manager is expected to make constructive suggestions about how to get the most work done in the prescribed hours.

In the rehearsal hall, the stage manager records the blocking in a specially configured copy of the play called the stage manager's *prompt book* (or simply, *book*). During rehearsals, actors sometime forget new blocking or execute old blocking instead. Using the official record in the prompt book, the stage manager can put everyone back on track. (Assistant stage managers usually stay "on book" during rehearsals to help the actors with their lines when they are first learning them.)

In rehearsal, the stage manager also takes notes from the director for the designers and technicians about any matter that pertains to the production. In an average rehearsal, props, sound, even lighting requirements change daily. As liaison between director, actors, designers, shops, and producer, the stage manager is responsible for expeditiously communicating all changes to each department head. As a stand-in for the director after the production has opened, the stage manager in the professional theatre can inform actors of any changes in their performance since rehearsals. The stage manager is also usually responsible for rehearsing replacement cast members.

To carry out these many and difficult responsibilities, stage managers write daily notes on rehearsals and performances that are distributed to all

Interview

ROY HARRIS, STAGE MANAGER FOR THE HEIDI CHRONICLES AT PLAYWRIGHTS HORIZONS AND ON BROADWAY, ON HIS PROFESSION.

I started my career as an actor and singer/dancer. After several years, I realized that I wasn't particularly good at it. I was okay, but didn't want to end up at the age of 50 or 60 disappointed, as an "unexpressed" person.

By accident I got a chance to be an assistant stage manager and discovered that I liked it. But shortly after that I left the business for nine years. I had a small child, and life was too complicated at that time for me to continue in the theatre. . . . None of the work I was doing really satisfied me. I found that I had to go back to the theatre.

In 1983 I came back to work as a stage manager. It was a slow process. I stage managed only three productions in the first year and a half. By 1985, I was lucky enough to work very consistently. A lot of that work has been off-Broadway.

When I first worked at Playwrights Horizons (it was then under the artistic leadership of André Bishop), I felt that I was in a great place. I loved what they stood for. Even if the play wasn't great, I knew that the production would be good. . . . From late 1986 through the end of 1989, when *The Heidi Chronicles* moved to Broadway, Playwrights Horizons was always home.

One of the most important things for any stage manager is the dissemination of information. The forms this information takes are contact sheets, rehearsal schedules, performance schedules (more often in not-for-profit situations), rehearsal reports, and performance reports. It is important that everybody know what is going on.

Rehearsal reports, for instance, record what takes place daily in rehearsal: what scenes were worked on, how the play is going, problems that are surfacing. Production notes in a rehearsal report tell what physical changes might have taken place that will affect the designers. Let's say, for example, a decision has been made in rehearsal that the costume of the woman in the first act has to be blue. All of the designers must know this, not just the costume designer. Is the set green, and how would that look with this new blue costume? How does this affect the lighting? If something is really important, I will call those involved in addition to providing the information in a written report.

As a stage manager, if you don't transfer information well, someone will miss something important. I learned this having made quite a few mistakes. If someone comes in and says, "Where is that prop?" and it has been out of the show for two weeks, the stage manager has not done the job properly, and has created unnecessary work for someone.

Stage management involves a lot of paperwork; I enjoy that. How you give out information is very important. I have developed a form for these reports over a period of years. Sometimes a stage manager is like a clerk!

The most important thing a stage manager does is deal with people. Any person of reasonable intelligence can call a show, but a good stage manager must deal with people, must anticipate what each actor needs, and must keep human relations as good as possible. Where I made the most mistakes when I was starting out—because it is the hardest area—was in working with stars or with people who think they are stars. If you make a mistake with an actor early on, it takes a long time to rectify it. You must take eccentricities into account whenever you work with anyone. You must approach each actor from the point of view of his or her needs.

For example, cast changes for *The Heidi Chronicles* involved a lot of work. The show was technically very involved. We spent a long time with all the backstage activity. After the first two companies that Dan [Sullivan] directed, an assistant director did the work on acting, and I taught the actors everything that happened backstage that intimately concerned them. By doing this, I learned how an acting moment might have to be shifted because of some technical need. This was very interesting to deal with.

In my current project [*The Sisters Rosenzweig*, also by Wendy Wasserstein], I had to put a new actor into a role. As I rehearsed the other actors with the new one, I had to do a balancing act: I had to let the new actor find her own way in, but she had to do so knowing that some moments were already working well. Usually two or three actors leave and are replaced at once. Putting in one was very odd. It took several weeks of performances before the show settled down.

I read *The Heidi Chronicles* over Thanksgiving weekend in 1987, a year before it went into rehearsal. I went in the following Monday and said to André Bishop, "Please consider me as first choice to stage manage this." They did. I was lucky. I met with Dan Sullivan, the director, we got along, and that is how it happened. The play dealt very honestly with the last 20 years of our lives. I wanted to do it because I liked it—not because I thought it was going to be a hit. It was a huge show for Playwrights Horizons. It nearly killed us. There was very little room backstage to store scenery not being used onstage. When it moved to Broadway, the show got even bigger. The chief difference was that on Broadway there was more room and it was mechanized and the mechanics were mostly computerized. At Playwrights it was entirely manual: one of my crew members had to crawl under the stage and push stairs out for actors to make an entrance from the house. He had to wait under the stage until the scene was over and pull the stairs back in. I felt so badly for him.

There weren't a lot of changes, other than the mechanics when we moved to Broadway. They cut about three minutes out of the last scene. The production got physically more beautiful and more efficient. It was a harder and more interesting production to call on Broadway. For instance, in the transition from scene 1 to scene 2, there were 16 cues in 11 seconds.

We did the technical rehearsals for *Heidi* on Broadway in four days—not very much time for such a huge show. For the first performance, I got to the stage manager's desk and discovered that my hands were shaking. I had to hold on to the desk. We had "teched" the show so fast that I didn't really know what the cues did yet; I knew where they went but not exactly what they did. I was worried that if something went wrong, I wouldn't know how to fix it! Pretty soon I learned what all the cues did, and I had a really good crew. When the scenery didn't move properly they took care of it.

A stage manager is responsible for maintaining the show after it opens, looking at the show as much as possible with the director's eyes. For example, if a scene doesn't look good, and it continues that way for several performances, I must convey that to the director and discuss how to deal with it. More of the burden falls on the stage manager when the director is not in town; when the director is in town, he or she will visit a show that is running perhaps twice a month and give notes to the actors.

departments. This provides everyone with information about any changes; even if a change does not appear at the time to affect another department, it may in the future (Figure 9.1).

Acting Rehearsals

Preparation

Most directors prepare some kind of notes for rehearsal. Some are as detailed as Stanislavski's prompt script for *The Seagull* that we saw in Chapter 3. Others, like Harold Clurman's "score," leave some questions open,

Figure 9.1
Production
notes from the
Playwrights
Horizons pro-
duction of *The
Heidi Chroni-
cles.*

THE HEIDI CHRONICLES

PRODUCTION NOTES #13
Monday, November 7, 1988

Props
NOTE: At the moment, we are NOT using a table in the
   Art
   Institute Rain Extravaganza. Only 2 folding chairs,
   one (1) picket sign, a clipboard, and a piece of
   plastic which will cover the two chairs and the
   picket sign. So you don't need to look for another
   table. HOWEVER, we will need two (2) more folding
   chairs that actresses bring on in this scene—can't
   use the ones from rap group as there's not time to
   strike them, since one scene follows the other.
   Clear? If not, see me.

We'd like a strap on Peter Patrone's umbrella so it can
   easily hang on back of chair.

What are the Pierre chairs like? How hefty? At the moment, Scoop is pulling the one from SR over to stage
   left to talk to Heidi. Is this gracefully possible?
   Are there arms on the chair?

Actors would like to use the green stuffed frog that
   we've got in rehearsal for the pediatric scene.
   Okay?

We'd like to be able to put the final box of books under the little child's table that's on the slide in
   pediatric unit. Is this possible? (Peter does this
   in the scene—he moves them from downstage left.)

(continued)

such as how the play will actually look onstage. Saxe Meiningen's drawing for the banquet scene in his production of *Macbeth* (Figure 9.2) shows another method of planning.

Max Reinhardt's *Regiebuches* were probably the most detailed prompt books in the recorded history of directing. In them he worked out, and wrote down, every detail of an upcoming production. Reinhardt's planning was concise and took everything into account, including facial expression,

***Figure 9.1,
continued***

In one of the boxes of Heidi's things, we need a skirt
    and blouse, perhaps a blanket, so that there's some
    soft fabric on top. Clear?
                        THE HEIDI CHRONICLES

PRODUCTION NOTES #13 (continued)

CARL, Tom Lynch says the one step unit will work, as
    the fire department rule is there must be four feet
    of clearance from the <u>back</u> of the chair. According
    to our semi-exact measurement, there's at least 4-
    1/2 feet from back of chair in first row.

<u>Sound</u>
We'd like to replace "Shake Your Booties," in the wed-
    ding scene (I,5) with "Get Up and Boogie."

Dan would like to use the one famous song (no one can
    remember its name) by Buffalo Springfield as the
    middle music in McCarthy Mixer (I,2). Other possi-
    bilities didn't work out.

<u>Slides</u>
In the second Prologue, we have now cut the second
    paragraph—the part involving Heidi's father—which
    means that we cut all the back and forth looking for
    the correct slide. Is this useful to know, Mr. M?
Dan asks, what is the progress on finding the <u>color</u>
    slide version of the Clara Peters self-portrait?

<u>Carl</u>
It may be necessary to have someone come in to work
    with Boyd and Joan on their fist fight in I,4—at the
    Art Institute. It needs to look really real, and Dan
    is concerned that no one get hurt. Boyd expressed

vocal intonation, physical position, emotion, the reactions of the other actors, all the stage decor (which he usually drew as well), costume descriptions, all the stage movement, lighting and lighting changes, music, and
how one scene changed into another.

One of Reinhardt's most noteworthy productions, *The Miracle* (a word-
less play with a musical score), was produced at the Century Theater in
New York in 1924 (Figure 9.3). The prompt book was complete down to the

Figure 9.2
The Duke of Saxe-Meiningen's drawing for the banquet scene from *Macbeth*.

last detail. Presumably, his descriptions reflect the way he worked with actors in rehearsals, and were very close to the final performance. The following are sample entries:

7. In the background a richly carved altar, with a golden shrine and candles seen through a grilled screen.
8. The eternal lamp burns before it.
9. A Cardinal's hat hangs above.
10. Altar, with table, to divide and open, with steps through it.
11. The floor is of large gray stones, some of which are tomb stones. In the center of the floor the stones are to be glass with lamps below, so wired as to spread the light from the middle outwards.
12. Flickering light from behind columns as from invisible candles throws fantastic shadows.
13. Shafts of sunlight, coming through the high windows at the right, projects patterns on the floor.
14. At left and right of auditorium, cloisters with vaulted ceilings and stone floors.
15. Chandeliers of various sizes in the auditorium to cast light downwards only, adding depth and mystery to the ceiling.
16. Several poles for flags and lanterns fastened to the seat ends in aisles of auditorium.
17. Panelling of balcony rail to show here and there between flags.
18. A clock above pulpit. This clock is to strike at various times during the dream parts, to suggest the existence of the church. Remember the sound before the clock strikes.

19. On top of the clock two figures to mark the hours, by striking a large bell between them. One of these figures symbolizes life; the other death.

20. Clerestory windows around upper part of auditorium. Choir stands and triforium openings below windows.

21. All doors have heavy bolts, locks and knockers to create business and noise.

22. Large keys on rings for various doors.

23. The doors immediately behind proscenium lead to sacristy.

24. The doors below the lodges lead to exterior.

25. Small midnight mass bell, near top of tower, to be rung from rope on stage floor.

26. Wind machines, thunder drums and voices also to be there.

27. When audience takes their seats, everything is dark.

28. The sound of a storm far away.

29. Soft candle-light in the auditorium, only where it is absolutely necessary, and flickering behind the columns around the altar screen.

30. Clusters of candle-lights in distant places in the auditorium and stage, high up in the tower to produce an effect of tremendous size and of incredible distance.

Figure 9.3
Setting by Norman Bel Geddes for the 1924 production of *The Miracle* at the Century Theater in New York City.

31. There are to be candles around the altar screen and on the altar itself. The candles should be of various lengths and the bulbs of very low voltage and of various pale colors.

32. In chapels tiny candles suggest side-altars against darkness. Prominent clusters of them unsymmetrically chosen. Flickering candles on the columns in the apse and cloisters throwing shadows.

Reinhardt took this notion to extremes, but any good director recognizes time limits and knows that advance planning will help in reaching the goals of a production. How that planning takes place varies both in its form on paper and in its implementation in the rehearsal hall.

Early Rehearsals

Early rehearsals are trying and exciting times for the actors and director. There are as many ways to investigate a play and its characters as there are actors, acting teachers, directors, and directing teachers.

The first rehearsal for the entire company (actors, director, and sometimes designers) is usually a *read-through* of the play from beginning to end by all the actors who have been cast. There are many other ways to begin the process, but the read-through is most common. Scene rehearsals and blocking, or staging, rehearsals follow the read-through.

Scene rehearsals allow the actors, along with the director, to explore the text of the play and further develop—then realize—the production concept through the acting. There are many ways to begin this process.

SCENE REHEARSALS   *Improvisation* is a technique through which actors can substitute their own words and actions for the words of the playwright, translating the latter into their own language. This helps some actors to gain a better, more personal understanding of the material. How might an actor improvise, through words or action, the opening scene of *A Streetcar Named Desire* from Blanche's entrance to Stella's return? How would you deliver Lady Macbeth's letter soliloquy in your own words?

Some actors and directors spend less preparatory time than others away from the actual words of the play, getting directly to work on the play as written. As we saw in the chapter on acting, a technique such as Stanislavski's guides the actor and director through the play moment by moment, through the use of intentions, objectives, affective memory, the given circumstances, and so on. These concepts provide the bedrock for most *scene work*—the process of investigating each moment of the play and creating a stage life for it.

We have noted how checklists or production notes are created by everyone involved in a production, and we have asked many questions about sections of dialogue in the five plays we have considered. These sorts of questions and their answers are often used as a springboard in scene rehearsals.

BLOCKING OR STAGING REHEARSALS   Some performances, like those of the *commedia dell'arte*, are improvised, but unless they are defined as such from the start, "set," or predetermined, staging is usually employed. Blocking requires rehearsal; the actors rely on each other to repeat the exact blocking every time. What would happen, for example, if Tesman neglected to close the curtain to shut out the light Hedda objected to? If Blanche, with the broken bottle in her hand, moved toward Stanley instead of away from him? Or if an actor in a duel slashed instead of parried? The consequences of missed blocking can sometimes be dangerous, and are almost always confusing.

There is rarely a single, set time for blocking a play. In early rehearsals, actors may move freely around the rehearsal ground plan, trying different staging ideas. The director is usually responsible for staging the production, but how rigidly this is adhered to, as we have seen, is a matter of personal preference. Generally, actors, the director, and sometimes the designers refine the staging as rehearsals progress. Because staging is so intimately connected with meaning, the choices will depend upon, and in turn influence, other production elements.

When Stella returns to find Blanche in her kitchen, many blocking alternatives are possible. If, for example, the kitchen has a table and four chairs, a small refrigerator and stove, and perhaps some counter space, the following options are only a few of those available:

BLANCHE: I've got to keep hold of myself!
   1) Blanche is seated again at the kitchen table.
   2) Blanche is still washing out the glass she used for whiskey, and is standing at the sink.
   3) Blanche is standing, looking out the door.

STELLA: Blanche!
   1) Stella calls out from outside before she enters.
   2) Stella sees Blanche first, says her name, then moves to her.
   3) Stella doesn't move toward Blanche at all.

BLANCHE: Stella, oh, Stella, Stella! Stella for Star!
   1) Blanche stays where she is, staring at her sister.
   2) Blanche moves to embrace Stella.
   3) Stella moves to embrace Blanche.

How do these different alternatives affect the meaning of the scene? How does the blocking do this? In the second group, the three options create three very different meanings for the audience. First, let us look at how these variations convey the relationship between Blanche and Stella.

1) If Stella calls from outside, it will appear that she is excited about Blanche's arrival and can't wait until she actually sees her to call out to her.

2) If Stella sees Blanche as she enters, says her name, and then moves toward her, it will seem that, while excited, Stella is approaching her sister with a sense of awe, or perhaps dismay that Blanche has arrived early.

3) If Stella doesn't move toward Blanche at all, we will assume that something is not quite right about their relationship, that Stella is truly upset about this early arrival, or that she is so surprised that she can't move.

Blocking can also establish focus onstage. In each of these three examples, the audience must be able to see Stella's response to Blanche's early arrival—they will already have seen Blanche's response to the situation—while simultaneously witnessing the change in Blanche as Stella actually appears. If the first option in each of the three groups is chosen, Stella will presumably move quickly, giving Blanche little time to adjust to her new circumstances. Blanche's adjustment will be the focus of this staging. With the second option in each group, the audience is given time to focus on both Stella and Blanche in an equal way; the sisters could easily be facing each other. With the third option, the audience will be required to focus on Blanche's response to her sister's apparent lack of response. Stella could even have her back to the audience and still maintain this focus.

How might you recombine these options to create a different focus based on the changes in relationship that would result? There are many ways to stage this scene, each of which would mean something different, if only slightly so. Nuances of performance grow out of the blocking rehearsal as well as the scene rehearsal. Usually, these rehearsals are combined in some way and together grow toward performance.

Rehearsing a Musical

Each part of a musical requires different rehearsal techniques. The actors are sometimes given "sides," which show only those sections of the musical in which they appear, along with enough of what comes before and after to help them place their part in context. This fairly antiquated process can create problems for the performer, who might consider only a tiny section of the musical without regard to the whole.

Chorus rehearsals are for singers and dancers; *book rehearsals* are for members of the company who have lines of dialogue. The lead performers in a musical usually have responsibilities in each area: speaking, singing, and dancing are all part of their roles.

The Run-through

At any point fairly well on in the rehearsal process, the director and actors can decide to *run through* the entire play. Sometimes they do this to gauge what is "working" and what is not. After the stops and starts of rehearsals, the actors finally have a chance to connect all the small moments they have been working on and to see how their characters develop throughout the course of the complete play. Run-throughs help set the appropriate rhythm and pace of a show. If a run-through occurs early enough in the rehearsal process, many adjustments can be made to communicate the point of view to the audience. Some run-throughs are not open to other members of the production staff and some are.

Immediately before the production moves into the theatre from the rehearsal hall, most productions schedule a run-through for the designers and technicians. Lighting designers watch and take notes on the blocking, on the emotional tone of a scene, on what lighting might be best where, on points in the play where characters turn lights on or off, and so on. Scenic designers watch for adjustments to the ground plan, for additions and changes in properties, and for information about scene changes. Costume designers look for staging that might be affected by costume (sitting in a late-nineteenth-century corset is different than sitting in a pair of blue jeans) and for quick changes. Wardrobe personnel, stagehands, and electricians come to run-throughs to plan how they will execute their responsibilities during the performance itself.

Rehearsals in the Theatre

Technical Rehearsals

Technical rehearsals exist for the purpose of setting, refining, and practicing everything that happens on stage in the production. A technical rehearsal allows the actors to become accustomed to the physical realities of the production in the theatre, and the designers, stage managers, and stagehands to work out how each event—onstage and off—will be accomplished, and by whom.

Many kinds of activities take place during technical rehearsals, including placing furniture and properties, the final working out of where scenery not in use will be stored, and determining how all light, scenery, sound, and other changes will be accomplished. The technical rehearsal is a slow, stop-and-go procedure. Any technical change needs to be rehearsed over and over again until it is done smoothly, quickly, and correctly.

The signal to change something in the theatre is called a *cue*, which is also the word for the change itself. The stage manager is responsible for "calling" or "throwing" the cue for any one of a number of purposes. A cue can be thrown:

- For an actor to enter (usually through the use of a cue light backstage)
- For an actor to say the next line (cue lines are usually used in technical rehearsals, not in performance)
- For scenery to be moved up and down or offstage to permit a new setting to come on and the old to be taken off
- For lights to change
- For the orchestra to begin playing
- For a change in recorded sound effects or music
- For the audience lights (houselights) to come on or off.

Here are some hypothetical cues for the transition from act 1 to act 2 of *The Seagull:*

- Scenic cues would be needed to remove the stage on which Treplev's play is performed, along with benches, trees, whatever represents the lake, etc.; then, the scenery for act 2 would be brought on, each piece in turn.
- Lighting cues for this transition would proceed from an evening "cue" in act 1, to "black" (no lights on), or some other transitional lighting, to a hot, daylight "cue" in act 2.
- Sound cues, if there are any, might go from cricket or night-bird sounds, to an absence of sound or music, to the sounds of daytime birds.

Technical rehearsals require a great deal of patience, particularly from the actors, who must repeat lines and actions connected to the cues many times over.

Dress Rehearsals

One of the main purposes of dress rehearsals, which are usually combined with or immediately follow the technical rehearsals, is to introduce costumes into the production. The *first dress rehearsal* is generally a long and complicated affair. This is the first time the actors have all the pieces of their costumes together during a performance. Learning to move in a costume and to integrate that knowledge with everything one has learned in rehearsals up to this point is time consuming, and a good actor will devote a lot of energy to the process.

During this period, costumes are reviewed by the costume designer, by the actors wearing the costumes, and by the director. Changes are made to

An important aspect of the dress rehearsal is the application of make-up by the actor or by a make-up artist. Here an actress applies elaborate make-up, which ages and distorts her face. Putting on make-up requires great skill, and can sometimes take hours.

help communicate the point of view to the audience. Scenic and lighting designers also continue their work during these rehearsals, refining, adding, and subtracting from their designs in the same way.

The first few dress rehearsals are stop and go, combining aspects of technical rehearsals with run-throughs of the play. Actors, technicians, wardrobe, and stage management people stop when they need to iron out a problem. The *final dress rehearsal* is almost always a run-through without unscheduled stops. This allows those involved to work through a problem, if one arises, as they would in the actual performance (which would be stopped only in the event of a life-threatening accident).

If there are costume changes in the production, they will be divided into average and quick changes. A *quick change,* as we saw in Chapter 6, is a change of costume that must take place in a very short period of time, sometimes in less than a minute. Costumes will be "rigged" in ingenious ways to facilitate this. Wardrobe people meticulously organize the costumes so that the change can be as rapid as possible. In some musicals, characters exit one side of the stage and enter on the other side, in a new costume, with lightning speed. In *The Heidi Chronicles,* actors move from one era to another from one scene to the next. At the end of one scene, Heidi wishes Peter a Merry Christmas; when the lights come up on the next scene, Heidi is seated onstage two years later on a warm afternoon.

Orchestra Rehearsal

One other form of rehearsal is the *orchestra rehearsal* for a musical. Because of the extremely high cost of every hour with an orchestra, technical rehearsals for a musical—like most other rehearsals—take place only with piano accompaniment. Once the orchestra is brought in, all attention focuses on ironing out problems within the orchestra and between the orchestra and singers. All other problems, except the most serious, have to wait for another time.

Scheduling Rehearsals

Acting Rehearsals

Acting rehearsal schedules show the daily layout of rehearsal hours, not what takes place during those hours (Figure 9.4). A stage manager, in consultation with the director, is responsible for scheduling what actually gets rehearsed on a given day.

Let us say that a production of *A Streetcar Named Desire* is in rehearsal, and the director wants to rehearse scene 1 of the play on a certain day. The stage manager must efficiently organize everyone's time so that no actors are left idle for long periods. This is the way the scene breaks down:

1) The scene opens with Eunice and another woman onstage. Stanley and Mitch come on, and Stanley hollers for Stella. Stella comes out to greet them and get the package. Stanley and Mitch leave. Stella follows. Blanche enters. Blanche and Eunice enter the house. Eunice goes to find Stella at the bowling alley, leaving Blanche alone. Stella comes back and joins Blanche.

2) After Stella and Blanche greet and discuss the condition of Stella's house and where Blanche is to sleep, Stanley and Stanley's friends, how much Stella loves Stanley, and the loss of their family estate, Stanley, Steve, and Mitch arrive outside the house.

3) Steve and Eunice yell at each other. Stanley enters the house and meets Blanche. They have a short scene together.

Each of these sections and subsections utilizes different actors and actresses. The actress playing Eunice, for example, is present at the beginning and end of the scene only. Stanley has a brief scene at the beginning and a slightly longer one at the end.

Figure 9.4
Acting rehearsal
schedule for the
Playwrights
Horizons pro-
duction of *The
Heidi Chroni-
cles*. Note that
the stage man-
ager calls the ac-
tor to rehearsal
only when
needed.

```
THE HEIDI CHRONICLES                 Mainstage 1988
REHEARSAL SCHEDULE

Wednesday, October 26, 1988
11:00-12:00     Monologues, etc.    Joan Allen
12:00-2:00      Act I, scene 2      Add Peter Friedman
                "McCarthy"
2:00-3:00       BREAK
3:00-5:00       Act II, scene 1     Joan, Ellen, Joanne,
                "Shower Scene"      Anne, Sarah Jessica
5:00-6:00       Act II, scene 3     Joan, Ellen
                "Restaurant"
6:00-7:00       " "                 Add Sarah Jessica
7:00            BREAK
***************************************************
****

Thursday, October 27, 1988
10:00-11:30     Act I, scene 4      Joan, Boyd, Joanne,
                Art Institute       Anne, Sarah Jessica
11:30-1:00      Act II, scene 2     Joan, Boyd, Peter,
                "Hello, N.Y."       Joanne, Vince, Sarah
J.
1:00-3:00       Act II, scene 5     Joan, Boyd, Vince
                "Pediatric Ward"
3:00-4:00       BREAK
4:00-5:00       Monologues, etc.    Joan
5:00-6:00       Act II, scene 6     Add Peter Friedman
```

The stage manager must decide approximately how much time will be
devoted to each section and must *call* the actors for rehearsal accordingly.
In this scene, it is likely that the longest period will be devoted to rehearsing the scene between Blanche and Stella. The stage manager might suggest
to the director that the beginning and end of the scene be rehearsed together since they employ the same actors.

Scheduling Technical Rehearsals

The stage manager is also responsible for scheduling hours during technical and dress rehearsals with the director, designers, general manager, or production manager. A typical technical rehearsal might be broken down as follows: "Scenes 1, 2 from 12–5 P.M., Scenes 3, 4 from 7 P.M.–12 A.M."

Again, the stage manager must set priorities within that period, or all the necessary work will not get done. For a production of *A Streetcar Named Desire,* that production schedule would need to take into consideration and schedule the following:

- Playing of taped pre-show music
- Timing and coordination of

  Darkening of audience lights (houselights out)

  Music for opening

  Actor's entrance upstage of curtain (or, if there is no curtain, in the dark)

  Curtain rising

  Lights up on beginning of scene 1

  Cue for Stanley and Mitch to make their entrance

  Adjustment of music so that actors' voices can be heard

  Cue for Blanche

  Cue for Stella to return when Blanche is in the correct position onstage

  Any incidental music or sound cues (street noises, more music, etc.)

  Cue for Stanley, Mitch, Steve, and Eunice

  Transition out of scene 1

Timing and coordinating these elements so that they work effectively together takes repetition, concentration, and a lot of time. For example, the first six items could easily take an hour or longer to time and properly rehearse.

The preceding examples are typical rehearsal schedules and, like everything else in the theatre, would be subject to change. Maximum acting rehearsal hours on Broadway and in regional theatres are broadly set by Actors' Equity, and the rules are strictly adhered to. Broadway technical and dress rehearsal hours are set by Equity, the musicians' union, and IATSE. In university and other nonprofessional theatres, individuals, rather than collective bargaining, determine time commitment and availability (Figure 9.5). This can present problems if, for instance, an overzealous director schedules too many hours of rehearsal when students have other academic commitments.

What takes place during rehearsals is always up to the company involved, and hopefully serves the needs of each individual.

Tentative PRODUCTION CALENDAR
February 5-March 11, 1989

January 17, 1989
THE HEIDI CHRONICLES

SUN	MON	TUES	WED	THURS	FRI	SAT
Feb 5	6 ELECTRICS SHOP SPOTTING prior	7 ORDER IN by January 27 to February 10	8	9	10 Pre-hang Elex	11
Feb 12	13 HOLIDAY	14 Hang Elex Install deck Sound & Projs Load in	15 Hang Elex Install Deck Company reh 12:00-5:00	16 Hang Elex Install Deck Company reh 12:00-5:00	17 Rest of Set Load in Company reh 12:00-5:00	18 Load-in, as needed
Feb 19 Load-in, as needed	20 HOLIDAY	21 Continue Load-in	22 Lites focus	23 Lites focus DRY TECH 7:00	24 DRY TECH 1:00-6:00 6:00-7:00 Break 7:00-Continue	25 DRY TECH* 1:00-6:00 7:00-Half-hour 7:30-12:00 DRESS/TECH
Feb 26 1:00-half/hour 1:30-6 TECH/ DRESS 6-7:30 Break 7:30-half/hour 8:00-12:00 T/D	27 1:00-half/hour 1:30-6 TECH/ DRESS 6-7:30 Break 7:30-half/hour 8:00-12:00 T/D	28 1:00-half/hour 1:30-6:00 T/D 6-7:30 Break 7:30-half/hour 8:00-12:00 T/D	March 1 1-6:00-reh,TBA 6-7:30 Break 7:30-half/hour 8:00-Preview 1	2 1-6:00-reh,TBA 6-7:30 Break 7:30-half/hour 8:00-Preview 2	3 1-6:00-reh,TBA 6-7:30 Break 7:30-half/hour 8:00-Preview 3	4 1:30-half/hour 2:00-preview 4 7:30-half/hour 8:00-preview 5
March 5 2:30-half/hour 3:00-preview 6	6 EQUITY DAY OFF	7 1-6-reh, as needed 7:30-half/hour 8:00-preview 7	8 1:30-half/hour 2:00-preview 8 7:30-half/hour 8:00-preview 9	9 6:00-half/hour 6:30-OPENING!	10 7:30-half/hour 8:00-performance	11 1:30-half/hour 2:00-performance 7:30-half/hour 8:00-performance

* If we should finish Dry Tech on Friday night, actors will be called on
Saturday, 2/25, at 1:00 for half/hour for full dress/tech rehearsal.

Stagehands
rigging a piece of
scenery.

Changing Scenery

Many plays require more than one setting. For example, multiple settings are required to perform *The Seagull, Macbeth, The Heidi Chronicles,* and almost any musical. A significant part of the magic of theatre lies in the way the stage can quickly be transformed from one place into another.

Moving or Shifting Flat or Painted Scenery

The simplest way to change from one set to another is by *gripping*. A *grip* is a stagehand who, by pushing, dragging, pulling, fastening, or unfastening pieces of scenery, changes the look of the stage. Over the centuries, many techniques developed in both the construction and rigging of scenic pieces have made gripping a very effective method of shifting lightweight (flat and/or painted) scenery. An experienced stagehand can move very tall flats (upwards of 35 feet!) efficiently without the aid of machinery.

Figure 9.5, opposite
Production calendar for the Plymouth Theater (Broadway) production of *The Heidi Chronicles*. ELEX = lights; DECK = special floor applied to existing stage floor (for this production only) to allow for easy movement of wagons and other scenic units.

Figure 9.6
A section of the
Madison Square
Theatre in 1879,
showing the
counterweight
system.

Flying refers to moving scenery up out of view, into the fly space above the stage, and back down onto the stage when needed. Flying is usually associated with flat or painted pieces, such as full-stage backdrops, but it can also be used to move even a fully dimensioned box set. Historically, flying has been accomplished in a variety of intriguing ways. The Greek theatre had a cranelike device called a *mechane,* which was used to fly actors up and over scenery. In the Middle Ages, pulleys were installed on the roofs of buildings so that various pieces (such as angels) could be flown in and out.

The illustration in Figure 9.6 of the backstage of the Madison Square Theatre in New York in 1879 shows an arrangement, not unlike that found in many theatres today, that uses a counterweighted system (note the weights on the bottom) to move two entire settings up and down. The same principle is used on single, flat pieces of scenery.

Shutters or *movable wings,* the scenic elements most popular in the Renaissance, inspired much experimentation with ways of moving scenery. One of the more ingenious was a system developed by Giacomo Torelli (1608–1678) called the "chariot and pole" shifting mechanism (Figure 9.7). Slots in the stage floor allow a tall piece of scenery to pass through from below. Above stage-floor level, the audience sees painted wings (Figure 9.8), while under the stage the "chariots" that hold the scenery ride on tracks and are controlled by a pulley system. An entire stage full of wings could rapidly move in and out of position simultaneously.

A contemporary fly system works in the same manner as the one at the Madison Square Theatre (see Figure 9.6). Although theoretically a large number of stagehands could pull on ropes to raise and lower a piece of scenery, adding weight instead of people makes the process more efficient.

Figure 9.7
A diagram of Torelli's "chariot and pole" shifting mechanism.

Figure 9.8
A sketch for a setting by Torelli as it would appear to the audience.

A *stage trap* is an opening in the stage floor through which an actor—or a piece of scenery or a prop—can pass up onto or down off of the stage. The trap itself is only an opening, and other devices must be used to move a large piece of scenery up or down. Traps were used in Shakespeare's time to permit the entrance and exit of ghosts, among other things. *Elevators,* moved today by means of hydraulics (fluids under pressure), are often used to move scenery or actors up through a trap.

An elevator stage in use at Berlin's opera house, 1926. This particular stage is completely divided into elevators, making entrances from below possible from virtually anywhere on stage.

A sketch of the set for Professor Higgins's study from the 1976 revival of *My Fair Lady,* designed by Oliver Smith. The set was composed of a number of wagons that together formed what appears to be a single piece.

Another commonly used method of changing scenery is by *wagon,* a device that rolls slightly above stage level and can carry all (in the case of a full-stage wagon) or part of a set. Wagons were used as early as the Greek theatre.

A *revolve,* or turntable, is a device that holds the setting that the audience sees, and also one or more others backstage that are ready to revolve into view. Often the revolution occurs in full view of the audience, an impressive effect (Figure 9.9). (Sometimes this is elaborated with concentric rings of revolves around a center, which allow scenery or actors to pass each other moving in different directions.)

Another interesting, but less often used, means of shifting heavy scenery is by *treadmill,* a piece inserted into the stage floor that usually moves along a plane parallel to the audience and carries actors, scenery, or both past each other.

How each piece moves, when, and by whom are critical to the visual success of a production. Whatever means are used—and there are usually several methods working together in any *scene shift*—the scenic designer,

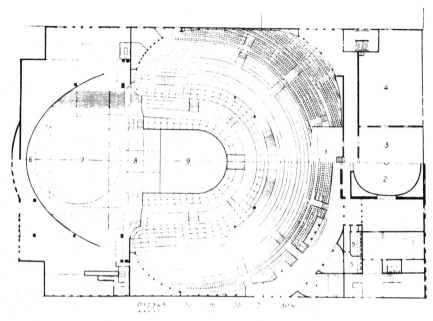

Figure 9.9
The plan for Max Reinhardt's Grosses Schauspielhaus. This huge theatre, seen here in plan view, used a full-stage revolve, which can be seen to the far left of the diagram.

These two settings for a production of the play *Noises Off* show the actors performing the play within the play (left) and their life backstage (right). The settings are on a revolve, or turntable, allowing one setting to "revolve" on as the other spins off.

The treadmill method of moving scenery, shown here in use in an 1889 production at New York's Union Square Theatre. The treadmill creates the illusion of a horse race without the horses.

technical director, and stage manager are responsible for putting together the *shift plan* or *shift plot* for a production. The shift plot for the original production of *The Heidi Chronicles* is shown in Figure 9.10.

Changing Lights and Sound

As we learned earlier in this chapter, a lighting picture onstage is called a lighting cue, but the cue contains both the actual level of each light and the time it takes to go from one picture—or cue—to another. This time or rate is referred to as the count, and is equivalent to a few seconds. Unlike scenery, stage lighting levels cannot be changed by mechanical means alone (except to a very limited extent, for instance, by placing an object directly in front of a light). Early scenery could be moved by clever mechanical contraptions like Torelli's chariot system, but early stage lighting such as candlelight or gaslight was not easily controlled. Stage lighting cannot be changed effectively without resorting to fairly complex, internal electrical means.

Figure 9.10
Two pages from
a sample shift
plot.

THE HEIDI CHRONICLES SHIFT PLOT—PLYMOUTH THEATRE
5/10/89

DECK	FLYS

ACT I PRESET—ONSTAGE:
    Podium ON—DR
    Trick Wall ON—UC

ACT I—Top of Show   **(#1)** Projection Screen IN

During Prologue:
    Folding chair ON—UR (slipstage)
    Trick Wall flips to basketball hoop DS/
    set 2 McCarthy posters US (1 man)

PROLOGUE to I-1 (Miss Crain's Dance)
                                (#2) DS Tabs OUT
(#1) DS slipstage to SR   Yellow Streamers IN (2 sets)
    (podium off SR/table on SL)   **(#3)** Projection Screen OUT
    Joan hand off jacket—UC   **(#3A)** DS Tabs IN

TRANSITION I-1 TO 1-2 (Miss Crain's Dance to McCarthy Mixer)
(#2) DS slipstage to SL   **(#4)** DS tabs OUT
    (punch table off SL/chips table on SR)   UR tab OUT
(#3) US slipstage to SL   Yellow Streamers OUT
    (garbage can on SL)   (2 sets)
                                   R/W/B Streamers IN (2 sets)

(Cue Lite #7)
    Trick wall—3 panels flip (3 men)   **(#5)** DS Tabs IN
    Joan add shawl—DL   **(#6)** UR Tab IN

TRANSITION 1-2 to 1-3 (McCarthy Mixer to Rap Group)
    UL-strike 2 folding chairs to SR   **(#7)** Projection Screen IN*
(#4) DS slipstage to SR (table off SR)   DR tab OUT
    US slipstage to SR   US tabs OUT
        (garbage can off SR/record player,   R/W/B streamers OUT
        sign, flagpoles, tray w/cookies   (2 sets)
        & cups, **Joanne & Anne** on SL)   **(#8)** Rap Wall IN
    UL—Chair rack ON   Hanging lamp IN**(Cue Lt #5)**
    DL—hand off coffee pot   **(#9)** US tabs IN
    Joan costume change—SL   DR tab IN
                             (#9A) Projection Screen OUT

[*]18 seconds for slides

DECK	*FLYS*

DURING 1-3:
    Trick Wall to storage SL
    Preset runner carpet USC
    Move marble topped table &   Pierre Masking Wall IN
      2 chairs to US Rap Wall

TRANSITION 1-3 to 1-4 (Rap Group to Art Institute)
(#5) DS slipstage to SL (bench on SR)   **(#10)** DS tab OUT
(#5A) US slipstage to SL (record player,   UL tab OUT
flags, 2 chairs, TV tray, **Ellen** off SL)
Joan, Joanne, Anne,   **(#11)** Art Institute drop IN
Cynthia add raincoats—DL   **(#12)** UL tab IN
    (#12.5) DS tabs IN

DURING 1-4:
Strike chairs & rack, record player,   Hanging lamp OUT
    2 flags
Preset Pierre Furniture: Rap Wall OUT
    Marble topped table, Settee, 4 chairs, Pierre Wall IN
    2 side tables, standing ashtray,
    2 pieces of carpet—US slipstage &
    thru doors

TRANSITION 1-4 to 1-5 (Art Institute to Wedding)
(#6) DS slipstage to SR (halfway)   **(#13)** DS tabs OUT
    (bench off SR/chair on SL)
    US slipstage to SR (chair, rug,   **(#14)** Projection Screen IN^{**}
    settee, 2 end tables on SL)   Border IN
    Slider Walls OUT   UL tab OUT
    (#15 & Cue Lt #4) Art
      Institute drop OUT
Joan & Boyd costume change—SL   **(#16)** UL tab IN
    (#17) Border OUT **(Cue Lt #5)**
(#7) DS slipstage to SR (chair on SL)   Projection Screen OUT
    DS tabs IN

END ACT I: **(#18)** Projection Screen IN
    Border IN
(#8) DS slipstage to SL (chair off SL)   DS tab OUT
    (#20) DS tab IN

^{**}12 seconds for slides

The introduction of electricity was a determining factor in the flexibility of stage lighting. As the desire for more and more elaborate lighting increased, various devices were developed that could control the amount of current sent to the light filament, thus controlling the amount of light output. The result is called *dimming.* The theatrical dimmer is similar to the small rheostat used in many homes. In the theatre, however, a single dimmer can control considerably more wattage, and many dimmers are grouped together and assembled in a control panel, which is operated by one—or at the most two or three—operators or electricians.

The theatrical dimmer allows enormous flexibility in lighting the stage. A designer, director, or electrician can move, or *fade,* from one stage picture to another, from one color to another, or from one source of light to another with great ease.

Although there are still a few mechanical dimming systems around today, which work by means of a control handle, *computerized,* or *memory,* dimming systems are most common. These allow a very large number of cues to be stored and then called up for viewing onstage as fast as it takes to punch in the command. During a performance, lighting cues are linked in sequence and operated by an electrician with a keyboard. Hundreds of dimmers, controlling hundreds of lights, can simultaneously move to different

A compact and user-friendly computerized control panel for stage lighting. To program a lighting cue the operator punches in light levels (and other information such as the speed of the cue) on the keyboard at right. When he or she is actually running the show—barring unforeseen complications—the operator need only push the "Go" button.

levels of intensity—even at individual rates. Changes can occur in different parts of the stage; for example, a sunrise can begin slowly, then even more slowly the stage can fill with light, while elsewhere an overhead light, perhaps left on from the night before, can be switched off, and so on. Many computerized systems can also create spectacular lighting effects such as flashing, chasing, and bouncing of lights. Combined with color and pattern, these can help to create an astonishing range of realistic and fantastic images: thunder and lightning, flickering candles, rolling clouds, almost anything imaginable (Figure 9.11).

These systems are very expensive (though less so than when they were first introduced) but they are important money savers on any production today. With a minimum of error it is possible to move quickly from any given moment in a production to another, saving time (and therefore money) during technical rehearsals. With earlier, more primitive systems, the electrician had to set (and reset) dimmers by hand, which was often difficult and always time consuming. For example, if it was necessary during a technical

Figure 9.11
A track sheet showing a light cue from the off-Broadway production of *Driving Miss Daisy*. The handwritten number beneath each channel number indicates the "reading" or level of intensity, of that channel in any given cue.

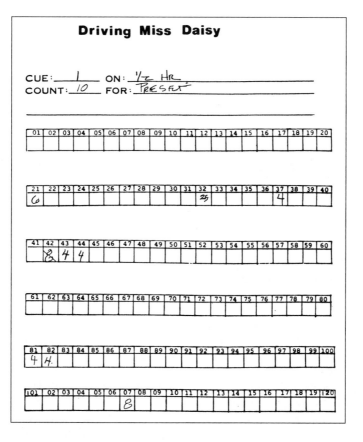

A sound console in operation. This is a manually controlled sound system, requiring the operator to move individual controllers each time the cue is performed.

rehearsal to go from a late part of the play to an earlier one, the electrician might have to retrace backward through all of the cues! With computerized systems, the electrician punches in the desired cue and the computer traces it back.

Sound in today's theatre is controlled in much the same way as stage lighting, although computerized sound control consoles are less prevalent than their lighting counterparts. Often sound and lighting are controlled from the same location in the theatre. Occasionally, they are controlled by the same operator if budgets are tight.

Preview Performances

A preview performance is one that an audience pays a reduced price to attend, with the understanding that they are not seeing the finished product. These performances give the production team added time to refine the show.

Seeing the production with an audience present has distinct advantages for the director, designers, playwright, and producers. Problems that were not apparent before are more obvious during a performance. Previews also help the actors to gauge audience response and adjust the timing of their line delivery accordingly. The presence of an audience gives everyone involved with a production a new perspective on the performance.

Theatrical unions, such as Actors' Equity, allow extended rehearsal time during the preview period. Once a production has opened to the critics, however, additional rehearsals can be extremely costly and basically rarely occur.

Suggested Readings

Elbert Gruver, *The Stage Manager's Handbook* (New York: Drama Book Specialists), 1975.

Motley, *Theatre Props* (New York: Drama Book Specialists), 1975.

Chapter TEN

The Audience and Performance

The Performance Space

Before a performance can take place, there must be a theatrical space in which to house it. Robert Edmond Jones defined theatre as a place for storytelling that has changed gears: in an effort to tell a story properly, the storyteller, out of frustration, finally says, "Let me show you!" Jones describes the theatre as an arrangement of seats put together in a way that allows the actor—or storyteller—to "reach out and touch and hold each member of his audience."[1] This simple requirement has led to many complex solutions, for the shape and size of the stage, or performance space, and these solutions have had a profound effect on the way an audience relates to and understands a production.

Although the vast majority of performance spaces are located indoors, they need not be. Sometimes there is no theatre per se, but instead a temporary space on a street or a hillside. The hill or the street itself, the surrounding buildings, or whatever can be carried by the actors might be the only scenery. The Greeks began producing plays as part of outdoor religious ceremonies. As time went on, they added bit by bit to the natural hillside used as the setting, creating a "house" in which scenery could be placed. Outdoor theatres can present greater problems for the performer and designer than indoor ones. There are many distractions outdoors—ambient light, the weather, one's neighbor, bugs—and the designer, architect, and performer must organize and use the space in such a way as to maintain the focus on the performance. Several basic types of performance space have evolved to solve this problem.

Outdoor Theatre

STREET THEATRE   Almost every period in history has had some kind of street theatre, a theatre for everyone that is cheap and accessible. Performances can take place almost anywhere. The performers are responsible for attracting an audience with little advance notice or advertising; tickets aren't sold ahead of time, and people simply gather around.

During the Middle Ages, for example, theatre took place inside and outside of churches, the center of medieval life. Performances often told the entire story of humankind from birth to death and beyond. Outdoor performances, much like pageants, took place over long periods of time—some lasting as long as 25 days! *Pageant wagons* moved past the audience, who

Figure 10.1
A medieval mystery play performed on a pageant wagon.

stood still as if watching a parade, or a series of *mansion stages* remained stationary while the audience passed by, viewing each one at a time in order, like an exhibit. Whether fixed or mobile, each stage contained its own world while telling its part of the larger story.

These outdoor stages had two important features in common. In the back was some kind of scenic picture or representation. In addition to serving as a decorative backdrop, this picture also became a place from which actors could enter and exit, and behind which they could wait, hidden from view of the audience. In front was an open playing space (Figures 10.1 and 10.2).

Commedia dell'arte companies performed wherever they felt they could gather an audience—usually in the streets, although sometimes they rented indoor spaces.

The New York Shakespeare Festival at one time had a mobile unit that toured the neighborhoods of New York City during the summer (Figure 10.3). Many kinds of plays were performed on it, from Shakespearean drama to musicals by Elizabeth Swados. The time needed to set up the stage was short, and often the neighborhood audience watched the preparations, which were almost as much a part of the show as the play itself. Apart from its motorized carrier, this stage is the modern equivalent of the medieval mansion.

Figure 10.2

A reconstruction drawing of an English pageant wagon. The drawing of the pageant wagon in Figure 10.1 shows what one might have looked like passing on the street. This illustration shows two reconstructed views of a wagon: in plan at the top, in section on the left. The drawing to the right is a section view of another, less formal, playing space that may have been set up along the route.

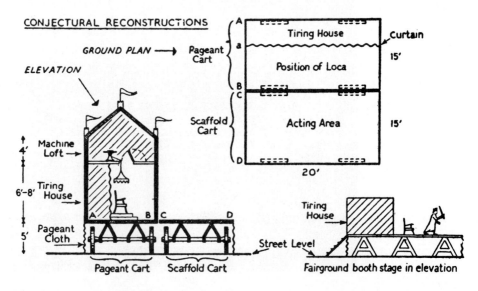

Figure 10.3
An etching by
Jacques Callot of
Zanni, or
Scapino, one of
the stock char-
acters in *Com-
media dell'arte*.

The New York
Shakespeare Fes-
tival's mobile
unit performing
in a New York
City neighbor-
hood.

The Bread and Puppet Theater in their performance of "Our Domestic Resurrection Circus" (August 1991). Note the use of overscale puppets and puppet heads, which produce a dramatic, shocking, fantastic effect in performance.

Today street theatre often serves a more overtly political purpose than it did in the past, but it uses the same basic forms that were used centuries ago. Now, as then, it can take place anywhere, in any natural or manmade outdoor setting. Peter Schumann's Bread and Puppet Theater, presents often highly charged political subjects through puppets and heavily masked actors in streets anywhere. The company's residence is now in Vermont, where its members perform in an outdoor festival each August.

AMPHITHEATRES   The amphitheatre, the most common venue for outdoor theatre, is based on concentric circles. The audience wraps around the smallest, inner circle in which the performance takes place; the performance space cuts a line across the circle at the back, leaving a space for entrances and exits. Seating for the audience is generally *raked*, that is, it rises quite steeply from the playing area, allowing those in the back rows to see easily over the heads of those in front. The amphitheatre evolved naturally from casual seating on a hillside, with the performance taking place below in a small valley.

At nearly the same time that Aristotle wrote his *Poetics* (c. 335–323 B.C.), the Theatre of Dionysus was furnished with a stone structure at the back of the playing space, giving it a permanent stage house (Figure 10.4).

Figure 10.4
A reconstruction drawing of the Theatre of Dionysus, late fourth century B.C.

Audience capacity was between 14,000 and 17,000 (roughly one quarter of the audience at a typical professional football game). Actors performed primarily in the circular center area (Figure 10.5).

The same shape exists today in theatres such as the Delacorte in Central Park, which has been home for many years to the New York Shakespeare Festival's free Shakespeare in the Park program. The shape of con-

Figure 10.5
Diagram showing the plan of the Theatre at Epidaurus.

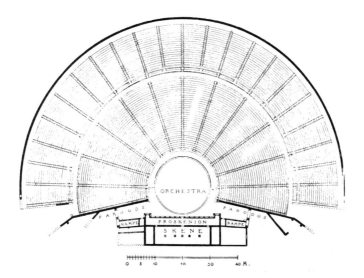

The ancient
Greek theatre at
Epidaurus took
the shape of an
amphitheatre.

temporary theatres is roughly the same as the ancient amphitheatre, but
the background varies according to choices made by the scenic designer.
Otherwise the basic relationship remains the same: a raked audience looks
down at a semicircular playing space backed by a decorative device.

Indoor Theatre

When theatre reappeared in Europe during the Middle Ages, it moved from
inside of churches to outside in marketplaces, and then back indoors again,
to theatres.

Another exam-
ple of an am-
phitheatre:
The New York
Shakespeare
Festival's Dela-
corte Theater in
Central Park,
New York City.

Scenery can be used inside and out, but the stronger the desire to create an environment that departs from the naturally occurring surroundings, the greater the need for scenery—and for a theatre building to house that scenery. A second factor is weather. Particularly in cold or wet climates, stage and audience need to be enclosed to insure that performances take place and are attended.

Over the centuries, in the Asian theatre as well as in the West, indoor performance spaces have evolved into roughly three shapes: the *proscenium* stage, the *thrust* stage, and the *arena* stage. Each has roots in outdoor theatre and represents the changing relationship of audience to performance.

PROSCENIUM   The term *proscenium* refers to a permanent archway separating the performance area (the *stage*) from the audience (the *house*). The proscenium allows scenery to be moved quickly from one position to the next, because the backstage space, with its machinery and stagehands, can easily be *masked*, or hidden, from the audience's view. The proscenium stage's front curtain, or *grand drape*, also reveals the scenery and actors to the audience. Productions in a proscenium theatre traditionally depend heavily on scenic effect (Figures 10.6 and 10.7).

Figure 10.6
The theatre at Drottningholm. The site of a royal residence in Sweden, the theatre at Drottningholm was built in the late eighteenth century, but was used only briefly used as a theatre. The building was rediscovered in 1921 after having been totally shut up for more than a century, and is an excellent example of an eighteenth-century proscenium house.

Figure 10.7
Talley's Folly, by Lanford Wilson, produced in New York in 1980 and designed by
John Lee Beatty. Beatty's rendering shows that the design is clearly meant for a
proscenium stage. The portal made to look like foliage mimics the shape of the
proscenium and contains the entire setting within that frame.

THRUST STAGE   A thrust stage, like an amphitheatre, literally thrusts the
performance into the space occupied by the audience. The audience surrounds the stage on three sides. Not surprisingly, this type of stage made its
first full-blown appearance as a permanent structure during the Elizabethan
period, when direct address to the audience in the form of soliloquies was
an important dramatic convention (Figure 10.8).

The Elizabethan thrust stage, reinterpreted many times, is in use today
in many theatres. The Guthrie Theater opened in Minneapolis, Minnesota,
in 1963. Its use of the thrust confirms the basic values of the form: the
arrangement of the audience in relation to the stage allows a close and un-
obstructed view from almost every seat.

Although the differences between the proscenium (which permits the
creation of a detailed and complete scenic illusion) and the thrust stage
(which relies more on the imaginative powers of actor and audience) are
critical, the conceptual line between the two is not as clear as it might
seem. Both are able to maintain the fundamental separation of actor and audience, a characteristic not always found in late-twentieth-century theatre,
for example.

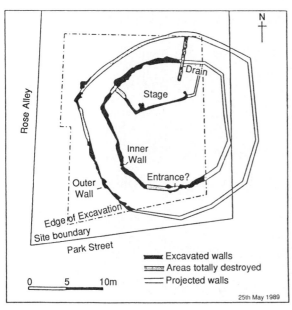

Figure 10.8
The Rose Theatre's ground plan after its alteration
in 1592, according to the 1989 excavation of the site.

The Milwaukee Repertory Theater's main
performance space, which is a thrust stage.
Exposed lighting equipment, steeply raked
seating, and minimal scenic decoration all
contribute to the audience's feeling of direct
involvement with the production.

The Guthrie
Theater in Min-
neapolis and its
version of a
thrust stage.

Like the Western thrust stage, the stage of the Noh theatre juts out into the audience and is surrounded by it on three sides; on the Noh stage, however, the illusion of realism is diminished even further. A traditional painting of a pine tree appears at the back of the stage in all Noh theatres. There is no other scenery. A long bridge (called the *hashigakari*) provides for extended (32 to 55 foot), formalized entrances onto the stage by the principal characters. An orchestra remains onstage in full view for the entire performance. Just as in the Elizabethan theatre, the responsibility for establishing change in place and mood belongs to the actor.

ARENA STAGE   With the audience on all four sides of the playing space, the arena stage, or "theatre in the round," is not as common as either the proscenium or thrust stage. The purpose of the arena stage—and of the thrust, though to a lesser degree—is to bring the audience into a more intimate relationship with the performance. The arena format can use only a minimal amount of scenery and requires that the actors perform to all four sides of the audience. These parameters preclude the kind of magical illusion that the proscenium's "picture stage" can create.

Actors enter and exit through *vomitoria*, a term from the Roman theatre that refers to covered corridors or entrances onto the stage (uncovered, these were the *paradoi* of Greek theatre) from beneath or through the audience area. The only other way onto the stage in an arena setting would be from above or from traps in the stage floor.

Adrienne Lobel's design for Arthur Schnitzler's *Undiscovered Country* at Arena Stage in Washington, D.C., shows the many possibilities for traffic flow, allowing the actor to face any side of the audience.

The designer Adrienne Lobel's setting for the Arena Stage production of *Undiscovered Country* (pictured above) helps to solve the central problem of staging in an arena theatre: how to allow each of the four sides of the audience a reasonable view of the actors. Ms. Lobel's arrangement of chairs allows each side of the audience to see at least one of two actors (in conversation, facing each other) or a side view of both actors. The actors also adjust their physical positions to allow the audience at least partial views of their faces.

Arena stages have one advantage that balances the problems they present. Every member of the audience is much closer to the actors than would be possible with either a thrust or proscenium stage in a theatre of equal seating capacity.

The Black Box or Flexible Theatre

As the urge for experimentation in the theatre grows, so does the need for different kinds of performance spaces. The followers of Brecht, Artaud, Grotowski, and Chaikin cut themselves off completely from the traditional actor-audience relationship, and the design of theatres became an active part of the experiment. Completely flexible theatre spaces have many names, the most popular being the *black box*—black because they are usually painted black, box because they are box-shaped and have no fixed or permanent seating.

Perhaps the most flexible performance space was the environmental theatre of Richard Schechner (b. 1934). The given space, whatever that

One of the earliest "found" or "flexible" spaces was used for the legendary production *Dionysus in '69,* performed in the Performing Garage in 1968. Audience and actors mix in a totally eclectic space. (Courtesy Fred W. McDarrah.)

might be (Schechner's was originally a garage in New York City), could be used in any way that made sense for the particular piece of theatre. Usually, performances used all the available space, including that normally occupied by the audience.

The idea of flexible performance spaces has made its way into more traditional theatres. Many resident theatres have second stages with flexible configurations; many colleges have black-box theatres set aside for experimental and student work.

Nontheatrical Spaces, Found Spaces, and Site-specific Productions

Street theatre has the great advantage of spontaneity. Some current theatrical experiments pursuing that sense can be found in spaces never meant to be theatres at all. Old warehouses, bars, mountaintops—any place appropriate for the production is used as a performance space. A site-specific production is performed in the actual setting for which the play was written; for example, a play set in a bar would be performed in an actual bar. The au-

Peter Brook's *Orghast at Persepolis* was developed cooperatively by the company and performed in this ancient, unchanged site. The actors responded to the performance space and created a theatrical piece around it.

dience is placed wherever there is room—usually in and around the performers.

A site-specific production of *A Streetcar Named Desire* might take place in a small, crowded apartment in a blue-collar section of a city like New Orleans—or New York City in summer.

Performance Style: The Actor-Audience Relationship

Style of theatrical performance is the means that best communicates the story artists want to tell. It has as long and exciting a history as playwrighting—although one that is more difficult to document.

If the goal of the production is to absorb the audience in the illusion of the world onstage, that goal can be achieved by a production that attempts to recreate everyday life or by one that does not. A production that does not resemble daily life as we experience it might not make a point of that difference. The audience can be aware of the play's *form*, such as Shake-

BASIC STAGE TERMINOLOGY

As noted, the meaning of these terms may vary with the kind of theatre. Figure 10.9 shows the section and ground plan of a university theatre.

The *stage* refers to the general onstage area or the area that encloses the stage. It includes:

- The *performance space:* the area from which the actor is visible to the audience during a performance. This area is not a constant, but is determined by the scenery for each production.

- The *backstage area:* the general space that includes the *wings*, the area upstage of the scenery, any storage area, and the dressing rooms. (During the Elizabethan period, when *Macbeth*

was written, this area was called the "tiring house.")

- The *wings:* the area immediately offstage of the performance space. It is in this area that the actor prepares for entrances and makes exits, and that the stage crew prepares for and makes scene and property changes. Scenery not in use can be stored in the wings. Quick costume changes can also take place here.

- The *dressing rooms:* rooms in which the actors dress for the performance. Some are private, some are shared by two or three actors, and some, called "chorus" dressing rooms, are meant for larger groups of actors.

Figure 10.9, below and opposite
Section and ground plan of the Adams Memorial Theater at Williams College. (Adapted from drawings by Cosmo Catalano.)

- The *fly space:* the area above the stage used to store scenery not presently in use, which also provides room for flown scenery in use onstage. In some theatres, there is a suspended catwalk system above both the audience and performance space from which lights, speakers, and sometimes pieces of scenery can be hung.

- The *fly rail:* offstage right or left, the place from which scenery is flown in and out.

- The *traps:* removable sections of the stage floor. With the addition of stairs or ladders, an open trap can provide for

entrances onto the stage from below or exits from above.

- The *traproom:* the area under the stage, sometimes used for scenic, lighting, and sound effects.

The *house* or *front of house* refers to the space occupied by the audience. It includes:

- The *pit:* the area directly in front of the stage, used for the orchestra in productions of a musical. In some theatres, it forms the dividing line between audience and performance space.

(continued)

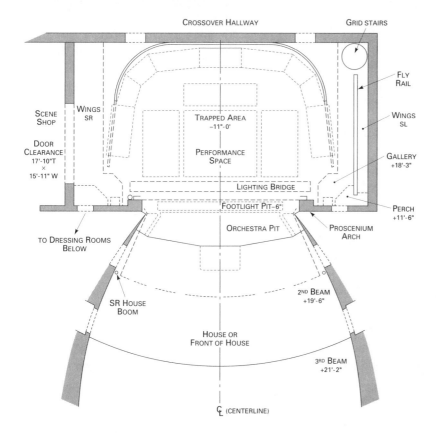

Photo 10.1
It was in the Presidential box at Ford's Theatre in Washington, D.C., that President Lincoln was shot in April 1865.

- The *orchestra:* the area on the main floor of a theatre with more than one seating level, offering the most direct view of the actors and the setting.

- The *balconies:* any seating area above the ground floor. There can be several balconies—up to four or five, but usually two. The *mezzanine* is the area in the front, lower section of the first balcony.

- The *boxes:* the areas to the extreme right and left of the first balcony in a proscenium theatre. An audience member seated in a box would be very close to the stage (see Photo 10.1).

- The *followspot booth:* an area above the top balcony from which followspots are operated.

- The *light booth:* contains lighting and sound controls and is sometimes the place from which the stage manager calls cues for the performance. When there is no actual booth, these functions are housed in the basement of the theatre, in one wing or another, or somewhere else out of the way.

- The *sound console:* this controls the recorded sound and microphones, and is sometimes located in the house, directly behind the audience.

speare's verse, without being conscious at every moment that they are witnessing a performance. Thus, they can be as easily absorbed by a production of *Macbeth* as by one of *Hedda Gabler, The Seagull, The Heidi Chronicles,* or *A Streetcar Named Desire.*

As Brecht showed, it is possible to place the audience in other emotional, psychological, or intellectual relationships with a performance. Whereas a seamless performance with continuous and linear action encourages total absorption in the illusion, a performance such as that of an episodic drama, in which the seams are shown, encourages the audience to think. The first type attempts to keep the audience involved and accepting of the circumstances of the drama; the second tries to provoke the audience to react, moment by moment, in a thoughtful or critical way. Neither occurs through the written play alone, but by means of the interaction of all the theatrical elements that go into creating a performance.

Styles of Performance

In order to illustrate performance style in terms of the actor-audience relationship, we will examine the following important historical examples:

- The chorus in Greek drama
- Direct address in Elizabethan theatre
- The movement toward realism and away from direct address in the late nineteenth century
- New relationships from the mid-twentieth century
- The musical theatre.

These are only a few examples of the many possible relationships between audience and performance. None is exclusive to a particular period, and is used only to indicate a dominant characteristic.

Addressing the Audience Indirectly

Greek theatre, known to us primarily from the few remaining tragedies and comedies of the fifth century B.C., employed the interaction between chorus and individual characters in addition to the interaction between characters. In the history of Western theatre this is unique. In the final scene of Euripedes' tragedy *Medea,* a chorus of women comments on Medea's murder of her children, which occurs offstage:

> O your heart must have been made of rock or steel,
> You who can kill
> With your own hand the fruit of your own womb.

Of one alone I have heard, one woman alone
Of those of old who laid her hands on her children,
Ino, sent mad by heaven when the wife of Zeus
Drove her out from her home and made her wander;
And because of the wicked shedding of blood
Of her own children she threw
Herself, poor wretch, into the sea and stepped away
Over the sea-cliff to die with her two children.
What horror more can be? O women's love,
So full of trouble,
How many evils have you caused already!

Presumably sung or chanted, the chorus's speech is a formalized response, although the murder occurs within their hearing. They do not attempt to stop Medea from killing the children, but pray to the Earth and Sun instead. They are not part of the plot, and are not expected to interact but rather to channel their reactions into commentary.

Medea's husband, Jason, enters and addresses the chorus not as a group of individual characters, but as a sounding board. He doesn't pause for a response to his questions, which are, in any event, rhetorical:

You women, standing close in front of this dwelling,
Is she, Medea, she who did this dreadful deed,
Still in the house, or has she run away in flight?
For she will have to hide herself beneath the earth,
Or raise herself on wings into the height of air,
If she wishes to escape the royal vengeance.
Does she imagine that, having killed our rulers,
She will herself escape uninjured from this house?
But I am thinking not so much of her as for
The children—her the king's friends will make to suffer
For what she did . . .

The chorus responds by informing Jason of the murder of his children. Its function is to:

- Interpret events for the audience
- Help convey information
- Give opinions
- Provide a break from the main action
- Tell the audience how to feel about the events of the play.

The chorus's constant presence and the nature of its responses create a link with the audience. Events are interpreted through the chorus, which, in this case, even provides a moral:

A relief sculpture of the poet Menander and theatrical masks, an important aspect of Greek and Roman theatre. Masked actors can project their voices and emotional intentions over a great distance. As in the Noh Theatre of Japan, the mask provides a recognizable framework—from within the mask the actor can express a more subtle, personal interpretation.

> Zeus in Olympus is the overseer
> Of many doings. Many things the gods
> Achieve beyond our judgment. What we thought
> Is not confirmed and what we thought not God
> Contrives. And so it happens in this story.

Thus, the audience is told not to feel secure or complacent, because the gods, who are all-powerful, sometimes change their minds for no apparent reason. Since there is no possible way for mere mortals to comprehend the rules, they must simply obey. In this play, the chorus communicates with the audience *indirectly*, interprets events as they happen, colors them with moral judgments, and speaks in one voice, as if for the community. Greek audiences attending a performance were probably absorbed by the production—and by the argument.

Addressing the Audience Directly

Elizabethan performers maintained a lively relationship with the audience and depended upon its imagination. Public playhouses such as Shakespeare's Globe Theatre maintained the basic actor-audience relationship developed in the Middle Ages, in which actors created a more or less direct relationship with the audience. Although actors no longer wandered through the audience as they had earlier, theatres in Elizabethan England were still relatively informal and rowdy. The relationship of permanent stage to permanent seating had been fairly well established, but the direct connection between audience and actor remained an important one.

The soliloquy, a standard feature of Elizabethan playwrighting, was more than a literary device; it took the actors out of the action onstage and put them directly in touch with the audience, in order to relay information about the characters' feelings, beliefs, and problems. It is thought that the soliloquy was so important in Elizabethan theatre that the actor came all the way downstage center and delivered it directly to the audience. Theatrical time was suspended so that matters other than plot could be examined. The Elizabethan soliloquy was clearly an aspect of performance, so much so that the actor may have taken a bow immediately after delivery.[2]

The *aside* is another device used to give the audience information directly, although it is much briefer. The aside is usually found in comedy. A character onstage, already engaged in the scene, turns aside and addresses the audience, which is thereby let in on a joke or some important piece of information.

Turning Away from the Audience

Stanislavski's method of training and rehearsing actors grew out of a need to establish a new relationship with the audience. Although the proscenium stage had eclipsed the Elizabethan thrust stage in England and on the continent, actors continued to play directly to the audience from the edge of the stage and in front of the scenery well into the nineteenth century.

André Antoine (1848–1953), an actor and producer of the Théâtre Libre (founded in Paris in 1887), was a major force in the movement toward a form that integrated the individual actor with both the other actors onstage—creating an *ensemble*—and the stage environment, thus vastly changing the actor's relationship to the audience. Antoine wanted theatre to represent the circumstances of the audience—an audience no longer made up exclusively of the upper classes—in a way they could immediately recognize. To do this, he felt that the actor needed to *turn away* from the audience and form a new relationship with the environment. This stage environment would be so realistically detailed that it would have a reality of its own, like a character in the play. It would resemble everyday life to such

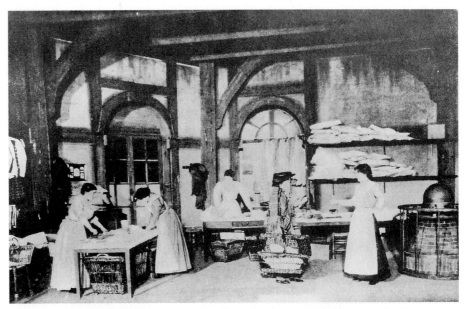

The 1906 production of *Op o' me thumb* at the Théâtre Antoine, Paris. The actors grouped "naturalistically" around workstations suggest to the audience that a fully active life existed before this moment and will continue when the play is over.

an extent that it would dictate the character's movements, not the other way around.

This is an extreme form of representational theatre. Looking at a slice of life as if through a keyhole, the audience sees behavior that looks absolutely lifelike. The actor, turning in to the environment and the ensemble, pulls the audience in, and the audience is totally carried along by the illusion.

Confronting the Audience

Brecht said that linear drama "involves the audience in an action," while his own epic drama "makes the audience an observer, but arouses its activity." Brecht's ideal audience-actor relationship was what he called "the street scene." The actor behaves like an eyewitness to an event, demonstrating "how a traffic accident took place. . . . The point is that the demonstrator acts the behavior of driver or victim or both in such a way that the bystanders are able to form an opinion about the accident."[3]

Following closely on Brecht's revolutionary idea, Julian Beck and Judith Malina founded The Living Theater in 1947. Like the Open Theater, theirs was a communal theatre in which everyone worked together, on a more or less equal basis. The company's revolution against the values and power

The Living Theater's production of *Frankenstein*. In a Living Theater production, the audience members' expectations are violated, challenging their sense of what theatre is. (Photo by Fred W. McDarrah)

structures of their time was expressed in a rejection of "traditional" theatrical performance styles, which they felt masked the real problems of life and deceived the audience.[4]

The Living Theater made the audience an *active participant* in its performances to such an extent that theatre became life. One of its many important productions was *The Connection* by Jack Gelber, which opened in New York City on July 15, 1959. The production broke every rule of traditional theatre. So real that it could barely be distinguished from life, it was nevertheless completely confrontational in the way it addressed the audience. Peter Brook, perhaps the greatest directorial force in today's theatre, describes a performance:

> When you go to *The Connection* in New York, you are aware, as you enter the building, of all the denial aspects of the evening. There is no proscenium—(Illusion? Well, yes, insofar as the stage is arranged like a squalid room, but it is not like a set; it is more as though the theatre were an extension of this room)—there is no conventional playwrighting. . . . But in *The Connection* the tempo is the tempo of life itself. A man enters—for no reason—with a gramophone. (Oh yes, there is a reason. He wants to plug it into the light socket.) He wants (apparently—he doesn't say so) to play a record. And as it's an LP we have to wait for it to finish—a quarter of an hour or so later. At first, our attitude as audience is fouled by our expectations. We can't truly savor the moment (enjoy the record for what it is worth, as we could in a room) because years of theatre convention have conditioned us to a different tempo: (Amazingly we cannot enjoy a record

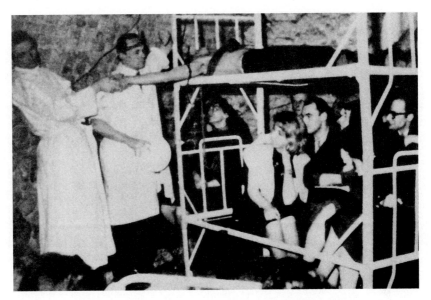

In *Kordion,* Grotowski arranges the setting for a mental institution and places the audience in the patients' beds—reversing their roles.

we would enjoy at home, because we have paid for our seat.) We sit waiting for the next contrivance that will—with seeming naturalness—interrupt the record and let us get on with . . . with what? That's the point.

For in *The Connection* there's nothing to get on with. And as we sit there, baffled, irritated and bored, suddenly we put ourselves in question. Why are we baffled, why are we irritated, why are we bored? . . . . the stage is paying us the supreme compliment of treating us all as artists, as independent creative witnesses. And the evening is as interesting as we choose to make it.[5]

Unlike Brecht's theatre, here there is no story, just life as theatre. What is real and what isn't? What is the audience's relationship with all of it? Although the performance turns away from the audience members, it simultaneously confronts them, demanding their responses, challenging their expectations of theatre.

Musical Theatre

The musical is arguably the most popular form of theatrical entertainment in the world today. It is generally the most expensive to produce and the most lucrative form as well. The use of music in theatre establishes a relationship between performance and audience that is different from any of those we have studied.

W. C. Fields, Ed Wynn, and Jimmy Durante were enduring stars of the vaudeville form.

Music played an important part in many periods of theatrical performance. In ancient Greece, music and dance actually preceded drama. But once theatre took the form in which situations were acted out, music became a complex accompaniment to both regular dialogue and choral passages. The Greeks evidently linked different kinds of music and dance to psychological or moral states.[6]

The Elizabethan theatre was nearly as rich in music as it was in dramatic literature. Incidental songs appeared in many plays. Elizabethan theatres had a permanent orchestra, usually with six musicians. They used trumpets to underline some entrances and exits, drums in battle scenes, and perhaps a musical accompaniment underlying many scenes.[7]

Musical performance evolved from opera and the ballad opera, and the use of incidental music in plays continued to take shape throughout the nineteenth and twentieth centuries, primarily in America. Several other forms—vaudeville, the musical revue, and the musical comedy—made their own contributions to the form we know today as the musical.

Vaudeville, a popular form of entertainment, consisted of a series of sketches that at first were interspersed with songs and had set time limits, presumably to keep them light. American vaudeville originated in places like Tony Pastor's Theater on Fourteenth Street in New York City, and often included comedy, acrobatics, song, and dance on one bill. Performers included personalities like W. C. Fields, Ed Wynn, Bill Robinson, Eddie Cantor, and Jimmy Durante.

The theatrical revue was typified by the Ziegfeld Follies, which was produced by Florenz Ziegfeld beginning in 1907. The revue comprised show girls in elaborate costumes (a forerunner of today's Las Vegas acts) and

Barbra Streisand portrayed the vaudeville comedienne Fanny Brice in the musical *Funny Girl.*

comic and vaudeville sketches (W. C. Fields and Eddie Cantor also starred in Ziegfeld productions). Among the famous performers to come out of Ziegfeld's theatre were the comedienne Fanny Brice (the inspiration for the Broadway musical *Funny Girl*), Mae West, Fred Astaire, Will Rogers, and Maurice Chevalier.

Beginning as musical comedies, early musical theatre was characterized by spectacular effects and many changes of scenery, lighting, and costumes. Gradually, the emphasis on dance and choreography grew.

Unlike opera, which is generally set entirely to music, the musical or musical comedy traditionally is split between music and dialogue, or *book.* The audience, whether or not it is directly addressed, also has a different relationship with the performers than it does in most other forms of theatre. The emotional or psychological states of characters, changes in their situation, and sometimes basic storytelling needs can all present the occasion for song and dance in a musical. The movement from dialogue to music can be celebratory, like an aside in a Molière comedy, or introspective, like a soliloquy in Shakespeare. A musical number often breaks sharply away from a scene, transporting the audience to another emotional level. The musical performer, likewise, must be able to make that shift both technically and emotionally. In recent years, the distinction between opera and

Showboat, written in 1928 by Jerome Kern and Oscar Hammerstein II. Although traditional in its use of staging and scenery (with echoes of vaudeville), *Showboat* had a "book" that told a single story. This scene depicts the act I finale—the wedding scene.

The musical is generally considered to be an American contribution, although musicals were written in England and the continent. Some very great composers have put their energy into musicals. George Gershwin (1898–1937) composed opera (*Porgy and Bess*, 1935) as well as more standard musicals (*Of Thee I Sing*, 1931). Conductor and composer Leonard Bernstein (1918–1991) composed *West Side Story* and *Wonderful Town*.

Showboat, written in 1928 by Jerome Kern and Oscar Hammerstein II, was the first major piece of musical theatre to establish a clear and coherent storyline. Rodgers and Hammerstein's *Oklahoma!*, produced in 1943 and considered the real turning point for the American musical,

took the story seriously and put together episodes for reasons other than spectacle or variety. The music, dance, and setting supported the story as well. After *Oklahoma!*, musicals began to be taken more seriously.

The musical continued as a popular form through the 1940s and '50s with productions such as Irving Berlin's *Annie Get Your Gun* (1946) starring Ethel Merman; Frank Loesser's *Guys and Dolls* (1950), which presented Damon Runyan's underworld figures and their "dolls" in dialogue and music; and Lerner and Lowe's *My Fair Lady* (1956) based on George Bernard Shaw's *Pygmalion*. *West Side Story*, produced in 1957, updated the tale of Romeo and Juliet, and combined

The American choreographer Agnes de Mille moved from classical ballet to the musical with her work on the 1943 production of *Oklahoma!* Her dance sequences show a strong balletic influence and play in integral part in the story.

West Side Story brought together some of the greatest talents of the mid-twentieth century to create a modern version of *Romeo and Juliet* in musical form. This knife fight, choreographed by Jerome Robbins, was another innovative use of dance in the musical.

the work of such talents as Leonard Bernstein (who composed the music), Stephen Sondheim (who wrote the lyrics), designer Oliver Smith, and director/choreographer Jerome Robbins.

In the 1960s, the American musical continued to build on the careful integration of dialogue, music, and lyrics in works such as *Fiddler on the Roof* (1964) and *Cabaret* (1966) directed by Harold Prince, who went on to direct opera and many other very successful musicals, in-

Based on the pyrotechnics of a young and accomplished circus performer, *Annie Get Your Gun*, produced in 1946, starred Ethel Merman, whose electrifying voice sang of the difficulty of her love and of leading a normal life in show business.

Hair, a musical about the 1960s generation, was bold and graphic in what was depicted on-stage. Produced by the forward-looking Public Theater, it enjoyed expected popularity off-Broadway, and a somewhat unexpected success on Broadway.

cluding *The Phantom of the Opera. A Chorus Line* (1975) was a landmark production in many ways. Produced jointly by the Shubert Organization and Joseph Papp's New York Shakespeare Festival, it established a precedent for commercial and nonprofit cooperation that allowed nonprofit theatres to earn money on Broadway, thereby becoming more financially independent and better able to produce other, less commercial work. The show also brought to prominence the po-

A Chorus Line, the longest running musical on Broadway, generated huge profits for the New York Shakespeare Festival that could be reinvested in new work at the Public Theater. The show told the story of dancers auditioning for a Broadway musical.

Classic musicals are often revived. *Anything Goes,* written by Cole Porter in the 1920s, was remounted in an award-winning production starring Patti LuPone in the late 1980s at the Vivian Beaumont Theater. Like *A Chorus Line,* the production was moved to Broadway for a long, successful run by a not-for-profit theatre.

Will Rogers' Follies, a musical based on the writings of humorist Will Rogers, returned to the roots of the traditional variety show—like the Ziegfeld Follies.

sition of director/choreographer, in this case, Michael Bennett, who would go on to work on such shows as *Dream Girls.*

British composer Andrew Lloyd Webber has had a long string of Broadway hits, perhaps the best known—and longest running—of which is *Cats* (1982), a musical based very loosely on the poet T. S. Eliot's *Old Possum's Book of Practical Cats.* Although scenic and lighting spectacle have always been an important part of the musical experience, this production, which took an unprecedented amount of time to prepare, led the way for bigger and more extravagant visual productions, such as *The Phantom of the Opera* (1987), also composed by Lloyd Webber; *Miss Saigon* (1991); and *Les Misérables.*

musical theatre has become increasingly blurred. Musicals like composer/lyricist William Finn's *Falsettos* use a kind of *sung dialogue*, in which there is no break between scene and song; in others, the break is not as distinct as it used to be.

Audiences presumably come to the theatre to be entertained, but they probably also come to be engaged. Whether they seek to reaffirm their own beliefs, to escape momentarily from the stress of real life, or to learn something new—or perhaps all three together—audiences must be engaged before anything at all can be communicated. All the performance relationships discussed in this chapter, and all the accumulated theories of playwrighting, acting, directing, and design, focus on finding the most engaging style of performance with which to communicate meaning or interpretation to the audience. Changing the style of a performance can be as disruptive to a point of view as changing the play itself would be. A Blanche or a Nina speaking directly to the audience would drastically change the audience's perception of the character and her world. A Lady Macbeth who breaks into song would do the same.

The audience provides the final element of performance. Whatever the production concept and point of view, individual audience members take away what they *choose*, as filtered through their individual points of view. Nevertheless, the possibility exists that an audience will be changed in some way simply by having experienced the production.

Suggested Readings

André Antoine, *Memories of Théâtre Libre*, translated by Marvin A. Carlson, and edited by H.D. Albright (Coral Gables, FL: University of Miami Press), 1964.

Edward Braud, *The Theatre of Meyerhold: Revolution on the Modern Stage* (London: Methuen), 1986.

Peter Brook, *The Empty Space* (New York: Avon Books), 1968.

Robert Brustein, The *Theatre of Revolt: An Approach to the Modern Drama* (Boston: LIttle, Brown), 1964.

Mary C. Henderson, *Theatre in America: 200 Years of Plays, Players, and Productions* (New York: Harry Abrams), 1986.

Conclusion

The Critical Point of View

*Thank God our art doesn't last. At least we're not adding
more junk to the museums. Yesterday's performance is
by now a failure. If we accept this, we can always
start again from scratch.[1]*
—Peter Brook

The Critic

Criticism in the theatre applies to both (1) the material brought to
bear in the interpretive process and (2) the response to a particular
production—in effect, an interpretation of an interpretation. The
first is intended for a small audience and is analytical in its approach.
It can be used by theatre artists before or during production. The second is popular criticism intended for the potential audience once a
production has opened to the public.

Critical material is brought to the interpretation of a play largely through the efforts of the dramaturge and the director, although any member of the production team may include scholarly criticism in his or her research efforts. This critical material can be useful at various stages of the interpretive process, because each piece of criticism represents yet another point of view, and therefore opens the play to further exploration.

Of course, there are so many different critical interpretations of some plays that not all of them could possibly be put to use in a single production. So much has been written about Shakespeare's plays that whole careers are devoted to studying the many critical points of view. *Macbeth* has been widely studied and written about by countless scholars. Two important twentieth-century critics, William Empson and Jan Kott, have written about the play from different points of view. Kott reduces the play to a single image:

> A production of *Macbeth* not evoking a picture of the world flooded with blood, would inevitably be false. . . . *Macbeth* has been called a tragedy of ambition, and a tragedy of terror. This is not true. There is only one theme in *Macbeth*: murder. History has been reduced to its simplest form, to one image and one division: those who kill and those who are killed. Ambition means in this play the intention and planning of murder.[2]

The experience of the play, Kott says, is like a bloody nightmare through which one wades. Most scenes take place at night, and everything—"both sleep and food"—has been poisoned. Macbeth, he says, is aware of the nightmare, and has only one dream: that there finally will be one murder that will end all murders and thereby end the nightmare. But the nightmare has no end. Once Macbeth has chosen to kill, he cannot control the fear that causes him to kill again and again. Macbeth feels no guilt, so in the end he simply takes as many people with him into death as possible. As to Lady Macbeth, Kott says that she "is taking her revenge for her failure as lover and mother. Lady Macbeth has no imagination."[3]

William Empson, exploring other issues in the play, provides a contrasting point of view. Concentrating on the question of whether or not the play was cut during Shakespeare's time (that is, whether or not today's text has fewer scenes than the original), he rejects the idea, posited by other major critics, that another scene preceded the first scene in the play that exists today. According to Empson, its presumed content—a discussion between Macbeth and Lady Macbeth about the murder of Duncan—has no foundation in the play. Empson justifies Macbeth's initial horror at the witches' prophecy as "an externalization of his secret, guilty daydreams; partly he feels exposed, but even worse he feels that the imaginary world has become real and must now be acted upon."[4]

Empson, like Kott, sees the play as a dark nightmare, but he sees the cause of the darkness quite differently. To Kott, the entire world of the play is dark. His Macbeth is aware that he is in a nightmare, but sees no viable way out. For Empson, the darkness is a symbol of Macbeth's refusal to see the consequences of his choice. Postulating that "the dramatic impression is that this kind of topic [murder] is practically the small talk of the Macbeth household," Empson reinforces his view that a conscious awareness exists from the beginning (and even before the beginning) of the play, and that although Macbeth tries to hoodwink himself into believing that he is not committing a moral crime, he knows that he is.

We might apply these points of view to questions about the nature of the world of the play, and what role fate and the witches perform in it. Is the world itself infected (as Kott's point of view assumes), or do the Macbeths infect it (as Empson thinks)? What effect does one have on the other? Who are the witches in Kott's view? In Empson's? In which interpretation does fate play the larger role?

These interpretations, if put to use, would drastically affect production choices. How would you imagine the witches from each of the two points of view? The Macbeths? Whom would you cast?

The popular critic writes daily, weekly, or monthly reviews about productions of plays, not about the written play as a separate entity (except in occasional thought pieces). Opening night is a time for celebration—the production is as complete as it ever will be—and also a time for anxiety. What will the audience think of the production? What will the critics think? Daily critics write their reviews immediately following the opening performance. How will this very rapid response affect the future of the production?

Like the scholarly critic, the popular critic brings a particular set of ideas about a play to the performance. David Richards, a drama critic for the *New York Times*, reviewed a production of *The Seagull*, presented by Tony Randall's National Actors Theater at the Lyceum Theater on Broadway, in December 1992 (Figure C.1). In it, he provided the potential audience with a sense of the overall quality of the production. He therefore considered the quality of the performances, the quality of the direction, and the quality of the interpretation. The review is, of course, subjective, but it is not always presented as such. Here is a summary of some of Richards's very well-considered points about the play:

- He says that the production did not strike a balance between the presentation of Russian provincial life and the "sorry souls" who are unfulfilled in love.
- He focuses on a "daisy chain" of unrequited love, making other issues in the play, such as the relationship of success to happiness, almost inconsequential.
- His point of view on the play is that "the poignancy comes from the inevitable frittering away of time, hope, youth and dreams."

This is a thoughtful and moving interpretation, but it is not the truth of the play for everyone.

Individual drama critics rarely concur on the meaning of a play or its production (see Figures C.2 and C.3 for two reviews of *The Heidi Chronicles*). Over time, the theatregoer comes to agree with certain critics, to disagree with others, and to identify a particular critic's personal quirks or tastes—in effect, to read the criticism critically.

The critic can also serve to put the production point of view in context. We have already considered what it means for an audience to see an unorthodox interpretation or one that runs counter to the wishes of the playwright. A critic can inform the potential audience, for example, that a production of *Macbeth* is set in Chicago in the 1920s, or that an actress is playing Hedda so aggressively that her suicide seems out of character.

Anyone can read a review of a production and decide whether or not to buy a ticket. This gives critics tremendous power over the success or failure of a production at the box office, especially considering how costly the average ticket to the theatre has become. In most cases, a poor box-office showing will hurt both a commercial and a not-for-profit production, and even an entire season's success. In the New York commercial theatre, a set of bad notices from important critics will almost surely close the show. Of course, the opposite is also true: a rave review can revive flagging ticket sales and keep a production running, or it can be responsible for a production's move to Broadway. Positive reviews were in large part responsible for *The Heidi Chronicles'* move from Playwrights Horizons, an off-Broadway, not-for-profit theatre, to Broadway.

Length of run and financial success is not an indication of a production's artistic merit. Many factors—the personal taste of a particular critic, the state of the economy, what other productions are running at the same time, awards won or lost, how well the play was advertised, how carefully money was managed—can shorten the life of a respectable or even a very good production.

Finally, audiences are critics as well. Why an audience likes a production is contingent upon many factors, including how involving, engaging, or entertaining the production is and how pertinent it and the play are to the audience's concerns. Some plays endure and can speak to audiences of any time or place. Others cannot and come to seem dated or irrelevant. Likewise, some productions appeal to audiences and some do not.

The Audience

Throughout this text we have carefully observed how an audience takes meaning from choices made onstage. We have seen how different Heddas emerge in different settings and in different costumes. We have examined how a particular physical presence or gesture, such as Blanche's controlled

'The Seagull'

If Ms. Akalaitis appears firmly on track at last, I fear we'll have to continue to settle for performances in lieu of productions from the National Actors Theater.

Tony Randall's well-intentioned company, which aims to bring the classics to Broadway, has just moved into the Lyceum Theater. Lovely theater, the Lyceum, but that's about it for sweeping changes. The first presentation of the troupe's second season, "The Seagull," is no different from last season's offerings. Here and there you'll spot an actor who's doing good work, and maybe a couple more who look to be on the right track. But there aren't enough of them to form what you would call an ensemble.

Unfortunately, most of the plays that Mr. Randall has chosen so far (Feydeau's "Little Hotel on the Side," Miller's "Crucible") are not the sort that can be rescued by a few good performances. If everybody doesn't function like clockwork in a Feydeau farce, nobody does, and let's not forget that "The Crucible" is an examination of *mass* hysteria. The shortcoming is even more grave when it comes to "The Seagull."

■

Like the rest of Chekhov's dramas, it's as much about the fabric of provincial Russian life at the turn of the century as it is about the sorry souls who can't wrest themselves free of the pervasive ennui or their paralyzing infatuation with the wrong person. The play, in fact, depicts a virtual daisy chain of unrequited love, starting with Madame Arkadina, the vain and aging actress who has attached a world-weary writer, Trigorin, to her entourage. He is quickly attracted to Nina, an idealistic young woman and aspiring actress who has a crush on Konstantin, Madame Arkadina's brooding son, although not for long. So it goes, around and around, which is to say nowhere. The poignancy comes from the inevitable frittering away of time, hope, youth and dreams.

The director Marshall W. Mason orchestrates a properly Chekhovian atmosphere—the silences that suddenly descend upon animated conversations, paralyzing the participants; the chirping of birds and crickets that mocks so much human misery; the muffled offstage noises that attest to more consequential goings-on elsewhere. Atmosphere is only part of it, though; the onstage events *are* the stuff of the play. They've got to be kept interesting, at the same time that they must be made to appear marginal, beside the fact. (Chekhovian drama is the drama of inattention, botched opportunities and the right truth uttered at the wrong time.)

■

All this presupposes a better-schooled cast than the current one. Tyne Daly's Arkadina is, regrettably, Mama Rose in "Gypsy" minus the songs. There's no insinuating charm here, no capriciousness, no wily femininity. The actress is like a sequined tank, flattening everyone before her. Mind you, it doesn't take a whole lot to flatten Ethan Hawke, who is simply out of his league and gives a dull and artless rendering of Konstantin, or Laura Linney, whose silvery beauty would seem to be her single claim on the role of Nina.

Two performances alone rise above the general mediocrity. Jon Voight, looking far more at home onstage than most movie stars, sees Trigorin for the true weakling he is. What the actor allows him, however, is a strong sense of self-loathing. The moments when he turns on himself for sacrificing so many years to his charming little talent as a writer are among the production's best. The other standout is John Franklyn-Robbins, Madame Arkadina's brother, who has arrived at the end of his long life, whiskers flying, memory collapsing, health broken. All that's left him are crotchety bluster and a lap robe. Whenever one of those actors gets to vent his remorse, the lethargic evening picks up.

Otherwise, on the lofty pretext of performing "The Seagull," the National Actors Theater is giving us a stageful of sitting ducks. ❑

Figure C.1
David Richards's review of the National Actors Theater Production of *The Seagull* at the Lyceum Theater on Broadway (New York Times, 13 December 1992).

Having been less enthusiastic than other critics about Wendy Wasserstein's *The Heidi Chronicles* Off Broadway, I hasten to point out that, reversing the pattern, it looks better and plays better on. Thomas Lynch has skillfully adapted his tongue-in-cheek scenery, Pat Collins has made her good lighting even more evocative, and the bigger space allows more room for the play's grand ambition to portray two decades of change in our society. A school dance looks more like a school dance, a pediatrics ward is more up to the old pediatrics, etc. And it's nice to bask in oversized slide projections in the hall where Heidi Holland—Wendy Wasserstein transmuted into a feminist art historian—lectures on women in art, even if the splendid Joan Allen mispronounces Sofonisba Anguissola as no art historian should.

The play chronicles Heidi's progress from a frightened but fast-quipping wallflower at a 1965 Chicago high-school dance, through becoming a timid on-looker at a New Hampshire Eugene McCarthy rally (1968), to being a Yale grad student in fine arts visiting a friend in Ann Arbor and shyly observing her consciousness-raising group in session (1970), then to a women-in-art protest march on the Chicago Art Institute (1974), and so on through thirteen scenes—all the way to 1989,

when Heidi moves into a commodious New York apartment and adopts a baby girl. Cautiously, she does not name her Sofonisba, Artemisia, or even Angelica, after one of her beloved women artists.

Here the first problem surfaces: the inconsistencies in Heidi's character. In contrast to her feminist and postfeminist friends, Heidi remains an almost Candide-like innocent, despite one of the sharpest and fastest tongues this side of the Pecos. When she lectures, however, her humor changes from vertiginous epigrams to patronizing down-home jokiness. Further, she seems to have an ample and diversified offstage sex life with one editor or another, yet is involved on stage with only a couple of unlikely men throughout.

There is Scoop Rosenbaum, a dazzling opportunist who goes from liberal journalism to putting out *Boomer*, the slickest of slickly upward-mobile magazines, and thence (as I understand it) into politics. Heidi has an off-and-on affair with him, but he wenches around and finally marries an intellectual 6 (instead of her 10)—a wealthy young woman who becomes a leading book illustrator, which is not bad for a 6. And there is Peter Patrone, as cynically scintillating at repartee as Scoop; he, however, beomes an earnest and distinguished young pediatrician.We follow him, a homosex-

ual, through a number of liaisons with men; as far as I can tell, he never sleeps with Heidi. But she is, for obscure reasons, enormously important to him as, in the end, we see him bitterly grappling with AIDS among both his special friends and his child patients.

Now, there are in life beautiful women who have weird problems with men, and witty women who are nevertheless shy; but to make them credible on stage takes a heap more than we are accorded here. When Miss W. had herself portrayed on stage by the portly, ethnic Alma Cuervo, she automatically spoke a good part of the truth; belief boggles at the elegant, glamorous Joan Allen in that role. Equally hard to take are the smart-aleck rapid-fire epigrams from almost everyone; this fits into the unrealistic, stylized milieus of Wilde, Coward, and Orton, but clashes with W.W.'s naturalistic ambience. Finally, the play is a mite too much of a survey course in women's studies; or, to put it bluntly, a check or even laundry, list. All the same, it is clever and funny and sometimes even wise, and there is, under Daniel Sullivan's direction, good acting from all, and much more than that from the subtly complex Miss Allen, the trenchantly ebullient Peter Friedman and Boyd Gaines, and the especially cherishable Joanne Camp.

Figure C.2
John Simon's review of the Broadway production of *The Heidi Chronicles* (New York Magazine, 27 March 1989).

THE WASHINGTON POST 3/14/89

Theater

The Life and Loves of 'Heidi'

On Broadway, Wasserstein's Baby Boomer 'Chronicles'

By David Richards
Washington Post Staff Writer

NEW YORK—Heidi Holland, the appealing heroine of "The Heidi Chronicles" is a keeper of the feminist faith who discovers that sometime when she wasn't looking, the church was dismantled right under her nose.

In 11 scenes, playwright Wendy Wasserstein takes her from a self-conscious adolescence in 1965 to single parenthood in 1989. As much as this observant play is Heidi's story, it is also the account of Wasserstein's generation—those who came to be known as the baby boomers. The play has the powerful scent of autobiography, but I suspect a good number of people are going to find reflections of themselves and their own peregrinations in Heidi's odyssey.

An off-Broadway hit earlier this season, "The Heidi Chronicles" has now been transferred to Broadway's Plymouth Theatre, where it continues to be a shrewd, funny and often moving work. Heidi (Joan Allen) is far too bright to be a Candide. But long after the contrary evidence has begun to mount up, she clings to the belief that this is the best of all possible liberated worlds.

Stumbling into a consciousness-raising session in Ann Arbor in 1970 (the scene is hilarious), she has to overcome her inherent reserve and a prissiness that sometimes manifests itself as causticity. Once over the hump, sisterhood strikes her as the path of the future: women supporting and celebrating one another. With so much empathy in the air, it is conceivable that even the men might come around.

There are two in Heidi's life—the engagingly cynical Peter Patrone (Boyd Gaines), whom she first meets by the punch bowl at a high school dance in Chicago; and Scoop Rosenbaum (Peter Friedman), the ambitious counterculture journalist, who comes on like gangbusters at a McCarthy for President mixer in Manchester, N.H. The play follows their fortunes, too. While Heidi is busy becoming an art historian, Peter turns himself into New York City's best obstetrician under 40 and Scoop founds the wildly successful Boomer magazine.

Neither, though, is able to fulfill Heidi's expectations of marriage as a partnership of equals. She learns that Peter is gay during a rally protesting the sexism of the Chicago Art Institute and has to accept him thereafter as a best friend. For a while, she has a fling with Scoop, but his fierce drive leaves no place for anything but the traditional wife, who stays home and stokes the embers of his ego.

Meanwhile, the country itself grows more acquisitive and self-centered. The idealism of the 1960s and '70s recedes. The women's liberation movement becomes the stuff of college courses. Heidi, eyes still shining, is left holding the bag.

The realization comes to her in a long monologue midway through the second act. She has been asked to address her high school alumni on the subject, "Women: Where Are We Going?"

Figure C.3
David Richards's review of the Broadway production of *The Heidi Chronicles* (*The Washington Post*, 14 March 1989).

And it dawns on her that she no longer has a compass, let alone an answer. Stepping from behind the lectern and taking the audience into her confidence, she confesses unhappily, "I feel stranded. And that wasn't the point. The point was, we're all in this together."

"The Heidi Chronicles" immediately brings to mind the extraordinary sequence in "The Search for Signs of Intelligent Life in the Universe" in which Lily Tomlin recounted the intertwining sagas of a handful of 1970s feminists. Like Tomlin, Wasserstein is charting the collapse of a collective dream. Like her, too, she has an acute awareness of fads and faddishness—the Miro posters, granola cookies and low-impact aerobic classes that date the passing times as accurately as any calendar.

At one point, Heidi, Peter and Scoop appear on "Hello, New York," one of those relentlessly inquisitive but unfailingly vapid morning TV talk shows, where they try to put the 1960s in perspective between commercial breaks. (Another hilarious scene.) Their segment is to be followed immediately, we learn, by one devoted to "Divorced Senate Wives Modeling Coats for Spring." Nice that, but no nicer than the observation that the essence of cool in 1965 was being able to twist and smoke at the same time.

Wasserstein is not one to bare her claws—or her teeth—in disappointment. Her writing is both sweeter and more sentimental than that in "The Search for Signs of Intelligent Life." "The Heidi Chronicles" ends with a quiet shrug: Heidi will carry on single-handedly, if she has to, with an adopted daughter. (Consider it symbolic that the sole piece of furniture in her new apartment is a rocking chair.) That's not exactly going out with a blaze of glory, dramatically speaking. But the play is so rewarding up to then that you forgive it a certain trailing off.

Insightfully directed by Daniel Sullivan, the cast is top notch. The doe-eyed Allen makes a wonderful Everywoman. Soft without being flaccid, bright without being cutting, she is perpetually bathed in vulnerability. The only hitch is that she is so winning you're not exactly sure why she can't win a man.

Scoop comes with first-class credentials as a wise-ass, who feels obliged to issue a running report card on the world and its inhabitants. (McCarthy qualifies, for example, as "a C-plus Adlai Stevenson.") The amazing aspect of Friedman's whirling dervish performance is that it is so likable. But then, so is Gaines, as the doctor whose already quick temper will be quickened by the AIDS crisis. The role is an affectionately conceived portrait of a homosexual, and Gaines endows it with a flair that is never patronizing.

Ellen Parker offers vivid counterpoint to Heidi, as a long-standing girlfriend who mutates with the times as Heidi can't. All the other parts—wives, lovers and strangers—fall to a quartet of performers. That they are nearly unrecognizable from one appearance to the next speaks of their skill. My program assures me, however, that Anne Lange is both the Junior League hostess cupcake at the Ann Arbor conciousness-raising and the magnolia-scented belle who marries Scoop and suffers his infidelities. In which case, she's a true chameleon.

Scoop puts the finger on Heidi's dilemma at their first meeting. She is, he informs her with characteristic bluntness, "a true believer, who won't realize it [the idealism of the 1960s] was a phase." Indeed, she won't. But maybe, she allows, the next generation will make the connections that she botched. Maybe, her adopted daughter and Scoop's son will meet in a plane over Chicago. Maybe . . .

Heidi is off and dreaming again.

elegance or uplifted arm, suggests a distinct point of view on a particular moment in the play. We have seen how one setting for *The Seagull* suggests the bottom of a well and another a serene park.

We have assumed that everyone in an audience perceives these choices and their meanings in roughly the same way. Barring color blindness, everyone sees the color red in much the same way and identifies it as such. The physical construction of the eye dictates this common understanding. A round ball is perceived as round by everyone, whatever it is called, and a hot stove will burn if we touch it. We begin to understand the truth about physical reality during childhood. We understand what we can see—and what we see in the theatre possesses the same kind of truth.

We can propose further that even the plot of a play is perceived in much the same way by everyone in an audience. The events leading up to Blanche's confinement in a mental institution can be catalogued from the text of the play in a very precise and unarguable manner. It follows that a particular sequence of events conveys the same meaning to everyone. Since one event necessarily follows the next, no story can turn out differently than it does. In the sequence lies the meaning, and everyone reading a play perceives that meaning in approximately the same way.

As we have seen, how this sequence of events is presented provides a context for the written play and the result is a point of view—the new meaning of that play in that particular production. Once again, if the production is effective, this meaning should be roughly the same for every member of the audience.

Where does this relentlessly logical process leave the audience? How does an individual who has witnessed a theatrical performance relate to the images and events onstage? Does the audience *function* in some way, or does it merely sit passively and let onstage events wash over it?

We have discussed the connections between the style of a performance and the audience's role. Should a production create the illusion of reality onstage or, as Brecht advocated, should it confront the audience and jar it into thought? Should the actors address the audience directly, as Elizabethan performers did, bringing it closer to the motivations of the characters? Which approach is more likely to effect change in an audience? Which is more likely to result in intellectual alertness or emotional absorption?

The audience provides the final element of performance. Whatever the production concept and point of view, audience members take away what they *choose*, as filtered through their individual points of view. What we remember of a production is the product of our personal reactions to and interpretations of what we have seen or read. As audience members, we are responsible for determining *what the meaning means for us,* and for deciding what to accept, what to reject, and what we will think about what has been presented, explicitly or implicitly, onstage.

If Blanche is presented as a liar and hypocrite, what will that mean to you, personally, as an audience member? If Hedda is spoiled? Lovborg a fool? Tesman an accomplished scholar? If Nina is not crafty enough to keep Trigorin as her lover? If Arkadina hates her son? If Lady Macbeth is unable to have children? If Heidi is no longer working at the time of the final scene? Once the audience perceives meaning, it reacts to it just as a reader reacts to words on a page.

Even rejecting another point of view can involve a more careful examination of one's own. For example, if you believe that single parenting is not a reasonable choice, a production of *The Heidi Chronicles* showing that Heidi will be an excellent parent because of her life experiences might make you think about the issue differently. What if a production of *A Streetcar Named Desire* emphasized the loss of something important, as did Kazan's production, rather than the Kowalskis' liberation from a problem relative? Even if you didn't particularly sympathize with Blanche or the Old South, would you have a greater understanding of the trauma of change? There is always a possibility that members of the audience, by experiencing a new point of view, might reconsider their own, and this possibility is the driving force behind the artists who present their interpretations.

To understand what you, as an audience member, take away from a performance, it is also necessary to consider what you are looking for. Some audiences look to the theatre for a different point of view; others want confirmation of their own. If you were interested in change, which of the five plays we have been studying would you choose to see? Which would you choose if you wanted your life to remain as it was?

Audiences in Eastern Europe under Communist domination had different needs than audiences in the same places have today. Theatre had to be tightly controlled to contain potential stirrings of unrest. *Macbeth*, for example, might be allowed in such a society, given the terrible ends of the two major characters. A play such as *The Heidi Chronicles*, however, might not be a likely choice. Musicals and light entertainment might be permitted, but a production of *Hedda Gabler* that emphasized the stifling of Hedda's freedom probably would not be.

In our country today, what are most of the members of the paying audience that keeps our theatres alive looking for in a theatrical event? In your view, what needs to be changed in our society? What changes are possible? What are we told needs to be changed? Is the prevailing wisdom that some things are unchangeable? Why do we "buy" certain productions and not others? As ticket buyers, we can be very much in control of what is produced. What are we looking for?

In Chapter 8, we examined the many considerations that lead to the decision to produce one play and not another. André Bishop, speaking as a not-for-profit artistic director, referred to instinct, a love of comedy, and a preference for the thematic interweaving of the personal and the social as factors that lead him to a play. Jane Harmon and Nina Kineally, speaking as commercial producers, said they are drawn to plays that speak honestly about the human condition, and to new American plays that are socially relevant. These general statements are eventually translated into specific choices. (André Bishop produced, among many other plays, *The Heidi Chronicles, Driving Miss Daisy,* and Stephen Sondheim's *Assassins*; Jane Harmon and Nina Kineally produced *Driving Miss Daisy* on Broadway.) Were it not for the preferences of such producers, and the funding they are willing to commit in support of their choices, plays such as *The Heidi Chronicles* might never see the light of day.

What is produced, or allowed to be seen, is usually a function of what can be funded. Why can a producer raise money for certain projects and not for others? First, it is easier to raise money for a project that does not challenge widely held beliefs than for one that does. Second, producers do not usually finance all (or any) of a project from their own personal funds. The not-for-profit producer relies on grants (public or governmental and private) and the commercial producer on investments by individuals or corporations. These backers, both not-for-profit and commercial, also have points of view that they wish to promote and others they do not. Much controversy has surrounded the way in which the National Endowment for the Arts (NEA) has awarded grants in recent years. An exhibit of photographs by Robert Mappelthorpe raised the question of whether or not public funds should be used to show material that was considered by some to be obscene (and by others to be extraordinary works of art). This controversy spread to the work of other artists as well, including some in the theatre. Several performance artists who addressed many of the same themes (some of them sexual) were denied grants. This touched off debate and conflict in the theatre as well as in the general community. Joseph Papp was so incensed that he turned down all NEA grants for the New York Shakespeare Festival.

Denying grants on the basis of content is unquestionably a form of censorship, just as is the choice of the producer—although the latter seems more personal. Part of the critical thinking of the audience member should focus on why a particular production was chosen in the first place. What point of view does it support? Who is the producer? What kind of funding was made available to this production, and why? How lavishly has it been produced? What was *not* produced?

In a sense, all theatre is an act of censorship. It is not possible to present all points of view in a single production, and it is unlikely that any theatre artist would wish to do so. Nevertheless, if only one or at most a few points of view can be conveyed onstage, it follows that many other interpretations are excluded. Theatre artists must take great care in choosing what to present to an audience. And audiences must take equal care in assessing what is presented to them.

Notes

Introduction

1. Antonin Artaud, *The Theater and Its Double* (New York: Grove Press), 1958, 31.
2. Jerzy Grotowski, *Towards a Poor Theatre* (New York: Simon and Schuster), 1979, 32.

Chapter One: *Interpreting the Play*

1. John Willett, ed., *Brecht on Theatre: The Development of an Aesthetic* (New York: Hill and Wang), 1964, 71.
2. Henrik Ibsen, "The Primacy of Character."
3. Ibid.
4. Janice Paran, "Redressing Ibsen," in *American Theater* (Nov. 1987), vol. 4, no. 8, 18.
5. Ibid, 19.

6. Theodore Buckley, trans., *Aristotle's Poetics* (New York: Bohn), 1914.

7. Ibid.

8. Barrett H. Clark, *European Theories of the Drama*, rev. ed. (New York: Crown), 1970, 515.

9. Ibid.

10. Augusto Boal, *Theatre of the Oppressed*, trans. Charles A. and Maria-Odilia Leal McBride (New York: Theater Communications Group), 1985, 155.

11. Clark, *European Theories of the Drama*, 112–113.

12. Martin Esslin, *Theater of the Absurd* (New York: Anchor), 1961, xvii.

Chapter Two: *Interpretation and Collaboration*

1. Peter Brook, *The Empty Space* (New York: Atheneum), 1968.

2. Toby Cole and Helen Krich Chinoy, eds., *Directors on Directing* (New York: Bobbs-Merrill), 1963, 364.

3. Toby Cole, ed., *Playwrights on Playwrighting* (New York: Hill and Wang), 1963, 167.

4. Arthur Bartow, ed., *The Director's Voice: Twenty-one Interviews* (New York: Theater Communications Group), 1988, 5.

5. Eileen Blumenthal, *Joseph Chaikin: Directors in Perspective* (New York: Cambridge University Press), 1984, 150.

6. Edward Gordon Craig, *On the Art of the Theatre* (New York: Theatre Arts Books), 1956, 58.

7. Ibid., 67.

8. Ibid., 99.

Chapter Three: *The Director*

1. Harold Clurman, *On Directing* (New York: Macmillan), 1972, 24.

2. Cole and Chinoy, *Directors on Directing*, 249.

3. Bartow, *The Director's Voice*, 133.

4. Ibid., 357.

5. Ibid., 273.

6. Ibid., 260.

7. Ibid., 111.

8. S. D. Balukhaty, ed., *The Seagull Produced by Stanislavski*, trans. David Magarshack (New York: Farrar, Straus & Giroux), 1952.

9. Oliver M. Sayler, ed., *Max Reinhardt and His Theatre* (New York: Benjamin Blom), 1968, 116.

10. Cole and Chinoy, *Directors on Directing*, 22–23.

Chapter Four: *The Actor*

1. Konstantin Stanislavski, *An Actor Prepares*, (New York: Theatre Arts Books), 1948..
2. Grotowski, *Towards a Poor Theatre*, 210.
3. Joseph Chaikin, *Presence of the Actor* (New York: Athenum), 1980, 22-23.
4. Max Reinhardt, "The Actor," in *Encyclopedia Brittanica* (1929), cited in *Actors on Acting.*
5. Robert Lewis, *Advice to the Players* (New York: Theater Communications Group), 1980, 4.
6. Laurence Olivier, *On Acting* (New York: Simon and Schuster), 1986, 26–27.
7. *Actors on Acting*, 142.
8. Oskar, Eustis, "Duet for One," *American Theater Magazine* (July/August 1989), 21.
9. Grotowski, *Towards a Poor Theatre*, 37.
10. Ibid, 77.
11. Yasuo Nakamura, *Noh The Classical Theater* (New York and Tokyo: Walker/Weatherhill).
12. Grotowski, *Towards a Poor Theatre.*
13. Lewis, *Advice to the Players*, 21.

Chapter Five: *The Scenic Designer*

1. Robert Edmond Jones, *The Dramatic Imagination: Reflections and Speculations on the Art of the Theatre* (New York: Theatre Arts Books), 1941, 27.
2. Ibid, 26.
3. Ronn Smith, *American Set Design 2* (New York: Theater Communications Group), 1991, 103.

Chapter Seven: *The Lighting Designer*

1. J. L. Styan, *Shakespeare's Stagecraft* (London: Cambridge University Press), 1967, 217.

Chapter Ten: *The Audience*

1. Jones, *The Dramatic Imagination*, 47.
2. J. L. Styan, *Shakespeare's Stagecraft* (Cambridge: Cambridge University Press), 1975, 72 and 73.
3. Bertoldt Brecht.
4. Julian Beck, *The Life of Theatre* (New York: Harper & Row), 1986, 12.

5. Peter Brook, *The Shifting Point 1946–1987* (New York: Harper & Row), 1987, 27.

6. Oscar G. Brockett, *History of the Theatre*, 6th edition (Boston: Allyn & Bacon), 1990, 27.

7. *Ibid.*, 179.

Conclusion

1. Brook, *The Shifting Point 1946–1987*, 56.

2. Jan Kott, *Shakespeare Our Contemporary* (New York: Doubleday), 1964, 87.

3. Ibid., 97.

4. William Empson, *Essays on Shakespeare* (New York: Cambridge Paperback Library), 1986, 151.

Play Summaries

Macbeth *by William Shakespeare (1564–1616)*

Considered one of the most important playwrights of all time, Shakespeare was also an actor and a member of a theatrical company that struggled for patronage and support throughout its existence. His plays have contributed much to our understanding of theatrical performance in the Elizabethan era, in addition to being a valued part of dramatic literature. Shakespeare's work has been and continues to be performed universally in nearly every language. The plays include tragedies, such as *Macbeth, Hamlet, King Lear, Romeo and Juliet, Othello,* and *Julius Caesar*; comedies such as *A Midsummer Night's Dream, Much Ado About Nothing, As You Like It*, and *The Taming of the Shrew*; and histories such as *Richard II, Henry V,* and *Richard III*. It is not known with certainty when *Macbeth* was written but most scholars date the play to 1605–06, with its first performance for King James I taking place in 1606.

Act 1, scene 1

On a heath, amidst thunder and lightning, three Witches gather, waiting for Macbeth. They will find him, they say, when "...the hurlyburly's done/When the battle's lost and won."

Act 1, scene 2

On the battlefield, Duncan, King of Scotland, and his son Malcolm, receive news from a messenger that their army has fought off a Norwegian invasion that had been abetted by traitors. Rosse and Angus, Scottish noblemen, arrive and report that "brave Macbeth" was largely responsible for this victory: he battled the Thane of Cawdor, a traitor to Scotland, and defeated him. Duncan decides to bestow the traitor's title on Macbeth.

Act 1, scene 3

On another heath near the battlefield, Macbeth and Banquo come upon the witches, who greet Macbeth by his title, Thane of Glamis; by the title he is about to receive, Thane of Cawdor; and as "Macbeth that shalt be King hereafter." The two men listen suspiciously, not knowing who or what these three are. The witches prophesize that Banquo will be the progenitor of kings; as Macbeth tries to ask more of them, they vanish.

Rosse and Angus arrive to report that Duncan has named Macbeth Thane of Cawdor. Macbeth, astonished, asks for and receives an explanation. His ambition begins to distract him. If this prophecy of the witches has come true, perhaps the other will as well and he will become king.

Act 1, scene 4

Macbeth, Banquo, Rosse, and Angus join the king, who has returned to his palace. Although pleased with Macbeth's performance on the battlefield, Duncan names his son Malcolm as heir to the throne. He tells Macbeth that he will visit Inverness, Macbeth's castle. Macbeth, unsettled by Duncan's decision regarding Malcolm, exerts great effort to conceal his "black and deep desires."

Act 1, scene 5

Lady Macbeth, at home at Inverness, reads aloud a letter from her husband, in which he tells her about the witches and their prophecies, and the fulfillment of the first of these. She speaks of her faith in these prophecies, but also expresses concern that Macbeth's nature will not allow him to grasp the opportunity.

A messenger arrives to inform her that Duncan is en route to Inverness. She sees in the king's visit a chance to gain the throne, and when Macbeth arrives shortly thereafter, speaks to him of murdering Duncan that evening. Macbeth neither agrees to, nor rejects this plan. He merely says, "We will speak further." Lady Macbeth appears to take responsibility for the plan and the execution of the deed.

Act 1, scene 6

Duncan and his entourage arrive at Inverness. Lady Macbeth greets them graciously.

Act 1, scene 7

As preparations continue around him, Macbeth tries to persuade himself that it would be wrong to murder Duncan. Lady Macbeth joins him and they argue. She accuses him of lacking courage and of having cruelly tempted her with the witches' prophecies. She tells him her plan: she will give enough liquor to the king's servants so that they will be too drunk to hear Duncan when he is struck. She will also make it appear that the servants themselves killed Duncan.

Act 2, scene 1

Banquo, wandering through the palace after midnight, comes upon Fleance, his son. Macbeth enters with a servant and suggests to Banquo that they discuss further the prophecies of the witches, some of which have already been fulfilled. Banquo agrees, with the understanding that he will not be a part of any wrongdoing.

The others depart, and Macbeth delivers a soliloquy that begins, "Is this a dagger which I see before me?," a dagger leading him to murder Duncan. He hears a bell that is obviously a signal worked out in advance with Lady Macbeth, and goes off to murder Duncan.

Act 2, scene 2

Lady Macbeth is waiting for Macbeth. She has managed to place the servants' daggers in a convenient and accessible place, but was unable to murder Duncan herself—which she presumably intended to do—because he reminded her of her father.

Macbeth joins her, having killed the king, but he has brought the bloody daggers with him. Lady Macbeth must take them back to the servants, because Macbeth is not able to do any more. As she returns, they hear knocking at the gate. She urges Macbeth to return with her to bed so that they will not be found awake at this late hour.

Act 2, scene 3

The porter is aroused by the knocking at the gate. Drunkenly, he makes his way to answer it. Lenox and Macduff, two generals of the Scottish army, are greeted first by the porter, then by Macbeth himself. When they go to greet the king, they find Duncan murdered. Macbeth, in feigned rage, kills the bloodied servants, as if in revenge for Duncan's murder. In the ensuing chaos, Lady Macbeth faints and is carried out. Malcolm and Donalbain, Duncan's sons, decide to flee, lest they be murdered as well.

Act 2, scene 4

Rosse and an old man discuss the awful events that have occurred. Macduff, reporting Malcolm and Donalbain's disappearance, tells the two that the sons have been accused of taking part in their father's murder. Macbeth has been named king and has left to be crowned.

Act 3, scene 1

Banquo, alone, speaks of his distrust of Macbeth. As Macbeth, Lady Macbeth, and the court enter, Banquo is recognized as the "chief guest" of a banquet they are preparing. Banquo says that he cannot promise that he will return in time from his afternoon business, and Macbeth presses him to do so.

Macbeth asks his servants to bring in two men who have been waiting outside the palace. He has recently persuaded them that Banquo cheated them and is their adversary. He now convinces them to kill Banquo and, because the witches predicted that Banquo's heir will become king, Fleance as well.

Act 3, scene 2

Lady Macbeth questions her husband's unhappy and distracted state and reminds him, "What's done is done." She urges him to hide what is in their hearts and he tells her to be particularly attentive to Banquo at the evening's feast.

Act 3, scene 3

In a park near the palace the murderers attack Banquo and Fleance. Banquo is killed, but Fleance escapes.

Act 3, scene 4

The banquet. One of the assassins reports Banquo's murder and Fleance's escape to Macbeth. Macbeth sees the bloody ghost of Banquo seated at the banquet table. He is so shaken by this vision that Lady Macbeth, after trying to bring him back to reality several times, finally must ask the guests to leave.

Macbeth and Lady Macbeth speak of the scene he just made, and of Macduff's absence from the banquet—a sign of revolt. Macbeth says he will consult with the witches.

Act 3, scene 5

The witches attend Hecate, who is angry with them for having met with Macbeth without her advice or consent. [This scene is generally considered to be a later addition to the play, and one not written by Shakespeare.]

Act 3, scene 6

Lenox and another lord review the recent events. Macduff has gone to England to join Malcolm. Together they will put together an army to oppose Macbeth, who all assume is responsible for Duncan's death. Macbeth, too, prepares for battle.

Act 4, scene 1

The witches are gathered around a boiling cauldron in a cavern, mixing the ingredients for a spell. Macbeth enters to learn what is to take place. They reveal three apparitions. The first is an armed head, which warns him to "beware Macduff." The second is a bloody child, who tells him that "none of woman born shall harm Macbeth." The third is a child crowned, who tells Macbeth that he "shall never vanquished be until / Great Birnan Wood to High Dunsinane Hill / Shall come against him."

Alarmed by the first apparition's message, Macbeth is somewhat encouraged by the other two. He asks if Banquo's heirs will ever be kings in Scotland, and is shown eight kings and Banquo following. The witches disappear, and Lenox arrives to tell Macbeth that Macduff has gone to join Malcolm as well. Macbeth decides that he must destroy Macduff's family.

Act 4, scene 2

At Macduff's castle Rosse attempts to help Lady Macduff understand why her husband has left her. Soon after he leaves, a messenger arrives and tells her to flee, but she has no time to do so. The assasssins sent by Macbeth murder her and her family.

Act 4, scene 3

In England, near the king's palace, Macduff finds Malcolm and sets out to convince him of the need to unseat Macbeth from the throne. Malcolm, at first suspicious of Macduff's loyalties, finally tells him that Siward, Earl of Northumberland, is standing ready with troops to move on Macbeth. Rosse arrives and must tell Macduff of the murder of his wife and children. Macduff, though shaken with grief, determines to revenge them by marching on Macbeth.

Act 5, scene 1

This scene is often referred to as the sleepwalking scene. Lady Macbeth, watched by a doctor and gentlewoman, walks in her sleep, speaking of things that deeply trouble her conscience. As she rubs her hands, she laments "Out, damned spot! out, I say!" She sees and smells the blood of Duncan on her hands. The doctor, who fears she may do harm to herself, asks that she be watched continually.

Act 5, scene 2

A group of Scottish rebels move toward Birnan Wood, where they are to meet up with Malcolm's English troops. Macbeth has enclosed himself in Dunsinane, his castle, but does not have much support from his own soldiers.

Act 5, scene 3

From within his castle, Macbeth takes comfort in the witches' prophecy that Birnan Wood must come to Dunsinane before he can be conquered. A servant tells him that ten thousand English soldiers have massed. He asks for his armor—he will fight to the end.

Act 5, scene 4

The Scottish and English troops have joined together near Birnan Wood. Malcolm instructs them each to carry a bough from the woods to conceal their numbers.

Act 5, scene 5

Macbeth, still confident that Dunsinane will keep out any attack, hears women crying and is told that his wife is dead. A messenger arrives to tell him that the woods look as if they are moving toward the castle. Macbeth begins to fear that the prophecies of the witches may be coming true, but resolves to fight to the death.

Act 5, scene 6

Malcolm and his army arrive at Dunsinane and rid themselves of their disguise.

Act 5, scene 7

Macbeth has moved out of the castle to fight. He kills Young Siward, then flees. Macduff enters looking for Macbeth. Malcolm enters with the elder Siward, who tells him that the castle has surrendered.

Act 5, scene 8

Macduff and Macbeth meet on the battlefield. Macbeth is still confident that the witches' prophecy cannot be fulfilled, but Macduff then tells him of the circumstances of his birth—he was "from his mother's womb untimely ripped." Macbeth at first refuses to fight him but, provoked by the thought of being captured and baited, challenges Macduff. The two exit fighting.

Malcolm and his troops enter and Siward learns of his son's death. Macduff enters bearing Macbeth's head. Malcolm has triumphed and will be crowned king.

Hedda Gabler *by Henrik Ibsen (1828–1906)*

Ibsen's plays grapple with issues of social or political importance. *An Enemy of the People* (1882), for example, tells the story of a doctor in a small impoverished town who discovers that the waters are polluted in a new hot-springs resort. The doctor investigates in spite of the financial loss to his town. *A Doll's House* (1879) examines one woman's dependent position in her household and traces the path by which she comes to leave her husband and children and seek her independence.

Ibsen's treatment of these issues transcends their time, and his plays remain popular with audiences today. His early works, including *Brand* (1865) and *Peer Gynt* (1867), were written in verse. Those that followed, including *A Doll's House, Rosmersholm, The Master Builder, The Wild Duck,* and *When We Dead Awaken,* were written in prose.

Act 1

The entire action of the play takes place in the drawing room of George and Hedda Tesman's house in Oslo. Another, smaller, room can be separated from the drawing room with a curtain. The time of year is autumn. The act takes place in the late morning.

Tesman and Hedda have returned the night before from a trip abroad—a prolonged honeymoon. We first see Tesman's Aunt Julia, who has arrived to greet them. The maid, Berte, who was Julia's maid for many years, expresses concern that she will not be able to please Hedda, her new mistress. Hedda, "General Gabler's daughter," was evidently quite spoiled by her father when he was alive. From Berte and Julia we also learn that Tesman has received the title "Doctor" from one of the universities where he studied abroad.

Tesman greets them warmly and affectionately. They chat about Hedda's excessive luggage, about Julia's new hat (bought to impress Hedda), about Aunt Rina's (Julia's sister's) declining health, and about the five-month wedding trip. Julia is anxious to know if Hedda is pregnant, but, unable to ask in a straightforward way, receives no straightforward answer. Instead, they talk about how much money the trip cost and how big and empty the house is. Julia had to post security for the furnishings, but says she is glad to help.

But there are more serious subjects to be dealt with. Tesman's most serious professional rival, Eilert Lovborg, has published a new book, amid some sort of unnamed trouble. They rejoice over the prospect of Tesman's competing, though as yet unwritten, book.

Hedda enters and they exchange polite greetings. Hedda complains that the curtains have been left open and "let in a whole flood of sunshine," but wants only the drapes drawn so that the fresh air will diffuse the scent of the flowers Aunt Julia has brought as a house gift.

As Julia prepares to leave, she remembers that she brought Tesman's old slippers for him. Hedda shows a distinct lack of interest in them, and makes a remark about Berte's having left "her old hat lying about," when the hat is actually Julia's new one. They bumble through apologies and misunderstandings and talk of how Hedda has "filled out," which she vehemently denies. To atone for her rudeness, Hedda invites Julia to visit in the evening.

After Julia finally leaves, Hedda and Tesman look at another welcome-home bouquet and see that it is from a Mrs. Elvsted, an old flame of Tesman's and an old schoomate of Hedda's. Just as they are discussing her possible connection to Lovborg, Mrs. Elvsted herself arrives. She is very upset. Lovborg, who has been tutor to her stepchildren for several years, has left her home and is in Oslo. She has come to ask Tesman to look after him. Hedda suggests that Tesman write Lovborg to let him know he is welcome. Tesman leaves the women alone as he goes off to write the letter.

Hedda is very anxious to get information about Lovborg from Thea Elvsted. Through their conversation we learn that Thea has actually left her husband and followed Lovborg. She has become his work "companion," just as Hedda herself, unbeknownst to Thea, once had been. Hedda wishes to keep all this secret from Tesman.

Thea leaves, but in a highly emotional state, just as Judge Brack pays a visit. As Hedda walks Thea to the gate, Brack talks with Tesman about the precariousness of his academic position, which is somehow connected to Lovborg's return. When Hedda returns, talk turns again to Lovborg and the fact that Tesman will receive his appointment only by competing with Lovborg.

After Brack's departure, Hedda asks Tesman what she will have to give up if he doesn't get the appointment: entertaining? a butler? a horse? She says no matter what, she will still have General Gabler's pistols. She goes off to look at them.

Act 2

Afternoon. Judge Brack arrives at the house by way of the garden to accompany Tesman to an evening party. Conveniently early, he finds Hedda, who is playing with her father's pistols. Their relationship is a jovial one. They speak lightly on several subjects, mainly the wedding trip. Hedda confesses to her growing boredom with Tesman, virtually inviting Brack's constant presence to ward it off. She even insists that Brack not use the word "love" in reference to her relationship with her husband.

Tesman arrives, complaining about the heat and loaded down with books, Lovborg's among them. He tells Hedda that Aunt Julia's visit will not be possible, because Aunt Rina has taken a turn for the worst. With that Tesman goes off to change.

Left alone once again, Brack and Hedda return to the subject of Hedda's unhappiness, which she calls her "boredom." She explains how she came to marry Tesman in the first place: she felt sorry for him, allowed him to escort her home, and—simply to make conservation—told him how much she would like to live in a house they were passing, the house they now inhabit. This house, she says, brought them together.

Brack wonders if Hedda shouldn't find some kind of vocation. She thinks only Tesman's entrance into politics would do for her. Brack laughs this off, suggesting that another vocation might be better. She harshly brushes aside the idea of motherhood, even though several earlier remarks implied that she is, in fact, pregnant.

Tesman enters, dressed for the party. They decide to wait for Lovborg, although Hedda says he could just as easily stay with her and Thea, who is also expected this evening.

Lovborg arrives, thanking Tesman for his letter. Talk immediately turns to his book and its success. Lovborg, himself, finds it thin; it is, he says, meant not to offend anyone, which accounts for its popularity. He has with him, however, a new book, the sequel, which he says is about the future of civilization.

After declining Brack's invitation to the party he is giving to celebrate Tesman's return, Lovborg agrees to have supper with Hedda and Thea. Hedda offers the men punch and, after Lovborg declines, Tesman and Brack retire to the side room for a drink before departing.

Hedda is left alone with Lovborg. To conceal their exchange, she takes out a photo album of her wedding trip. Tesman moves in and out of the room, bringing things to Hedda, so she and Lovborg carry on what becomes a very intimate conversation in fits and starts. Lovborg unfolds their prior relationship for the audience. He insists that their relationship was one of working comrades, and that love was its basis. She says that she only wanted a taste of what was forbidden to her, his wild life and his work. They speak of how she threatened to shoot him the last time they were together, and why she stopped herself.

Thea is ushered in. Hedda places herself between Thea and Lovborg on the settee. She encourages Lovborg to take a drink to prove that he is truly a reformed alcoholic, but he is firm in his resolve and declines. Hedda chides Thea for being so anxious about him. Thea is very upset that Hedda has betrayed her confidence and that Lovborg now knows she didn't trust him. Lovborg, in response, takes the offered drink.

As Brack and Tesman prepare to depart, Lovborg decides to join them. He promises to return later to escort Thea home. Thea frets over Lovborg, and Hedda reassures her. Thea, however, feels that Hedda has another agenda, and Hedda admits that she does—she wishes to control a human destiny. In a jubilant moment she embraces and teases Thea, saying that perhaps she will burn Thea's hair after all, as she used to threaten to do when they were schoolgirls together. Thea tries to leave, but Hedda drags her into the dining room.

Act 3

Seven o'clock in the morning. Thea and Hedda are asleep in the parlor, wrapped in blankets on the sofa and an armchair. The fire in the stove has burnt out. The men have not returned from their party. Thea and Hedda soon awaken and try to guess where the men might be. Thea is frantically worried; Hedda is brusque and dismissive of Thea's hysteria.

As Berte comes in to start the fire, Tesman arrives home, surprised to see Hedda up so early. At her insistence, he tells her the events of the evening, exclaiming most over the parts of Lovborg's book that Eilert read to him. "I believe it's one of the most remarkable things that has ever been written," he says. After the reading, however, the gathering turned into an "orgy," with a drunk Lovborg making speeches about the woman who inspired his work. As they left the party together to walk Lovborg home, Tesman picked up the manuscript, which Lovborg had dropped carelessly. He has held onto it for fear that Lovborg would lose it again in his drunken state.

Tesman is called away by a note from Aunt Julia informing him that Aunt Rina is dying. Hedda, in the flurry of his departure, says that she will safeguard the manuscript, knowing that there is no copy.

Just as Tesman is leaving, Brack arrives to tell Hedda of Lovborg's further exploits. After Brack left him, Lovborg, still very drunk, and some of the others went to visit a woman of not quite decent reputation. There Lovborg discovered that the manuscript was missing. A fight ensued and Lovborg accused the woman of stealing it. She, of course, denied it and sent for the police. Lovborg was taken to jail. Brack has come to the Tesmans to make certain they do not welcome Lovborg to their home. He fears guilt by association if the public learns that Lovborg was at his home the previous evening. Hedda begins to understand that Brack really wants Lovborg out of Tesman's house so that he—Brack—can be "cock-of-the-walk."

Brack departs through the back way. As Hedda begins to look at Lovborg's manuscript, he arrives and pushes past Berte to get in. Thea has woken and rushes in to find them. Lovborg tells her that their relationship is over, that he has torn up the manuscript.

Thea departs alone, leaving Hedda and Lovborg together. He confesses to her that he didn't destroy the manuscript but lost it, and that he intends to kill himself. Hedda asks him to "make it beautiful" and gives him one of her father's pistols. She tells him to "use it now." They say goodbye and Hedda takes the manuscript from its hiding place. She opens the stove and burns it.

Act 4

Evening. Aunt Julia has come to find Tesman, who is not yet at home. Aunt Rina has just passed away, and Hedda and Julia discuss Julia's future now that she is alone.

Tesman rushes in, distracted, and Julia leaves to finish the burial preparations. Tesman has found out about Lovborg's visit that morning. He wants to return the manuscript to Lovborg and Hedda confesses that she has burned it. Tesman becomes hysterical, but his mood changes when Hedda tells him that she burned it for his sake. She hints at her possible pregnancy. They decide that the fate of the manuscript will be their secret.

Thea returns, frantic about the rumors she has heard about Lovborg. Brack returns to confirm that Lovborg is dying in the hospital. He tried to kill himself. They are all terribly upset; only Hedda sees beauty in his act. As they mourn Lovborg and the loss of his manuscript, Thea tells them that she has retained all of the notes used to put together the book; she and Tesman might be able to piece them together. They leave Hedda and Brack alone to pursue this idea.

Brack reveals to Hedda that Lovborg is already dead, not shot through the heart, as he said before, but through the bowels. Perhaps the gun discharged accidentally. As they are speaking, Tesman and Thea return, and Hedda and Brack continue their conversation in whispered tones. Brack knows that the pistol Lovborg used belonged to Hedda. As long as he keeps silent, there will be no way for the police to identify the pistol—and no scandal. Hedda realizes that she is under Brack's control, that she is no longer free.

Hedda excuses herself to lie down on the sofa in the other room, but is soon heard playing a wild dance tune on the piano. Tesman asks her not to play that music on a night of mourning. He suggests to Thea that they work at Aunt Julia's in future so as not to disturb Hedda, whom he will leave in Brack's care. Hedda overhears them. They hear a shot from the other room and rush in to discover that Hedda has killed herself.

The Seagull *by Anton Chekhov (1860–1904)*

Chekhov, roughly a contemporary of Henrik Ibsen's, began his dramatic career writing short comic stories to support his family while he was studying medicine. Chekhov was a practicing physician prior to committing himself full-time to playwriting. *The Seagull,* written in 1896, was his third work to be produced. It opened on October 17, 1896 at the Alexandrinski Imperial Theatre in St. Petersburg and was not a success. This was in part because the audience knew his humorous stories and expected something similar, and in part because the actors performed in a style inappropriate to Chekhov's material. The production missed the subtle relationship of sound and silence that the play demanded.

The Seagull was remounted on December 17, 1898, by the Moscow Art Theatre under the direction of Konstantin Stanislavski, who also played the role of Trigorin. It was a perfect partnership. The company's work moved away from the melodramatic style of the nineteenth century, as Chekhov sought to do in his writing. Its production of *The Seagull* marked the beginning of an important and successful collaboration: the Moscow Art Theatre produced Chekhov's other great works as well: *Uncle Vanya* (1899), *The Three Sisters* (1901), and *The Cherry Orchard* (1904).

Act 1

Early evening. The setting is a park near a lake on an estate in the Russian countryside owned by Sorin, an elderly gentleman. A stage has been erected in the park, presumably surrounded by benches or some kind of seating arrangement for spectators.

The central event of this act, the one that prompts the gathering of all the characters, is the performance of a play written by Konstantin Treplev, Sorin's nephew, who lives on the estate year round. The play is to be performed by Nina Zarechnaya, a young woman who lives across the lake. Treplev is in love with her.

The characters begin to gather for the event. First Masha and Medvedenko arrive and briefly exchange their points of view on their relationship: she is miserable, he loves her anyway. Treplev arrives with Sorin and is nervous about everything connected with the performance, particularly Nina's arrival and his mother's devotion or lack of it. He looks over the stage that has been erected and surveys the setting.

Nina arrives and, amid talk of Treplev's love for her and her nervousness about the impending performance, the two begin their preparations.

Paulina and Dr. Dorn arrive. Although not married (Paulina is married to Shamrayev, estate manager for Sorin, and is mother to Masha), the two have been engaged in an ongoing romance for some time. The last to arrive are Arkadina, Treplev's mother, and Trigorin, a famous writer and her lover. Arkadina, herself a well-known actress, comes to her brother's estate each summer.

The curtain goes up on Nina, alone, with the moonlit lake as background. She delivers a monologue that comprises the entire play, speaking of ancient images, Satan, and the like. Arkadina interrupts and Treplev, furious with her, stops Nina in midspeech, brings down the curtain, and runs off.

At first angered by Treplev's response but then feeling nostalgic for her past summers by this lake, Arkadina finally expresses concern about her son. Masha goes to look for him just as Nina comes out from behind the curtain. She shyly greets Trigorin, with whom she is very impressed. She leaves, and all but Dorn return to the house. Alone, Dorn speaks of his admiration for Treplev's play, which the others have rejected.

Treplev joins him and is encouraged by Dorn's support. Masha arrives, having followed Treplev all over the park. He leaves to find Nina, and Masha confesses her love for him to Dorn.

Act 2

A croquet lawn near the main house of the estate on a sunny summer afternoon. The characters are presumably spending some leisurely time out of doors. Casually, even languidly, events that have taken place over a few week's time—and consequent shifts in relationships—are revealed.

Arkadina, Dorn, and Masha chat and read to one another in the bright sunlight. Arkadina tries to cheer up Masha, who says, "I drag my life like an endless train behind me," by telling her how to dress and take care of herself.

Nina, Sorin, and Medvedenko join the group. We are reminded of Sorin's ill health and Dorn scolds him for smoking and drinking sherry. Shamrayev, with Paulina, joins them and disrupts the pleasures of the day by demanding to know how he is to provide Arkadina with the carriage horses she has requested for a drive to town. He insists he needs the servants, and says the horses and harnesses are in the field for the harvest. They argue shrilly and Arkadina marches out, enraged. She has decided to depart for Moscow.

Shamrayev, Sorin, and Nina exit, leaving Dorn and Pauline. She begs him to take her away from the husband who has just made such a horrible scene. He replies that he is too old to change.

Nina comes from the house to report that Sorin is having an asthma attack and that Arkadina is crying. As she speaks, she hands Dorn some flowers she has just picked. Pauline, in a jealous rage, tears them up and exits. Dorn follows Pauline into the house. Nina, alone, speaks of the strange events taking place and of Trigorin, a famous writer who prefers to spend all day fishing.

Treplev enters with a gun and a dead seagull. He tells Nina that he killed the bird and will kill himself the same way, and soon. They see Trigorin coming from a distance. Treplev is clearly jealous, both of Trigorin and of Nina's response to him. He leaves as Trigorin approaches.

Nina and Trigorin talk intimately and at length—she, about how wonderful it must be to be so famous; he, of the pressures of fame to do more and more, to be better and better. Finally, Arkadina calls him from the house and announces that they are staying after all.

Act 3

The dining room of the main house—a central area, more like a corridor than a room, through which the occupants of the house pass. Trigorin eats lunch while Masha speaks to him of her still unrequited love for Treplev. Suitcases and boxes surround them, indicating that someone is about to depart. In the course of this dialogue we learn that Treplev has attempted to shoot himself, and that he has challenged Trigorin to a duel. As a result, Arkadina has decided to leave at once.

As Masha, rather melodramatically, says goodbye to Trigorin, Nina appears to give him a present: a medallion with an inscription and the title of his latest book. As someone else approaches, she makes a hurried exit, requesting that he see her briefly before she leaves.

Arkadina and Sorin return as Trigorin leaves to find the source of the inscription on Nina's medallion. Sorin tries to convince Arkadina to give her son some money, so that new clothes and travel abroad might relieve his depression. She argues that she cannot afford to help Treplev any more because as an actress she has many expenses. Sorin, whose health has been shaky throughout, begins to faint. Arkadina shouts for help and Treplev—his head bandaged after his suicide attempt—and Medvedenko come to the rescue. Medvedenko escorts Sorin to another room to lie down, leaving Arkadina and Treplev alone.

Treplev asks his mother to change his bandage and their dialogue begins peacefully enough. Arkadina begs him not to try "anything so stupid again" and Treplev promises not to. He says he did it in a moment of despair, one that presumably will not be repeated. They talk a bit of the past, of Treplev's childhood. Finally, Treplev complains that he has no one left in the world but her, and she is totally under the influence of Trigorin. This sets off a violent argument. Arkadina accuses him of jealousy and mediocrity. He tears off the bandage she has been carefully applying and accuses her of acting in "miserable third-rate plays!" The quarrel escalates until finally she accuses him of being a "nonentity," after which she begs his forgiveness and the two make up.

As Trigorin reenters, Treplev departs, promising to drop his demand for a duel.

Trigorin begins the next, and pivotal, scene by asking Arkadina to stay for a few more days. She tells him that she knows he is attracted to Nina, that she is what holds him here, and that he must stop. Trigorin asks her to let him go. Arkadina, on her knees, begs him not to leave her. She insists he belongs to her and that she is the only one who appreciates his greatness. He gives in and the grand exit begins.

The household staff gather for their tips, and all but Trigorin, who hangs back, exit noisily. As Trigorin finds a last reason to delay, Nina enters and tells him that she has decided to run away to Moscow to pursue her career on the stage. He hurriedly gives her his address and they kiss.

Act 4

Two years later. A drawing room in the same house on Sorin's estate on a rainy, windy evening. Masha and Medvendenko, as at the beginning of act 1, are the first to enter. They have since married and have a baby. Sorin is even more ill and cannot tolerate being left alone. He wants Treplev with him at all times. Masha, it seems, has been staying overnight on the estate rather than going home. She and her mother make up a bed here in the study for Sorin.

Treplev, now a published writer, is asked by Pauline to be kinder to Masha and abruptly leaves the room. From an adjoining room, he can be heard playing a melancholy waltz on the piano.

Sorin is brought in by Dr. Dorn along with Medvedenko, who seems unable to leave. Arkadina, also in residence to care for her ailing brother, has gone to the station to pick up Trigorin. While they wait for her, they talk idly, stumbling on the subject of Nina, who, Treplev relates, ran away from home and went to live with Trigorin in Moscow. She had a child, but the child died. Trigorin tired of her and went back to Arkadina. Nina has also had something of a stage career but by all accounts is not a very talented actress. She is currently staying at the inn in town. She writes Treplev occasionally and always signs herself "the seagull."

Arkadina and Trigorin return from the station. After briefly greeting Treplev, and complimenting him on his published writing, Trigorin sits down with the others to play cards before dinner. Treplev declines, saying he is going out for a stroll.

During the card game there is talk of Treplev, who is once again playing the piano—of his strange style of writing and of Dorn's continued belief in him. When the game is finished, all but Treplev go in to dinner.

Alone, Treplev speaks of his writing, which he sees as a failure. He hears someone outside and finds Nina there. She comes inside with him, crying, and demands that he lock the doors so no one else can enter. She is distraught and speaks in a rambling, incoherent manner about the past and their lost love, about Trigorin's lack of faith in her, about her work as an actress, which she believes is her calling. She finally confesses her enduring love for Trigorin, which is driving her mad. She contrasts that love with the innocence of the evening on the lake when she performed Treplev's play. She repeats part of it for him, then runs out into the storm.

Treplev methodically tears up his manuscript, unlocks the doors, and leaves the room. The others return for an after-dinner drink. A shot is heard coming from the room to which Treplev has escaped. Dorn goes off to investigate, returns, and announces to the others that a bottle of medicine probably exploded in his bag. He takes Trigorin aside to tell him that he must take Arkadina out of the room because Treplev has once again shot himself.

A Streetcar Named Desire *by Tennessee [Thomas Lanier] Williams (1914–1983)*

Williams, a prominent American playwright, grew up in St. Louis, Missouri, during the Great Depression and, as a young man, made a difficult living working in a factory. His first successful play, *The Glass Menagerie*, was produced in New York in 1945. The role of the mother, Amanda, was immortalized by the great actress Laurette Taylor.

A Streetcar Named Desire (1947) premiered in a Broadway production directed by Elia Kazan, and starring Jessica Tandy as Blanche DuBois and Marlon Brando as Stanley Kowalski. (Kazan also directed the well-known film of the play, starring Brando and Viven Leigh as Blanche.) Williams's other important plays include *The Rose Tatoo* (1950), *Summer and Smoke* (1948), *Camino Real* (1953), and *Cat on a Hot Tin Roof* (1955).

The play takes place in and around a building in New Orleans that contains two flats, one upstairs and one down. The building lies in a poor section of the city on a street called Elysian Fields, which is situated between railroad tracks and the river.

Scene 1

An early evening in the beginning of May. Stanley Kowalski and his friend Mitch enter from around the corner. Stanley calls for his wife, Stella, who comes out to greet him. After the couple exchange a few words, Stanley and Mitch head for the bowling alley, followed shortly thereafter by Stella.

Blanche DuBois enters around the same corner carrying a slip of paper bearing her sister Stella's address. She seems confused and Eunice, the upstairs neighbor, asks if she is lost. Blanche has come to the right place, the home of her sister, but it seems she has arrived unexpectedly and is dismayed by the surroundings. Eunice lets Blanche in to Stella's apartment so that she can rest from her journey and then goes to find Stella.

Left alone, Blanche discovers a bottle of whiskey in a half-opened cabinet and has a drink. She carefully washes and replaces the glass when she has finished. She is clearly upset about something.

Stella returns and the sisters greet each other warmly. They seem not to have seen each other for some time. Stella offers Blanche a drink and, after some protest, she accepts. Blanche then questions Stella about her living conditions and Stella quietly defends herself. Finally, Blanche brings up the subject of her early arrival. She has taken a leave of absence from her teaching job and, because of exhaustion, has left before the term was out.

They talk about how each other looks, and how they will all fit into the small apartment, which has only two rooms and a bathroom. This leads to a discussion of Stanley, whom Blanche has never met. We learn that Stanley was in the military and that Stella is devoted to him. The conversation then turns to the fate of their family plantation, Belle Reve. After Stella left to make her own living, Blanche stayed on and took care of the remaining family members until they all had died. Now, the money is gone and the plantation lost. Blanche becomes very upset and accuses Stella of abandoning her. They apologize to one another.

Stanley returns with Mitch, who leaves for home after confirming a poker party for the following evening. Stanley enters the flat and greets Blanche, whom he seems not to know much about. We learn that Blanche was married long ago, and that her young husband died.

Scene 2

6:00 p.m. the following evening. Blanche is soaking in a hot bath. As Stella gets ready to go out, she and Stanley discuss the loss of Belle Reve. Stanley wants to know how Blanche lost Stella's inheritance, pointing to the old inexpensive furs and jewels that Blanche has brought with her as proof that she squandered the money. Stella and Stanley argue.

Blanche enters, ready to dress for her evening out with Stella. Stanley demands an explanation about Belle Reve. He digs through her trunk, looking for papers. Blanche, furious and upset when Stanley finds love letters from her husband, finally gives him the papers he is looking for. In the course of their argument, Stanley tells Blanche that he is protecting his wife's rights because she is going to have a baby. Stella, who has been listening from the front steps, joins Blanche and they leave.

Scene 3

Tennessee Williams titled this scene "The Poker Night." As it opens, Stanley, Steve, Mitch, and Pablo are playing poker. From much semidrunken talk we learn that Stanley is losing and that Mitch has a sick mother who is waiting up for him. Stella and Blanche appear on the street as Mitch heads for the bathroom. They enter and Stella introduces Blanche. Stanley suggests that the women leave them to their poker but Stella asks him to end the game because it is 2:30 a.m. Blanche meets Mitch on her way into the bedroom.

The two women discuss Mitch and Stanley's relative merits. As they undress, Stella warns Blanche that she is standing directly in the light and can be seen by the men. She moves away. Stanley expresses annoyance at the women's talk and laughter and, when Blanche turns on the radio, he storms into the bedroom in a drunken rage and turns it off.

Mitch excuses himself one more time and, on the way to the bathroom, runs into Blanche again. They make polite conversation on a number of subjects and he places the colored paper lantern Blanche has just bought over the bare bulb for her. Blanche again turns on the radio, and this time Stanley throws it out the window. Stella, very angry, asks everyone to leave and Stanley hits her. The men hold him back while Blanche and Stella run upstairs to Eunice; then they throw Stanley under the shower and leave.

Stanley, distraught, goes outside calling for Stella. Finally, she comes down and they enter the dark apartment together. Blanche follows, but is stopped from entering the apartment by Mitch, who has been waiting around the corner. The two have a cigarette together on the landing.

Scene 4

Early the following morning. Blanche returns to the apartment to find Stella lying in bed. Stanley has gone out to "get the car greased." Blanche is frantic about the night before and tries to convince Stella to leave. Stella insists that she has no desire to leave Stanley, even as Blanche continues to dream up schemes by which they might escape. We learn that Blanche is virtually penniless. Out of a kind of desperation, she tells Stella what she thinks of Stanley. In her famous speech, she describes him as an animal and implores Stella not to "hang back with the brutes!" Stanley, who has returned and overheard Blanche's words, enters and greets them both, pretending not to have heard.

Scene 5

A warm evening around 7 p.m. Blanche and Stella are waiting for Stanley and Mitch. When Stanley arrives, he asks Blanche if she knows someone named Shaw, who says he met her at the Flamingo Hotel in Laurel, Mississippi. She denies knowing him, but admits knowledge of the hotel—a cheap place where she says she would never be seen. When Stanley leaves the room, a panicked Blanche asks Stella what people have been saying about her. She admits that the past few years have been difficult for her, but says that Mitch, whom she has been dating, could provide the peace she needs. Stella reassures Blanche and goes out with Stanley. A young man rings the bell, collecting for the newspaper. Blanche flirts with and then kisses the young man. She tells him to run along, saying, "It would be nice to keep you, but I've got to be good—and keep my hands off children." He leaves just as Mitch arrives for their date.

Scene 6

2:00 a.m. the same evening. Mitch and Blanche return from their date, which has not gone well. Blanche invites Mitch in for a nightcap; Stella and Stanley have not yet returned. She leaves the lights off, lighting a candle instead. They speak awkwardly and he embraces her. Blanche objects, saying she has "old-fashioned ideals." They talk about Stanley's attitude toward Blanche. She tells Mitch how much Stanley hates her and asks if he has said anything to Mitch about her. Mitch asks how old she is, saying his mother wants to know, and they talk about love and devotion: Mitch's devotion to his dying mother and Blanche's love for the boy she married, who, it turned out, was bisexual. She tells the story of the night he killed himself, and why: "It was because—on the dance-floor—unable to stop myself—I'd suddenly said—'I saw! I know! You disgust me'" Mitch embraces her, saying, "You need somebody. And I need somebody, too. Could it be—you and me, Blanche?"

Scene 7

The middle of September, late in the afternoon. Stella prepares for her sister's birthday celebration while Blanche takes a bath. Stanley tells Stella that Blanche has been lying to them all along, that she lived at the Flamingo Hotel after the loss of Belle Reve, and that she was asked to leave. Blanche was fired, according to Stanley, for having an affair with a 17-year-old student.

Stella tries to explain Blanche's behavior to Stanley, citing her tragic marriage, but Stanley pays little attention. He warns Stella not to expect Mitch at the birthday party because he told him Blanche's story. Stanley bangs on the bathroom door and when Blanche comes out, she senses that something is very wrong.

Scene 8

Three quarters of an hour later. Blanche is trying to tell stories to ease the tension at dinner. Stella criticizes Stanley who, enraged, throws his plate to the floor, shouting that he is the king in his household. He storms out to the porch.

Blanche asks Stella what happened while she was in the bathtub and why Mitch did not come to supper. While Blanche tries to phone Mitch, Stella goes out to Stanley, who assures her that once Blanche leaves and the baby is born, everything will again be all right. They go back inside and Stella lights the candles on Blanche's birthday cake.

Stanley and Blanche quarrel. The phone rings but the call is for Stanley, not Mitch for Blanche. Stanley then presents Blanche with a birthday gift—a bus ticket back to Laurel. Stella, furious, tells Stanley that "nobody, nobody, was tender and trusting as she was. But people like you abused her, and forced her to change."

Stanley repeats his complaint that he and Stella were happy before Blanche arrived. Stella's labor pains begin and she asks him to take her to the hospital.

Scene 9

Later that evening. Blanche is alone in the flat. Mitch arrives and she tries to greet him, but he brushes past her. Blanche desperately tries to please him. She complains that she hears in her head the music they played when she accused her young husband.

Asked why he missed the birthday dinner, Mitch tells Blanche that he hadn't intended to see her again at all. They quarrel and Mitch begins to question Blanche about why they only have dates in the evening, in dark places. Saying that he has never had a really good look at her, Mitch tears the paper shade off the bare bulb, turns on the light, and shines it in her face. He turns it off and says he doesn't care that she is older than he thought, but is angry that she lied to him about her old-fashioned morality. She says, "I don't want realism, I want magic! I tell what *ought* to be truth."

Mitch has checked Stanley's story himself because he didn't believe it was true. Blanche hysterically acknowledges that it is, but tells him how much their relationship has changed her. Mitch grabs her, demanding what he's been "missing all summer." He says he doesn't want to marry her because she's not clean enough to bring home to his mother. Blanche screams "Fire! Fire! Fire!" to get him away from her and out of the house.

Scene 10

Later the same night. Blanche has been drinking since Mitch left. She is now dressed in an old ball gown and a rhinestone tiara. She talks aloud to herself, obviously reliving late-night parties of her youth.

Stanley enters and Blanche asks after Stella. The baby hasn't been born yet, and Stanley has come home to get some sleep. Blanche tells him she has received a wire from an old admirer and is trying on clothes to bring on a cruise with him. Stanley takes off his shirt and opens a quart of beer. He offers Blanche a drink, suggesting that they "bury the hatchet." She declines.

Blanche tells Stanley that Mitch returned earlier with a box of roses to ask her forgiveness, but she gave him his "walking papers." Stanley says that he knew she was a liar all along. Blanche picks up the phone, trying to locate the beau, Shep Huntleigh, who is supposedly coming to rescue her. She tells the operator: "In desperate, desperate circumstances! Help me! Caught in a trap!" She tries to flee the bedroom, terrified of Stanley, who goes after her. She smashes a bottle at the neck, so she can "twist the broken end in [his] face!" Stanley closes in on her, saying, "We've had this date with each other from the beginning!"

Scene 11

Several weeks later. A poker game is being played by the same men as in the earlier poker scene. In the bedroom, Blanche, Eunice, and Stella are packing Blanche's belongings. The newborn baby is upstairs. Blanche comes in from the bathroom, waiting for a phone call and selecting clothing for an imaginary journey. Stella tells Eunice that she chose to believe Stanley's version of events because if she believed Blanche, she could not go on living with her husband. She doesn't know if she has done the correct thing.

Stella and Eunice help Blanche dress and try to get her to eat some grapes. Although Blanche seems ready to go somewhere, Stella is anxious to keep her in the bedroom. "She's going to walk out before they get here."

Blanche invents a story about dying from eating an unwashed grape, on the sea, looking into the blue eyes of a ship's captain. As she finishes the story, a doctor and a matron arrive to take Blanche away. They ring the doorbell, but wait outside while Blanche finishes dressing. She goes out to greet them, but is understandably confused because the doctor is not the beau of her imagination. She runs back into the bedroom and the doctor and matron follow.

Stella begs them not to hurt Blanche, and Eunice assures her that she has done the right thing. The doctor vetoes the matron's suggestion that they use a strait-jacket and Blanche takes hold of his arm. "Whoever you are—I have always depended on the kindness of strangers." They depart together, passing through the kitchen and the poker party. Stanley comforts Stella, and the poker game continues.

The Heidi Chronicles *by*
Wendy Wasserstein (b. 1949)

The Heidi Chronicles was first produced in Seattle in 1988. It then moved off-Broadway to Playwrights Horizons in New York City, and then to Broadway. The play received the Pulitzer Prize for Drama in 1989 and a Tony Award for Best Play. Wasserstein's other plays include *Uncommon Women and Others* (1977), *Isn't It Romantic* (1983), and *The Sisters Rosenzweig* (1992).

    The Heidi Chronicles takes place during an era of intense social change (1965–1989), and each of its characters is thrown into the turmoil of the times: Heidi, a professional woman who becomes a single mother; Susan, who becomes an executive superwoman; Peter, a gay man who begins to find his rights; and Scoop, who spouts liberal ideas but shows little regard for the women in his life.

Act 1

This act is prefaced by a prologue set in a lecture hall in New York City in 1989, where Heidi is presenting an art history lecture. Act 1 follows Heidi from 1965 to 1977.

Scene 1
Heidi and her friend Susan are attending a high school dance. Susan attempts to find the most efficient way to attract boys. Heidi doesn't seem to be able to catch on to the necessary techniques. First she introduces Susan to a boy who asks *her* to dance. He quickly departs. Next she ridicules Susan's "ladies choice" as someone who can merely smoke and dance the twist at the same time. Susan waves goodbye and goes off on her conquest. Heidi sits down to read and a fellow named Peter comes over to talk. They communicate by speaking like the characters in the novel Heidi is reading. Finally, they dance.

Scene 2
1968, another dance, this time a fundraiser for Eugene McCarthy's presidential campaign. Here Heidi meets the second important man in her life, Scoop Rosenbaum. He has an odd habit of "grading" everything, such as the potato chips ("B- Texture, C+ Crunch"). Scoop tells her that he is going to pick up Paul Newman at the airport, and asks if she would she like to go along. They argue over Scoop's Marxist interpretation of the work of the

contemporary artist. He asks her to go to bed with him. Instead they go off together, presumably to find Paul Newman.

Scene 3

A church basement in Ann Arbor, Michigan, in 1970. Heidi attends her first meeting of the Huron Street Ann Arbor Consciousness-raising Rap Group with Susan, who is already a member. The discussion centers around subjects just beginning to surface in the early 1970s: women's oppression in the home, sexual freedom, women in the marketplace. As the individual members talk about their problems, those who listen express their deep support: "Susan, I'm so proud of you," "I love you Fran," and so on. Finally, the group turns to Heidi. Susan tells them, "My friend Heidi is obsessed with an asshole." Heidi talks about her three-year "off-and-on" relationship with Scoop. She sees that Scoop is not the best choice for her and that Peter would be better. She knows she allows Scoop to define her self-worth. Following her revelation, the group joins hands and sings a camp song, then quickly change to Aretha Franklin's "Respect."

Scene 4

1974, outside the Chicago Art Institute. The occasion is a demonstration for "women in art." It is raining. Heidi speaks through a bullhorn. Peter joins her. It is obvious that they have not seen each other in a long time. Heidi has asked him to meet her in front of the museum because she will only be in town for a short while. Peter is now a medical intern and Heidi has been writing her dissertation. As they banter in their usual way, Peter takes the opportunity to tell Heidi that he is gay and currently involved with a child psychiatrist named Stanley. Just then the other women rejoin them and insist that Peter not be allowed to march on the curator's office, because he is a man. Heidi chooses to stay with Peter, and finally admits that she is hurt that he is not "desperately and hopelessly" in love with her. Teasing each other, they manage to overcome this new hurdle together, but just then Mark, a waiter whom Peter has recently met, arrives for lunch. Heidi hands Mark a picket sign and the three decide to march regardless of the other women's objections.

Scene 5

1977, the ballroom of the Hotel Pierre. The occasion is Scoop's marriage to Lisa Friedlander. Susan, Peter, Heidi, and Molly (who has come with Susan) stand together in an empty room, next to the one where the wedding celebration is taking place. They gossip about the bride and groom. Scoop enters. He wants them—"the most interesting people at this party"—to go into the other room and join in the festivities. Susan and Molly do so, leaving Peter, Scoop, and Heidi to predict Susan's doomed future: instead of working for a woman's collective, as she is now doing, she will be working on Wall Street in two years. Peter asks Scoop if he is really in love as Lisa joins them. She is an illustrator of children's books that are very popular in Peter's waiting room (he is a pediatrician), but she is debating whether or not to continue working after she has children of her own. Annoyed at Scoop's lack of interest in dancing with her, she asks Peter instead and off they go, leaving Heidi and Scoop to discuss why they couldn't manage to keep their relationship together. Although they decide that they didn't want the same things, they dance together to Sam Cooke's "You Send Me." Scoop tells her that he will always love her.

Act 2

The Prologue opens again in 1989, in a lecture hall at Columbia University where Heidi is presenting another art history lecture. Her subject is Lilla Cabot Perry, an American Impressionist.

Scene 1
Scoop and Lisa's apartment, 1980, on the day of the memorial for John Lennon in Central Park. Scoop and Lisa have been married for about three years and are about to have a baby. Susan and Heidi are attending the baby shower along with two new characters, Betsy and Denise. As Lisa opens presents, we learn that Scoop is now the publisher of a magazine called *Boomer*; Susan has accepted a new job in Los Angeles as a film producer ("They wanted someone with a feminist and business background"); and Heidi has written a book called *And the Light Floods in from the Left*, teaches at Columbia, and has left behind a man she was to marry in London, because he didn't want to leave England. The phone rings and Lisa goes to answer it. It is Scoop saying he is still working. While she is out of the room, the others discuss Scoop's most recent affair and whether or not Lisa knows about it.

Scene 2
A television studio in 1982. Scoop, Peter, and Heidi are preparing to appear together on a talk show that will cover "the Sixties social conscience, relationships, Reaganomics, money, careers," and Peter's sexuality. The program begins with questions asked fairly equally of all three participants, but as it continues, Heidi, who is seated between the two men, is interrupted more and more frequently—until she can barely finish a sentence. When the taping ends, they wait to go to lunch. Heidi is furious at being cut off. She calls Peter and Scoop "the cynic and the idealist," and suggests they could easily be regulars on the talk show. She escapes to a lunch with a woman artist. Peter and Scoop, left alone, find themselves at odds and unable to communicate.

Scene 3

A trendy New York restaurant in 1984. Susan and Heidi are having lunch. Susan is now a television producer and Heidi has just received a grant to do a "small show of Lilla Cabot Perry." Although Heidi believed they were meeting to talk about life, Susan has invited Denise (Lisa's sister from scene 1), who is now working for her. The purpose of the lunch is to convince Heidi to work as a consultant on a new television sitcom pilot about a "way-out painter," "an uptight curator," and a "dilettante heiress in a loft." They want to depict these three young women as funny and successful, and as having avoided the mistakes Susan and Heidi supposedly made. Since Heidi doesn't think they made so many mistakes, she declines the offer.

Scene 4

1986, the Plaza Hotel. Dr. Heidi Holland, a distinguished alumna from Miss Crain's School, is introduced as the speaker. The topic she is to address is "Women, Where Are We Going?" Heidi begins by confessing that she has no prepared speech, and in a very funny passage, describes the superwoman/supermom that she might have been, which would have given her an excuse for being so ill-prepared. She goes on to explain why she doesn't have a prepared speech. She describes the women in the locker room of her aerobics class: each makes Heidi envious, from the "hot shots" to the gray-haired fiction writer who extolls brown rice. She is jealous even though she doesn't particularly like these women, and she doesn't want to feel she belongs to a generation of women who made terrible mistakes. She tells her audience that she feels stranded and that she "thought the whole point was that we wouldn't feel stranded."

Scene 5

The Children's Ward of New York Hospital, 1987. It is midnight on Christmas Eve. Heidi arrives in the darkened waiting room with boxes of records, toys, and books. She is greeted by Ray, a young doctor. She explains that she is making a donation. Peter enters, surprised at Heidi's unannounced appearance. She tells him that she has come to see him because she is leaving the following day to take a job in the Midwest. Peter is very disturbed by this news, and by everything else. As Heidi attempts to find the real cause of his unhappiness, Peter begins to speak about the hospital unit he established for immune-deficient children, about all the funerals of young men he attends, and about his friend Stanley's newly diagnosed illness. He needs Heidi to stay with him and she decides she must do that. They wish each other a Merry Christmas.

Scene 6

New York City, 1989, a white, freshly painted room with sunlight streaming in from a window on the left. Seated in a rocker, Heidi reads a book galley. She greets Scoop, who has come to visit her in her new apartment. With Lisa out of town, Scoop has come to tell Heidi he has just sold *Boomer* because he doesn't have anything important to show his children. Nonchalantly, he lets her know that he has actually come to see the baby she recently adopted. He feels that if she could do that courageous deed, he could certainly do more than he has done. He asks her if she is happy. Heidi says she is made happy by the thought that things might be a little more equal for their children than it was for them. She brings in Judy, the new baby, to meet him. Scoop has to rush away because he is missing his own fourth grader's school play. As he leaves, Heidi rocks Judy and sings "You Send Me." The stage directions tell us that the final image is a slide of Heidi holding Judy in front of a museum banner for a Georgia O'Keefe exhibit.

Glossary

Actors' Equity Association: the union that represents professional actors and stage managers.

alienation effect *(verfremdungseffekt)*: a term used by Bertolt Brecht to describe a method of cutting through theatrical illusion in performance. The actor comments on the character rather than identifying with or trying to bring to life that character. *See also* **epic theatre.**

artistic director: in the nonprofit theatre, the person who usually selects the plays to be produced in a season (often directing several of them) and who ultimately is responsible for the finished production.

backdrop: a painted or unpainted piece of cloth or canvas that covers the upstage (rear) wall of the theatre.

blocking: see **staging.**

call-backs: the second stage of the audition process to which those actors who impressed the director and producer at the initial reading have been invited back to read for their parts again, often with the actual candidates for the other roles.

commedia dell'arte: a type of dramatic comedy popular in sixteenth- and seventeenth-century Italy in which performances were improvised around outlines called scenarios that included the basic plot, location of the action, and characters. Commedia used recognizable stock characters, each of whom wore the same kind of costume and exhibited the same traits from production to production. Examples of stock characters are Pierrot (the innocent servant), Harlequin (a clown), and Pantalone (an old father).

dialogue: a dramatic structure in which there is a conversation or exchange of ideas between two or more characters. *See also* **monologue, soliloquy.**

dimmer hookup: a chart that provides information about how each light is to be connected and controlled, where it is to be focused, what kind of instrument it is, and what color it is. Also called a *channel hookup.*

dramaturge: although long established in Europe, this position is relatively new in American theatre; the dramaturge assists the director in the selection and critique of the text or translation to be used; locates and evaluates research material; advises the director, actors, and designers on the period in which the play takes place or the history of the play and its performances; and may write the program notes and critical essays about the play. In regional theatre, the dramaturge is usually in residence, often serving as well as the company's *literary manager,* who reads new scripts and helps select the plays to be performed in a season.

drape: the cut of a garment, the way in which a costume is fitted to the actor.

epic theatre: Bertolt Brecht's dramatic ideal, by which he sought to engage the intellect, not the emotions, of the audience through such techniques as the *alienation effect.* In its departures from dramatic convention and the illusion of onstage reality, epic theatre had a political impetus, keeping the audience alert to the possibilities of social change. *See also* **alienation effect.**

episodic structure: organization of a play by which the story unfolds through a series of scenes, usually involving many changes in time, setting, and situation. The plots of episodic plays do not necessarily follow a simple cause-and-effect relationship and often show many different views of the central issue of the play. *See also* linear structure.

exposition: information about a character or about events before or outside the action of the play conveyed to the audience through dialogue

floodlight: a lighting instrument consisting of a light bulb, shield, and reflector. Lacking a lens system, the floodlight produces a general wash of light. *See also* **spotlight.**

fly: to lift scenery out of view into the masked area (flyspace) above the stage.

general manager: the person who oversees the budget of a commercial production, monitoring all expenses, including funds spent on advertising and audience development.

grip: a stagehand who manually moves the scenery in a scene change; to *grip* is to move scenery manually.

ground plan: a map of the setting as seen from above, indicating exits, placement of furniture, masking, and so on.

improvisation: performance that is not tied to the words and actions of a scripted play but is rather a spontaneous response to the circumstances of the performance. The actors usually begin only with a situation and basic character relationships, although the improvisation may be loosely tied to plot outlines worked out in rehearsal or previous performances. Also, a means of developing a character in rehearsal in accordance with the text, but not yet connected to specific lines of dialogue.

light plot: a scaled drawing of the lighting instruments in the theatre in plan view (i.e., seen from above) that indicates exactly where the lights are to be placed and in what configuration, and that shows the relationship of the lights to the scenery.

linear structure: organization of the play by which each element of the plot builds logically on the last in a cause-and-effect relationship, reaching an inevitable climax and resolution. Plays that follow a linear structure usually contain a limited number of settings and characters, a brief time span, and a single central problem. *See also* **episodic structure.**

managing director: the person responsible for all financial matters in a non-profit theatre, including negotiating the contracts of those working on a production, securing funds, and balancing the theatre's expenditures against projected box office earnings and other revenue.

model: a representation of the stage or scenery built to scale (usually one half inch on the model equals 1 foot onstage) to show how the design will look in three-dimensional space.

monologue: an extended speech by one character within hearing of any other characters present in the scene. One of the foremost practitioners of this form in contemporary theatre is Spalding Gray, whose performance pieces such as *Swimming to Cambodia* consist entirely of long, autobiographical monologues.

Noh (also **Nō**): a stylized form of Japanese theatre dating from the fourteenth century whose use of masks and ritualized movement and gesture greatly influenced twentieth-century avant-garde theatre artists such as Jerzy Grotowski.

objective: the term used by Konstantin Stanislavski to describe what a character wants or is trying to achieve in a given scene in a moment of a play, or in the play as a whole. Stanislavski believed that to present a character truthfully onstage, an actor must work out the objectives behind the character's words and actions, and each of these objectives must be specific, active, and appropriate to the play.

organic mask: a term used by Jerzy Grotowski to describe a kind of mask created solely by fixing the facial muscles into a set emotional expression for the character portrayed. This fixed expression is meant to depersonalize the character and present a more universal human characteristic.

paint elevation: a scaled painted drafting depicting how the scenery will be painted.

performance art: a new kind of theatrical performance that combines dance, visual art, and the spoken word. Performance artists rely less on written text—or even speech itself—than on the total impact of the performance.

plot: a series of actions, incidents, or situations through which the story of a play and its implications are communicated.

Poetics: one of the most influential documents on the theatre, written by Aristotle c. 335-323 B.C. In it, Aristotle set forth his definition of tragedy, the exact meaning of which has been disputed ever since, partly because only a fragment of the original text has survived and partly as a result of translation.

point of attack: the place in the larger story at which the playwright has chosen to begin the plot. Generally, the later the point of attack, the more exposition is required.

presentational drama: theatrical performance that acknowledges the artifice of the stage world and is less concerned with preserving the illusion of onstage reality. An actor breaking out of a scene to address the audience directly is an example of this style. *See also* **representational drama.**

preview: a public performance of the play before the official "opening night." Audience members usually pay a reduced ticket price and are aware that what they are seeing is not the finished product. Critics do not review preview performances.

producer: in commercial theatre in America, the person responsible for the financial side of a production, including raising the money needed for production costs. One production often has more than one producer. (In the British theatre, the term *producer* is roughly equivalent to the American stage director.)

production concept: a plan that sets out the specific way in which the artists working on a production will communicate the shared point of view to the audience. The production concept integrates and orchestrates all the production elements and serves as a blueprint for everyone involved in mounting the production.

production notes: information gathered by the director, stage manager, or designers through research, a reading of the script, and the rehearsal process to fulfill the needs of the play and the production point of view. Also called a *checklist* or a *shopping list.*

property (prop): an object or article that is carried onstage by an actor or is part of the setting, excluding painted scenery and costumes. (Articles perceived as belonging to a costume, such as eyeglasses or canes, are called *costume props.*) Some props are integral to the scenic or costume design; some (such as the bottle Blanche breaks in *A Streetcar Named Desire* or the letter Lady Macbeth reads in *Macbeth*) are required by the words and actions of the play or suggested by an actor's interpretation of a character.

regional theatre: professional, nonprofit theatres across the country that together make up our national theatre. Also called *resident theatre.*

rendering: a painted representation of the lighting, setting, or costume used by the designer to communicate the design to the director and other production collaborators.

representational drama: theatrical performance that attempts to preserve the illusion of onstage reality by recreating the surface behavior and appearance of everyday life. *See also* **presentational drama.**

run-through: a rehearsal of the entire play from beginning to end, usually without stops.

sense memory: Stanislavski's term for the process by which an actor draws on emotions or passions in the actor's own life that parallel those of the character being played. Drawing on one's own experiences is thought to allow the actor to reexperience these feelings during performance.

soliloquy: an extended speech in which a character gives voice to internal thoughts or feelings. By dramatic convention, the audience understands that this speech is not addressed to or heard by any other character onstage.

spine: Stanislavski's term for the primary motivation that drives a character's actions in the play, and which should be expressed as an active verb. Also used by Harold Clurman to state one's interpretation of the main action of the play.

spotlight: a lighting instrument with a lens system in addition to the lightbulb, reflector, and shield. The lens system allows the designer to control and shape the light. *See also* **floodlight.**

stage, arena: performance space surrounded on all sides by the audience; also called *theatre in the round.*

stage, black box: a flexible performance space with no fixed or permanent seating. Developed for experimental theatre in the 1960s, this theatre allows the size and relative location of the performance area and the audience space to be changed for each production.

stage, proscenium: a performance space separated from the audience by a permanent archway—the proscenium arch—which has the effect of distancing audience members from the action of the play, as though they were looking through an invisible "fourth wall."

stage, thrust: a performance space surrounded on three sides by the audience, providing more of a sense of intimacy.

stage directions: text that accompanies the dialogue of a written play in which the playwright may specify onstage actions and entrances and exits or provide character descriptions.

staging: the predetermined way in which the actors move onstage in performance. Some directors set the staging to create stage pictures through the actors' movement; others allow the staging to evolve in rehearsal. Also called *blocking.*

Theater of the Absurd: a phrase coined by Martin Esslin to describe the innovative work of playwrights writing at about the time of his 1961 book of the same name. These plays have no plot, no clear beginning or ending, and often unrecognizable characters whose behavior is mechanical, repetitive, illogical, and inappropriate. Although the works generally contain comic moments and ludicrous circumstances, the underlying theme is gravely serious—the futility and absurdity of modern life.

value: a term used by designers to describe the relative brightness of an object onstage.

willing suspension of disbelief: the process by which an audience gives itself over to the illusion of theatrical time and space.

wing: a space to the left or right of any stage, out of view of the audience or a vertical piece of scenery that masks this backstage or offstage area and the actors entering or exiting it.

Credits

Photo Acknowledgments

Page numbers are given in boldface. Positions of photographs are indicated in the abbreviated form as follows: top (t), bottom (b), left (l), right (r), and center (c).

Carter   **70**—William Gibson/Martha Swope Associates   **71**—Paulo Netto   **75 & 76**—Courtesy The Guthrie Theater   **81** (t)—Martha Swope   **81** (b), **82, 97, & 106** (l)—The New York Public Library for the Performing Arts   **106** (r)—Eileen Darby   **107**—Courtesy The Guthrie Theater   **108**—The New York Public Library for the Performing Arts   **110**—The Granger Collection   **113** (l)—Inge Morath/Magnum Photos, Inc.   **113** (r)—Sylvia Plachy   **117**—© The Board of Trustees of the Victoria and Albert Museum   **119**—The Bettman Archive   **120**—Photo by Ken Friedman. Courtesy Berkeley Repertory Theatre   **121**—Courtesy Williamstown Theatre Festival   **122** (l)—Mary Ellen Mark/Library   **122** (r)—Phill Niblock   **123** (l)—National Museum, Tokyo   **123** (r)—Japan National Tourist Organization   **124** (l)—From *NOH The Classical Theater* by Yasuo Nakamura published by Walker/Weatherhill, NY & Tokyo.   **124** (r)—Courtesy Japan Performing Arts Center, Tokyo. Photo by Katsuaki Furudate   **125**—Courtesy Japan Performing Arts Center. Photo by Masaru Miyauchi   **126**—Anita & Steve Shevett   **132**—Courtesy George Tsypin   **135**—From *Le Décor de Théatre* by Denis Bablet   **140**—NOVOSTI   **141**—The New York Public Library for the Performing Arts   **142**—Jaromir Svoboda, photographer. From *The Scenography of Josef Svoboda,* Wesleyan University Press. Photo courtesy Jarka M. Burian   **143** (t)—Courtesy George Tsypin   **143** (b)—Courtesy John Arnone   **145** (tl)—The New York Public Library for the Performing Arts   **145** (tr) & (b)—From *The Theatre of Robert Edmond Jones,* edited by Ralph Pendleton, Wesleyan University Press   **147** (l)—From *Elements of Style* edited by Stephen Calloway and Elizabeth Cromley. Simon & Schuster © 1991   **147** (c)—Library of Congress   **147** (r)—Courtesy The Historic New Orleans Collection, Museum/Research Center, Acc. No. VCS sq 42   **148**—© Joel Gordon   **149**—Marc Bryan-Brown   **152** (t)—Courtesy Clinton Turner Davis   **152** (bl)—Courtesy Adrienne Lobel   **152** (br)—Photo by Will Gulette, The Old Globe Theater, San Diego. Courtesy Hugh Landwehr   **153** (l)—© T. Charles Erickson   **153** (r)—Theatre Arts Collection, Harry Ransom Humanities Research Center, The University of Texas at Austin   **154** (l)—P. Gontier/The Image Works   **154** (r)—Dawn Murray   **155** (t)—© Chris Bennion   **155** (b)—From *Le Décor de Théatre* by Denis Bablet   **156**—From *History of the Theatre* by Oscar G. Brockett   **157** (tl)—The Metropolitan Museum of Art, The Elisha Whittelsey Collection, the Elisha Whittelsey Fund, 1951. (51.501.27)   **157** (tr) & (b)—Reproduced by permission of His Grace The Duke of Devonshire and The Trustees of The Chatsworth Settlement   **158** (t)—From *Le Décor de Théatre* by Denis Bablet   **158** (b)—Martha Swope   **159** (t)—Dawn Murray   **159** (b)—Courtesy Wenger Corporation   **162**—The New York Public Library for the Performing Arts   **163** (l)—Martha Swope   **163** (r)—Richard Feldman   **165**—Harvard Theatre Collection   **166**—Clemens Kalischer   **169** (t)—Dan Bosler/Tony Stone Worldwide   **169** (bl) & (br)—Wide World Photos   **171**—John Springer Collection/Bettmann Archive   **172**—Museum of Modern Art/Film Stills Archive   **179** (l)—Photo by Louise Dahl Wolfe, Courtesy of the Design Laboratory, Fashion Institute of Technology, New York   **179** (r)—1947 "Femina" Christian Dior. From *Fashion Through Fashion Plates 1771-1970* by Doris Langley Moore. © 1971 Clarkson N. Potter Inc., NY   **180**—Martha Swope   **182, 183, & 186** (l)—The New York Public Library for the Performing Arts   **186** (r)—The New York Public Library for the Performing Arts. Photo by Henry Grossman   **187**—© T. Charles Erickson   **189** (l) & (r)—Bulloz   **189** (c)—1890 "The Queen" Adolf Sandoz. From *Fashion Through Fasion Plates 1771-1970* by Doris Langley Moore. © 1971 Clarkson N. Potter Inc., NY   **190**—From *Fashion Through Fashion Plates 1771-1970* by Doris Langley Moore. © 1971 Clarkson N. Potter Inc., NY   **191**—Dawn Murray   **192**—Lisa Ebright   **193**—From *The Blue Book of Men's Tailoring* by Frederick T. Croonberg. © 1977 Van Nostrand Reinhold Co.   **197** (t)—Greg Pease/Tony Stone Worldwide   **197** (bl)—Sydney Byrd/Tony Stone Worldwide   **197** (br)—G. Gardner/The Image Works   **198 & 199**—From *Le Décor de Théatre* by Denis Bablet   **203** (l)—© T. Charles Erickson   **203** (r)—Martha Swope   **211**—The New York Public Library for the Performing Arts   **215** (t) & (bl)—Kliegl Bros.   **215** (r)—Courtesy ETC/LMI. Electronic Theatre Controls, Inc.   **216**—Kleigl Bros.   **217** (tl)—Théâtre de l'Odéon, Paris, 1925. From *Twentieth Century Stage Decoration*   **217** (tr)—© T. Charles Erickson   **217** (b)—Hope Wurmfeld   **218** (l)—© T. Charles Erickson   **218** (r)—Courtesy The Guthrie Theater. Photo by Michal Daniel   **219**—Reprinted with the permission of Atheneum Publishers, an imprint of Macmillan Publishing

Company and the Estate of Jo Mielziner from *Designing for the Theatre* by Jo Mielziner. Copyright © 1965 by Jo Mielziner **226**—Courtesy The Guthrie Theater **227**—© Chris Bennion **235**—Courtesy Arena Stage **237**—Courtesy New York Shakespeare Festival **241**—Courtesy National Endowment for the Arts **247**—Courtesy Actors' Equity Association **248** (l)—Courtesy Playwrights Horizons **248** (r)—Courtesy Shubert Organization **254** (t)—Lisa Ebright **254** (b)—Martha Swope **261**—From *Directors on Directing* **262**—From the Scientific American 1924 **268**—Burt Glinn/Magnum Photos, Inc. **273**—Lisa Ebright **274**—From the Scientific American 1884 **275** (t)—Dawn Murray **275** (b)—From *History of the Theatre* by Oscar G. Brockett **276** (t)—Theatermuseum, Osterreichische Lichtbildstelle, Austria **276** (b)—From *Twentieth Century Stage Decoration* **277**—The New York Public Library for the Performing Arts **278** (t)—From *History of the Theatre* by Oscar G. Brockett **278** (b)—Martha Swope **279**—From *History of the Theatre* by Oscar G. Brockett **282** & **284**—© T. Charles Erickson **287**—From *History of the Theatre* by Oscar G. Brockett **288**—Courtesy of Routledge & Kegan Paul, Ltd. **289** (t)—From *History of the Theatre* by Oscar G. Brockett **289** (b)—George E. Joseph **290**—Ronald T. Simon **291**—From Dorpfeld, Griechische Theatre (1896) **292** (t)—Courtesy Greek National Tourist Organization **292** (b)—George E. Joseph **293**—Photo by Beata Bergstrom. Drottningholm Theatre Museum **294**—Courtesy John Lee Beatty **295** (tl)—Courtesy Museum of London **295** (tr)—Courtesy Milwaukee Repertory Theater. Photo by John Nienhuis **295** (b)—Courtesy The Guthrie Theater. Photo by Robert Ashley Wilson **296**—Japan National Tourist Organization **297**—Photo by George de Vincent. Courtesy Arena Stage **299**—Tony Stone Worldwide **302**—Culver Pictures **305**—The Art Museum, Princeton University. Museum purchase, Caroline G. Mather Fund **307**—From *Le Décor de Théatre* by Denis Bablet **309**—Odin Teatrets Forlag **310**—Culver Pictures **311**—John Springer Collection/Bettmann Archive **312**—Culver Pictures **313** (tl) & (tr)—Theatre Arts Collection, Harry Ransom Humanities Research Center, The University of Texas at Austin **313** (b)—Culver Pictures **314**—George E. Joseph **315**—Martha Swope **Color pages following page 82: 1** (t)—Richard Feldman **1** (b)—Dennis Stock/Magnum Photos, Inc. **2**—Martha Swope **3** (t)—Richard Feldman **3** (b)—William B. Carter **4** (t)—Richard Feldman **4** (b)—George E. Joseph **Color pages following page 114: 1**—Carol Rosegg/Martha Swope Associates **2** (t) & (c)—© Chris Bennion **2** (b)—Richard Feldman **3**—© Chris Bennion **4**—Richard Feldman **Color pages following page 210: 1** & **2**—Courtesy James Scott **3** & **4** (t)—Courtesy Arden Fingerhut **3** & **2** (b)—Reprinted with the permission of Atheneum Publishers, an imprint of Macmillan Publishing Company and the Estate of Jo Mielziner from *Designing for the Theatre* by Jo Mielziner. Copyright © 1965 by Jo Mielziner. **Color pages following page 242: 1**—Gerry Goodstein **2** & **3** (t)—Marc Bryan-Brown **4**—Gerry Goodstein

Literary Acknowledgments

Page numbers are given in boldface following acknowledgments.

Actors' Equity Assocation. "Standard Minimum Production Contract to be issued only to actors performing as stage managers or assistant stage managers" and "Standard Minimum Production Contract to be issued only to actors performing as principals" reprinted by permission of Actors' Equity Association. **247**   American Repertory Theatre. Statement by the American Repertory Theatre, Robert Brustein, Artistic Director. Reprinted by permission. **51**   Bartow, Arthur. From *The Director's Voice* by Arthur Bartow, copyright © 1988 by Arthur Bartow. Reprinted by permission of Theatre Communications Group Inc. **50, following page 82, 83**   Beckett, Samuel. From *Waiting for Godot* by Samuel Beckett. Copyright © 1954 by Grove Press Inc. and renewed 1982 by Samuel Beckett. Reprinted by permission of Grove/At-

Index

Page numbers followed by f denote figure or photograph.